Ready-to-Use

P.E. ACTIVITIES

for Grades 3-4

Joanne M. Landy · Maxwell J. Landy

PARKER PUBLISHING COMPANY

West Nyack, New York 10995

Library of Congress Cataloging-in-Publication Data

Landy, Maxwell J.
    Ready-to-use P.E. activities / Maxwell J. Landy, Joanne Landy.
      p. cm.
    Contents: bk. 1. For grades K–2—bk. 2. For grades 3–4—bk.
  3. For grades 5–6—bk. 4. For grades 7–9.
    ISBN 0-13-673054-X (v.1)—ISBN 0-13-673088-4
    1. Physical education for children—Curricula. 2. Physical
education for children—Planning. I. Landy, Joanne. II. Title.
III. Title: Ready-to-use PE activities.
  GV443.L334   1992
  372.86—dc20

              92-21049
              CIP

Printed in the United States of America

10 9 8 7 6   10

*Dedicated in loving memory of my husband and a dear father, Maxwell
J. Landy, and to our children Max, Jr., and Nikki. Thank you, Max
and Nikki, for your loving support, enthusiasm, and for being
wonderful role models for our program!*

ISBN 0-13-673054-X (v.1)   ISBN 0-13-673088-4

PARKER PUBLISHING COMPANY
West Nyack, New York 10994

On the World Wide Web at http://www.phdirect.com

About the Authors

Maxwell J. Landy, PED, New South Wales, B.S. and M.Ed., University of Oregon, Associate Professor Emeritus, University of Regina, Canada, was actively involved in the field of physical education for 39 years. For 18 of those years, Max served as a K–12 P.E. specialist and consultant in Canadian and Australian schools. For 20 years, he taught at the university level, where he developed innovative programs in physical education and health, specializing in the P.E. internship program. Max passed away on May 7, 1991.

Joanne M. Landy, B.Ed., University of Regina, has 15 years of experience as an elementary and high school P.E. specialist in the Saskatchewan school system. She also became involved as a demonstration P.E. teacher in liaison with the University of Regina, Faculty of Education pre-internship and internship programs, and presented at several workshops for elementary and secondary teachers. Joanne and her two children now reside in Perth, Western Australia.

Max and Joanne co-presented at several major P.E./Health conferences in Canada, the United States, and Australia. In 1988 they were involved in the USA National Fitness Foundation–Youth Fitness Camp in Los Angeles, spearheaded by John Cates of UCLA. Between them they combined over 50 years of Physical Education teaching knowledge and experience to produce the *Complete Physical Education Activities Program*.

Forewords

It is with extreme pleasure that I submit this foreword on behalf of Max and Joanne's wonderful contribution to improve the health and fitness of our youth.

I first met Joanne and Max in 1986 when they were selected as faculty members of a model youth fitness camp sponsored by George Allen's National Fitness Foundation.

During the camp, I had the opportunity to observe first hand the wonderful physical education materials that Joanne and Max had created. Classroom teachers, with no formal physical education training, were able to immediately involve their students in "fun" activities that emphasized all of the components of fitness. User-friendly lesson plans provided the teachers with games and activities for the progressive development of motor skills. Students, teachers, administrators, and parents soon became advocates of quality daily physical education.

I am delighted that the Landys have published their wonderful *Complete Physical Education Activities Program.*

In the United States, the level of youth fitness has continued to decline over the past several years. Physical education specialists and classroom teachers have been searching for physical education materials that will address the individual health and fitness needs of children while developing self-confidence and self-esteem. Joanne and Max have provided the materials that can put "quality" into daily physical education.

John Cates, Supervisor
Department of Physical Education
University of California, San Diego
Assistant to Arnold Schwarzenegger
Chairman, President's Council
**   Physical Fitness and Sports**

I am proud to say that Max Landy was, before his unfortunate death in 1991, one of my closest personal and professional friends. I had the pleasure of working with Max at the University of Regina from 1978–1980. He was my mentor, and out of this a lasting friendship developed with both him and his wife Joanne. I came to know and appreciate both Max and Joanne as two very extraordinary physical educators. I was impressed by their dedication to the profession and, in particular, to the development of a physical education program which they believed worth working and sacrificing for. Their goal was to develop a "user friendly, activity oriented" curriculum for teachers, designed to help promote a physically active lifestyle among children and youth. Their commitment to this work has been long-term in nature, spanning more than twelve years. After Max's death, Joanne carried on to see their project come to fruition. Now it is available for all of us in their new series of books, the *Complete Physical Education Activities Program*.

To me, this series is first of all a jumping off place for the inexperienced teacher of physical education, whether a classroom teacher or a physical education specialist, who is desirous of specific ideas as to what to teach and how to go about teaching it. In this regard, an especially unique and attractive characteristic of these teaching units/books are the many delightful cartoon-like illustrations designed to clarify the correct action, organization, and/or arrangement of students. In addition, teaching instructions are written in step-by-step form and can be read directly to students. My more than twenty years of in- and pre-service work with teachers indicates that this is exactly the kind of direction they will most benefit from. Their initial teaching experiences will prove enjoyable for both themselves and their students, thus encouraging further involvement. Their students can only benefit!

Although the *Complete Physical Education Activities Program* is of most obvious help to the teacher who has not had an in-depth background in physical education, it is a time-saver even for the experienced physical education teacher. It contains a myriad of practical, ready-to-use, and easy-to-follow activity ideas. These are organized sequentially to ensure proper progressions and allow for individualized teaching. The curriculum is divided into warm-up, fitness, core, and closing activity sections. This organization permits a flexibility and facility in lesson planning which would not be possible if detailed lesson plans were provided. The teacher is able to compile complete, well-balanced lesson plans merely by selecting activities from the various sections. Thus, teachers are encouraged to be creative in their implementation efforts.

Max and Joanne have skillfully blended together traditional activity ideas with more current ones in an effort to preserve the very best that both have to offer. However, they offer more than an academic approach. They provide many new and meaningful activity ideas, including many new, fun-packed fitness activities, which have evolved from their more than fifty years of teaching physical education in Australia and Canada. Notably, their curriculum has been field-tested in Regina schools where it received high ratings from the many teachers and student-teachers who used it. Finally, it is divided into four books or teaching units, each tailored to the specific developmental needs of the students at that level. Thus, teachers need only purchase the book(s) appropriate for their grade level.

Through Max and Joanne's professional dedication and hard work, we have moved one step closer to providing quality daily physical education experiences in our schools. They have provided teaching units which will no doubt be used by a great many classroom teachers and physical education specialists who believe that physical activity is important for our children and youth. If the ultimate utility of information lies in its ability to enhance the quality of human experience, then their work represents a substantial contribution to the literature. I am honored that Joanne has asked me to write this foreword and wish her every success in this and all her future endeavors.

Dennis Caine, Ph.D.
Western Washington University

About *Ready-to-Use P.E. Activities for Grades 3–4*

This practical resource is one of four books presenting a unique curriculum for elementary and middle/junior high school educators entitled *Complete Physical Education Activities Program* (CPEP). The curriculum is designed to help classroom teachers and P.E. specialists successfully prepare and teach interesting, fun-packed physical education lessons in a sequential co-educational program. It includes the following specialized teaching units, each tailored to the specific developmental needs at the particular level:

Book 1   *Ready-to-Use P.E. Activities for Grades K–2*

Book 2   *Ready-to-Use P.E. Activities for Grades 3–4*

Book 3   *Ready-to-Use P.E. Activities for Grades 5–6*

Book 4   *Ready-to-Use P.E. Activities for Grades 7–9*

The CPEP curriculum provides a comprehensive continuity program from kindergarten through grade 9, with a strong emphasis on the *fitness* component. It is based on sound education principles, research in motor learning, exercise physiology, and teaching methodology and meets the requirements as a delivery system and resource for current P.E. curricula in the United States and Canada. Its primary objectives are:

- to foster in children a love of physical activity and play
- to instill a need for physical fitness in each child
- to develop coordination, grace, and control
- to provide opportunities for increased responsibility in planning, organizing, and leadership
- to give children as wide a skill, games, and dance experience as possible
- to present opportunities for children to belong to a group in which each child is accepted
- to provide experiences which will develop initiative, self-reliance, self-worth, loyalty, honesty, kindness to others, and a love of learning
- to develop a sense of fair play and cooperation in children and the ability to work in groups, leading to increased cultural understanding
- to provide opportunities for integration of P.E. with other subject areas: language arts, math, social studies, science, health, music, and art

For your convenience, Book 2 in the curriculum is subdivided into eight sections, including: Introductory Activities, Fitness Activities, Movement Awareness, Rhythms and Dance, Play Gymnastics, Games Skills, Special Games, and Closing Activities. This organization allows you to compile complete, well-balanced lesson plans in minutes merely by selecting activities from the various sections, thus saving valuable lesson preparation time.

Each book in the curriculum also provides a special section entitled "How to Prepare Lessons Using These P.E. Activities," which explains (a) how to prepare a Yearly/Weekly P.E. Plan, (b) how to prepare a Daily P.E. Plan, and (c) how to record the activities taught. By following the lesson format described in this section, you can use and reuse the program activities in an endless number of combinations with other activities. Moreover, many of the activities contain variations and suggested modifications, thus providing valuable repetition and reinforcement and sufficient material for an entire year of daily physical education.

Other features of the "Complete Physical Education Activities Program" curriculum include the following:

Time Allocation:

Flexibility is a key feature of the program, as the format allows you to select and adapt activities that may be taught within the allotted time.

Indoor-Outdoor:

Activities have been provided for both indoor and outdoor learning stations.

Coeducational:

All of the activities in each level book are suitable for both boys and girls.

Illustrations:

Cartoon-like, stick figures supplement the activity directions throughout. All measurements, diagrams, and ground markings are written in standard and metric measurement to fit the needs of educators in the United States and Canada.

Basic Equipment:

Most of the program activities can be taught using standard equipment already available in elementary/middle schools. Some enrichment activities may require additional items such as juggling scarves, parachutes, peacock feathers, and scooters.

By presenting K–9 students with a variety of challenging, stimulating activities during each lesson throughout the year, this P.E. program will help you create enjoyable, success-oriented experiences that reach every child. Moreover, the program provides for the mainstreaming of atypical children within the context of the regular physical education lesson. Special attention has been given to (a) social interaction and the improvement of self-concepts, cooperation, and sportsmanship; (b) fitness and skill development; and (c) acquisition of basic fundamentals through conceptual learning.

Interaction of the four F's—FUN, FITNESS, and FRIENDSHIP through the FUNDAMENTALS of physical education—stimulates children to want to participate in physical activities not only during their school years, but for the rest of their lives.

Joanne Landy
Maxwell J. Landy

Contents

Section 4 RHYTHMS AND DANCE 91

Section 2   FITNESS ACTIVITIES 33

Section 3   MOVEMENT AWARENESS 59

Section 7 SPECIAL GAMES. 307

Section 8 CLOSING ACTIVITIES **339**

How to Prepare Lessons Using These P.E. Activities

The following discussion gives you suggestions for using this resource to prepare stimulating, well-balanced physical education activities for your students. Specifically, it provides a description of the different types of activities presented in Sections 1 through 8, a sample activity illustrating the easy-to-follow organization used for all activities in the program, and directions for creating your own yearly/weekly P.E. teaching plan. Included are a filled-in sample Yearly/Weekly Plan Chart along with a reproducible blank chart, plus a Class Record Sheet to help you evaluate the progress made by each class during the year.

DESCRIPTION OF THE ACTIVITIES

Sections 1 through 8 present a wide range of activities for creating a stimulating variety of daily P.E. lessons.

▪ Warm-Up Activities (Sections 1 and 2)

Introductory Activities

The first activity of the lesson is intended to produce a state of physical and mental readiness. This Introductory Activity produces a *general warm-up,* increasing blood flow to the major muscle groups. Mentally, it helps to get children excited about participating in the activities that follow.

Fitness Activities

The Fitness Activity functions as a *specific warm-up* and, when used in combination with an introductory activity, develops overall fitness with emphasis on cardiovascular endurance and muscular strength and endurance.

▪ Core Activities (Sections 3–6)

Movement Awareness

The activities in this section help to develop the movement principles of space awareness, body awareness, effort awareness, and relationships. Themes are used to set tasks that ask "what, where, how can, and who can?" The children respond to the task or problem by exploring and experimenting at the floor level, on low apparatus, or on large apparatus, with or without equipment.

Rhythms and Dance

The Rhythms and Dance activity is intended to develop creative expression, rhythmic movement, musical appreciation, and active listening skills. Muscular growth and coordination are improved; space awareness, body awareness, effort awareness, and social skills are improved in an atmosphere of fun. Through the rhythm and dance section, specific music suggestions are provided; otherwise, lively popular music is suggested.

Play Gymnastics

The Play Gymnastics activities progressively develop muscular strength and endurance, flexibility, balance, and overall coordination. The children also develop self-confidence, improved posture, and safety awareness.

Game Skills

Game Skills activities develop the abilities children need to participate in most traditional games, such as soccer, volleyball, basketball, softball, and football as well as more innovative games, such as parachute play, scooter play, and juggling. The Games Skills activities are arranged in units that you could plan to teach over a two- or three-week period.

▪ Special Games (Section 7)

Relays, low-organized games, and tabloid sports activities develop leadership, cooperation, self-esteem, creativity, and a sense of fair play. The emphasis throughout the activities in this section is on fun and teamwork, not winning or losing.

▪ Closing Activities (Section 8)

After a vigorous physical workout, the Closing Activity serves as a quiet, cool-down activity and leaves children ready to continue with classroom work.

Each activity in the program is presented in a functional, easy-to-follow format, as illustrated by the following sample:

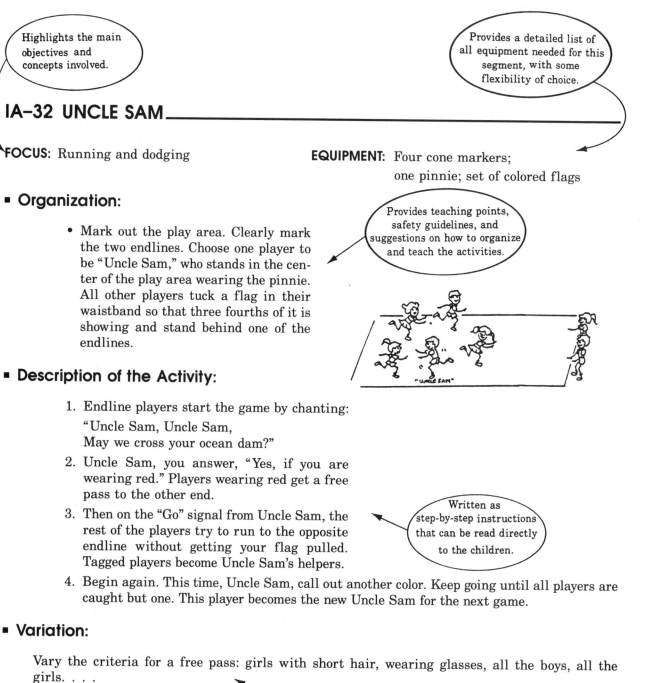

Highlights the main objectives and concepts involved.

Provides a detailed list of all equipment needed for this segment, with some flexibility of choice.

IA–32 UNCLE SAM

FOCUS: Running and dodging

EQUIPMENT: Four cone markers; one pinnie; set of colored flags

■ **Organization:**

• Mark out the play area. Clearly mark the two endlines. Choose one player to be "Uncle Sam," who stands in the center of the play area wearing the pinnie. All other players tuck a flag in their waistband so that three fourths of it is showing and stand behind one of the endlines.

Provides teaching points, safety guidelines, and suggestions on how to organize and teach the activities.

■ **Description of the Activity:**

1. Endline players start the game by chanting:
   "Uncle Sam, Uncle Sam,
   May we cross your ocean dam?"

2. Uncle Sam, you answer, "Yes, if you are wearing red." Players wearing red get a free pass to the other end.

3. Then on the "Go" signal from Uncle Sam, the rest of the players try to run to the opposite endline without getting your flag pulled. Tagged players become Uncle Sam's helpers.

Written as step-by-step instructions that can be read directly to the children.

4. Begin again. This time, Uncle Sam, call out another color. Keep going until all players are caught but one. This player becomes the new Uncle Sam for the next game.

■ **Variation:**

Vary the criteria for a free pass: girls with short hair, wearing glasses, all the boys, all the girls. . . .

Provides additional ideas to modify or extend the activities.

Preparing the Yearly/Weekly Plan

It is important that the physical education program be planned ahead of time, whether for a two-week unit, a season, or even a year. Yearly planning allows you to meet long-range objectives, to use facilities and equipment to their utmost, and to consider seasonal activities and special days.

■ Developing the Yearly/Weekly Unit Plan

To develop the yearly/weekly plan, select the activities from the suggestions listed on the Scope and Sequence Chart and the Table of Contents of each section, and then prepare a Weekly Unit Plan Chart. Refer to the Sample Yearly/ Weekly Plan Chart for Core Activities (page xviii). The chart shows the school year divided into a sequence of 40 weekly units and, when completed, should give you an outline of the order in which the material will be taught. A blank sample Weekly/Yearly Plan Chart is provided for you on pages xx and xxi.

Although decisions made on the Yearly/Weekly Unit Plan Charts will provide reliable, concrete guidelines, your decisions should never be regarded as irreversible and certainly may be changed as circumstances require.

■ Developing the Daily Lesson Plan

There are five basic steps in preparing a lesson using the "Complete Physical Education Activities Program" system:

STEP 1: Decide how much time is allocated to your lesson. Each part of the lesson can vary in length according to the objectives and focus of the lesson.

STEP 2: Select an activity from the Introductory Activities section, then one or more activities from the Fitness section.

STEP 3: Decide on the Core Unit to be taught by referring to the appropriate week on the Weekly Plan Chart. Then select the appropriate activities from the core sections of Movement/Rhythms and Dance, Gymnastics, or Game Skills.

STEP 4: Select a related game from the Game Skills section or the Special Games section.

STEP 5: Select a cool-down activity from the Closing Activities to finish the lesson.

NOTE: It is not necessary that all the material in an activity be taught in one lesson. You may decide to use two or three lessons to cover all of the tasks on that particular activity.

■ Gathering the Equipment

To make a list of all of the equipment needed for each lesson, refer to the Equipment List on the top right-hand corner of each activity. Check that all of the equipment listed is indeed available for use. Prior to the lesson, designate children to bring out and arrange the equipment in the activity area.

■ Recording the Activities Taught

When all of the tasks or components in an activity have been taught, you can circle the number of the activity on a photocopy of the Class Record Sheet provided on page xxii. By referring to the Record Sheet, you will quickly be able to evaluate the class's progress throughout the year.

SAMPLE YEARLY/WEEKLY PLAN CHART

WEEK 1 Date	WEEK 6 Date	WEEK 11 Date	WEEK 16 Date	WEEK 21 Date
Orientation week IA: Signals Starting Positions GS: Hoop Play SG: L-O Games CA	Fit: Aerobics; e.g. Aerobic Circle stunt Breaks GS: Rope Play Short Rope Skill CA	Rope Play; Formation Jumping Volleyball station Wk. Volleyball Tourney Volleyball Lead-up Games	GS: Combative Pl. GS: Basketball Tourney SG. Tabloid	IA: Warm ups Fit: Strengtheners GS: Hockey Stick skills & Related Games CA: Stretches

WEEK 2 Date	WEEK 7 Date	WEEK 12 Date	WEEK 17 Date	WEEK 22 Date
IA: Warm-up Activities & Games GS: Frisbee Play Juggling SG: Relays	FIT 12-min w.o. #1 & 2 cooperative stunt breaks GS: Long Rope Skills SG: Jump the Shot	Fit: 4-corner warmup Limber & Loosen GS: Basketball (Dribbling & Footwk) Fit: Cool-Down	Fit: Aerobic Rout measuring H.R.'s Gym: Balance & Supports GS: Scooter Play & Relays	R& D: Novelty Dances, Fundamen tal Rhythms GS: Hockey Skills & Related Games Relays

WEEK 3 Date	WEEK 8 Date	WEEK 13 Date	WEEK 18 Date	WEEK 23 Date
IA: Tag-Type Game FIT: Equipment Breaks GS: Scoop Plays Related Games CA	Fit 12-minute workout #3, #4 GS: Volleyball Skill & Related Games (setting, bumping) CA	IA: Warmup Activities & Games GS: Basketball sk. & Related Games (Passing & Receiving) SG Relays	IA: Tag-Type eg. Heart Attack Fit: Strengtheners GS: Parachute Play Gym Pyramid Building	Fit: Aerobics Limber & Loosen Gym: Balance Bench & Beam CA

WEEK 4 Date	WEEK 9 Date	WEEK 14 Date	WEEK 19 Date	WEEK 24 Date
Fit: Aerobic Rout. Limber & Loosen GS: Football Skill & Related Games CA	IA: Tag Type Games Alertness Type GS: Volleyball Skill & Related Games (serving & Re- ception) CA	Fit: Charlie Brown's Circuit GS: Basketball S. (Shooting & Defense) & Related Games CA	School break	Tourneys; Volleyb., Basketb. Hockey SG: L-O games Fitness Testing

WEEK 5 Date	WEEK 10 Date	WEEK 15 Date	WEEK 20 Date	WEEK 25 Date
IA: Warm-up, e.g. grass drills, astronaut run Fit Muscle-Bone signals GS: Football Skills Fitness Testing	IA: Exercise Hunt Joker's Wild GS: Volleyball sk. (Blocking, Defense) & Related Games CA	Fit: 12 minute workout #5 & #6 GS: Baketball Sk. (Rebounding, Blocking Out) Lead-up Games	school break	R& D: Novelty & Folk Dances Gym: Rotations SG: Relays

YEARLY/WEEKLY PLAN CHART

WEEK 26 Date	WEEK 31 Date	WEEK 36 Date	WEEK Date	WEEK Date
Fit: Charlie Brown's Circuit Gym: Rotations SG: L-o Games	spring break	Fit: Milk Routes GS: Soccer Lead-up Games Station Work CA		
WEEK 27 Date	**WEEK 32 Date**	**WEEK 37 Date**	**WEEK Date**	**WEEK Date**
Fit: 12 minute workouts #7, #8 Design a Workout Gym: Springing & Landing CA	R&D: Rhythmics Fit: 12 minute Walk-Run test SG: L-o Games CA	Fit: Prediction & Cross-Country Runs GS: Softball Play & Related Games (pitching, ba??ing)		
WEEK 28 Date	**WEEK 33 Date**	**WEEK 38 Date**	**WEEK Date**	**WEEK Date**
Fit: Workouts Per Group Gym: Climbing, Hanging, Swinging SG: L-o Games	R&D: Square Dancing Dance-making GS: Paddle Play & Related Games CA	SG: L-o games GS: Softball Play Lead-up Games Station Work		
WEEK 29 Date	**WEEK 34 Date**	**WEEK 39 Date**	**WEEK Date**	**WEEK Date**
IA: Tag-Type R&D: Folk Dances Gym: Station Work CA	IA: Geronimo Paper Route GS: Soccer Skills Dribbling, Trapping Related Games	Fit: Limber & Loosen GS: Track & Field Running Relays Fit: Cool-Downs		
WEEK 30 Date	**WEEK 35 Date**	**WEEK 40 Date**	**WEEK Date**	**WEEK Date**
Fit: Aerobics Bench-Step Test GS: Paddle Play Easter Tabloid	IA: Tag-Type GS: Soccer Skills (kicking, Goalkeeping) Related Games CA	Track & Field Tabloid Favorite Games		

YEARLY/WEEKLY PLAN CHART

FEBRUARY		MARCH		APRIL		MAY		JUNE	
WEEK 1	Date	WEEK 1	Date	WEEK 1	Date	WEEK 1	Date	WEEK 1	Date
WEEK 2	Date	WEEK 2	Date	WEEK 2	Date	WEEK 2	Date	WEEK 2	Date
WEEK 3	Date	WEEK 3	Date	WEEK 3	Date	WEEK 3	Date	WEEK 3	Date
WEEK 4	Date	WEEK 4	Date	WEEK 4	Date	WEEK 4	Date	WEEK 4	Date
WEEK 5	Date	WEEK 5	Date	WEEK 5	Date	WEEK 5	Date	WEEK 5	Date

YEARLY/WEEKLY PLAN CHART

SEPTEMBER		OCTOBER		NOVEMBER		DECEMBER		JANUARY	
WEEK 1	Date	**WEEK 1**	Date	**WEEK 1**	Date	**WEEK 1**	Date	**WEEK 1**	Date
WEEK 2	Date	**WEEK 2**	Date	**WEEK 2**	Date	**WEEK 2**	Date	**WEEK 2**	Date
WEEK 3	Date	**WEEK 3**	Date	**WEEK 3**	Date	**WEEK 3**	Date	**WEEK 3**	Date
WEEK 4	Date	**WEEK 4**	Date	**WEEK 4**	Date	**WEEK 4**	Date	**WEEK 4**	Date
WEEK 5	Date	**WEEK 5**	Date	**WEEK 5**	Date	**WEEK 5**	Date	**WEEK 5**	Date

Book 2: Ready-to-Use P.E. Activities for Grades 3–4
Class Record Sheet

Class: _____

Year: _____

Level: _____

Teacher: _____

INTRODUCTORY ACTIVITIES

1	2	3	4	5	6
7	8	9	10	11	12
13	14	15	16	17	18
19	20	21	22	23	24
25	26	27	28	29	30
31	32	33	34	35	36
37	38	39	40	41	42
43	44	45	46	47	48
49	50				

FITNESS ACTIVITIES

1	2	3	4	5	6
7	8	9	10	11	12
13	14	15	16	17	18
19	20	21	22	23	24
25	26	27	28	29	30
31	32	33			

RHYTHMS & DANCE

1	2	3	4	5	6
7	8	9	10	11	12
13	14	15	16	17	18
19	20	21	22	23	24
25	26	27	28	29	30
31	32	33	34	35	36
37	38	39	40	41	42
43	44	45	46	47	48

SPECIAL GAMES

1	2	3	4	5	6
7	8	9	10	11	12
13	14	15	16	17	18
19	20	21	22	23	24
25	26	27	28	29	30
31	32	33	34	35	36
37	38	39	40	41	42
43	44	45	46	47	

MOVEMENT AWARENESS

1	2	3	4	5	6
7	8	9	10	11	12
13	14	15	16	17	18
19	20	21	22	23	24
25	26	27	28	29	30
31	32	33	34	35	36
37	38	39	40	41	42
43	44	45	46		

PLAY GYMNASTICS

1	2	3	4	5	6
7	8	9	10	11	12
13	14	15	16	17	18
19	20	21	22	23	24
25	26	27	28	29	30
31	32	33	34	35	36
37	38	39	40	41	42
43	44	45	46	47	48
49	50	51	52	53	54
55	56	57	58		

CLOSING ACTIVITIES

1	2	3	4	5	6
7	8	9	10	11	12
13	14	15	16	17	18
19	20	21	22	23	24
25	26	27	28	29	30
31	32	33	34	35	36
37	38	39	40	41	42
43					

GAME SKILLS

1	2	3	4	5	6	7	8	9	10	11	12	13	14
15	16	17	18	19	20	21	22	23	24	25	26	27	28
29	30	31	32	33	34	35	36	37	38	39	40	41	42
43	44	45	46	47	48	49	50	51	52	53	54	55	56
57	58	59	60	61	62	63	64	65	66	67	68	69	70
71	72	73	74	75	76	77	78	79	80	81	82	83	84
85	86	87	88	89	90	91	92	93	94	95	96	97	98
99	100	101	102	103	104	105	106	107	108	109	110	111	112
113	114	115	116	117	118	119	120	121	122	123	124	125	126
127	128	129	130	131	132	133	134	135	136	137	138	139	140
141	142	143	144	145	146	147	148	149	150	151	152	153	154
155	156	157	158	159	160	161	162	163	164	165	166	167	168
169	170	171	172	173	174	175	176	177					

Introductory Activities

The first activity of the P.E. lesson should help produce a state of physical and mental readiness in children. It provides a general warm-up, increasing blood flow to the major muscle groups, and helps spark excitement about participating in the subsequent activities.

This section offers 50 possible Introductory Activities, including:

IA-1 ORGANIZATION SIGNALS

FOCUS: Class management; formations   **EQUIPMENT:** None

ORGANIZATION:

- Organization Signals mobilize the class, arranging children in various formations quickly and without confusion. Used constantly and spontaneously, these Signals will improve class control. Call out each Organization Signal and use the corresponding hand signal simultaneously. As the children become familiar with the signal's action, simply use the hand signal.

DESCRIPTION OF ACTIVITY:

1. **Listening Circle:** Run quickly to sit cross-legged in a circle near and facing me. (*Hand Signal:* Point with your index finger to the floor near you while circling the other index finger overhead.)

2. **Listening Line:** Run quickly to stand side by side in a line near me. Space yourselves at arm's length and face me. (*Hand Signal:* Point with your index finger to a line near you, and then extend your arms sideways at shoulder height.)

3. **Quiet Signal:** Immediately stop what you are doing and raise one hand. Give me your full attention. (*Hand Signal:* Hold one hand overhead. Wait until all are quiet and paying attention.)

4. **Homes:** Run to a free space in the play area and sit cross-legged there, facing me. Check your spot so that you cannot touch anyone or anything. Remember your home. (*Hand Signal:* Make a roof overhead with hands. Mats or hoops could also be used as "Homes.")

5. **Endline:** Run quickly to one end of the play area and stand in a line, equally spaced apart, facing me. (*Hand Signal:* Point with index finger to one end of play area and extend arms sideways at shoulder level.)

IA–2 FORMATION SIGNALS

FOCUS: Class management

EQUIPMENT: Chart paper;
marking pen;
and masking tape

ORGANIZATION:

- Formation Signals organize players into partners, small groups, or lines. Call out each action and use accompanying hand signal simultaneously. Establish four equal teams at the beginning of the year. List the names of the players of each team on chart paper, and tape the chart to the wall. Select a leader and co-leader for each team. Change leaders and co-leaders often throughout the year so that each team member has a turn at both positions.

DESCRIPTION OF ACTIVITY:

1. *Groups:* Quickly sit in a group with the number of players I call; for example, "Groups of 2!" or "Groups of 5!" (*Hand Signal:* Hold up the same number of fingers as players in each group.)

2. *Lines:* Leaders, run with your team to the side of the play area and sit cross-legged there, facing me. Other team members, quickly find your leader and sit cross-legged in a line behind him or her. Space yourselves evenly apart. Leader, sit at the front of the file and co-leader, sit at the back. (*Hand Signal:* Extend arms in front, parallel to each other and to the floor.)

VARIATION:

Waves: Call Lines signal and use its hand action; then move to one side of the lines and have players turn to face you.

FOCUS: Class management; circle formation **EQUIPMENT:** Lively music; tape or record player

ORGANIZATION:

- Movement Signals quickly get players moving. Call out combinations of formations and locomotor movements such as "Activity Circle, slide clockwise!" or "Scrambled Eggs, run!" Use hand signals as well. Change locomotor movements frequently throughout the activity. Players could: jog, skip, hop, slide-step, leap, gallop, or run backwards. Motivate players with lively music.

DESCRIPTION OF ACTIVITY:

1. **Scrambled Eggs:** Run helter-skelter in any direction. Remember, don't touch anyone as you move! (*Hand Signal:* Roll hand over hand.)

2. **Activity Circle:** Jog clockwise (or CCW) around play area in single file. Stay in your original order; don't pass anyone. (*Hand Signal:* Circle one arm overhead in a clockwise [or CCW] direction.)

VARIATIONS:

a. Use "Scrambled Eggs" signal with different directions, pathways, and levels (call "Scrambled Eggs, run sideways!" or zigzag, high, and low), or, with different walks (call "Scrambled Eggs, crab-walk!" or lame-dog walk and bear-walk); enhance spatial awareness by calling "Scrambled Eggs, jog in a small space," ". . . jog in a smaller space," ". . . jog in an even smaller space."

b. **Switching Sides (Movement Signals Game):** Mark out play area with cone markers. Divide the class into two equal teams. Start with each team standing behind opposite endlines of play area, facing each other. Ensure that players are well spaced along the lines to avoid collisions. Adjust the running distance and the number of runs to class level. Use a variety of locomotor skills such as walking quickly, running with arms in the air, hopping, skipping, galloping, moving on all fours, etc. On signal "Switch Sides," both teams must change sides to sit cross-legged just behind the opposite line; the first team to do so earns one point. Play each game to five points.

IA-4 SIGNALS GAME

FOCUS: Alertness; listening skills

EQUIPMENT: None

ORGANIZATION:

- The game of Signals consists of a locomotor movement and a simultaneous verbal and hand signal. Encourage players to respond quickly by issuing a challenge such as "You owe me three jumping jacks (push-ups, or any task) if you are last!"

- Regard the "You owe me three!" challenge as good sportsmanship, not as punishment. Caution children to watch where they are going at all times.

DESCRIPTION OF ACTIVITY:

1. Run quickly. Run slowly. Skip high. Crawl low. Now Clear the Deck! Get off the floor as quickly as possible to stand on a bench, a chair, the climbing frame, and so on. (*Hand Signal:* Open arms overhead.)

2. Gallop in a new direction every time I call "Change!" Now Hit the Deck! Lie face down as quickly as possible on the floor or ground. (*Hand Signal:* Point to the floor with both hands.)

3. Walk like a robot. Waddle like a duck. Crabwalk. Now Corners! Run to any corner of the play area, or where any two lines cross, and sit cross-legged there. (*Hand Signal:* Cross arms overhead.)

4. Walk backwards in pairs, holding hands. Hop in pairs. Now Iceberg! Stop immediately and freeze like a statue. (*Hand Signal:* Make a fist overhead.)

VARIATIONS:

a. When playing Signals indoors, use the markings on the play area floor as part of the game. For example, call "Red lines!" and stand on a red line when you want players to sit cross-legged there.

b. Challenge players to keep alert by signalling with hands only.

c. Substitute other previously taught signals such as "Scrambled Eggs!" or "Activity Circle!"

IA–5 STARTING POSITIONS

FOCUS: Class management; personal space awareness   **EQUIPMENT:** None

ORGANIZATION:

- Starting Positions are used to quickly organize and position the class for any activity. Teach the following positions; then have the children practice the positions by calling them out in random order and in quick succession. Stress correct body posture.

DESCRIPTION OF ACTIVITY:

1. **Long Sit:** Sit with legs outstretched and together. Lean back on hands for support.

2. **Hook Sit:** Sit with legs together, knees bent, and feet flat on the floor. Lean back on hands for support.

3. **Wide-Sit:** Sit with legs outstretched and comfortably apart. Lean back on hands for support.

4. **Cross-legged Sit:** Sit with legs crossed and arms resting on knees.

5. **All Fours:** Support your weight on hands and knees.

6. **Front Support:** Support weight on hands and toes, with face down. Hold body straight.

7. **Front-Lying:** Lie face down with legs together and arms at sides, chest level.

8. **Back-Lying:** Lie face up with legs together and arms at sides.

9. **Hook-Lying:** Lie on back with knees bent so that feet are flat on floor. Arms are relaxed at sides.

10. **Back Support:** Sit with legs outstretched and together. Lean back on hands for support, bend elbows slightly, and then raise trunk to take weight on hands and heels. Hold body straight.

11. **Squat:** Stand; bend knees to raise heels from the floor. Place hands between knees and rest them on floor.

12. **Stand Tall:** Stand with feet comfortably apart and toes turned out slightly. Arms are at sides.

VARIATION: As part of the Signals Game, combine Starting Position signals with Organizational signals; for example, "Scrambled Eggs, skip." "Iceberg, long sit!"

IA–6 SHIP AHOY!

FOCUS: Listening; alertness

EQUIPMENT: None

ORGANIZATION:

- Have players imagine that the play area is a Ship. You are the ship's Captain and they are the crew. Teach the players the meaning of the nautical terms "Bow," "Stern," "Starboard," and "Portside." Then as Captain, give two signals: a signal to run to different parts of the ship such as the bow or the stern, and then a signal to perform an action. Explain and demonstrate signals before the game begins. At first, point in the direction players should move when they forget which part of the ship is which. When learned, mix up the signals to keep players alert.

DESCRIPTION OF ACTIVITY:

1. ***Run to the Bow!*** (Run to front end of play areas.)

   Lifeboat! Form groups of three players and pretend to row to shore.

2. ***Hop to the Stern!*** (Hop to other end of play area.)

   Captain's coming! Stop and salute your captain.

3. ***Skip to Port!*** (Skip to left side of the play area as you face the bow.)

   Periscope! Lie on your back and raise one leg.

4. ***Jump to Starboard!*** (Jump to right side of play area as you face the bow.)

   Crew overboard! Grab someone's arm and hold on.

5. ***Power-walk to the bow!***

   Crow's Nest! Climb up any object.

6. ***Leap to the Stern!***

   Radar! Run with hands up and make beeping noises.

7. ***Roll to Starboard!***

   Sharks! Link a body part with another player until everyone is joined together.

VARIATIONS:

a. Have players suggest other signals; for example, "Swab the deck!" (Players pantomime scrubbing the floor area.)

b. Use gymnastic equipment for players to mount in such signals as "Crow's nest!" or swing from ropes on the signal "Pirates."

c. Substitute another theme such as "In the Jungle" or "In the Wild West."

IA–7 TAKE A CHANCE

FOCUS: Aerobic warm-up; listening

EQUIPMENT: Deck of "Take-a-Chance" cards; one short rope per player; background peppy music; tape or record player

ORGANIZATION:

- For this warm-up activity, you will need to make a deck of Take-a-Chance cards: On each index card, print an exercise task and the number of times the task should be repeated. To play Take-a-Chance, fan the deck of cards and ask one player to "take a chance." That player selects a card, reads it aloud, and then leads the class through the movement described. After the class has completed the task, another player selects a card. Continue in this way until you feel your class is sufficiently warmed up. Emphasize doing the exercises slower and well, rather than rushing to finish first.

- These cards can be used as "Breaks" (see Fitness Activities) at any time during the lesson, throughout the school year.

- The following are some suggestions for card tasks.

DESCRIPTION OF ACTIVITY:

- Touch each wall and then sit cross-legged in the middle of the play area.

- Touch each sideline; then return to long-sit in your home.

- Jump a rope 30 times.

- Do four push-ups in each corner of the play area.

- Jog three laps CCW (counterclockwise) around the play area.

- Give "high ten's" to ten different players.

- Touch ten different lines on the floor with your left foot and right hand.

- Do a two-body part-balance with a partner.

- Do eight sit-ups at four different lines.

- Do 20 Jumping Jacks together with a partner.

- Touch in order a bench, a door, a mat, and a rope.

- Do eight half jump-turns on the spot.

- Step up and down a bench 20 times.

- Exercise of boys' choice.

- Exercise of girls' choice.

- Exercise of Teacher's choice.

VARIATIONS:

a. Have different players choose cards, but lead the exercises yourself.

b. Distribute blank index cards and have each player write a new Take-a-Chance card.

IA–8 FRIENDSHIP LINK-UP

FOCUS: Running; friendship

EQUIPMENT: Lively music;
tape or record player

ORGANIZATION:

- Have players find a partner, hold hands, and scatter.

DESCRIPTION OF ACTIVITY:

1. When you hear the music, this is the signal to begin. Run with your partner in open spaces, keeping in time with the music.
2. When the music stops, you stop. On the signal "Change!" quickly find another couple. One partner hold hands with one of the other pair. You are now partners. The two outside players then link up to become a new pair as well. Move together in time with the music.
3. Continue changing partners like this each time the music stops and you hear the signal "Change!" If I call "Change, skipping," change partners and—still holding hands—skip together in time with the music. I may also call: "Change, hopping"; "Change, sliding"; "Change, running backwards."

VARIATION: Have players greet each other when they meet a new partner: "Hello, Matt!"; "Hello, Amy!"

IA–9 ARTFUL DODGER

FOCUS: Running and dodging; alertness; fair play

EQUIPMENT: Lively music;
tape or record player

ORGANIZATION:

- Discuss the meaning of the word "dodge" (to move quickly aside; to change direction to avoid something or someone; to get away from). Discuss the meaning of the word "mark" (to follow; to shadow; to stay close to). In this game we will practice being a good Dodger and a good Marker. Explain that many simple games as well as organized sports involve the skills of dodging and marking. Have players find a partner and stand back-to-back in a home space. The taller partner is the Dodger; the other, the Marker.

DESCRIPTION OF ACTIVITY:

1. When the music starts, Dodger, run away from your Marker. Marker, chase your Dodger, trying to stay within an arm's reach of the Dodger at all times.
2. When the music stops, everyone FREEZE! (stop immediately on the spot where you are). Now, Marker, reach out without moving your feet and touch your Dodger. If you can, then change roles.
3. As soon as you hear the music, begin the game again. Who will be the Dodger and Marker this time when the music stops?
4. Now find a new partner and continue the game when the music starts.

VARIATIONS:

a. Allow Marker to take a pivot step in any direction when trying to touch his or her Dodger.
b. Use other locomotor movements such as walking forward, walking backwards, side-stepping, galloping, and skipping.
c. Play the game in pairs—one pair is the Dodger; the other pair is the Marker.

FOCUS: Running and dodging; alertness; fair play

EQUIPMENT: Four cone markers; one beanbag

ORGANIZATION:

- Use the cone markers to mark out the play area. Choose one player to be IT and hold the beanbag. All other players scatter throughout the play area. Emphasize that players play by the rules. Encourage good use of space and awareness of the safety of others.

DESCRIPTION OF ACTIVITY:

1. *Poison Tag:* On signal "GO!" IT try to tag the other players on different parts of their bodies with the beanbag. Players, when tagged by IT, you must hold onto the "poisoned" part or the place where you were tagged; then you can also try to poison other players. Game ends when all players have been poisoned.

2. *Nose and Toes Tag:* On the signal "GO!" IT try to tag the other players with your beanbag. Players, you are safe from being tagged if you are holding your nose with one hand and your foot with the other and are moving. If tagged, you become the new IT, pick up the beanbag, and the game continues.

3. *Stork Tag:* Players stand like a stork to avoid being tagged.

4. *Turtle Tag:* On the signal "GO!" IT, chase the other players. Players, when IT comes near, avoid being tagged by quickly lying on your back with your arms and legs raised in the air (like a turtle on its back). As soon as IT has gone by, spring to your feet and keep running. If you are tagged, you become the new IT.

5. *Back-to-Back Tag:* On the signal "GO!" IT, chase the other players. Players, you are safe for five seconds only when you stand back-to-back, elbows linked, with another player. As soon as you feel safe or your five seconds are up, separate and run in free space until IT comes near again. Then find a new partner and stand back-to-back. If you are tagged, you become the new IT.

6. *Arch Tag:* (Have all players find a partner, hold hands with their partner, and scatter. Choose one pair to be the IT pair.) On the signal "GO!" the IT pair, try to tag as many other pairs as possible. A tagged pair must jog on the spot while facing each other with arms raised to form an arch. You can only be freed by another pair running through your arch.

VARIATIONS:

a. Have more than one IT.

b. Have each IT wear a colored pinnie or banner to identify themselves.

IA-11 PARTNER TAG

FOCUS: Running and dodging; partnerwork; fair play

EQUIPMENT: Four cone markers; set of colored banners; lively music; tape or record player

ORGANIZATION:

- Have players find a partner, hold hands, and scatter. Choose one pair to be the "Chasers" and wear banners. Remind pairs to run to open spaces to avoid others. Emphasize that the hand-hold may not be broken during the game.

DESCRIPTION OF ACTIVITY:

1. On the signal "GO!" Chasers, attempt to tag the other pairs. Either of the IT pair may make the tag.

2. If you are tagged, you also become chasers and each must wear a colored banner.

3. We will play until the last pair has been tagged.

VARIATION: Have pairs link up until they become a group of four. Only the end players may tag.

IA-12 DOUBLE TROUBLE

FOCUS: Running and dodging; alertness; partnerwork

EQUIPMENT: See activity IA-11.

ORGANIZATION:

- Choose one player to be IT and wear a colored banner. Everyone else scatters. Emphasize that pairs must keep their hand-hold throughout the game.

DESCRIPTION OF ACTIVITY:

1. On the signal "GO!" IT, chase the other players. IT, if you tag a player, then that player must put on a banner and join hands with you. Now chase others as an IT pair.

2. IT pair, if you tag someone else, then that player must wear a banner and join hands with you, too. Continue as an IT group to chase the free players.

3. As soon as four players are holding hands in the IT group, split into two IT pairs, who join hands and give chase.

4. Continue the game until all players are running in pairs.

VARIATION:

For a large class, begin the game with two or more ITs and increase the size of the playing area.

IA–13 PARTNERSHIP

FOCUS: Aerobic warm-up; partnerwork

EQUIPMENT: One whistle;
four benches;
15 mats;
lively music;
tape or record player

ORGANIZATION:

• Scatter several mats around the play area, and position a bench on each side of the play area. Have players find a partner of equal size and scatter. One partner leads and the other follows the leader's actions. They change roles whenever you blow the whistle. Do so every 30 seconds to ensure that players have several opportunities to be the leader. At first, have the Partnership activity last for three minutes; then gradually increase the duration of the activity as children's fitness levels improve.

DESCRIPTION OF ACTIVITY:

1. When the music starts, Leaders, begin exercising. Followers, copy your Leader's movements. Try the sample exercise routine, repeating each exercise for ten seconds. Then try your own exercise ideas!

2. *Sample Exercise Routine:*
   — Side-step around the play area.
   — Jump and kick.
   — On one whistle blast, change roles.
   — Skip with high arm swings in and out of the mats.
   — Do bench push-ups. Now do mat sit-ups.
   — On one whistle blast, change roles and continue activity.
   — Grapevine-step (cross one foot in front of the other; then step that foot behind as you move sideways).
   — Leap over mats around the play area.
   — On one whistle blast, change roles again.
   — Do "high-ten" jumps (jump to clap partner's hands overhead).
   — On two whistle blasts, find a new partner.

IA–14 FOLLOW THE LEADER

FOCUS: Aerobic warm-up; leadership

EQUIPMENT: Lively music;
tape or record player

ORGANIZATION:

• Form groups of four to six players. Have each group choose a leader to start the fun run. Players stand in a file behind their leader. Emphasize that groups not interfere with other groups. Encourage leaders to use their imaginations; be creative.

DESCRIPTION OF ACTIVITY:

1. At the start of the music, follow your Leader doing whatever he or she does. Stay in order and in line, and try to keep in time with the music.

2. Leader, think of movements and activities for your Followers to do:
   — Run in different ways; crawling; hopping; twisting; rolling; dodging; jumping.
   — Move forward; backwards; sideways; diagonally.
   — Do animal walks such as the bear walk; seal walk; crab walk; kangaroo hop.
   — Do exercises such as sit-ups; push-ups; jumping jacks; knee bends.
   — Do dance steps of any dances you have done.

3. On the signal "Change" (after about 30 seconds), the next player in the line, take over as the new Leader to continue the activity. Old Leader, join the end of the line.

IA–15 THREE DEEP

FOCUS: Running and dodging

EQUIPMENT: One beanbag or small ball;
lively music (optional);
tape or record player

ORGANIZATION:

- Choose one player to be the Chaser. Choose another player to be the Runner. Everyone else finds a partner. Partners scatter around the play area and stand in single-file formation.

DESCRIPTION OF ACTIVITY:

1. On signal "Go!" all pairs, jog on the spot. Chaser, try to lightly tag the runner.
2. Runner, to save yourself from being tagged, stop in front of any pair. As soon as you join a pair, the last player in the file becomes the new Runner and sprints away to avoid the Chaser.
3. Chaser, when you tag a Runner, change roles and continue the activity. Remember, waiting players, to jog on the spot. Neither the Chaser nor the Runner should touch the other pairs during the game.

VARIATIONS:

a. Designate two Runners and two Chasers.
b. Have Runner carry a beanbag or ball and pass the object to the third player in the line, who then becomes the new Runner.

IA–16 BRONCO TAG

FOCUS: Running and dodging

EQUIPMENT: None

ORGANIZATION:

- Divide the class into groups of three players. In each group, players stand in single-file formation and hold onto the hips of the player in front, to form a Bronco: The first player is the head; the second player, the middle; and the third player, the end. The remaining players, or one group of three, are the Loose Tails. To start the game, have the Bronco groups scatter throughout the play area and the Loose Tails stand in the middle of the play area.
- Continue the game until you feel the players are sufficiently warmed up.

DESCRIPTION OF ACTIVITY:

1. On signal "Go!" each Loose Tail, try to hook onto the last player of a Bronco group. Meanwhile, the head player of a Bronco, try to swing your group away from the Loose Tail to protect the end player.
2. If a Loose Tail does hook onto an end player, then the head player becomes the new Loose Tail and tries to hook onto a Bronco.
3. If a Bronco group comes apart while being chased by a Loose Tail, then the Tail may immediately join the Bronco group, and the head must become the new Tail.

VARIATION:

Loose Caboose: Play game as above, except that each group of three forms a Train: First player is the Engine; second, the Coal Car; and third, the Caboose.

FOCUS: Running and dodging; accuracy throwing

EQUIPMENT: One beanbag or Nerf™ ball per player; four cone markers

ORGANIZATION:

- Use the cone markers to mark out a large rectangular play area.

DESCRIPTION OF ACTIVITY:

1. **Wasps!:** (Have players find a partner; then have one partner of each pair get a "stinger" [beanbag]. This partner is the "Wasp.") On signal "Wasps!" Wasp, chase your partner trying to hit him or her below the waist with the stinger. If you are hit, you then pick up the stinger to become the new Wasp and chase your partner.

VARIATIONS:

a. Have the Wasps touch the partner with the stinger.

b. Every player is a Wasp who can sting anyone. When hit, that player must perform some exercise, such as three jumping jacks, to get back in the game. A loose beanbag on the floor may be picked up by anyone.

c. The whole class is chased by several Wasps and, when hit, those players must perform a stunt or dance step to get back in the game.

2. **Galloping Lizzie:** (Choose one player to be "Lizzie," who has a beanbag [or Nerf™ ball] and stands in the center of the play area. Have all other players scatter.) On the signal "Gallop Lizzie," Lizzie *gallop* around the play area trying to hit the other players below the waist with the ball. Players, you may tease Lizzie by going as close as possible, and then running away. If you are hit by the ball or go out of bounds, do five jumping jacks on the spot to get back into the game. Only Lizzie may touch the ball throughout the game. The fifth player to be hit by Lizzie becomes the new Lizzie, and the game continues.

VARIATIONS:

a. Instead of galloping, have Lizzie skip or fast walk.

b. Have two Lizzies, but only one ball. The Lizzies may pass the ball to each other to get a better shot and have to take it in turn to score. How many players can you hit before 1½ minutes are up and two new Lizzies take over?

3. **Bounce Ball Tag:** (Choose two to three players to be the "Throwers." Have each get a Nerf™ ball and stand in the middle of the play area. Have the rest of the class scatter. If indoors, allow the ball to bounce off a wall before hitting a player.) On the signal "Bounce Ball," the Throwers, bounce the ball on the floor to hit the players below the waist. Players, if you are hit by one of the balls, form a bridge on the floor with your hands and feet. You can be freed by having one of the other players slide under your bridge. A player cannot be hit while freeing another player.

IA-18 COOPERATIVE SHUTTLE WARM-UP

FOCUS: Aerobic warm-up; listening

EQUIPMENT: Several cone markers;
lively music;
tape or record player

ORGANIZATION:

- In this Warm-Up, partners take turns moving in different ways to the opposite side of the play area, touching a required body part to the floor. Have players find a partner and, as a pair, stand in single-file formation at one side of the play area.

DESCRIPTION OF ACTIVITY:

1. When the music starts, the first partner, move quickly to the opposite side, touch the floor with the body part I call, and then quickly return using the same movement to tag your partner.
2. Waiting partners, jog in place until your partner tags you; then repeat the action and return to tag your partner.
3. Keep going until everyone has repeated the following tasks:
   — Run forward; touch both hands.
   — Run backwards; touch both knees.
   — Hop on one leg; touch one elbow and one knee. Hop on the other leg to return.
   — Crab-Walk: Move in the back-support position; touch hips.
   — Lame-Dog Walk: Run on hands and feet, with one leg raised; touch ear.
   — Seal-Walk: Walk on hands in front support position, dragging feet; touch head.
   — Bear-Walk: Walk on hands and feet, moving right arm and leg forward, then left arm and leg forward; touch seat.

SEAL WALK

BEAR WALK

IA-19 STICKY HANDS

FOCUS: Aerobic fun run; partnerwork; friendship

EQUIPMENT: Several cone markers;
lively music;
tape or record player

ORGANIZATION:

- Have players find a partner and join hands. When the music starts, the pairs run together anywhere in the play area until you signal that they must change partners. Change partners often at first; then, as the warm-up progresses, increase the time the pairs run together before they stop to change partners.

DESCRIPTION OF ACTIVITY:

1. Run! Now on signal "Sticky Hands!" drop hands and find a new partner. Greet your new partner by name; for example, "Hi, Abby!" or "Hi, Jimmy!" Join hands and run together.
2. On signal "Sticky Hands!" drop hands and find another partner. Again greet your new partner by name, join hands, and run.
3. At the end of the activity, walk around the play area with your last partner, gently swaying from side to side.

VARIATIONS:

a. Substitute other movements for running: skip, side-step, power-walk.
b. Substitute a different way of greeting a new partner: shake hands; say "Good day!", link elbows and skip around twice; give each other a "High Ten!" (jump to touch hands); share a friendly hug.
c. Interview your partner as you run together, asking questions such as: "What is your favorite sport?"; "How many brothers do you have?"

IA-20 UNCLE SAM

FOCUS: Running and dodging; listening

EQUIPMENT: Four cone markers;
one pinnie;
set of colored flags

ORGANIZATION:

- Mark out the play area. Clearly mark the two endlines. Choose one player to be "Uncle Sam," who stands in the center of the play area wearing the pinnie. All other players tuck a flag in your waistband so that three quarters of it is showing and stand behind one of the endlines.

DESCRIPTION OF ACTIVITY:

1. Endline players, start the game by chanting:
   "Uncle Sam, Uncle Sam, may we cross your ocean dam?"
   Uncle Sam, you answer by saying:
   "Yes, if you are wearing blue."
2. Players wearing blue get a free pass to the other end. Then on the signal "Go" from Uncle Sam, the rest of the players try to run to the opposite endline without getting their flag pulled. Tagged players become Uncle Sam's helpers.
3. Begin again. This time, Uncle Sam, call out another color. Keep going until all players are caught but one. This player becomes the new Uncle Sam for the next game.

VARIATIONS:

a. Vary the criteria for a free pass: girls with short hair, wearing glasses, all the boys, all the girls, etc.
b. If tagged, the player has to do five repetitions of an exercise before re-entering the game.

IA-21 FIRE ALARM!

FOCUS: Running and dodging; listening

EQUIPMENT: Four cone markers;
set of colored flags

ORGANIZATION:

- Mark out the play area with two well-defined endlines. Choose one player to be the "Fire Chief," who stands in the middle of the play area. Have all other players, the "Firefighters," stand behind one of the endlines and number off from one through four.

DESCRIPTION OF ACTIVITY:

1. Fire Chief, begin to call out the numbers one, two, three, or four; but Firefighters, do not move until the Chief calls "Fire!" after your number. For example, on the signal "two, Fire!" all the two's will run to the opposite end of the play area.

2. Fire Chief, try to tag as many Firefighters as you can. A tagged Firefighter will become your helper. The last one tagged becomes the new Fire Chief for the next game.

3. When the Fire Chief calls "Fire Alarm!" then all the players must run.

VARIATIONS:

a. The Chief may call out more than one number at a time.
b. Use flags tucked into players' waistbands that must be pulled out in order to be caught.

IA-22 GERM BUG

FOCUS: Chasing and dodging

EQUIPMENT: Three beanbags (sponge or tennis balls); four cone markers

ORGANIZATION:

- Define the boundaries of the play area. Choose three players to be the Germ Bugs. Each Germ Bug holds a beanbag in his or her hand and stands in the middle of the play area to start the game. The rest of the players are "ordinary Bugs" who scatter throughout the play area.

DESCRIPTION OF ACTIVITY:

1. On the signal "GO!" Germ Bugs, chase the other "Bugs" anywhere in the play area and try to touch them with the beanbag.
2. Bugs, if you are touched by the Germ Bug, you become "Dead Bugs" and must get into the "dead bug position" by lying on your back with hands and feet in the air and wiggling all over!
3. Another Bug may come along and free a "dead bug" by forming a bridge over this player and holding the position for three slow counts.
4. Bugs, you are safe from being tagged as long as you are in the "Stork Stance" (by holding one foot with the opposite hand). You may stay in this position as long as you want or until you loose your balance.
5. The fourth "ordinary Bug" to be touched by a Germ Bug becomes the new Germ Bug, and the old Germ Bug becomes an "ordinary Bug." The game continues until a warm-up effect has been reached.

IA-23 WOLF ON THE PROWL

FOCUS: Running and dodging; spatial awareness

EQUIPMENT: Several cone markers; one flag per player (optional)

ORGANIZATION:

- Use cone markers to mark the middle third of the play area as the Wolf's Den. Have all players stand side-by-side at either end of the play area; then have one player go to the Wolf's Den. That player is the Wolf and all other players are Rabbits. The rabbits have "tails" (flags tucked into back of shorts).

DESCRIPTION OF ACTIVITY:

WOLF'S DEN

1. Rabbits, run through the Wolf's Den to the other end of the play area. Tease the Wolf as you go, shouting "Wolf, wolf, you can't touch me!" Once you enter the Wolf's Den, you must continue through to the opposite end before running back to where you started.
2. Wolf, try to tag any Rabbit who runs into your Den. You may also chase the Rabbits outside your den, but only for three steps. Tagged Rabbits become Wolves, join the Wolf pack, and help tag other Rabbits.
3. The game continues until all Rabbits are caught. The last rabbit caught is the Wolf in the next game.

IA-24 CLEAR THE FIELD

FOCUS: Aerobic warm-up; agility; fair play

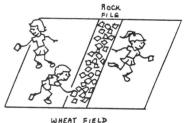

EQUIPMENT: All available beanbags (or deckrings); several cone markers; lively music; tape or record player

ORGANIZATION:

- Use cones to mark out the rock pile, an area in the middle of the play area, which is a wheat field. Scatter all available beanbags within the rock pile area. The beanbags are "rocks" that players will take one by one to the other side of the field.
- To begin, divide the class into two equal "work crews." They stand at opposite ends of the play area. As players become more fit, increase the length of the play area.

DESCRIPTION OF ACTIVITY:

1. When the music starts, everyone run to the rock pile and pick up one rock each. Run with it to the opposite end of the play area and place it there. Then run back to the rock pile and repeat the action. Remember to take only one rock at a time and to place, not throw, the beanbags!
2. After all the rocks have been cleared from the rock pile, take the rocks from your end to the other end.
3. When the music stops, freeze on the spot. If you are carrying a rock, take it to the other end of the field and return to your end. Now count the number of rocks at your end of the field. Which crew worked harder to clear the field? The work crew with more rocks wins the game.

IA-25 GIVE AWAY

EQUIPMENT: All available beanbags (or deckrings); several cone markers; two hoops; one mat per player; lively music; tape or record player

ORGANIZATION:

- Place a hoop in the middle of the play area and fill it with beanbags. Have players find a partner and get a mat to share. Help partners space mats equally around the hoop and about five meters (15 feet) away from it. Pairs then sit on mats and decide which partner will go first.

DESCRIPTION OF ACTIVITY:

1. When the music starts, first partner, run to the hoop, get a beanbag, and return to your mat. Place the beanbag on the mat and sit down. Second partner, pick up the beanbag from your mat and run with it to the hoop or to another pair's mat. Place the beanbag there, return to the mat, and sit down.
2. Meanwhile, other players will have placed beanbags on your mat. Taking turns, pick up a beanbag from your mat and run to place it in the hoop or on another pair's mat. You may pick up only one beanbag at a time! One partner must remain on the mat at all times.
3. Continue until the music stops. Now count the number of beanbags on your mat. The pair with the fewest beanbags wins.

IA-26 INDIANAPOLIS 500

FOCUS: Aerobic fun run; fair play

EQUIPMENT: 15 cone markers;
lively running music;
tape or record player

ORGANIZATION:

- Distribute cones evenly around an oval racetrack that is about the size of a basketball court. Begin the race by having runners stand at the cone markers, with no more than three runners at each cone. To encourage runners to compete only with themselves, before the race have them estimate how many laps they think they will run in three minutes. Compare estimate with actual number of laps after the race.

DESCRIPTION OF ACTIVITY:

1. Pretend that you are a racing car driver, revving your engine at the start of a race. Select a name for your car and tell me what it is. Now tell me how many laps you think you can run. Count the number of times you pass your starting cone.
2. As soon as the music starts, begin running CCW around the racetrack. Overtake other runners only on the outside of the track. If you cannot keep a running pace, then turn off and walk around the inside of the cone markers. Re-enter the traffic in a free space when you are ready.
3. If you bump into another player, your racing car has crashed and you must go to the repair pit in the middle of the track. Do ten jumping jacks there; then return to the race wherever you left it.
4. If you knock over a cone marker, set it up again before running on. Slow to a walk when the music stops and tell me how many laps you ran.

VARIATION: Gradually lengthen the time the music plays to increase the number of laps players run. If space permits, set up two racing tracks. Which team can accumulate more laps?

IA-27 SWAP SIDES

FOCUS: Aerobic warm-up; listening skills

EQUIPMENT: Four cone markers;
balls (optional)

ORGANIZATION:

- Divide the class into four equal groups: A, B, C, and D. Assign each group to stand on a line on one side of a square court, marked out by cone markers.

DESCRIPTION OF ACTIVITY:

1. On the signal "AC," all players in groups A and C swap sides as quickly as you can. On the signal "BD," all players in groups B and D change sides as quickly as possible.
2. On the signal "AB," all players in groups A and B swap sides; on the signal "AD," all players in groups A and D swap sides; on the signal "BC," all players in groups B and C swap sides; and on signal "CD," all players in groups C and D swap sides.
3. On the signal "ABCD," *all* groups swap places moving carefully to the opposite side.

VARIATIONS:

a. Vary the way players swap sides by adding a movement to the group signal: "AC, SLIDE!" (Crab Walk; Seal Walk; Frog Hop; Lame Dog Walk, and other Animal Walks; skip; hop; walk backwards; roll; crawl; leap).
b. Work "Ball Skills" into the game by having the players roll, carry, bounce, or kick the ball as they swap sides.

IA-28 CROWS AND CRANES

FOCUS: Alertness; agility; listening

EQUIPMENT: Eight cone markers; one flag per player

ORGANIZATION:

- Mark out the play area with two center lines about one meter (3 feet) apart and two safety lines about 20 meters (60 feet) apart from each other. The safety lines should be at least 4 to 5 meters (12 to 15 feet) from the end walls or any other obstruction. Have each player tuck a flag in the waistband so that it hangs loosely and can be easily seen. Then divide the class into two equal teams, the "Crows" and the "Cranes." Have each team stand, facing the other, on one of the center lines. Players should space themselves evenly along the line.

DESCRIPTION OF ACTIVITY:

1. Crows, your safety line is behind you; Cranes, your safety line is behind you. You cannot be caught if you are on or beyond your safety line.
2. I may call either "C-C-C-Crows!" or "C-C-C-Cranes!" If I call "Crows," all the "Crow" players chase the Cranes, trying to pull as many flags as possible before the Cranes can reach their safety line.
3. All Cranes who had their flag pulled, replace the flag in their waistband and join the Crows' team. Both teams quickly return to their center line to listen for the next signal. Which team will have more players at the end of the game?

VARIATION: Vary the locomotor movements used when one team is chasing the other: gallop; skip; hop; jump; slide; crab walk; dog walk.

IA-29 SNATCH THE FOX'S TAIL

FOCUS: Chasing and dodging

EQUIPMENT: One flag per pair; one flag per player (optional); lively music; tape or record player

ORGANIZATION:

- Have players find a partner and stand two meters (six feet) apart. One partner in each pair is the "Fox" and tucks a flag into the back of the waistband so that it hangs out like a tail. The other partner is the "Hound."

DESCRIPTION OF ACTIVITY:

1. On signal "Tallyho!" each Hound, chase your Fox and try to snatch the Fox's tail.

2. If you succeed, tuck the tail into your waistband and run away from your partner. You are now the Fox and your partner is the Hound.

3. After a few minutes, find a new partner and begin the activity again.

VARIATIONS:

a. Give flags to everyone except two or three players. They are the Hounds and try to snatch flags from other players. Tagged players become Hounds and help tag others.
b. The player whose flag is snatched must do five repetitions of an exercise of his or her partner's choice before continuing the game.

IA–30 POMPOM PULL-AWAY

FOCUS: Aerobic warm-up; chasing and dodging

EQUIPMENT: One flag per player; four cone markers

ORGANIZATION:

- Mark out the play area with a safe zone at each end. Clear the play area of obstacles such as benches, chairs, and other equipment. Select one player to be IT, who stands in the middle of the play area. Have all other players tuck a flag in the back of their waistband so that two thirds of the flag is showing and stand at one end of the play area.

DESCRIPTION OF ACTIVITY:

1. On the signal "POMPOM PULL-AWAY!" called out by IT, all players try to run to the safe zone at the opposite end of the play area before IT can pull your flag.
2. Players tagged, you become IT's helpers and join IT in the middle of the play area. Don't forget to return your flag to me.
3. Now all ITs, shout together, "Pompom Pull-Away!" and players again try to run to the opposite safe zone.
4. Continue in this way until only one player is left. That player becomes IT for the next game.

VARIATIONS:

a. Start with more than one IT.
b. Have players start at either end; all players must change ends when "Pompom Pull-Away" is called.

IA–31 PAC-MAN TAG

FOCUS: Running and dodging; alertness

EQUIPMENT: One banner per player; one beanbag per player; several cone markers

ORGANIZATION:

- Use cones to mark two circular safe zones near either end of the play area. Divide the class into two equal teams: "Pac-Men," who wear banners diagonally across the chest and hold a beanbag each; and "Ghost Monsters," who also hold a beanbag each.

DESCRIPTION OF ACTIVITY:

1. Players, you may run only on the lines marked on the play area. Ghost Monsters, you may jump from line to line and may rest within the safe zones at either end of the play area for a "three pac-man" count; then you must run again. Pac-Men, you must not guard the safe zone.
2. On signal "Go!" Pac-Men, try to "zap" Ghost Monsters by lightly tagging them with your beanbag.
3. Tagged Ghost Monsters, jog on the spot until you are able to tag a Pac-Man and free yourself. When you are tagged a second time, you become a Pac-Man, put on a Pac-Man banner, and must chase other Ghost Monsters. Continue in this way until all Ghost Monsters are Pac-Men.

VARIATIONS:

a. Reverse roles—Ghost Monsters are IT.
b. Have players invent their own rules.

IA-32 SWAT TAG

FOCUS: Running and dodging; alertness

EQUIPMENT: One swatter (towel, masking tape); four cone markers; six hoops

ORGANIZATION:

• Mark off a large rectangular play area and scatter six hoops throughout this area. Make a swatter by rolling up a towel and taping it at both ends and in the middle with masking tape. Select one player to be IT, who holds the swatter and stands in the middle of the play area. Everyone else scatters around the play area.

DESCRIPTION OF ACTIVITY:

1. On the signal "Run!" free players, move around the play area by running. IT, give chase trying to gently swat a player on his or her backside. Then immediately after the "swat," drop your swatter and run away. The swatted player now picks up the Swatter and becomes the new IT. Continue in this way.
2. The hoops are "safety homes." Only one player at a time may be inside a hoop, and you may stay for only a five-second count.
3. After every two minutes of play, I will stop the game. Those players who did not become IT will earn five points. Keep track of your points. Who will have the most points at the end of the game?

VARIATIONS:

a. Have more than one swatter.
b. Give a different movement signal after each stoppage of play, such as "Skip!"; "Side-step!"; "Walk backwards." IT must move the same as the other players.
c. Increase or decrease the playing area.

IA-33 OCTOPUS

FOCUS: Running and dodging

EQUIPMENT: One beanbag or Nerf™ ball; one flag per player (optional)

ORGANIZATION:

• Choose one player to be the "Octopus," who holds a Nerf™ ball and stands in the middle of the play area. Other players, the "Fish," stand side-by-side at one end of the play area. Change the Octopus every two minutes during the game. Have Fish "swim" across using different locomotor movements.

DESCRIPTION OF ACTIVITY:

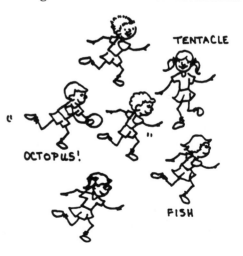

1. When the Octopus calls "Swim, Fish, Swim!" everyone run to the opposite end of the play area. Octopus, try to tag players by touching them with your Nerf™ ball as they "swim" past you.
2. Tagged players and those who run outside of the play area, jog on the spot. You may swing your arms like the tentacles of an octopus and try to tag other players as they run by, but you must not move from your spot. Tentacle, then change roles with any player you tag.
3. Free players, when you reach the opposite end, jog on the spot, waiting for the Octopus to signal "Swim, Fish, Swim!"—then run again. The game continues until all players have been caught.

IA–34 FOUR-CORNER WARM-UP

FOCUS: Aerobic warm-up

EQUIPMENT: Four or more cone markers; posterboard and marking pens; lively music; tape or record player

ORGANIZATION:

• In "Four-Corner Warm-up," players move continuously around the boundaries of the play area. Each time they turn a corner, they begin a new type of movement. Place a cone marker at each corner of the play area. Write different movements on posterboard to make activity signs. Lean an activity sign against each of the four cone markers. Arrange signs so that players perform quick movements along the long sides and slow movements along the short sides of the play area. Signs must be visible to incoming players. Have players stretch before starting and after the warm-up is completed. Start and stop the activity with music. Adjust the boundaries of the play area to match the players' fitness levels. Have players scatter evenly around the track.

DESCRIPTION OF ACTIVITY:

1. *Long Side Movements:* jog; skip; slide-step; run backwards; grapevine step.
2. *Short Side Movements:* hop; jump; crab-walk; lame dog walk; seal walk.

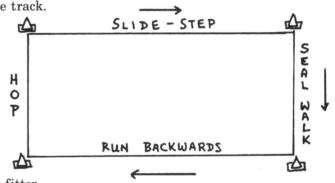

VARIATIONS:

a. Repeat circuit in opposite direction.
b. Increase the length of time on the course or the size of the play area as players become fitter.
c. *Six- or Eight-Corner Warm-Up:* Place more cone markers and locomotion signs around the perimeter of the play area. Alternate long-quick and short-slower movements.

IA–35 ASTRONAUT RUN

FOCUS: Aerobic fun run

EQUIPMENT: Lively music; tape or record player

ORGANIZATION:

• During "Astronaut Run," children move continuously around a circle, alternating locomotor movements, which include walking, running, jumping, side-stepping, and skipping. Explain that faster runners can pass, but only on the outside of the circle. Start and stop the activity with music, allowing music to play for three or four minutes in beginning sessions. Gradually increase the duration and intensity of movement as the children's fitness levels improve. Have children space themselves evenly around a large circle. The following are some movement ideas.

DESCRIPTION OF ACTIVITY:

— Jog clockwise with good posture. Snap fingers overhead as you run.
— Hop, changing feet every three or four hops.
— Walk backwards, clapping hands above head, in front, and behind. Repeat clapping pattern.
— Jump from side to side as you move forward.
— Walk on your toes, heels, and the inside and outside of your feet.
— Bear-Walk (on hands and feet, moving right arm and leg forward, then left arm and leg).
— Walk with giant cross-over steps.
— Skip with high arm swings.
— Side-step, facing outward for eight counts; then side-step, facing inward for eight counts. Repeat pattern.

VARIATION: Intersperse running with "Aerobic Circle" signals (see Fitness Activities).

IA-36 THE BLOB!

FOCUS: Running and dodging; cooperation   **EQUIPMENT:** Four cone markers

ORGANIZATION:

• Use the cones to mark out the boundaries of a large rectangular play area. Choose one player to be the "Blob," who stands in the middle of the play area; all other players scatter.

DESCRIPTION OF ACTIVITY:

1. On the signal "Go!" Blob, chase free players, trying to tag them with a light one-hand touch.
2. A tagged player must hook onto the Blob by holding hands. Now Blob, try to tag other free players, using only your free hand to make the tag. If the Blob breaks apart, no tagging can happen until it is joined together again.
3. As more players are tagged, the Blob will grow bigger and bigger! Blob players, do not break your hand-hold as you give chase. Only the end players may tag with their free hands. Free players may not break through the Blob by running through the arms.
4. The last player to be tagged becomes the Blob for the next game.

VARIATIONS:

a. When the Blob becomes too big, split it into two smaller Blobs.
b. Begin the game with two or three "baby Blobs."

IA-37 SNAKE AND THE HUMMINGBIRD

FOCUS: Aerobic warm-up; cooperation   **EQUIPMENT:** Four cone markers

ORGANIZATION:

• The boys form a chain by holding hands or linking arms to form a "Snake" and make a "hissing" sound. The girls, the "Hummingbirds," scatter over the play area, making a "humming" sound.

DESCRIPTION OF ACTIVITY:

1. On the signal "GO!" the Snake tries to capture a Hummingbird by encircling it. When caught, the Hummingbird must join the Snake.

2. Hummingbirds cannot break through the chain or go under the arms. Play until the last Hummingbird is caught.

3. Let's play the game again. This time the girls form the Snake; the boys become the Hummingbirds.

VARIATION:

For a large class, have more than one Snake.

IA-38 TEAM COLORS TAG

FOCUS: Running and dodging

EQUIPMENT: Four sets of colored flags;
stopwatch;
one whistle;
chalkboard and chalk or chart paper and marking pens;
cone markers

ORGANIZATION:

• Divide the class into four equal teams and have each team choose a captain. Team captains distribute a set of colored flags among their team members, who tuck flags into the back of their waistbands so that most of the flag shows.

DESCRIPTION OF ACTIVITY:

1. Each team, choose an exercise that you can ask the other three teams to do when you tag them, such as sit-ups, push-ups, or jumping jacks.

2. Listen for your team's color. When your color is called, your team is IT and has one minute to "tag" as many of the other players as possible by pulling a player's flag. The pulled flag is returned to the tagged player and tucked into the front of the waistband.

3. Tagged players and anyone else who runs outside the play area, do the exercise the IT team has chosen. Continue to do the exercise until one minute is up.

4. Change the IT team. Listen for another color to be called. When you hear your team's color, remind players of the exercise you want them to do when you tag them. Continue the game until each Team has been IT.

VARIATION: Count the number of players each team tags and record team scores. Which team will earn the best score?

IA-39 NUMBER TAG

FOCUS: Running and dodging;
listening

EQUIPMENT: One marking pen;
one numbered beanbag per player in a basket;
cone markers

ORGANIZATION:

• Number beanbags, one for each player. Then have player pick up a beanbag out of the basket and find a free space.

DESCRIPTION OF ACTIVITY:

1. Hold your beanbag so no one else can see what number you have. Jog around the play area.
2. On signal "Homes!" find a free space and jog on the spot. I will call out five numbers. When your number is called, you are IT.
3. All ITs, raise your hand so that everyone can see who you are. Now, on the count of five, chase free players and try to hit them below the waist with your beanbag.
4. Tagged players or anyone else who runs outside the boundaries of the play area must do jumping jacks on the spot, until everyone else is doing them, too.
5. To start a new game, trade your beanbag with another player, check your new number, then jog around the play area again, and listen for the signal "Homes!"

IA–40 HOOP AEROBICS

FOCUS: Aerobic warm-up; strength

EQUIPMENT: One hoop for every player; suitable music; record or tape player

ORGANIZATION:

- Have every player get a hoop, find a home, and sit in the hoop. Suggestions follow.

DESCRIPTION OF ACTIVITY:

—Leave your hoop. Can you leap over ten different hoops and return to sit in your own hoop? Who can be the quickest?

—Visit ten hoops, placing your right hand and left foot in each. Then return home.

—Hopping on one foot only, land in a hoop; change your hopping foot and hop into another hoop. Continue until you have visited eight hoops. Then hop back to your home.

—Crab Walk (on hands and feet, facing upward) to six different hoops, sitting down in each one. Return home and curl up in your own.

—Jump in and out of your hoop as you move around it. Jump to another hoop and repeat, jumping in the opposite direction around the hoop; then jump home.

—Pick up your hoop in both hands, stand and stretch upward with it. Then lower it so that you are now inside of it, holding the hoop at waist level. Run once around the play area; as you pass me place your hoop over my arms and sit in the middle of the play area.

VARIATIONS:

a. Vary the number of repetitions to the fitness level of the class.

b. Repeat using different locomotor movements: skipping, sliding, walking, galloping.

IA–41 MAT-ERCISE

FOCUS: Aerobic warm-up; strength; stretching

EQUIPMENT: One mat per player; lively music; tape or record player

ORGANIZATION:

- Have players get a mat and hook-sit facing you. Suggestions follow.

DESCRIPTION OF ACTIVITY:

—The mat is your home. Leave your home and touch ten different mats with your right hand and left foot. Then quickly jump home.

—The mats are now puddles of water. Run and leap over as many mats as you can before I signal "Freeze!" How many mats did you go over? Now skip home.

—Run to four different mats and do eight sit-up hugs on each mat. Then hop home. (To do a sit-up hug, begin in back-lying position with hands stretched overhead. Gently curl up to hug your knees to your chest; then gently curl down to starting position.)

—Run to six different mats and do four knee push-ups on each mat. Then walk backwards home.

—Long-sit on your mat. Cross your ankles and reach for the toes. Hold for ten seconds; then change the top leg and repeat. Now in back-lying position, stretch in a long narrow shape for ten seconds; roll into back-lying position, and stretch in a wide shape for ten seconds.

VARIATION: Have players suggest "mat-ercise" activities.

IA-42 GRASS DRILLS

FOCUS: Aerobic warm-up

EQUIPMENT: Popular music; tape or record player

ORGANIZATION:

- Grass drills, commonly used in football training, require players to alternate aerobic or running-type movements with ground exercises. Emphasis is on agility and quickness. Arrange the class in scatter or semi-circle formation. Check the spacing. Start and stop the activity with music, allowing the drill to continue for about two to three minutes at first. Increase the time as fitness levels increase. Alternate any locomotor movement with a grass drill. Select different players to lead the class.

DESCRIPTION OF ACTIVITY:

- On the signal "Jog!" jog in place with knees high and clap for 20 seconds; then "Front!" (quickly lie face down).
- On the signal "Rope Jump!" pantomime rope jumping in place for 20 seconds; then "Back!" (quickly lie on your back).
- "Jumping Jack"; "Turtle" (lie on back with feet up).
- "Sprint in place"; "Curl-up" (hold modified V-sit position).
- "Straddle Jumps"; "Push-up" (hold the front-support position).
- "Side-Kicks"; "Seal" (in front-support position, raise body and drag feet).
- "Cross-over steps"; "Crab" (in back-support position, bend knees and lift hips).
- "Twist-Jumps"; "Bridge" (hold the back-support position).

IA-43 DOUBLE CIRCLE RUN

FOCUS: Aerobic fun run

EQUIPMENT: Popular music; tape or record player

ORGANIZATION:

- Have players form a double circle in which one circle is inside the other. Players stand facing a partner in the opposite circle. Ensure partners are evenly spaced around the circle.

DESCRIPTION OF ACTIVITY:

1. When the music starts, partners, turn to face opposite directions and begin running around the circle. As you approach your partner, raise your inside hand and "give five" (slap hand lightly) to each other.
2. On signal "Change direction!" turn and run the other way. This time, "give five" to your partner with your other hand.
3. When the music stops, everyone stop and jog in place. Players in the outer circle, jog right one position to meet a new partner. "Give ten" by lightly slapping both partner's hands. Outside partners, turn to face clockwise; while inside partners, turn to face counterclockwise. Jog in place waiting for the music to start.
4. When you hear the music, everyone run in your circle pattern. Raise your inside hand and "give five" to your new partner. Change direction on signal, and continue the activity as before.

VARIATIONS:

a. Substitute running for other movements such as skipping, side-stepping, and jogging backwards around the circle.
b. Change signal to "Give high fives!" (jump to touch hands) or "Give high tens!" (jump to touch both hands); "Salute!" (salute like a soldier); "Right Swing!" (link right elbows, skip around twice).

IA–44 TREES OF THE FOREST_____

FOCUS: Chasing and dodging; alertness

EQUIPMENT: Two beanbags (or sponge balls)

ORGANIZATION:
- Choose two players to be the "Hunters"; all other players are "Rabbits," who stand side-by-side at either end of the play area ("Briar Patch"). Hunters get one beanbag each and go to the middle of the play area.

DESCRIPTION OF ACTIVITY:

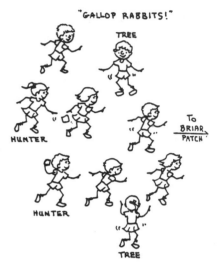

1. Hunters, think about different ways you could ask the Rabbits to move, such as hopping, running, or side-stepping. During the game, one Hunter at a time will call out a movement and everyone will act it out.
2. On Hunter's movement signal, Rabbits, repeat this movement all the way to the other Briar Patch. Meanwhile, Hunters, moving in the same way, try to hit the Rabbits below the waist with your beanbag before they can reach the Briar Patch. You may run only to fetch your beanbag.
3. Tagged Rabbits or anyone else who runs outside the boundaries of the play area, jog on the spot. You are now a Tree of the Forest and, keeping your feet rooted to the spot, may try to tag any Rabbit that comes near. A Rabbit tagged by a Tree also becomes a tree.
4. Free Rabbits, when you are safe in your Briar Patch, Hunters will return to the middle of the play area and call out a new movement. The game continues in this way until only two Rabbits are free. They become the Hunters for the next game.

VARIATIONS:
a. When a Tree of the forest tags a Hunter or a free Rabbit, they change roles.
b. Hunters are not allowed to throw the beanbag, but may only tag a Rabbit by touching the Rabbit with the beanbag.

IA–45 SQUIRRELS AND NUTS_____

FOCUS: Aerobic warm-up; fair play

EQUIPMENT: All available beanbags, deckrings and jump ropes; four hoops

ORGANIZATION:
- Divide class into four equal groups of players, who are the "Squirrels." Place a hoop, the "Tree Hole," in each corner of the play area and assign a group to each corner. Place all the "Nuts" (beanbags, deckrings, and jump ropes) in a pile in the center of the play area, which is the "Forest."

DESCRIPTION OF ACTIVITY:

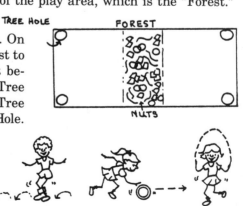

1. On signal "Scamper!" run around in general space. On signal "Feeding Time!" quickly scamper to the Forest to pick up a Nut. If your Nut is a beanbag, place it between your ankles and jump back to put it in your Tree Hole; if your Nut is a deckring, roll it back to your Tree Hole: if your Nut is a jump rope, skip back to your Hole.
2. Always return from your Hole to the Forest to collect another Nut by scampering on hands and feet. You may only carry one Nut at a time.
3. The game ends when there are no more Nuts left in the Forest. Which Squirrel group can collect the most number of Nuts?

VARIATION: Allow Squirrels to "steal" Nuts from other Tree Holes, but only one Nut at a time!

IA-46 SNOWBALL TAG

FOCUS: Running and dodging; accuracy throwing

EQUIPMENT: One folding mat per pair;
six small sponge balls;
lively music;
tape or record player

ORGANIZATION:

• Have players, working in pairs, get folding mats, carry them to free spaces in the play area, and stand them upright in a zig-zag position as snow forts. Choose six players to be IT; then have each IT player get a sponge ball, which will be a snowball. IT players go to the middle of the play area; everyone else scatters.

DESCRIPTION OF ACTIVITY:

1. When the music starts, ITs chase the free players and try to hit them below the waist with your snowball.

2. Free players, use the snow forts and duck behind to avoid being hit. Whenever a snowball hits you below the waist, even when you are behind a snow fort, you are tagged.

3. A tagged player, immediately change role with the IT player who hit you, pick up the snowball, and continue the chase.

4. Remember how many times you were hit. Who can be hit the fewest times before the music stops?

VARIATION:

Players choose a partner and take turns trying to hit each other with snowballs.

IA-47 KINGS AND QUEENS

FOCUS: Running and dodging; fair play

EQUIPMENT: Four sets of different colored banners

ORGANIZATION:

• Choose two boys to be "Kings" and two girls to be "Queens"; the other players are the "Soldiers," who the Kings and Queens will try to "knight" or tag. Give each King and Queen a set of colored banners to wear around their necks. There should be enough banners for all players. Have Kings and Queens then stand in the middle of the play area. Soldiers scatter.

DESCRIPTION OF ACTIVITY:

1. On signal "Go!" Kings and Queens, start chasing the Soldiers. Try to tag them with a light, two-handed touch on the shoulder. Knight each tagged player with a banner, placed around the neck. Knights, help your King or Queen tag other Soldiers.

2. When you are tagged by a Knight, jog on the spot until that Knight's King or Queen runs over and officially knights you by placing a banner around your neck.

3. Continue until all players are knighted. The King or Queen with the most Knights wins the game.

IA-48 EXERCISE HUNT

FOCUS: Aerobic warm-up; groupwork; fair play

EQUIPMENT: One photocopied list of exercises per group; four folding mats; benches; music with a strong 4/4 beat; tape or record player

ORGANIZATION:

- Prepare a list of ten fitness exercises following the suggestions below and photocopy the list for each group of five to seven players. Explain that groups may do exercises in any order, as long as they finish all of them. Before anyone in the group can move on to the next exercise task, every player in the group must have completed the immediate task.
- Play music to start the activity. As groups finish the Exercise Hunt, have them stretch out in the middle of the play area.

DESCRIPTION OF ACTIVITY:

Indoor Exercise Hunt:

1. Touch four different benches.
2. Shake hands with ten different players who are not a member of your team.
3. Do 20 jumping jacks.
4. Curl up 16 times.
5. Touch 12 different lines around the play area with your left knee and your right elbow.
6. Join hands in a circle and together recite your favorite Christmas carol or nursery rhyme as you walk in a clockwise direction.
7. Run once around the play area clapping your hands in time to the music.
8. Do ten bent-knee push-ups.
9. Sit down; stand up. Repeat eight times.
10. Hold hands and slide-step to each corner of the play area.

Outdoor Exercise Hunt:

1. Touch a tree, a fence, and a swing.
2. Squat in single-file formation. Last player leapfrog over other players, then squat at front of the line. As a group, do a total of 20 leapfrog jumps.
3. Do eight curl-ups at three different trees.
4. Crab-walk from one path to another path nearby.
5. Crawl under five different playground objects.
6. Run once around the perimeter of your school grounds.
7. Run around three garbage cans located around the school.
8. Touch four benches. Do three push-ups at each.

IA-49 GERONIMO

FOCUS: Fun run

EQUIPMENT: Four cone markers;
lively music;
tape or record player

ORGANIZATION:

- Place one cone marker at each corner of a rectangular race course (about the size of a basketball court). Form four equal teams. Have each team stand in single-file formation at a different corner of the race course. The player at the front of each file is the Leader.

DESCRIPTION OF ACTIVITY:

1. When the music starts, each team, run forward around the race course. Stay in the same order and do not pass each other. Leader, set a steady pace that can be maintained throughout the run.
2. Last runner, sprint forward on the inside of the course, passing all your teammates. As you join the front of your team, yell "Geronimo!" At this signal, the last player in the line will repeat your action and then shout "Geronimo!"
3. Continue this running pattern until the music stops; then walk slowly around the course, inhaling and exhaling deeply. Original Leaders, count the number of "Geronimo" yells your team makes, and compare your score with other teams. Which team will be the best "Geronimo team"?

VARIATION: Increase the time the music plays to improve fitness levels.

IA-50 PAPER ROUTE

FOCUS: Aerobic fun run

EQUIPMENT: Playground equipment;
stopwatch (optional);
wall map (optional)

ORGANIZATION:

- A "Paper Route" is a jogging route around the block, playground, or nearby park; anywhere that is interesting and challenging. It is a fun alternative to running laps. Gradually lengthen the route so that the children run continuously for at least ten minutes. When out of the school, insist on street safety; use crosswalks and sidewalks.

DESCRIPTION OF ACTIVITY:

Today we're going to run a Paper Route around the playground. We will start with a steady jogging pace. Stay with the rest of the group and follow my directions.
— Run around the swings. Pull yourself across the jungle gym, down the slide, and weave in and out of the goal posts. Keep together!
— Stop at the grass area and do eight sit-ups, eight push-ups, and sixteen arm-circles.
— Skip for twenty paces; slide-step for twenty paces right, slide-step for twenty paces left; hop right foot for ten hops, left foot for ten hops; then run backwards for twenty paces.
— Repeat the course, or add other activities.
— Run back to the starting point; then slow to a walk for one minute.
— How hard was your heart working? While still walking, hold your fingers to your wrist and count the number of pulse beats. Your target heart range should be thirty to forty beats in fifteen seconds.
— Now do three different stretches, holding each stretch for ten seconds.

VARIATIONS:

a. *Team Run:* Divide into teams. Have teammates encourage each other so that their team finishes with the best accumulated time.
b. *Cross-Country Run:* On a wall map of the country, record the distance the class, the grade, or the whole school runs each day. Plot the runner's progress from your community across the country.

Section 2

Fitness Activities

The daily Fitness Activity serves as a *specific warm-up* and, used in conjunction with an introductory activity, builds overall fitness, with emphasis on cardiovascular endurance and muscular strength and endurance.
This section presents an assortment of 33 Fitness Activities.

FA-1 ORGANIZATIONAL BREAKS

FOCUS: Class organization; listening

EQUIPMENT: Benches; mats

ORGANIZATION:

- A "break" is a short informal activity which, when introduced spontaneously throughout lessons, provides for efficiency in class organization and mobilization and in the collection and dispersal of equipment. Breaks can also be used for relief, a change of tempo, alertness training, extra fitness, challenge, and fun. They need not be related to any other part of the lesson. Organizational breaks provide transition between lesson segments and efficient mobilization of the class for the next activity. Use these breaks without warning repeatedly throughout the lesson to increase the activity of the class. Try the examples below, but adapt to your own situation.

DESCRIPTION OF ACTIVITY:

1. On signal "Go!" run CW around the play area, doing four jumping jacks in each corner; then find a partner and sit cross-legged in the middle of the play area.
2. Find a partner and stand back-to-back. On signal "Go!" race your partner CCW around the play area, touching with your right knee and left elbow the middle of all four sidelines; then return to your starting place. The slower partner owes you five sit-ups.
3. Do eight Bench-Steps at four different benches; then stand arm's length apart on this sideline.
4. Touch a mat, a rope, a door, a bench with a different body part each time; then quickly hop to the big circle and hook-sit in groups of three. Go!
5. On signal "Go!" quickly skip to one end of the play area; then log roll toward the middle of the play area, jump up and lie down three times in a row, and then run to the listening circle where I am standing. Go!

FA-2 EQUIPMENT BREAKS

FOCUS: Equipment organization; listening

EQUIPMENT: Balls; jump ropes; benches; climbing chairs; mats; bats; softballs; bases

ORGANIZATION:

- Equipment Breaks provide time between parts of the lesson for equipment set-up, collection, and dispersal. Safety in handling equipment should be emphasized and taught. The fourth break demonstrates how equipment set-up can be a group activity with each group responsible for designated equipment. Divide your class into four equal teams, with a leader for each team. Try these examples, but adapt to your own situation.

DESCRIPTION OF ACTIVITY:

1. Dribble your basketball with your nondominant hand once around the play area in a CW direction. Then drop the ball into the cart and sit in your teams, leaders on the red line.
2. Touch a sideline; then get a jump rope, take it to your home, and skip 25 times in place. Go!
3. Quickly get into groups of three. One player get a base; another player get a softball from the basket, and the third player get a baseball bat from the cart. Find a free space for your group to practice batting, pitching, and retrieving the ball.
4. Number off one, two, three, four: One's, collect folding mats and lay them out in one corner of play area; two's, collect a ball each, place the ball between your ankles, and jump to this sideline. Place all the balls on the line. Three's, carry the benches and two climbing chairs to the middle area; four's, collect long ropes, two beachballs, one short rope. Place these at the end of the play area.

FA–3 TEMPO CHANGE BREAKS

FOCUS: Class organization; alertness training

EQUIPMENT: Indoor or outdoor play area; one rope per player; Take-a-Chance cards

ORGANIZATION:

- Tempo Change Breaks provide a change of pace. Use them to get players moving quickly again after a period of inactivity or to ensure that exercising in all the fitness component areas occurs. Reinforce the names of these Breaks so that players will remember them to save time explaining when you use them later. When teaching outdoors, adapt these breaks to the playground equipment and play area available. Try the following examples, but adapt to your own situation.

DESCRIPTION OF ACTIVITY:

1. On signal *"Compass!"* touch one finger to the floor and run around it five times; then try to balance on one leg for five seconds. Repeat using the other hand and running in the opposite direction.

2. On signal *"Corkscrew Stand!"* stand tall while folding your arms and crossing your feet. Now try to sit down in back-lying position. Can you stand up without unfolding your arms and legs?

3. On signal *"Touch!"* touch the five objects I name; then sit in the listening circle. Who can be the quickest to finish? Touch a mat, a door, a red line, a bench, and a ball.

4. Stand tall with your arms at your sides. Slowly to the count of ten, drop down to a squat position. On the signal *"Blastoff,"* jump as high as you can into the air.

5. On signal *"Shake Break,"* shake the body part that I call out: right hand; left hand; right leg; left leg; both hands; both legs; head; all over! (Vary the starting position: standing; long sitting; back lying; front lying; moving in free space.)

6. On signal *"Sticky Popcorn,"* quickly bounce like popcorn popping in the pan and move toward each other to link up and form a "Popcorn Ball." Can you do this before I count to ten?

7. On signal *"Step-Ups!"* do ten step-ups on each of four different benches. On signal "Hang!" hang on a piece of climbing apparatus for as long as you can.

8. On Signal *"Wall Jump!"* stand sideways to a wall. Jump to touch the highest point you can reach on the wall. Repeat three times. Can you reach higher each time?

9. On signal *"Pepper Jump!"* get a rope and do 50 quick jumps with your rope.

10. On signal *"Take-a-Chance!"* pick a card, read the task aloud, and perform it with everyone else. (Refer to Introductory Activities, activity IA–7.)

VARIATION: Use any of the other "Organizational Signals" from the Introductory Activities in Section 1 as Breaks.

FOCUS: Class organization; partnerwork; listening

EQUIPMENT: One ball per pair; two to four benches

ORGANIZATION:

- Use Partner Breaks spontaneously to generate an atmosphere of fun and challenge and to enhance listening skills. Spontaneity will come more easily if you teach players the names of the Breaks and repeat them often. Also use any previously taught short activity as a Break, provided that the activity can be introduced quickly by name.

DESCRIPTION OF ACTIVITY:

1. On signal *"Action sports!"* quickly find a partner. Move around the play area, copying the sport actions of your partner. On "Change!" find a new partner and repeat the activity.

2. When I call *"Leapfrog!"* place your hands on your partner's back and straddle-jump over your partner. Repeat this action from one end of the play area to the opposite end.

3. When I call *"Benches!"* race your partner to touch each bench with both hands and return to your home space to toss a ball to each other ten times.

4. On the signal *"Saw Logs!"* face your partner and, holding both hands, place your right foot forward. Jump to change the forward foot and create a "sawing-like" action. Repeat this 16 times.

5. When you hear *"Elbows!"* link elbows with your partner and skip to each corner of the play area. At each corner, swing right elbows once around, and then swing left elbows once around in a circle. Return to sit cross-legged on the big circle when finished.

6. On the signal *"Poison Ball,"* the partner with the ball, chase the other partner, and try to touch him or her with the ball. If you tag your partner, he or she becomes the new chaser. Remember to watch where you are going.

7. On signal *"Knee Box!"* face your partner and try to touch your partner's knees. Dodge quickly to avoid contact, but stay in a confined area.

8. On signal *"Body Builders!"* stand facing your partner. Pretend that you are a muscle-bound weight-lifter posing in a contest. Copy what your partner does; then change roles.

VARIATION: Refer to "Combatives" in Section 6, Game Skills, for other partner activities that can be used as Breaks.

FA-5 STUNT BREAKS

FOCUS: Class organization

EQUIPMENT: None

ORGANIZATION:
- Stunts provide excellent breaks and a change of pace. Call out a Stunt Break immediately before changing to the next activity. Teach players the names of these stunts and reinforce their learning by repeating the stunts often. Substitute any Animal Walk that you have already taught.

DESCRIPTION OF ACTIVITY:

Pogo Springs
Inchworm
Rockers
Log Rollers
Hoppo Bumpo
Thread the Needle
Spinning Tops
Bouncing Ball
Wicket Walk
Bucking Bronco

FA-6 COOPERATIVE STUNT BREAKS

FOCUS: Class organization; partnerwork

EQUIPMENT: None

ORGANIZATION:
- In these Stunt Breaks, partners cooperate together as they work in pairs. The key to the success of these Breaks is in the spontaneity and unpredictability of their use. Substitute any Gymnastic stunt that players could do in pairs.

DESCRIPTION OF ACTIVITY:

Backward Get-Up

Wring the Dishrag

Wheelbarrow Walk

Scooters

Centipede Walk

Bouncing Ball

Snake Roll

Three Legs

Shadowing

Foot Walk

Pair Rowing

FA-7 LIMBER AND LOOSEN

FOCUS: Large muscle mobilization

EQUIPMENT: Music with a strong 4/4 beat; tape or record player

ORGANIZATION:

- This workout warms the large muscle groups: *H*ead; *F*orward trunk; *A*rms and shoulders; *B*ack; *L*ateral trunk and *L*egs (H-F-A-B-L-L or "Health and Fitness Allows Better and Longer Life!"). Each lesson should begin with a proper warm-up! The warm-up phase should last for about four to five minutes to prepare the body for the vigorous aerobic phase to follow; to prevent injury, stress, and strain to the body; and to increase the children's ability to perform movement skills. Have players scatter around the play area. They should stand tall with feet comfortably spread apart, tummy muscles tight, pelvis tucked under, back straight, head up, and shoulders relaxed. Knees should be loose throughout the warm-up, and players should pulse them in time to the music.

DESCRIPTION OF ACTIVITY:

1. ***Head Nods:*** Gently turn your head from side to side as if saying "NO!"; then slowly move your head up and down as if nodding "YES!" Repeat this sequence two more times.

2. ***Shoulder Shrugs and Rolls:*** Shrug your shoulders four times. Alternate right and left shoulder shrugs eight times. Then roll both shoulders forward four times and backwards four times. Repeat sequence once more.

3. ***Twisters:*** With knees slightly bent and feet still, twist upper body from side to side, pushing the opposite hand out to that side. Repeat eight times.

4. ***Arm Circles:*** Gently circle arms forward so that hands cross in front eight times.

5. ***Traffic Lights:*** Hold your arms sideways at right angles with fingers pointing upward and squeeze shoulder blades together. Repeat four times. Repeat another four times with your fingers pointing downward. Repeat sequence once more.

6. ***Y-Stretches:*** Stand tall with legs apart and knees slightly bent. Stretch each hand, in turn, overhead and to the opposite side. Let the other hand support on hip. Hold each stretch for ten seconds; do not bob or jerk. Repeat eight times.

7. ***Leg Sways:*** Stand with feet wide apart. With hands on hips, lean to each side, bending the knee on that side. Repeat eight times. Now touch elbow to opposite knee as you do eight more Leg Sways.

8. ***Knee Circles:*** Keeping knees and feet together, slowly circle knees CW four times; then CCW four times. Repeat this sequence once more.

9. ***Calf Stretch:*** From front-support position, raise the hips and push the heel of one foot to the floor, and then the heel of the other foot. Repeat eight times. Bend your knees and slowly roll up to starting position.

10. ***Foot Circles:*** Balance on one foot and hug the other thigh to your chest. Circle the foot four times; then change legs and repeat. Do this sequence once more.

FA-8 MUSCLE SIGNALS

FOCUS: Major muscles of the body

EQUIPMENT: Chart of the muscles of the body; muscles-of-the-week chart; muscle signs

ORGANIZATION:

- In this activity, teach ten major muscles of the body and their location. A large chart depicting the major muscles could be used. Create a "Muscle-of-the-Week" chart and each week highlight one of the muscles. Introduce these major muscles in your health class. Have children locate each muscle on a diagram and discuss its function. Encourage players to learn to say each muscle's name properly and to spell it correctly.

- To begin, have players stand tall in their own home space.

DESCRIPTION OF ACTIVITY:

1. How many muscles do you have in your body? **600!** What is the strongest muscle? **Your heart is the strongest! It is about the size of your fist and is located in the center of your chest.**

2. Let's learn the names of eight more major muscles. On signal "Scrambled Eggs," run helter-skelter in any direction. On signal (name of the muscle), stop and touch the muscle I name:

   — **Biceps:** top muscles of the upper arm

   — **Triceps:** underneath muscles of upper arm

   — **Rectus Abdominus:** stomach muscles

   — **Quadriceps:** front muscles of the thigh

   — **Hamstrings:** back thigh muscles

   — **Gastrocnemius:** calf muscles

   — **Gluteus Maximus:** buttock muscles

   — **Deltoids:** shoulder muscles

3. **Busy Muscles:** When I call out the name of a major muscle, quickly find a partner and touch that muscle to your partner's muscle. Each time a new muscle is called, find a new partner and repeat.

VARIATION:

Dancing Muscles: Divide the class into eight groups and secretly assign each group a muscle; for example: Group 1, the Heart muscle; Group 2, the Biceps; Group 3, the Triceps; Group 4, the Quadriceps, and so on. Have each group create a dance to show the rest of the class how the muscle works. Have the other groups guess what the muscle is.

FA–9 BONE SIGNALS

FOCUS: Major bones of the body; basic functions

EQUIPMENT: Chart of the skeletal system; bone-of-the-week chart

ORGANIZATION:

- In this activity, teach the names of the major bones of the body, their location, and their basic functions. Use a large wall chart of the Skeletal System and create a "Bone-of-the-Week" chart that will focus on one particular bone for that week. Introduce these major bones in your health class. Have players locate the bones on a diagram of the skeleton and discuss their functions.

- To begin, have players scatter and stand in their own free space.

DESCRIPTION OF ACTIVITY:

1. How many bones do you have in your body? **Your skeleton is composed of 206 bones!** What are the three basic functions of bones? **Bones support and protect the other body systems; store minerals such as calcium and phosphorus; and produce cells for the circulatory system.**

2. *Busy Bones:* Let's learn the names of the major bones. Find a partner and stand beside him or her. I will call out the name of a major bone. Try to touch this bone to your partner's. On signal "Busy Bones," find a new partner and be ready to touch the new bone to your partner's as I call out its name.

   — *Cranium:* bones of the head
   — *Mandible:* jaw bone (the strongest bone)
   — *Clavicle:* collar bone
   — *Scapula:* shoulder blade
   — *Sternum:* breast bone
   — *Humerus:* upper arm bone
   — *Ulna and Radius:* lower arm bones
   — *Carpal bones:* wrist bones
   — *Metacarpal bones:* bones of the hand
   — *Phalanges:* finger bones
   — *Femur:* upper leg bone (the longest bone)
   — *Patella:* knee cap
   — *Fibula:* outer bone of lower leg
   — *Tibia:* inner bone of lower leg
   — *Tarsal bones:* ankle bones
   — *Metatarsal bones:* foot bones
   — *Phalanges:* toe bones
   — *Ribs:* bones of the chest
   — *Vertebrae:* bones of the spine

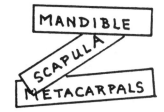

VARIATION:

Bone Charade: Divide the class into groups of three to four players. Write the names of the bones above on pieces of paper, place into a container, and have the leader of each group draw for a bone. Have each group, in turn, pantomime their bone's actions, while the other groups try to guess what the bone is in a 30-second time limit.

FA-10 10-MINUTE WORKOUT 1

FOCUS: Leg, arm, shoulder, and abdominal strength

EQUIPMENT: One mat per player; music with a strong 4/4 beat; tape or record player

ORGANIZATION:

- For this workout, which warms, stretches, and strengthens the major muscle groups, have players begin by standing in a line at one end of the play area.

DESCRIPTION OF ACTIVITY:

1. **Robot Warm-Up:** On signal "Robot!" move around the play area with stiff, "robot-like" actions. On signal "Haywire!" you begin to fly all over the place. Your radar "beeps" keep you from bumping into other robots.

2. **Cross-Jumps:** Stand tall with your hands on hips. Jump to cross one foot in front of the other; jump again to cross the other foot in front. Do 20 of these jumps.

3. **Sunflower:** Begin in back-lying position with feet and hands wide apart. Curl up to hug your knees to your chest; then return to starting position. Do 14 more in this way.

2.

3.

4. **Walking Push-Ups:** In front-support position, walk hands right four times, left four times, toward feet four times, and ahead four times. Repeat this sequence three times.

5. **Crocodile Crawl:** In front-lying position, push with your lower arms to move from one side of the play area to the opposite. Imagine that you are crawling through swamp-land!

4.

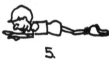

5.

6. **Shadow Boxer:** Stand tall with one foot forward and the other foot back. On signal "Box!" alternately punch into the air with your hands while changing your foot positions with each arm "punch."

6.

7. **Dead Bug Stretch:** Begin in back-lying position with your hands and feet in the air. Grab your ankles and gently hold this stretch for ten seconds. Relax, stretching into a long pencil shape; then do another ten-second "Dead Bug Stretch."

8. **Robot Rest:** You are a robot again. Oh-oh! Your batteries are running down. You are programmed to R-E-S-T! Sit cross-legged and press your knees to the floor for ten seconds. Relax; then repeat two more times.

7.

8.

FA–11 10-MINUTE WORKOUT 2

FOCUS: Leg, arm, shoulder, and abdominal strength; trunk mobility

EQUIPMENT: Lively music; tape or record player

ORGANIZATION:

- This workout warms, strengthens, and stretches the large muscle groups. Have players scatter around the play area and stand tall in their homes.

DESCRIPTION OF ACTIVITY:

1. **Super Star Warm Up:** Begin by jogging on the spot. I will call out the names of several different sports. You become a star player of that sport moving around the play area without touching anyone. For example, on signal "Basketball!" pantomime dribbling a basketball on a fast break down the floor. (Other signal suggestions are: "Hockey"; "Karate"; "Boxing"; "Tennis"; "Horse Racing"; "Hang-gliding.")

2. **Clock Walk:** Begin in front-support position. Keeping your feet on the spot, "walk" your hands around the clock. Repeat, moving in the opposite direction. If I am standing at 12 o'clock, move your feet to 3 o'clock; 6 o'clock; 9 o'clock.

3. **Bicycling:** Begin in hook-sit position with your weight supported on your elbows. Show me how you can move your feet as if pedalling a bike down the street. Can you pedal in front for eight counts? to the right side for eight counts? to the left side for eight counts? Repeat this sequence again.

4. **Swimmers:** Begin in front-support position. Raise your right hand off the floor, bringing it back to touch your left hip. Return your hand to place; then repeat this action using your left hand. Do 20 Swimmers in this way.

5. **Ankle Taps:** Begin in hook-lying position on a mat. As you sit up, bring your left knee toward your chest. Touch right hand to left ankle and return to starting position. Repeat, sitting up to touch left hand to right ankle. Can you do 20 Ankle Taps in this way?

6. **Side Leg-Lifts:** Get a mat and lie on your right side with legs straight. Place your left hand flat on the floor out in front. Let your head rest in the hand of your right arm, bent at the elbow. Now raise and lower your left leg eight times. Roll over to your other side and repeat leg lifts with your right leg.

7. **Runner's Lunge Stretch:** Step forward with one leg, bending the knee directly over the ankle. Take your weight on either side of this foot, and slide the other leg straight out behind you. Check that your knee is bent at a right angle and that your foot is flat on the floor. Can you feel a stretch in your hip and in the upper thigh of your back leg? Hold for ten seconds; then change legs and repeat.

8. **Cross-Leg Stretch:** Begin in long-sit position with your legs crossed. Gently reach forward and "walk" your fingers along your legs until you can grasp your toes and hold them for four seconds away from you. Cross your legs the other way and repeat the stretch.

FOCUS: Leg, arm, shoulder, and ankle strength

EQUIPMENT: Suitable music; tape or record player

ORGANIZATION:

- This workout warms, strengthens, and stretches the major muscle groups of the body and teaches the players a variety of "Animal Walks" that, once learned, could be used as "breaks" in the lesson. Have players begin by standing at one end of the play area.

DESCRIPTION OF ACTIVITY:

1. **Bridges and Tunnels:** Number players one or two. All players with the number one are the "bridges"; all those with the number two are the "tunnels." Move around the play area by skipping (galloping, side-stepping, hopping, running backwards). On the signal "Bridges!" one's quickly make bridges by taking your weight on hands and feet; two's crawl under as many bridges as you can before the signal changes. On signal "Tunnels," two's stand with legs wide apart, while one's crawl under as many tunnels as you can before the signal changes.

2. **Seal Walk:** Begin in front-lying position with your hands behind you and turned slightly outward. Taking your weight on your hands, move from one side of the play area to the other side, dragging your feet behind you and making "seal-like" noises.

3. **Camel Walk:** Take your weight on your hands and feet. Travel forward by moving the right hand and leg together, and then moving the left hand and leg together. Extend the middle of your back to look like a camel's hump.

4. **Monkey Walk:** Show me how you can walk on your hands and feet making "monkey-like" sounds. Show me how a monkey scratches itself; eats a banana!

5. **Crow Hop:** Begin in the squat position and spring with both feet together, from one side of the play area to the other making "crow-like" sounds. Can you change direction and speed as you crow hop along, using your arms as wings?

6. **Chicken Walk:** In squat position, put your arms between your legs and around the outside to grasp your ankles. Make chicken sounds.

7. **Elephant Walk:** Bend forward, holding both hands, and let both arms dangle together in front of you. This is your trunk. Show me how you can walk forward with slow lumbering movements, letting your trunk swing from side to side.

8. **Kicking Horse:** Begin in the squat position. Take your weight on your hands and kick your legs upward into the air.

9. **Butterfly Stretch:** Sit tall with the soles of your feet touching. Grasp ankles with your hands and gently press your elbows against your knees for ten seconds. Relax, gently pulsating your legs like "butterfly wings," and then repeat stretch again.

FOCUS: Leg, arm, and abdominal strength

EQUIPMENT: One mat per player; music with a strong 4/4 beat; tape or record player

ORGANIZATION:

- This workout warms and strengthens the major muscle groups. Have players stand in a line, spaced arm's length apart, at one end of the play area.

DESCRIPTION OF ACTIVITY:

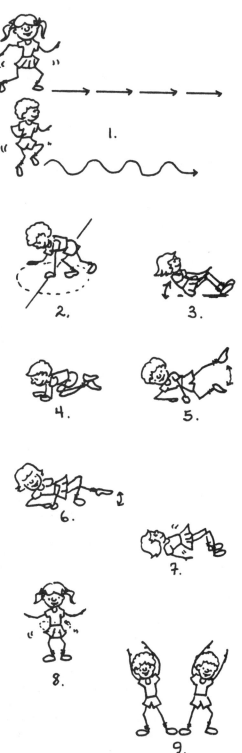

1. **Giant Strides:** How many "giant strides" will it take you to cross the play area to the opposite end? Can you return in fewer strides? Count the number of "hops" you will take to move to the opposite end of the play area. Can you return to your starting line in fewer hops? Repeat, using "jumps"; then "skipping-steps."

2. **Grinder Warm-Up:** On signal "Grind Away!" run to the opposite sideline, place one palm on the floor, and quickly walk in a complete circle around your hand; then run back to the starting line. Walk around your other hand. Do six crossings in this way.

3. **Curl Ups:** In hook-lying position on a mat, with your hands resting on your upper legs and your heels on the floor, slowly curl up, sliding your hands up your legs until the wrists are just past your knees. Then slowly curl down to starting position. Take four counts to curl up and four counts to curl down. Repeat curl-ups 24 times.

4. **Cross-Over Knee Push-Ups:** Kneel on all fours with hands directly below shoulders; cross feet at ankles. Now walk your hands forward, keeping your back flat and hips low. Bend elbows, slowly lowering your chest to mat; then push up to starting position. Repeat ten times.

5. **Side Leg-Lifts:** Lie on your left side with the left lower leg bent. Place left lower arm and right hand flat on the mat in front for support, roll hips forward, and lift trunk. Now raise and lower top right leg eight times. Change sides and repeat.

6. **Inside Leg-Lifts:** Bend top right leg and cross it in front of bottom left leg so that right foot rests flat on floor near the left upper leg; then lower and raise left leg eight times. Change sides, leg positions, and repeat.

7. **Seat Lifts:** In hook-lying position with hands at your sides, raise and lower your hips off the mat 12 times. Keep your lower back in contact with the mat.

8. **Belly-Button Swivels:** Stand tall with feet shoulder-width apart and feet glued to the floor. Place hands on hips. Now, holding upper body still, trace a circle with your belly button. Circle four times in one direction, then four times in the opposite direction. Repeat this pattern three times. Remember to hold your upper body still.

9. **Corner Stretch:** Standing tall with feet shoulder-width apart, raise hands overhead. Slowly lean to side, opening chest to front. Hold three seconds. Return to starting position and lean to other side. Repeat eight times, alternating sides.

FA–14 10-MINUTE WORKOUT 5

FOCUS: Agility; tummy, leg, arm, shoulder, and back strength; lateral and forward trunk flexibility; partnerwork

EQUIPMENT: Twelve cone markers; one beanbag per pair; suitable music; tape or record player

ORGANIZATION:

- This workout involves working in pairs to warm, strengthen, and stretch the major muscle groups. Using cone markers, mark off six sets of parallel lines equally spaced apart, as illustrated. Have players find a partner about the same size and stand one behind the other at one end of the play area.

DESCRIPTION OF ACTIVITY:

1. **Line Shuttle Run:** On signal "Run!" each partner, in turn, run forward to touch one foot to each of the five lines in front of you, returning each time to touch the starting line before running to the next line. Repeat this Line Shuttle twice.

2. **Partner Ski Jumps:** Begin in standing position on the same side of the line, facing your partner and holding both hands. Show me how you and your partner can together do 20 "Ski Jumps" by jumping across the line and back again for one count.

3. **Twist and Touch:** Stand back-to-back about one giant step apart. Without moving your feet, turn to the same side and touch partner's palms; turn to the other side and touch palms again. Continue this pattern for 16 touches.

4. **Hand Pull:** Face each other in long-sit position, with the soles of your feet touching. Bending at the knees, reach forward to grasp each other's wrists. Now gently try to lean backwards. Hold this position for ten seconds. Relax, and then repeat.

5. **Partner Curls:** Begin in hook-sit position, facing your partner. Interlock legs by hooking your feet around your partner's. On signal "Curls!" curl down together and curl up together. Can you and your partner do 20 curls in this way?

6. **Kangaroo Dodge:** Face your partner, arms folded across the chest. Hold a beanbag between your feet. Hop like a kangaroo around your partner, dodging each other and faking directions. Can you do 20 kangaroo hops without losing your beanbag?

7. **Churn-the-Butter:** Face your partner, raise arms to sides and join hands. Lower arms on one side, while raising them on the other side. Turn under raised arms, away from each other. Continue turning back-to-back, raising the other pair of arms and turning under them to starting position. Do three turns in this direction; then do three reverse turns.

8. **Tick-Tock:** Stand back-to-back with your partner, arms and legs wide apart, and join hands. Together gently lean to one side, hold for five seconds, and then lean to the other side and hold for another five seconds. Repeat this stretch two more times.

FOCUS: Leg, arm, and shoulder strength and flexibility; partnerwork

EQUIPMENT: Music with a strong 4/4 beat; tape or record player; one beanbag per pair; one laundry basket

ORGANIZATION:

• Have players find a partner about the same size.

DESCRIPTION OF ACTIVITY:

1. ***Beanbag Jog:*** Run, tossing the beanbag back and forth to each other. If your beanbag drops to the floor, pick it up and, holding hands with your partner, sprint once around the play area; then continue to jog and toss. Which pair will have dropped the beanbag the least times? Then one partner quickly put the beanbag in the basket, while the other finds a free space.

2. ***Hoppo Boppo:*** Stand side-by-side with your partner and hold the outside leg behind your back with your outside hand. Link inside elbows with your partner and hop together around the play area. Reverse direction and hopping leg every eight hops.

3. ***Backward Get-Up:*** Sit back-to-back with elbows linked and legs outstretched. Gently push against each other so that you rise to standing position. Now slowly sit down again. Repeat three times.

4. ***Bicycle Pumper:*** Sit facing your partner with the soles of your feet touching. Lean back on your hands for support and lift your legs off the floor. Working together, move your legs in a pedalling action. Can you pedal your legs together in the reverse direction?

5. ***Spinning Tops:*** Stand facing your partner with feet touching. Grasp partner's wrists with both hands and lean back until arms are straight. Slowly circle together, increasing speed until you are spinning together. Spin CW; then as soon as you feel dizzy, reverse directions.

6. ***Circle Knee Springs:*** Face your partner, clasp hands, and squat. Spring-turn in a full circle to the right; then repeat to the left. Repeat three times with a different partner each time.

7. ***Teeter-Totter:*** Facing your partner with legs bent, gently sit on each other's feet. Then holding onto your partner's upper arms, rock back and forth together. Raise your feet as your partner rises from the floor, keeping your feet under your partner's seat.

8. ***Partner Long-Sit Stretch:*** Hook-sit facing your partner with feet touching and knees bent. Clasp hands and slowly try to straighten legs. Hold for 20 seconds; then repeat two more times.

9. ***Wring-the-Dishrag Stretch:*** Have partners face each other, raise arms to sides, and join hands. Now they turn out to stand back-to-back and stretch arms to sides for ten seconds. Then turn back in to face each other and stretch for another ten seconds. Repeat three times.

FA-16 MEASURING THE HEART RATE

FOCUS: Technique of monitoring heart rates

EQUIPMENT: One stopwatch or several digital wristwatches

ORGANIZATION:

- Have players sit quietly in the Listening Circle. Discuss how one's Aerobic Fitness level is related to how efficiently the heart works. We can measure this efficiency by recording our "Resting Heart Rate" (the rate at which your heart is beating or pulsing at rest). The pulse is the blood rushing through the arteries after each heartbeat. Explain and demonstrate how to take heart rates; then have players monitor their own heart rates. Let them also take a partner's heart rate. If players have digital wristwatches, have them take their own heart rates. Have players take their heart rates in the classroom as a daily activity.

DESCRIPTION OF ACTIVITY:

1. *At the Neck:* Place your three middle fingers on the "carotid artery" located on either side of the neck, just below the chin. Never use your thumb because it has a pulse of its own. Do not press too hard on the artery, as it may alter the heart rate. On signal "Go!" count the number of beats you hear in 30 seconds until I say "Stop!" Then multiply your score by two to determine the number of beats per minute. This is your "resting heart rate." The lower this pulse rate is, the better.
2. Now find a partner. Practice taking each others' heart rates. Find a new partner and repeat.
3. Now jog around the play area for two minutes. On signal "Go!" quickly listen to your heart rate. Is there a difference? Why? This is your "working heart rate."

FA-17 THE FITNESS GAME

FOCUS: Fitness components workout

EQUIPMENT: Lively background music; tape or record player; set of activity cards; one mat and one rope per player

ORGANIZATION:

- Prepare on index cards a variety of endurance, strength, agility, and flexibility tasks. Color-code the cards according to the fitness component areas: GREEN—Endurance; RED—Strength; YELLOW—Agility; BLUE—Flexibility. To ensure that a balanced workout occurs, have players select cards from each of these component areas. Players perform the exercise, and then return to their homes to jog in place. Suggestions follow.

DESCRIPTION OF ACTIVITY:

—Touch the middle of each wall or sideline. Use a different locomotor movement to get to each wall.
—Do four Jump Turns in each corner of the play area.
—Hop to four different mats and do eight sit-ups at each one.
—Slide-step along the diagonal of the play area and gallop along the width (figure-eight pattern).
—Touch five pieces of equipment in play area with a different body part each time.
—"Glue" your feet to the floor and walk your hands in a circle around your feet.
—Do a Partner Stretch together.
—Give eight different players a "Crab Walk greeting" by touching bottom of your foot to the bottom of another player's.
—Jump rope 30 times as quickly as you can.
—Do whatever your Teacher tells you to do, twice!

VARIATION:

Design a "Fitness Game" for outside, using the available space and equipment in your school area.

FA–18 AEROBIC CIRCLE

FOCUS: Cardio-respiratory endurance; leadership

EQUIPMENT: Music with a strong 4/4 beat; tape or record player

ORGANIZATION:

- Have players form a large circle and space themselves at arm's length around it, facing the middle. Discuss the meaning of the word "aerobic" (with oxygen). Cardio-respiratory endurance activities are aerobic. Ask children to give you examples of aerobic activities: walking, running, rope jumping, biking, swimming, skating, cross-country skiing. Ask each player to think of an aerobic activity. Explain that, when pointed to, each player will come to the middle to lead the class through the activity for 16 counts. Each Leader then has eight counts to point to the next leader and return to the circle; everyone else jogs in place. At the end of the warm-up, have players take their pulse rate for 15 seconds.

DESCRIPTION OF ACTIVITY:

— Jog, clapping hands above head; behind; and in front.
— *Sailor Jumps:* Jump with one leg forward and the other back while swinging arms in time to the music.
— *Jumping Jacks:* Jump legs and arms apart sideways, then together.
— *Combo Jacks:* Alternate Jumping Jacks and Sailor Jumps.
— *Side Kicks:* Kick legs from side to side and wave with hands.
— *Seat Kicks:* Kick buttocks.
— *Mule Kicks:* Kick straight legs behind.
— *Front Kicks:* Kick legs out in front.
— *Skier Jumps:* Jump from side to side.
— *Bell Jumps:* Jump forward and back.
— *X-Jumps:* Jump to cross and uncross ankles.
— Pantomime rope jumping.
— Use any locomotor movements to "move" circle CW or CCW.
— "Cool" dancing!

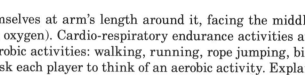

"SIDE-KICKS"

FA–19 AEROBIC SNAKE

FOCUS: Cardio-respiratory endurance; copying

EQUIPMENT: See activity FA–18.

ORGANIZATION:

- In this aerobic activity, children move through several different movement patterns. Vary the locomotor movements used as the "snake" moves in different patterns around the play area: walk forward, backwards; gallop (either foot leading); side-step facing one direction, then the other; skip forward; hop, alternating feet every four counts. Have children stand in single-file formation at arm's length from each other. Create various running patterns such as moving up and down the length of the play area; back and forth across the width; from one diagonal corner to another; in concentric circular patterns ("Coil the Snake"). Emphasize staying in original order throughout the activity and moving in time to the music. Have children cool down by walking once around the play area and listening to their heart beats. Discuss the importance of the heart needing regular activity to stay healthy.

DESCRIPTION OF ACTIVITY:

— Clap in time to the music as we walk forward in our long aerobic snake. Let me hear the snake "hissss . . ."
— Jog and snap your fingers to the beat of the music. Let's pretend this is our snake "rattling."
— Follow me around the play area as we move in different patterns. Can you keep all parts of the snake moving together?

PATTERNS

VARIATION:

Dancing Snake: Use dance steps such as Grapevine step; Step-Hop; Scottish step; Bunny Hop step.

FA-20 SWIM ROUTINE

FOCUS: Cardio-vascular endurance; rhythm-sense

EQUIPMENT: Selected music such as the Beach Boys' "Surfin' Safari"; tape or record player

ORGANIZATION:

- This routine provides a fun aerobic activity while enhancing sense of rhythm. Have children find their own home space and face you. Make sure that everyone can see you. Emphasize that children cannot touch others as they move, and that they should try to move in time with the music. Have players take their working heart rates for 15 seconds immediately after stopping the activity.

DESCRIPTION OF ACTIVITY:

1. Let's pretend that our play area is the beach and we are going to go for a swim! On signal **"Beach!"** jog anywhere around the play area for 16 counts. Change directions often.

2. On signal **"Front Crawl!"** stay on the spot while lifting one arm then the other up, forward and around to eight slow counts, just as if you were swimming in water.

3. On signal **"Back Crawl"** lift one arm then the other up, back and around for four slow counts; then repeat for eight quick counts. Now place your hands on hips, and jump with feet together for two counts to the left side, then two counts to the right side. "Push" your hips out to that side each time.

4. On signal **"Beach!"** jog in free space again for 16 counts.

5. On signal **"Breast Stroke"** stay on the spot while bringing straight arms together forward and then opening them to each side for eight slow counts.

6. Repeat the sequence in part 3. Then on signal **"Beach!"** jog again in free space for 16 counts.

7. On signal **"Sidestroke!"** stay on the spot as you roll hand over hand; then extend one arm upward and at the same time the other arm downward. Repeat this action, alternating arms for eight slow counts.

8. Repeat sequence in part 3; then jog in place for another eight counts while you do your own "Swim" stroke, such as the "Dog Paddle," until the music ends.

VARIATION:

Butterfly: Add this swim stroke to the routine in part 8 above by having children jump forward while at the same time throwing their arms back, around, and forward for eight slow counts.

FA-21 AEROBIC PARTNER SIGNALS

FOCUS: Cardio-vascular endurance; partnerwork; listening

EQUIPMENT: Music with a strong 4/4 beat; tape or record player

ORGANIZATION:

- To begin, have players find a partner and start jogging in place together.

- When the music starts, partners move in a CW direction around the play area, listening for a Signal to change partners or perform a partner activity. Demonstrate and have partners practice each exercise. Suggested signals follow.

DESCRIPTION OF ACTIVITY:

— *Two-Handed Swing:* Take partner's hands and skip in a circle four times in each direction.

— *Elbow Swing:* Hook right elbows and circle your partner four times. Change elbows and do another four swings in the opposite direction.

— *Partner Change:* Release hands, bow to partner, and jog to a new partner.

— *Partner Shuffle:* Join hands with new partner and side-step together eight times in each direction. Repeat.

— *Partner Step-Hops:* Hold inside hands and place outside hands on hips. Step on your right foot and then hop on that same foot; step on the left foot; then hop on the left. Do eight Step-Hops in a CW direction, and then eight Step-Hops in a CCW direction. Repeat.

— *Rocker Steps:* Continuing to hold hands, hop twice on the left foot while raising the right foot forward; then hop twice on the right foot, while raising the left foot behind. Repeat.

— *Pulse Check:* On this signal, stop and quickly find your pulse. Count the number of heart beats in 15 seconds and multiply by four. Did your heart have an aerobic workout?

— *Aerobic Partners:* You and your partner create a partner activity of your own!

SWINGS

BOW

SHUFFLE

STEP-HOPS

ROCKER STEPS

PULSE CHECK

AEROBICS!

FA-22 AEROBIC HOOPS

FOCUS: Leg, arm, and shoulder strength

EQUIPMENT: One hoop per player; music with a strong 4/4 beat; tape or record player

ORGANIZATION:

- This activity strengthens the large muscle groups. Have players get a hoop, place it on the floor, and face you.

DESCRIPTION OF ACTIVITY:

1. *Hoop Warm-Up:* Step inside your hoop and jog 16 times. Then jump twice in the following directions: to the front, inside, to the back, inside, to the right of the hoop, inside, to the left of the hoop, and inside again. Jog in the hoop 16 times and clap hands; then repeat jumping pattern.
2. *Hoop Hops:* Hop on right foot in and out of your hoops in a CW direction; then change hopping foot and direction.
3. *Hoop Trunk Circles:* Hold hoop in front and trace its shape with big movements. Change direction.
4. *Hoop Pulses:* Raise hoop overhead parallel to the floor, and lower it four times. Bend knees in time with the music each time you lower the hoop. Raising and lowering hoop, bend to the right, straighten, and then bend to the left. Repeat this sequence four times, pulsing knees with each repetition.
5. *Hoop Step-Kicks:* Place hoop on the floor. Step and kick legs while circling hoop. Change direction.
6. *Hoop Stretches:* Hold hoop overhead and stretch to the right; hold for ten seconds; then stretch to the left and hold for ten seconds. Repeat.

FA-23 AEROBIC ROPES

FOCUS: Cardio-vascular endurance; strength; equipment manipulation

EQUIPMENT: One short rope per player

ORGANIZATION:

- Have players get a rope, check it for proper length, and find enough space to turn rope freely. Take heart rates readings before and after workout. Add to the routine by adapting other rope tricks (see rope plays in Section 6, "Game Skills"). To start, have players pulse knees in time with the music.

DESCRIPTION OF ACTIVITY:

1. *In Flight:* Holding rope handles in one hand, jog in place, and repeat each of the following rope turns eight times: circle rope overhead like a helicopter's blade; in front like a propeller; on each side like the wheel of a car; in front in a figure-eight pattern. Change hands and repeat. Remember to keep your feet moving!
2. *Levels:* Pulse knees and continuously circle rope overhead four times at each of the following levels: sit, lie down, sit up again, and finally stand. Change hands and repeat. Try the same routine with only two repetitions at each level.

HELICOPTERS

3. *Fancy Footwork:*
   - Circle rope overhead and touch alternate heels to the floor eight times; then circle rope in front and do eight jumping jacks.
   - Circle rope on each side while doing eight Pogo Springs (jump one leg forward and the other back).
   - Pulsing knees, swing rope in front in a figure-eight pattern eight times, then add a twist jump while doing eight more figure-eight's.
   - Repeat the Fancy Footwork sequence, alternating hands every fourth count.
4. *Break Step:* Hold one rope handle in each hand. With hands together, swing rope to one side; then open hands and jump through rope. Swing rope to the other side, and then open hands and jump through rope. Repeat four times.

PROPELLERS

FA-24 ARM BUILDERS

FOCUS: Arm and shoulder strength

EQUIPMENT: One mat per player;
four to five benches;
music with a strong 4/4 beat;
tape or record player

ORGANIZATION:

- Discuss the two major muscles involved when doing arm exercises and their location: the "Biceps" (front muscles of upper arm) and the "Triceps" (underneath muscles of lower arm). *"Bi*ceps" consist of two bundles of muscles working together; *"Tri*ceps" consist of three muscle bundles working together. Discuss the importance of having strong arm muscles: to carry out daily work and play, such as taking out the garbage, raking the lawn, hanging and swinging on playground apparatus, throwing a football; and meeting unforeseen emergencies. Emphasize that children breathe rhythmically as they exercise; exhaling as they push up and inhaling as they lower themselves to the mat. Gradually increase the number of repetitions. Have players get a mat and find a home space.

DESCRIPTION OF ACTIVITY:

1. *Wall Push-Up:* Stand, facing a wall, with feet a comfortable distance from it. Lean forward with hands flat against wall and shoulder-width apart. Bend and straighten arms to push away from wall. Repeat 12 times.
2. *Knee Push-Ups:* Begin on all-fours position on your mat. Keeping your hands shoulder-width apart and fingers pointing ahead, lean forward and lower chest to mat; then push up to starting position. Remember to keep your back flat throughout the push-ups. Repeat 12 times.
3. *Triceps Push-Ups:* In back-support position, slowly bend and straighten arms. Repeat eight times.
4. *Full Push-Ups:* In front-support position, hands shoulder-width apart and fingers pointing ahead, lower until chest almost touches mat; then push up to starting position, keeping back flat and pelvis tilted forward. Repeat eight times.
5. *Bench Push-Ups:* Place hands on bench in full push-up position and bend and straighten elbows to lower body to bench. Repeat 12 times.
6. *Triceps Stretch:* Sitting tall, hold one straight arm across body and gently pull elbow towards body with opposite hand. Hold ten seconds; then change arms and repeat.

FA-25 SEAT SHAPERS

FOCUS: Mid-body strength

EQUIPMENT: One mat per player;
music with a strong 4/4 beat;
tape or record player

ORGANIZATION:

- Review the name of the buttock muscles ("Gluteus Maximus" muscles) and why it is important to keep them strong. (These muscles give support to lower back and hip area.) Have players sit on a mat, facing you.

DESCRIPTION OF ACTIVITY:

1. *Seat Waddles:* Sitting with legs outstretched and feet together, raise arms in front. Can you snap fingers and move hips forward in time with the music using only your seat muscles? Move backwards; sideways.
2. *Hip Tilts:* In hook-lying position, gently squeeze buttocks as you tilt hips forward and back 12 times. Remember to keep your lower back flat on the mat. Squeeze feet and knees together. Repeat another 12 times.
3. *Seat Lifts:* In hook-lying position, gently lift and lower your hips off the mat 12 times. Then squeeze your buttocks as you lift hips upward and hold for ten seconds. Repeat once more.
4. *Hugger Stretch:* From hook-lying position, lift legs off the mat; cross feet right over left and grasp ankles with opposite hands. Hug knees to chest ten seconds. Relax. Repeat, crossing left foot over right.

FA-26 TUMMY TOUGHENERS

FOCUS: Abdominal strength

EQUIPMENT: One mat per player; music with a strong 4/4 beat; tape or record player

ORGANIZATION:

- Discuss the importance of maintaining strong rectus abdominis muscles: to prevent lower back pain and misalignment of the lower back area; to protect the vital organs in that area; and to keep an attractive figure. Throughout the following abdominal exercises, emphasize that players breathe evenly, exhaling as they curl up and inhaling as they curl down. For exercises 4, 5, 6, and 7, ensure that the back is kept flat against the mat to prevent lower back strain. Encourage them to move smoothly and rhythmically. Increase the number of repetitions as players gain abdominal strength. Have players get a mat and sit in long-sit position.

DESCRIPTION OF ACTIVITY:

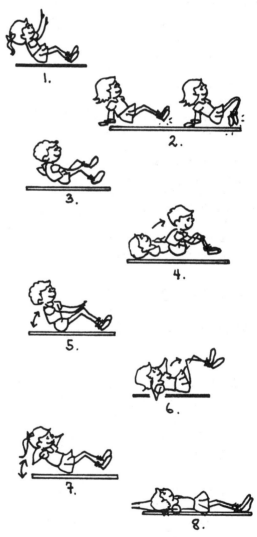

1. *Climbers:* Begin in hook-sit position. Lean back slightly until you feel your abdominal muscles tighten; then move arms as if climbing a rope. Repeat 20 times.

2. *Heel-Toe Taps:* Begin in hook-sit position on mat. Extend your legs to touch your heels to the floor in front of you; then draw your legs in to touch your toes to the mat near your seat. Repeat 12 times.

3. *Ankle-Tap Curl-Ups:* Begin in hook-lying position on mat. Lift head and shoulders slightly off mat; then curl forward to touch opposite hand to the inside of the opposite ankle. Slowly curl downward to mat; then curl upward again. Repeat 16 times.

4. *Sunflower Sit-Ups:* Begin in back-lying position on mat, with arms and legs wide apart. Curl forward to hug your knees towards your chest. Then slowly curl downward to starting position. Repeat 16 times.

5. *Curl-Ups:* Begin in hook-lying position, hands resting on thighs. Curl your body upward, tucking chin to chest and rounding back. Continue to slide hands up thighs until wrists are just past your knees. Slowly lower shoulders to mat. Repeat 12 times.

6. *Elbow-Knee Curl-Ups:* Begin in hook-lying position. Raise feet and cross them at ankles, so that your knees are bent to a 90-degree angle. With fingers at ears, curl up to touch elbows to knees. Repeat 16 times.

7. *Sit-Ups:* Begin in hook-lying position, with hands interlocked behind your head and weight on the heels of the feet. Sit up to touch elbows to knees; then return to starting position. Repeat 16 times.

8. *Abdominal Stretch:* Lie back and stretch your arms overhead and legs straight out. Hold for ten seconds. Pause and repeat.

VARIATIONS:

a. *Elbow-Knee Curl-Ups:* Have players interlock hands behind head and then curl body upward, toward the knees, with the chin leading. Emphasize that elbows are kept out to the sides.

b. In Sit-Ups, have a partner hold the performing partner's feet.

FA-27 HIP HONERS

FOCUS: Mid-body strength

EQUIPMENT: One mat per player; music with a strong 4/4 beat; tape or record player

ORGANIZATION:

- Have players get a mat and kneel on all-fours. Players should keep head low and distribute weight evenly over hands and knees throughout these exercises.

DESCRIPTION OF ACTIVITY:

1. *Fire Hydrants:* On all-fours, with hips square and right knee bent, raise right leg to side and lower it again. Repeat eight times; then change legs.
2. *Hip Flexors:* Lie on your right side with your head resting on your right hand and your left hand flat on the mat in front of you for support. Do not lean forward. Raise and lower your left leg 12 times. Roll over onto your other side and repeat leg raises. The knee should point ahead, not upward, throughout the exercise.
3. *Skyscrapers:* Kneel on all-fours, lower weight to forearms, and tighten abdominal muscles. Raise bent leg behind and push the heel of the foot to the ceiling eight times. Change legs and repeat.
4. *Sit and Tuck Stretch:* Begin in half-hook, half-long-sit position. Cross the bent leg over the straight leg. Gently press with both hands against the knee of the bent leg, pulling it toward the opposite shoulder. Do not pull your shoulder to the knee. Hold for ten seconds. Change legs and repeat.

FA-28 LEG SHAPERS

FOCUS: Lower body strength

EQUIPMENT: See activity FA-27.

ORGANIZATION:

- Review the two muscles of the upper leg and their location: the "Quadriceps" (four muscle bundles of the front thigh) and the "Hamstrings" (back muscles of the thigh). The back muscles of the lower leg are called the "Gastrocnemius." Discuss the importance of having strong leg muscles: used for all our daily work and play such as walking, biking, stair-climbing; for kicking a football or soccer ball; for meeting unforeseen emergencies. Have players scatter and face you.

DESCRIPTION OF ACTIVITY:

1. *Mountain Climbers:* In front-support position, bring the right knee up under chest and extend the left leg backwards. Quickly switch leg positions, keeping in time to the music. Repeat 16 to 24 times.
2. *Leg Crankers:* To strengthen the hamstring muscles, begin in the all-fours position. Raise and lower the right straight leg eight times; then repeat with the left leg. Repeat sequence again.
3. *Thigh Lifts:* Begin in the half-hook, half-long-sit position on your mat. Raise and lower the extended leg eight times. Reverse leg positions and repeat.
4. *Wall Sit:* Lean with your back against a wall and your heels about 30 centimeters (12 inches) away from it. Then slide down, bending knees until they are at right angles and you are in a sitting position. Hold for 20 seconds; then release. Repeat.
5. *Ankle Builders:* In long-sit position on your mat, circle one ankle CW four times; then change direction. Repeat with other ankle. Do this sequence three times. Now flex your ankles by pointing toes toward you; out; away from each other; together; for four counts each direction. Repeat this sequence three times.

FA-29 COOL-DOWN STRETCHES _____

FOCUS: Overall body suppleness

EQUIPMENT: One mat per player;
relaxing music;
tape or record player

ORGANIZATION:

- The "cool-down" phase is a continuation of activity, but at a slower pace and should never be omitted! This phase should last for at least five minutes to allow the heart rate to return to its normal rate. Stretching and toning activities are included to further improve strength and increase one's flexibility. Discuss the meaning of "Flexibility" (joint mobility or suppleness): the range of movement around a joint and its muscles. Discuss why it is important to stretch: to warm up the muscles for aerobic activity; to prevent injury; to maintain the elasticity of the muscles. Name the different muscles involved in each stretch. When stretching, emphasize the following: Breathe normally while holding a stretch, don't hold breath; avoid any bouncing, bobbing or jerking motions; hold stretch for at least ten seconds and gradually try to increase the time. Stretch often, daily! *Homework Stretch:* Have players do stretches at home and teach each of the following stretches to their parents, relatives, or friends.

DESCRIPTION OF ACTIVITY:

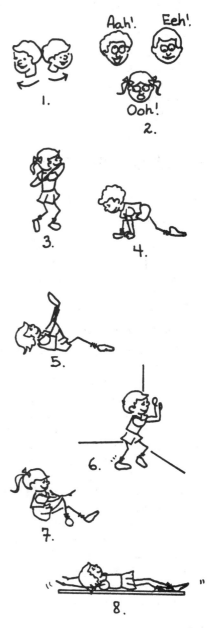

1. *Head and Eye Rolls:* Rotate eyes as you turn your head gently from side to side. Then keep your head still as your eyes look upward then downward. Can you make your eyes follow in a circular path?
2. *Face Stretch:* How many different ways can you twist and contort your face in 20 seconds? Then smile to relax your facial muscles. Now try making these sounds for five seconds each: "Aaah!"; "Eeeh!"; "Oooh!"
3. *Shoulder Stretch:* Standing tall, reach behind your head and down your back as far as you can with your left hand. Try to grab the fingers of your right hand coming up, palm out, behind your back. Hold for ten seconds. Reverse hand-hold and repeat stretch.
4. *Sprinter Stretch:* Begin in the all-fours position on a mat. Move one leg forward until the knee of the front leg is directly over the ankle. Extend the other leg back, shifting the weight up onto the toes and ball of the back foot. Place both hands on the inside of the bent knee. Hold this stretch for ten seconds; then gently pulse the extended leg's knee to the mat. Reverse leg positions and repeat stretch.
5. *Hamstring Stretch:* Begin in hook-lying position on the mat. Raise your right leg upward and grasp it at the ankle with both hands. Gently press the leg toward your chest for ten seconds. Repeat, stretching the other leg.
6. *Calf Stretch:* Stand facing wall. Press your forearms to wall and rest your head on back of hands. Step forward with one leg, bend knee, and place foot flat on floor with toes pointed forward. Straighten the back leg and press the heel to floor. Slowly push forward until you feel a stretch in the calf of the back leg. Hold for 20 seconds; then change legs.
7. *Back Stretch:* Begin in half-hook, half-long-sit position. Cross the bent leg over the straight leg. Gently press the opposite elbow against the outside of the bent knee. Hold this position for ten seconds. Reverse leg and elbow positions and repeat stretch.
8. *Diagonal Stretch:* In back-lying position, stretch your right hand overhead while at the same time pointing the toes of your left foot. Hold for ten seconds; then repeat stretching with the left hand and right foot. Then stretch in as long a shape as you can make for ten seconds!

FA–30 OBSTACLE COURSE

FOCUS: Cardio-vascular endurance; strength; coordination

EQUIPMENT: Chart paper;
marking pens;
masking tape;
six traffic cones;
one springboard;
five or six folding mats;
six jumping ropes;
three balance benches;
four softball bases;
music with a steady beat;
tape or record player

ORGANIZATION:

• Set up equipment at stations around the play area. Start with about eight stations; then gradually increase the number as players' fitness levels improve. Add other obstacles until the number of stations equals at least half the number of players in the class. Prepare a "Stretch Chart" showing the stretches players know and post it on a wall in the stretch area. Begin by "walking" players through the obstacle course so that they know what to do at each station. Encourage players to move quickly, but safely, through the course. Try to avoid "bottlenecks" or places where the activity slows down; keep the players moving! Have players pair off and go through the Obstacle Course in 15-second intervals. Suggestions follow.

DESCRIPTION OF ACTIVITY:

—**Bench Walk:** With feet on bench and hands on floor, walk the length of a bench.

—**Spring and Tumble:** Jump from the springboard, land on both feet, bending at your knees, and do two forward rolls along the mats.

—**Rope Jump:** Do 20 Pepper Jumps with the short rope.

—**Base Run:** Run around the bases once, touching each one in turn.

—**Cone Weave:** Run in a zig-zag pattern in and out of cones.

—**Bench Step-Ups:** Step up and down 20 times.

—**Tunnel Crawl:** Crawl through a tunnel as quickly and carefully as you can.

—**Hoop Jump:** Jump, feet together, from hoop to hoop.

—**In and Out:** Climb in and out of containers as quickly, yet carefully, as you can!

—**Stretch Wall:** After completing the course, go to "Stretch Wall" and do the stretches on the chart.

VARIATIONS:

a. Reverse the direction of travel.

b. Have players go through the course holding hands with a partner.

FA-31 CREATIVE OBSTACLE COURSE

FOCUS: Aerobic warm-up; imagination; cooperation

EQUIPMENT: Cone markers and scooters;
balance benches and climbing chairs;
tables and chairs;
carpet squares;
beanbags;
mats;
ropes;
hoops;
music with a strong 4/4 beat;
tape or record player

ORGANIZATION:
- Divide the class into groups of about five to six players. Have each group begin by sitting cross-legged in a line at one end of the play area. Assign each group a set of equipment. Rotate groups about every two minutes. Discuss with the class what an obstacle course is.

DESCRIPTION OF ACTIVITY:
1. On the signal "Go!" each group collect your equipment and, working together in front of your line, create an obstacle course that stretches to the other end of the play area. Return to the starting position when your obstacle course is completed.
2. When you hear the music play, each group travel through your obstacle course until the music stops; then quickly return to sit in your starting position.
3. On the signal "Rotate!" each group move to the obstacle course on your right as your group faces the opposite end of the play area. Each time we change, the first group must march together around the play area and say in unison, "I will never smoke! I will never smoke! . . ." until the group reaches the last obstacle course. Each group continue in this way until all obstacle courses have been visited.

VARIATION: Have the leader of each group decide how the group will move through the obstacle course. Everyone in the group copies the leader. After each rotation, a new leader takes over. Ensure that each player gets the opportunity to be a leader.

FA-32 OUTDOOR OBSTACLE COURSE

FOCUS: Cardio-vascular endurance; strength

EQUIPMENT: Playground equipment;
school environment;
stretch chart;
string

ORGANIZATION:
- Using the playground apparatus and equipment, set up an obstacle course of about ten stations. Carefully check the equipment for any faults. Try to avoid "bottlenecks" or places where the activity slows down. Keep the players moving! "Walk" the players through the course, explaining the task to be performed at each station. Encourage players to move quickly, but safely, through the course. Prepare a "Stretch Chart" showing the stretches players know and post it on a tree. Suggestions follow.

DESCRIPTION OF ACTIVITY:
— Swing on a fixed apparatus such as a swing or horizontal bar.
— Cat walk (on all-fours) along a bench.
— Climb up, across, and down a vertical grid such as a climbing ladder or dome.
— Crawl through a vertical tire or pipes.
— Run around the bases of a baseball diamond.
— Run up and down a sloped area.
— Climb up and slide down a slide.
— Climb through a jungle gym.
— Zig-zag through a line of trees.
— **Stretch Tree:** After completing the course, go to the stretch tree and do the stretches on the chart.

FOCUS: Aerobic endurance; strength; flexibility

EQUIPMENT: Activity station signs;
music with a strong 4/4 beat;
tape or record player;
four cone markers;
one or two benches

ORGANIZATION:

- Set up eight to ten Fitkid exercise stations around the perimeter of the play area, positioning them in a circle, oval, or rectangle. Make station signs that depict vigorous, continuous exercises on posterboard that can be folded in half and then made to stand on its own. Laminate the signs to improve their durability. To begin, explain how to perform each exercise, emphasizing correct technique; then have a maximum of four players go to each station. Play music to begin and stop activity. At first have players perform the exercise for 30 seconds, with ten seconds to rotate; then gradually increase the activity time. Have players take their heart rates immediately after the circuit is completed.

DESCRIPTION OF ACTIVITY:

1. **Swimmers:** In front-support position, lift your right hand back to touch your left hip, return to place; then lift your left hand back to touch your right hip. Continue in this way.

2. **Jump-Turns:** Jump and turn in the air so that you are facing in the opposite direction. Repeat four times; then do four jumps turning the other way.

3. **Line Push-Ups:** Begin in the front-support position with both hands behind a line. Place one hand, then the other, in front of the line; then place one hand after the other behind the line.

4. **Tummy Tightener:** Sit in long-sit position. Lean back slightly and pretend to climb a rope hand-over-hand.

5. **X-Jumps:** Place your hands on your hips, feet wide apart. Jump and cross your feet right over left; jump and cross your feet left over right.

6. **Crab-Walk Dance:** From hook-sit position, place your weight on your hands and feet, lifting your bottom off the floor. Now lift one hand off the floor to touch your opposite knee; then lift the other hand to touch the opposite knee.

7. **Figure-Eight Run:** (Place two cone markers 5 meters [15 feet] apart. Set up two identical stations.) Slide in a figure-eight pattern around the two cone markers.

8. **Bench-Steps:** Step up onto the bench with one foot; then step up with the other foot so that you are in the standing position on the bench. Now step the first foot off the bench, followed by the second foot. Repeat this stepping pattern.

9. **Bench-Jumps:** Stand on one side and near to one end of the bench. Clasp the sides of the bench; then jump with feet together onto the bench; jump off to the other side. Jump back onto the bench, jump off to the starting side. Repeat this jumping pattern.

10. **Stretch Time:** Do your favorite stretch and hold it for at least ten seconds.

VARIATION: Have players run once around the play area before continuing to the next station.

Section 3

Movement Awareness

The Movement Awareness activities help to develop the movement principles of space awareness, body awareness, and effort awareness and relationships. These are used to set tasks that ask *What? Where? How can?* and *Who can?* The children respond to the task or problem by exploring and experimenting at the floor level, on low apparatus, or on large apparatus, with or without equipment.

This section offers 46 Movement Awareness activities, including:

MA-1 ORIENTATION TO PERSONAL/GENERAL SPACE _____

FOCUS: Space awareness; safety training; listening

EQUIPMENT: None

ORGANIZATION:

- This section is a forerunner of the sections on "Rhythms and Dance," "Gymnastics," and "Game Skills" and, therefore, should be taught first. The concepts, principles, and movement vocabulary can then be directly applied to these areas; in fact, to all forms of human movement. The four basic themes of Movement Awareness are: "Space Awareness," "Body Awareness," "Effort Awareness," and "Relationships," which are integrated throughout the CPEP program.

- As in Book 1, these themes are further divided into subthemes, which provide a wide variety of movement experiences, and are sequentially arranged. Beginning with floor tasks and progressing to manipulative equipment and apparatus, children work individually, with a partner, and in groups. Revise the signals, formations, and starting positions from Section 1, activities IA–1 through IA–6. To begin, train the children to move safely in general space, to identify a personal space and boundaries, and to develop good listening skills. Establish your start and stop signals and insist that on the "Freeze!" signal, they are to stop immediately—no sliding, no bumping.

DESCRIPTION OF ACTIVITY:

1. Find your own home or personal space. Check your space. Can you touch anyone else or anything? If so, move to a free space. Explore moving different body parts in your home space.

2. **"Scrambled Eggs!":** Leave your home and move in and out of each other. Now you are travelling in general space. Don't touch anyone. "Freeze!" Quickly return to your home and hook-sit facing me. Now leave home and travel in a different way. No collisions! "Freeze!" Return home in a different way again. "Freeze!" there.

3. Explore moving about in general space on different body parts: one foot; hands and feet; seat and feet; one knee, one foot and one hand. "Freeze!" Now move slowly with one body part leading. "Freeze!" Travel quickly with another body part leading. (Repeat several times.)

4. Find a partner and explore moving together in personal space. Now move together in general space. "Freeze!" Quickly return home. Find another pair and join hands to form a group of four. Sit in a circle in your home space. On signal "Corners!" each group, touch the four corners of the play area with a different body part each time; then return home to sit cross-legged in a circle again. Don't forget to hold hands while you move and watch out for other pairs.

5. Now let's explore the boundaries of the play area. Touch the sidelines with both elbows; gallop to touch opposite endlines with one knee and one hand; slide to diagonally opposite corners and touch with any three body parts; then find a home in the play area. How quickly can you step outside of the boundaries? Jump inside the boundaries; then return to your home.

MA-2 SETTING UP/DISMANTLING APPARATUS; COLLECTING/ DISPERSING EQUIPMENT_____

FOCUS: Space awareness; safety training

EQUIPMENT: One bench per group;
chairs;
hoops;
tables;
mats;
box horse;
springboard;
basket of beanbags;
cart of play balls;
cone markers;
climbing apparatus

ORGANIZATION:

- Form groups of five; each group with a Leader. Teach children how to lift, carry, arrange, collect, and put away the equipment and apparatus safely and efficiently.

DESCRIPTION OF ACTIVITY:

1. To begin, Group 1 will demonstrate how to correctly lift and carry a bench: With one child on each end and three children on the sides of the bench, all facing the same direction; bend your knees, and together lift the bench with both hands, keeping your backs straight. Walk, not run, over here, lowering the bench into place slowly. Do not drop. Make sure no toes are underneath!

2. Now each group lift and carry your bench to the place I point to. Set it there carefully; then straddle-sit on the bench one behind the other, facing me. Well done!

3. Group 3 will demonstrate how to bring out the climbing ropes and set up the climbing frame.

4. Now Group 1, your job is to bring out 12 hoops and scatter them around the play area.

   — Group 2, place the cone markers around the boundaries of the play area, spacing them one giant step apart.

   — Group 3, bring out six folding mats and place them under the climbing ropes and climbing frame.

   — Group 4, bring out the basket of beanbags and cart of balls and place them in the center of the play area.

   — Group 5, carry two chairs, one table, one box horse and set up an obstacle course at this end of the play area.

   Let's observe how each group arranged the equipment. Have you any suggestions for improving it?

5. **_Follow-the-Leader:_** Leaders, take your group in and out, over and under, on and off, across, through and around, up and down the apparatus and use the equipment that has been set out. On signal "Change," the next team member becomes the leader. Remember to move safely at all times.

6. Now class, it is time to put all the equipment away! Each group, please return the equipment to its proper place. Group 2, you will put away the climbing frame; Group 4, you will look after the climbing ropes, as well.

MA-3 EXPLORING DIRECTIONS

FOCUS: Space awareness

EQUIPMENT: One drum

ORGANIZATION:

- Review the term "Directions": movement that is forward, backwards, sideways, up, down, and diagonally on different body parts, in personal and general space. To begin, have children stand in their homes, facing you.

DESCRIPTION OF ACTIVITY:

1. Show me how you can travel **forward** on different body parts: feet; back; tummy; seat and feet; hands and feet; on any three body parts. Change body parts on each drum signal.

2. Travel **backwards** in general space on different body parts: on your seat; back; tummy; hands and feet, facing upward or facing downward. Watch where you are going so that you don't bump into anyone!

3. Travel **sideways** to the right on two body parts; to the left on the same body parts. Repeat using different body parts. Make different parts lead the way. How can you travel **diagonally** on different body parts? Make different parts lead the way.

4. **Direction Game:** Every time you hear a drum beat, change direction. Now change body parts you are moving on as well as direction, on each drum signal.
5. **Direction Story:** Using different directions and body parts, make a story with a *Beginning*, a *Middle* part, and an *Ending*. Practice your story; then I will ask you to perform it in front of the class.

MA-4 EXPLORING PATHWAYS AND PATTERNS

FOCUS: Space awareness

EQUIPMENT: Posterboard and marking pen or chalkboard and chalk

ORGANIZATION:

- A "Pathway" is the track that the body makes as it travels about in general space, on the apparatus, and through the air. A "Pattern" is a predictable pathway or route. On posterboard or chalkboard, draw the different *pathways*: zig-zagged, curved, straight, winding, and spiral; and *patterns*: circle, triangle, square, rectangle, figure-eight, diamond shape, a letter, a number. Have children begin in their own homes.

DESCRIPTION OF ACTIVITY:

1. **Pathways:** Look at this picture of a zig-zagged pathway (sharp angled turns). Show me how you can travel around the play area in this way, changing directions, and then return to your home. Try not to touch anyone.
2. Now travel in a straight pathway on four body parts. "Freeze!" Change direction and travel a straight pathway on three body parts. (Repeat several times.) Can you wind your way back home? Look at this picture of a curved pathway. Show me how you can travel in this way, making small curves; then large curves. Zig-zag your way home.
3. **Patterns:** Can you travel in a circular pattern, just in your personal space? Repeat, making your pathway bigger and bigger. Show me how you can travel in general space in a square pattern; a rectangular pattern; a triangular pattern; a figure-eight; a spiral pathway. Use different body parts as you travel in these pathways, and change directions often.
4. **Pathway/Pattern Story:** Choose three different pathways or patterns you have learned. Put them together to create a story (or Sequence) so that you have a Beginning, a Middle, and an Ending. Finish in your home space. Practice. (Have children draw their "Pathway Story" on paper.)

MA-5 COMBINING DIRECTIONS/PATHWAYS/PATTERNS

FOCUS: Space awareness

EQUIPMENT: Posterboard and marking pen or chalkboard and chalk; drum (optional)

ORGANIZATION:

• Children explore various ways of combining directions, pathways, or patterns they have learned. Use posterboard pictures to show examples that they can try. Provide ample opportunity for them to create their own combinations. Have children begin in their homes.

DESCRIPTION OF ACTIVITY:

1. You have learned to travel in different directions, pathways, and patterns. Now let's experiment with combining these. Look at the following pictures. Can you use different body parts as you move? Examples:

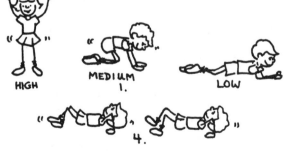

Directions	Pathways	Patterns
—backwards	—zig-zag	—circular
—sideways	—curving	—square, rectangular
—forward	—spiral	—triangular
—backwards	—winding	—figure-eight, letter
—diagonal		

2. Now put together your own direction and pathway/pattern combination. Travel in this way and finish in your home.

3. **Direction and Pathway/Pattern Story:** Show me how you can put together any three directions/pathway/pattern combinations to create a sequence. Practice. Then, while the girls watch, boys show us your sequences; then girls, it's your turn. For example: Beginning—backwards, zig-zagging, on tippy-toes; Middle—circular CW, on hands and feet; Ending—sideways, figure-eight, on feet.

MA-6 EXPLORING LEVELS

FOCUS: Space and body awareness

EQUIPMENT: None

ORGANIZATION:

• Children explore moving in personal and general space, at different levels from high, to medium, to low, in different pathways, and directions on different body parts. Have children begin in their homes.

DESCRIPTION OF ACTIVITY:

1. **Levels:** Show me how you can be at a high level in your personal space. Now move to a medium level; then to a low level. Now move from low to high level.

2. Let's explore taking different body parts from a high level, to a medium level, to a low level: feet; nose; elbows; hands; tummy; etc. Reverse the levels and repeat.

3. **Levels, Directions, and Pathways/Patterns:** Try the following sequence. Travel in a forward direction at a high level, in a winding pathway. "Freeze!" Move backwards at a medium level, in a circular pathway. "Freeze!" Return home by moving sideways at a low level, in a straight pathway. Now you create your own sequence.

4. **Partner Levels:** Find a partner and a free space. Begin with one partner at a high level and the other at a low level. Change levels by moving around, over, under each other. One partner be the leader; the other, the follower. Leader, travel about, changing levels, directions, pathways/patterns. On signal, switch roles.

MA-7 EXPLORING RANGES

FOCUS: Space and body awareness   **EQUIPMENT:** None

ORGANIZATION:
- Review the meaning of the term "Range": refers to how close one thing is to another. A range can be near to, far from; long, short; large, medium, small; wide, narrow. Children explore ranges in personal and general space, noticing how their body shape also changes. Have children begin in their homes.

DESCRIPTION OF ACTIVITY:

1. In your home, make a shape with your hands and feet far away from your body; near to your body. Is your new shape small or large? Make a shape with your head and feet near to each other. Can you make another shape with your feet near your head? Make a shape with two body parts far away from each other and two other body parts near to each other.

2. Travel in general space, staying far from your classmates. As soon as you come close to someone, spring away. Now be near to someone as you travel around the classroom. Move about in general space, using the biggest movements you can make; the smallest movements.

MA-8 CONTRASTING MOVEMENTS

FOCUS: Space awareness   **EQUIPMENT:** Benches

ORGANIZATION:
- Working in pairs, children learn about contrasting terms and how to use these terms in a variety of movement patterns. Some tasks are suggested below. Children find a partner and stand together in a home space.

DESCRIPTION OF ACTIVITY:
1. *Above (over)—Below (under, beneath):* Shake your hands above your head; below your head. Make a bridge over your partner; make a bridge under your partner.
   - *Across (along)—Around:* Jump across your partner. Move around him or her. Travel along a bench. Hop around the bench.
   - *Around clockwise (CW)—Around counterclockwise (CCW):* Side-step around your partner in a CW direction. Skip around your partner in a CCW direction.
   - *Between—Alongside of:* Stand alongside of your partner. Crawl between your partner's legs.
2. *Forward—Backwards—Sideways:* Travel in a forward direction, then backwards, then in a sideways direction with your partner.
   - *Right—Left:* First partner travel to your right; the second partner travel to your left.
3. *Heavy—Light:* Run lightly; run heavily.
   - *Big (large)—Small (tiny, little):* Travel in a big shape; travel in a small shape.
   - *Round (curved)—Flat (straight):* First partner make a round shape; second partner make a flat shape. Then switch roles.
   - *Wide—Narrow (thin):* First partner make a wide shape; second partner make a narrow shape. Then switch roles.
4. Others: Fast–Slow; Smooth–Jerky; Near to–Far from; Relaxed–tensed.
5. *Opposite Game:* I will give you a contrasting term. You must move to the opposite term. For example, "stretch to the right side" (you stretch to the left side).

MA-9 USING MANIPULATIVE EQUIPMENT

FOCUS: Space awareness;
manipulation and control

EQUIPMENT: Beanbags;   deckrings;   ropes;
hoops;   batons;   balls

ORGANIZATION:

- Children explore manipulating and controlling equipment in personal and general space, while moving in different directions, pathways/patterns, levels and ranges. Organize children to bring out the equipment. Have each choose a piece of equipment and find a home space. After a few minutes, have them trade equipment.

DESCRIPTION OF ACTIVITY:

1. In your home, show me how you can hold the equipment with your knees; your feet; under your chin; under your arms. How many different ways can you hold your equipment high? at a medium level? a low level? Move your equipment far from you; close to you. Make a funny shape while holding your equipment.
2. Put the equipment on the floor and move in different directions around it: backwards; sideways; forward. Show me how you can move the equipment using different body parts. Try moving with your equipment far from you; close to you.
3. Everyone collect a ball. Show me how you can bounce the ball in place while you skip CW in a circular pattern around the ball.
   — Travel forward at a high level, bouncing your ball in a zig-zag pathway. "Freeze!" Control your ball. Now travel backwards as you bounce your ball at a low level. "Freeze!" Change from one level to another while bouncing your ball.
4. **Buddy Equipment:** Find a partner and choose a piece of equipment. Explore different ways of moving this equipment between you as the two of you travel, changing directions, pathways/patterns, and levels. Remember to watch out for others. Trade your equipment with another pair and repeat the task.

MA-10 TRAVELLING ON APPARATUS

FOCUS: Space awareness

EQUIPMENT: Mats;   cone markers;
benches;   box horse or tables;
hoops;   climbing frame
chairs;

ORGANIZATION:

- Children explore ways of travelling on the apparatus in different directions, pathways, ranges, and levels. Have teams collect and arrange the equipment throughout the play area. Remind players about the safety procedures for lifting and carrying the equipment and setting up the climbing apparatus. Children begin by standing near a piece of equipment.

DESCRIPTION OF ACTIVITY:

1. Move in different directions in general space without touching the apparatus or any person. On the signal "Freeze!" squat down low and stay very still. Are you in control? Now move in a different pattern to each piece of apparatus. (Repeat several times.)
2. Show me how you can travel over, under, along, on and off, around, and through the apparatus: changing directions, pathways or patterns, and levels. For example, move forward on your tummy along the bench; climb a square pattern on the climbing frame; zig-zag in and out of the hoops; roll sideways in a straight pathway along a mat; move on hands and feet over the box.
3. **Apparatus Game:** Travel on the apparatus, keeping your body near to the apparatus as you go. Now try travelling keeping your body parts far from each other. On the signal "Freeze!" make yourself long (wide, narrow, rounded, small, large) on the apparatus. Watch where you are going at all times. (Repeat several times, varying the "freezing" shape.)

MA-11 RUNNING, FAKING, AND DODGING _____

FOCUS: Space awareness; locomotion; footwork

EQUIPMENT: Chairs;
hoops;
cone markers;
drum

ORGANIZATION:

- In this section, the basic locomotor movements are further explored through a variety of movement tasks, incorporating previous themes of directions, levels, pathways/patterns, and ranges. Review the terms "Dodging" (quickly darting away from someone or something); "Faking" (pretending to move in one way, but actually doing the opposite); and "Marking" ("shadowing" a player as closely as possible). To begin, have children find a home space.

DESCRIPTION OF ACTIVITY:

1. **Walking Warm-Up:** Walk about in general spacing, making quick changes of direction every time you hear my drum beat. Remember good "walking style": Let your heel touch first, and then rock to ball and toes of foot; keep your head up; shoulders down; tummy tucked in; feet moving straight ahead; and swing your arms slightly.

   — Walk on different parts of your foot: toes; heels; inside; outside; toes turned in; toes turned out; tiny steps; giant steps; cross-over walks.

   — "Mood walks": happy, mad, sad, tired, frightened, cautious, etc.

2. Now run on the balls of your feet into free spaces, making quick changes of direction on one drum beat and freezing on two drum beats. Don't bump into anyone!

3. Choose a partner and stand together in a free space. The taller partner stay in this space, while the shorter partner runs away. Now shorter partner, run up to your home partner, stop, and change direction. How close can you come without touching your partner? This is called dodging.

   — Repeat, gradually running faster toward your partner, and then darting off in another direction. Change roles after three dodges.

4. Repeat the task in part 3, but this time look one way, and then dart off in the opposite direction. This is called a head fake. Are you in control when you change direction quickly?

5. **Equipment Dodging:** (Have children scatter chairs, hoops, and cone markers throughout the play area.) Practice your running, faking, and dodging the various obstacles. Remember to watch where you are going!

VARIATIONS:

a. Play "Artful Dodger" from Section 1.

b. Refer to Section 1 for several "tag-type" games to reinforce dodging concept.

MA-12 JUMPING AND HOPPING

FOCUS: Space awareness; locomotion; coordination

EQUIPMENT: Mats; ropes; hoops; wands

ORGANIZATION:

- Review the terms "Jumping" (the action of pushing off with both feet and landing on both feet) and "Hopping" (the action of springing from one foot and landing on the same foot). Children explore jumping and hopping in personal and general space in different directions, pathways/patterns, and levels on the floor, and then using different equipment. Remind children to use their arms for forward motion and balance, to spring off the balls of their feet, and to land lightly bending at the knees, ankles, and hips to absorb the force of the landing. Have children start in a home space.

DESCRIPTION OF ACTIVITY:

1. In your home, jump low; jump high; higher! Can you alternate low and high jumps? Jump and land with your feet sideways apart; jump and land with your feet together again; jump and crisscross your feet sideways; jump and click your heels in the air.
   — Jump-Turns; quarter turns; half turns; three-quarter turns; full turns. Jump in either direction.

2. Hop in place on your right foot four times; then hop four times on your left foot. Hop three times on each foot; two times; once.
   — On your right foot, hop forward four times; hop backwards four times to place; hop to the right four times; hop to the left four times. Repeat on left foot.
   — Hop, holding the free foot in different positions: right hand holding right foot behind; left hand holding right foot behind; holding the free foot in front; to the side.

3. Stretch a rope along the floor. Jump back and forth over the rope from one end to the other end. Jump backwards to the start. Hop back and forth over the rope; change hopping foot to return.

4. *Using Equipment:* Place a hoop on the floor. Jump in and out of it in different ways. Repeat by hopping in and out of your hoop.
   — Have a partner hold a wand just off the floor. Jump over it. How high can you safely jump?

MA-13 JUMPING AND HOPPING GAMES

FOCUS: Partner- and groupwork; alertness

"Footsie"

EQUIPMENT: One hoop per child; one "footsie" per child; one long rope; one deckring

ORGANIZATION:

- To make a "Footsie" or an ankle jumper, you will need one small plastic container with lid; 1–1.2-meter (4-foot) piece of rope; one large plastic bleach bottle; and one roll of masking tape. Cut out a small hole in the side of the small container. Place one end of the rope through this hole and knot it to prevent it from slipping out. Tape or glue the lid securely shut. Cut a 2.5-centimeter (1-inch) strip out of the bleach bottle to make the ankle ring. Tie the other end of the rope to it.

DESCRIPTION OF ACTIVITY:

1. *Footsie:* (Each player scatters and positions the ankle jumper on the foot.) Practice jumping over the rope as it swings CW; CCW. Now find a partner. While one partner wears the footsie and keeps the rope turning, the other partner jumps over it. Exchange roles after a while. Raise the ankle ring so that the rope will swing higher, and repeat the above tasks.

2. *Hoop Hopping:* (Divide the class into groups of four or five and have each group collect six hoops.) Arrange your hoops on the floor in any pattern that you wish. Now try hopping through your hoops in a follow-the-leader formation. Visit other groups and hop through their hoop pattern. Two groups, combine your hoops to create even more interesting patterns. Then explore hopping through the pattern. Visit other hoop patterns.

3. *Jump the Rope:* Form one large circle and space yourselves arm's length apart. Jump over the rope (long rope with a beanbag or deckring tied at one end) as I stand in the center and swing it under your feet.

MA-14 HOPSCOTCH GAMES

FOCUS: Space awareness; hopping and jumping

EQUIPMENT: One beanbag per child; floor tape or chalk

ORGANIZATION:

- Use floor tape to mark out two identical Hopscotch patterns for each Station as shown. Divide the class into groups of four or five; assign two groups to a station and allow them to practice hopping through the pattern. Explain the rules of the game: Take turns to play; use beanbags to toss; lose your turn if you step on a line, toss your beanbag on a line or the wrong space, change your hopping foot, or land on both feet in other than the allowed space; take your turn again when the other players in your group have had their turn. Rotate groups every ten minutes to a different Hopscotch station.

DESCRIPTION OF ACTIVITY:

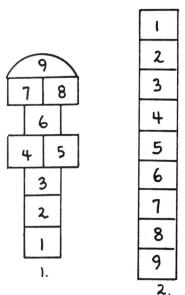

1. *Half-Moon Hopscotch:* Toss your beanbag into the first square; then hop into this square, pick up your beanbag, and hop out. Now toss your beanbag into the second square. Hop into the first square, then into the second square, pick up your beanbag, and then hop into the first square and out. Continue in this way, up and back down. In spaces 4 and 5, 7 and 8, and 9 ("half-moon" space), land with both feet on the ground at the same time.

2. *Ladder Hopscotch:* Toss your beanbag into the first square. Hop over this square into the second square, pick up the beanbag, and hop into the first square and out. Now toss the beanbag into the second square. Hop into the first square, over the second, and into the third square. Turn around, pick up your beanbag, and hop into the second and first squares and out. Continue in this way, up and then down the ladder.

3. *Shuffleboard Hopscotch:* Stand on one foot and toss the beanbag into the first square. Then hop over this square into all of the other spaces: Land with one foot in spaces 1, 4, 7, and 10 (change hopping foot here); land with two feet in spaces 2 and 3, 5 and 6, 8 and 9. Upon reaching square 2 on the return, lean forward and pick up your beanbag; hop into square 1 and out. Continue in this way.

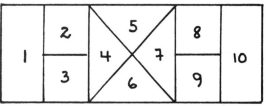

4. *Snail Hopscotch:* Toss your beanbag into the first space. Hop into that space, pick up your beanbag, and hop out. Now toss the beanbag into the second space; again pick up your beanbag and hop back into the first space, and then out. Continue until you reach the last space. Land with both feet in the center of the "snail," and then begin again, working your way from the last space to the first.

5. *Tournament Hopscotch:* Kick your beanbag into the first space. Hop into this space and kick your beanbag into the second space, using your hopping foot. Continue in this way, using as many kicks as necessary until you reach the tenth space. Now kick your beanbag out and hop out. In spaces 1 and 2 and 4 and 5, land with both feet on the ground, one in each space. A two-foot landing can also be used in the seventh space.

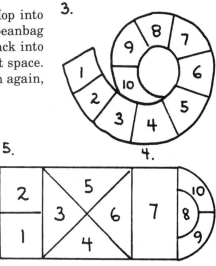

VARIATION:

If outside, use chalk on the tarmac or sidewalk surface and draw the different Hopscotch games.

MA-15 SKIPPING, SIDE-STEPPING, GALLOPING; SLIDING, CREEPING, CRAWLING

FOCUS: Space awareness; locomotion; partnerwork

EQUIPMENT: One hoop per child; pictures of wide, long, round, twisted shapes; benches; chairs; tables; mats; one drum

ORGANIZATION:

- Review the term "Skipping" (a series of "step-hops" performed by alternating the feet). Remind children that skipping is done on the balls of the feet with the arms swinging in opposition to the legs. Emphasize smoothness and rhythm, not distance and speed. Also review "Side-Stepping" (movement to either side in which the leading foot steps sideways, while the other foot quickly follows). Side-stepping is a graceful, smooth, and controlled movement, also done on the balls of the feet. "Galloping" is a forward movement with one foot always leading and the other foot following.
- "Sliding" is the action of moving the whole body in as low a position as possible; "Crawling" is the action of moving on hands and knees; "Creeping" is the action of moving one body part slowly after the other.
- To begin, have children skip to a home space.

DESCRIPTION OF ACTIVITY:

1. Skip forward in general space, in and out of your classmates, changing directions on the drum signal. Good! Now skip backwards. Watch where you are going! Repeat, side-stepping; galloping.
   — Skip in different pathways and patterns. Repeat by side-stepping; galloping.
2. Do something different with your hands as you skip: Clap your hands; snap your fingers; raise them high in the air. Show me what you can do with your arms as you side-step: Hold them out sideways at shoulder level and circle your arms or move them up and down; swing them inward; swing them outward. Now gallop with one foot leading; on my drum beat, let the other foot lead.
3. **Hoop Shapes** (Scatter hoops throughout the play area.) On signal "Skip!" (or "Side-Step!" or "Gallop!"), skip around the hoops without touching them. On the loud drum beat, jump inside a hoop and make a "hoop shape" from the picture I am showing to you.
4. Find a partner and, holding hands, skip side-by-side, changing pathways and directions on my drumbeat signal. Explore other ways of skipping together: backwards; around in a circle holding hands; linking elbows and skipping in opposite directions.
   — Side-step together in different ways: face-to-face; back-to-back; side-by-side; around in a circle holding hands; etc. Now explore galloping together in different ways.
   — Repeat movement tasks in groups of three or four.
   — Create a Skip-Gallop-Side-step story with your partner.
5. Slide on different body parts: tummy, back, seat, and feet. Crawl in different directions. Creep on different body parts. Freeze on the loud drum beat. Make a Slide-Crawl-Creep story.
   — With a partner create a story using all six of these locomotor movements!
6. (Scatter several obstacles throughout the play area.) Crawl or creep around obstacles. Crawl under or over an obstacle; crawl through a low opening. Slide along a bench; under or over an obstacle. Move to each obstacle by skipping, galloping, or side-stepping!

MA-16 SPRINGING AND LANDINGS

FOCUS: Space awareness; flight; landings

EQUIPMENT: Low box; hoops; cones; mats; chairs; benches; wands

ORGANIZATION:

- Discuss the term "Flight" (the action of springing to eject the whole body into the air). There are three components of flight: the take-off, flight, and landing. "Leaping" is the action of springing from one foot and landing on the other foot. Emphasize the using of the arms to get good height and landing "softly" on the toes, balls, and then heels of the feet, bending at the hips, knees, and ankles to cushion the impact.

DESCRIPTION OF ACTIVITY:

1. In your home, from a standing start show me how high you can spring into the air. How can you use your arms to help you spring even higher?
2. On signal, travel about in general space. Show me how many ways you can "fly" as you move. How can you get your whole body in the air?
   — Explore ways of taking off and landing on your feet: from one foot and landing on two feet; from one foot to the same foot; from one foot to the opposite foot; from two feet to one foot; from two feet to two feet. Remember to land softly, bending at the knees!
3. Show me how you can leap in general space in different directions.
   — Leap and turn in the air so that you land softly, facing in the opposite direction. Repeat, turning in the opposite direction.
   — Show me how you can spring into the air, make a shape, and land softly.
4. *Flight Sequence:* Find three different ways to take off, fly, and land softly. Practice your sequence. Then we will observe each other's.
5. *Stand and Spring:* How far can you spring? Experiment with your feet close to each other; shoulder-width apart; feet wide apart; arms at your sides; arms swinging. Which is best?
   — How far can you go in three springs in a row?
   — Stand just behind your mat. Can you spring over the width of your mat? Can you spring over the length of your mat?
6. *Run and Spring:* Run toward your mat. Spring from one foot and judge your take-off point so that you can land in the middle of your mat.
   — Repeat, springing from your other foot. Which take-off foot feels more comfortable?
7. *Hop, Step, and Jump:* Practice this sequence. Hop from your right foot to your right foot; step onto the other foot, and spring to land on both feet. Now try again, hopping on your left foot to start. Which feels better for you? Repeat from a running approach.
8. *Flight Using Apparatus*—Suggested tasks:
   — Explore different ways of jumping onto a bench; springing off a bench and landing; leaping over a bench.
   — Explore different ways of springing for height (making shapes, turning) from a box horse; vary the landings.
   — Spring over the obstacles, such as mats, hoops, low boxes, chairs, hurdles (wand resting on two cones), in different ways.

MA-17 LOCOMOTION STATIONS

FOCUS: Space awareness;
locomotor movements

EQUIPMENT: Hoops;   chairs;   wands and standards;
cones;   low box;   climbing apparatus;
basketballs;   ropes;   mats
benches;

ORGANIZATION:

- Children further explore using different locomotor movements learned in a variety of stations such as those suggested below. Encourage them to change directions, levels, pathways/patterns, and ranges. Divide the class equally, depending on the number of stations. Have each group set up (and later put away) a station under your direction. Groups rotate to another station every four to five minutes. Remind children to move safely at all times.

DESCRIPTION OF ACTIVITY:

Station 1 Travel across the bench in different ways: walking backwards; running on toes; skipping; side-stepping; hopping; crawling; creeping; jumping. Spring off the bench to land softly in different ways on the mat.

Station 2 (Set up the climbing frame and place safety mats under it.) Travel in different pathways and directions on the frame. Crawl through the frame. Move across the beam in different ways. Jump off from a low level.

Station 3 (Scatter several chairs in this area and place a cart of balls nearby.) Get a ball and walk while bouncing the ball in and out of the chairs. Repeat running and bouncing the ball in and out of the chairs; skip and bounce the ball; side-step and bounce the ball.

Station 4 (Use bench, low box, cones, mats, hoops, wands and standards, and ropes to set up an obstacle course.) Travel along the bench by jumping on and off of it; leap over a hurdle; spring off a box horse and land facing the opposite way; hop back and forth over a rope; crawl through a hoop; side-step in and out of the cones.

MA-18 MAKING MOVEMENT SEQUENCES

FOCUS: Sequence-making;
space awareness

EQUIPMENT: Various available equipment and apparatus

ORGANIZATION:

- Review the term "Sequence" (a "movement sentence" with a beginning, a middle part, and an ending). In this activity, children invent their own Locomotion sequences using the different locomotor movements they have learned. Their sequence should involve movement through general and personal space, remembering levels, directions, pathways, speed, body parts, and shapes. Provide opportunity for children to observe each other.

DESCRIPTION OF ACTIVITY:

1. Show me how you can do the following three-action word sequence:
   — CREEP lightly on your toes; at a high level; in a curvy pathway;
   — CRAWL quickly forward in a straight pathway; at a medium level;
   — SLIDE backwards, slowly; on your tummy; then stop in a curled shape.
2. Now, it's your turn. Make up a three-action word sequence of your own. Practice it; then you can perform your sequence for the rest of the class.
3. Have children scatter various equipment throughout the play area, such as mats, benches, hoops, cones, chairs, etc. Have them practice their sequence using the equipment. For example, SLIDE on your back in a backwards direction along the bench; spring off with a HALF JUMP-TURN, landing in a wide high shape.

MA-19 RELATIONSHIPS OF BODY PARTS

FOCUS: Body awareness

EQUIPMENT: Deck of "Body Parts" cards

ORGANIZATION:

- The "Body Part Task Game" is designed to develop children's awareness of their bodies. Children should be able to identify and locate the different parts; know their usage; isolate different parts; know where one body part is in relation to other parts and to their environment; discriminate between right and left; and put right and left body parts together in cross-lateral combinations.
- Make a "Body Part Task" deck of cards by printing the following tasks on index cards (12.5 by 7.7 centimeters or 5 by 3 inches). Add ideas of your own!

DESCRIPTION OF ACTIVITY:

1. **Body Part Task Game:** I will ask one player to draw a card from the deck of cards. That player read clearly and loudly the task to be performed; then everyone try to do it.
2. SAMPLE TASKS:
   - Touch your right foot to your left shoulder.
   - Touch the soles of your feet together.
   - Move only your upper body. Move only your lower body.
   - Swing your hips from side to side.
   - Touch your right ear to a wall.
   - Grab your left ankle with your right hand and hop in place.
   - Touch your back to a ball.
   - Shrug your shoulders up and down.
   - Touch your nose to your left knee.
   - Sit, with legs wide apart. Reach with your right hand toward your left toes, then your left hand to right toes.
   - Nod your head to say "Yes!"; "No!"
   - Touch your right elbow and left knee to a bench.
   - On your tummy, grasp your shins and rock.
   - Stand and grab your right foot with your left hand.
   - Make a happy face! Yawn . . . Blink your eyes.

3. **Busy Bees:** Have everyone find a partner and scatter. On signal "Busy Bee!" find a new partner and "shake right hands." Players will shake hands, and then wait for the next direction, such as: "sit back-to-back"; "give high five's with your left hands"; "stand toe-to-toe, then heel-to-heel"; "stand seat-to-seat"; "touch right knee to partner's left ankle"; "link left elbows and skip around twice"; etc.

MA–20 BODY SHAPES AND BASES

FOCUS: Body awareness; bases of support   **EQUIPMENT:** One mat per child

ORGANIZATION:

- Children explore supporting the body in different shapes on a variety of bases, and at different levels. Review the basic shapes: round, narrow, wide, and twisted, flat, and pointed. Discuss the terms "Base of Support" (part or parts of the body that support the body weight); "Points" (small base such as elbows, knees, head, feet); and "Surfaces" (large bases such as the back, seat, side or stomach). Have children get a mat and take it to a home space.

DESCRIPTION OF ACTIVITY:

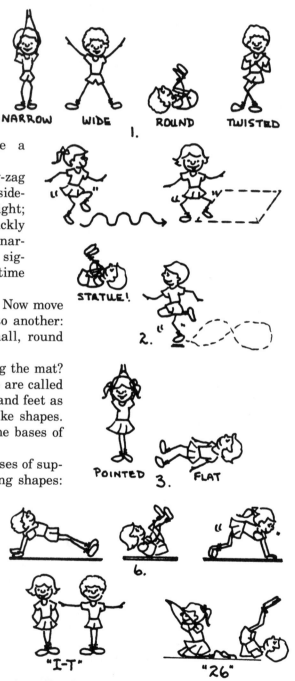

1. In your home, show me a long, narrow shape (like a pencil) at a high level; at a low level.
   — Now change your shape to a wide shape (like a wall). Change from low level, to medium, to high level.
   — How can you make a round, curled shape (like a ball) at a medium level? at a low level?
   — Who can show me a twisted shape (like a corkscrew) at a high level? at a low level?

2. **Statue:** On the Locomotion Signal (run in a zig-zag path; walk backwards; skip in a winding pathway; side-step to the left in a big square; hop in a figure-eight; etc.), perform the task. On the signal "Statue," quickly freeze in the shape I call (round, wide, twisted, narrow), and hold until you hear the next "locomotion signal." Form your shapes at a different level each time (wide high, twisted medium, narrow low . . .).

3. How can you make a flat shape? a pointed shape? Now move about, changing shape as you go from one level to another: Travel in a tall, pointed shape; change to a small, round shape; then change to a twisted, rolling shape.

4. Curl up on your mat. Which part of you is touching the mat? Find other parts on which you can be curled. These are called Bases of support. Take your weight on your hands and feet as the bases of support, and make different bridge-like shapes. Make different shapes using just your hands as the bases of support.

5. Small bases of support are called Points. Large bases of support are called Surfaces. Try making the following shapes:
   — Explore making wide shapes using different surfaces; different points.
   — Explore making narrow shapes using different surfaces; different points.
   — Explore making round shapes; twisted shapes using different surfaces; different points.

6. Make a Shape Story which has a beginning, middle, and ending changing directions, pathways/patterns, levels, and body bases.

7. **Word and Number Shapes:** Find a partner and together create the shape of simple words such as "O-N," "I-T," "B-E," "A-M."
   — Repeat with different two-digit number combinations: "36," "81," etc.
   — Get into groups of three or four. Together form simple three- or four-lettered words such as "C-A-P," "S-N-O-W," "B-I-R-D." Use different bases of support.

MA-21 DYNAMIC BODY SHAPES

FOCUS: Body awareness; sequence-making

EQUIPMENT: One mat, one hoop, one rope, and one chair per child

ORGANIZATION:

- Children explore different combinations of shapes in personal and general space. Shapes can be created by rounding one body part while stretching wide or narrow or twisting another part: wide top, long bottom; long top, wide bottom; twisted top, round bottom. Provide ample time for children to develop and practice their shape sequences and opportunity for children to observe each other's sequences. To begin, have children find a home space.

DESCRIPTION OF ACTIVITY:

1. In your home space, make your body into a wide, stretched shape at a high level. Show me how many different ways you can move in that shape (forward, backwards, sideways, turning around and around, jumping, hopping, etc.).
   — Find ways of moving in a curled, round shape in your personal space.
2. Show me how you can make a wide shape with your upper body and a long shape with your lower body. Now try a long top and a wide bottom.
   — Try a twisted top and round bottom; a round top and a wide bottom.
   — Make a wide top and a twisted bottom.
3. Show me how you can skip in a wide shape; roll in a long, narrow shape; walk in a twisted shape. Move in different ways on your hands and feet in a wide shape; a long shape; curled; twisted.
4. **Using Equipment** (Have children scatter mats, hoops, and ropes throughout the play area.) Make a wide shape on your mat; a round shape in your hoop; a long shape on your rope. (Repeat several times, changing levels and bases.)
5. **Shape Sequence:** Select your Beginning Shape; add a travelling action to take you from one equipment to another; make your Middle shape; add a different travelling action to take you to the equipment; and there hold your Ending shape for five seconds. Practice this sequence several times until you feel comfortable and confident with it. **Sequence-Building:** Add a twisted shape on a chair, and another travelling action.

MA-22 CONTRASTING SHAPES

FOCUS: Body awareness; partnerwork

EQUIPMENT: One mat per child

ORGANIZATION:

- Children explore the contrasting shapes of stretching and curling on different bases of support in personal and general space.

DESCRIPTION OF ACTIVITY:

1. Get a mat and find a home space. Stand on your mat and curl different parts of your body (arms, legs, fingers, back, etc.). Can you stretch those same body parts? Using your seat as the base of support, curl and stretch your body. Find other bases of support and curl and stretch your body.

2.

2. Show me how you can curl up on one part of your body and stretch out on another part. For example, curl your legs while stretching your upper body.
   — Experiment with different bases of support.
3. Travel in general space with your body stretched; curled. Show me how you can move about continuously changing from being curled up to being stretched out.

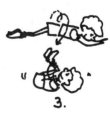
3.

4. Find a partner. First partner stretch out, while the second partner curls up. Then the first partner curl up while the second partner stretches out. Continue stretching and curling using different body bases.

MA–23 BODY SHAPES ON APPARATUS

FOCUS: Body and space awareness

EQUIPMENT: Benches; mats; box horse; springboard; horizontal bar; ladder; climbing frame; ropes

ORGANIZATION:

- Children explore creating body shapes using a variety of bases while balancing or travelling on apparatus. Have children set up the apparatus and check that safety mats are in place and apparatus is stable. Emphasize that children move safely at all times, always in control. The following tasks are suggested. Adjust to your own situation.

DESCRIPTION OF ACTIVITY:

1. **Benches:**
   - Starting at one end, move along the bench keeping one shape; then return in another shape. Slide along the bench, keeping a body shape.
   - Travel along the bench, stretching and curling as you go.
   - Balance on a bench on different bases, making wide shapes; curled shapes.
   - Travel along the bench making a sequence of three different body shapes. Change the base of support each time.

2. **Mats:**
   - Travel across one mat in one shape and across another mat in a different shape. Travel by rolling in a variety of shapes.
   - Create a sequence of three bases of support with a different shape for each base.

3. **Box Horse, Springboard:**
   - Arrive on the box in a round shape. Jump off in a different shape.
   - Taking the weight on your hands, move onto, over, and off the box, emphasizing the shape of your lower body—curled, wide, long.
   - Take off from two feet, make a shape in the air, and land softly on both feet in the same shape.

4. **Horizontal Bar, Ladder:**
   - Hang, travel, swing, or balance in a variety of shapes.

5. **Climbing Ropes:**
   - Hang on one rope, making a round shape; long; wide; twisted; the top long and the bottom curled; the top curled and the bottom wide; etc.
   - Repeat tasks hanging on two ropes.
   - Swing on one rope, in a stretched shape. Land on a mat in a contrasting shape—curled.
   - Make a sequence of three different shapes while hanging on one rope.

6. **Climbing Apparatus:**
   - Hang on the climber making a round shape; a wide shape; long; twisted.
   - Hang with your upper body wide and your lower body, long; with your top curled and your bottom wide; top long and bottom twisted; etc.
   - Travel on the climber, changing from one shape to another.
   - Stretch and curl as you travel on the climber.
   - Make a sequence of three different shapes.

MA-24 BODY SHAPE SEQUENCES

FOCUS: Body and space awareness; sequence-making

EQUIPMENT: None

ORGANIZATION:

- Children explore making movement sequences of body shapes in personal and general space. Have children find a home space.

DESCRIPTION OF ACTIVITY:

1. Starting from a round shape, stretch to a long shape, then to a wide shape, and finish in a twisted shape. Start from other shapes. Remember to stay in your home space.
2. Show me how you can do the following Body Shape Sequence in your home: Beginning—Jump from a crouched position; Middle—Stretch to a wide shape in the air; Ending—Land softly in a curled shape.
3. Create three different shapes on different bases of support. Can you join these together smoothly? Try this: Make a long, high shape on your feet; to a curled shape on your knees and elbows; to a wide, low shape on your tummy, legs, and arms.
   — Repeat, but this time create a different shape for your upper body than for your lower body; for example, round top and wide bottom.
4. Travel about the floor in four different ways. Show a change of shape for each way: Skip in a wide shape; crawl in a curled shape; jump in a twisted shape; and finish by a roll in a long shape.
5. Can you make a Body Shape Sequence using all round shapes? all wide shapes? all narrow shapes? all twisted shapes? Include three different ways of travelling in your sequence.

MA-25 SYMMETRICAL/ASYMMETRICAL SHAPES

FOCUS: Body awareness; movement terms

EQUIPMENT: None

ORGANIZATION:

- Discuss "Symmetry" (even, balanced, matching, equal, same). Symmetrical movements involve both sides of the body moving together to do exactly the same thing at the same time and in the same way. These movements occur in an up-down; forward-backwards direction. "Asymmetry" (uneven, lop-sided, different, irregular). In asymmetrical movements, corresponding body parts are not used in the same way at the same time. One side of the body becomes more active, or active in a different way from the other side. Any turning, twisting, or sideways movement is asymmetrical. The top half of your body may be asymmetrical in shape and movement while the lower half is symmetrical, and vice versa.

DESCRIPTION OF ACTIVITY:

1. Make a stable base on your feet. Make a shape so that each arm and leg match each other. This is called a symmetrical shape. Make other symmetrical shapes. Does each arm and leg match the other? Change your base of support (knees, seat and hands, back, stomach, etc.) and make symmetrical shapes.
2. Using your feet again as the base of support, twist your body; turn it sideways; bend to the other side. These are asymmetrical shapes. Now try to make your body look lop-sided or asymmetrical by using one hand and the opposite foot as a base; one foot as the base. Use other bases of support (knee, side of your body, elbow and knee, etc.) and make asymmetrical shapes.
3. How can you travel keeping your body symmetrical? Use different bases. For example, two-foot jumping; forward rolling; bunny jumps; etc.
   — Run, jump in the air, showing a symmetrical shape in flight. Repeat.
   — Run, jump in the air, showing an asymmetrical shape in flight. Repeat.
4. Begin with a symmetrical balance, change to an asymmetrical balance. Repeat, using different bases of support. Start with an asymmetrical balance and change to a symmetrical balance.

MA-26 SYMMETRICAL/ASYMMETRICAL SEQUENCES_____

FOCUS: Body and space awareness; sequence-making   **EQUIPMENT:** None

ORGANIZATION:

- Children create sequences using symmetrical and asymmetrical actions. Ensure that children have sufficient time to create and practice their sequence. Provide opportunity for children to observe each other's sequences.

DESCRIPTION OF ACTIVITY:

1. Run, jump, using a symmetrical take-off and landing.
    — Run, leap, using an asymmetrical take-off and landing.
    — Run, spring with a symmetrical take-off; asymmetrical landing.
    — Run, spring with an asymmetrical take-off; symmetrical landing.

2. Create a sequence that uses a symmetrical take-off and landing and an asymmetrical position in flight.
    — Make a sequence that uses an asymmetrical take-off and landing and a symmetrical position in flight.
3. Make a travelling sequence using symmetrical movements.
    — Make a travelling sequence using asymmetrical movements.
    — Combine symmetrical and asymmetrical movements to create a travelling sequence.

MA-27 SYMMETRICAL/ASYMMETRICAL ACTIONS ON APPARATUS_____

FOCUS: Body and space awareness   **EQUIPMENT:** Benches;   springboard;
several mats;   climbing ropes
box horse;

ORGANIZATION:

- Children explore travelling and balancing symmetrically and asymmetrically on various apparatus. Ensure that apparatus has been properly set up and safety mats are in place. Emphasize that children perform the tasks safely—always in control.

DESCRIPTION OF ACTIVITY:

1. *Benches and Mats:*
    — Travel along the bench on your back using your hands symmetrically on it. Repeat, but travel on your front.
    — How can you travel along the bench using your arms asymmetrically? (use one hand on the bench and the other on the floor)
    — Move along the bench using your hands and feet asymmetrically; symmetrically.
    — Balance symmetrically on the bench; balance asymmetrically.
    — Show me symmetrical movements on the bench and asymmetrical movements on the mat. Repeat, but in reverse.
    — Make a sequence of travelling and balancing actions that are only symmetrical; only asymmetrical.
2. *Box Horse, Springboard:*
    — Travel over the box using your hands symmetrically; asymmetrically.
    — As you travel onto and over the box, keep your body symmetrical; asymmetrical.
    — Use symmetrical and asymmetrical take-offs and landings.
    — Balance on the box in symmetrical shapes; asymmetrical shapes.
    — Take off from a springboard, making symmetrical shapes in the air; making asymmetrical shapes; land in the same way as your flight shape.
3. *Climbing Ropes* (Single or Double): (One rope often produces asymmetrical actions; two ropes, symmetrical actions.)
    — Climb, using symmetrical movements; asymmetrical movements.
    — Hang, showing symmetrical shapes; asymmetrical shapes.

MA-28 STATIC BALANCES

FOCUS: Body awareness; weight-bearing   **EQUIPMENT:** One mat per child

ORGANIZATION:
- Children explore stationary or static balances, both symmetrical and asymmetrical, on different bases. Have children get a mat and find a home space.

DESCRIPTION OF ACTIVITY:

1. Balance on a one-body-part base. Change to another body base and balance (seat, one foot, tummy, back). Hold your balances for three seconds. Repeat with two-, three-, and four-body part balances. Which balance gives you a better base of support? These balances that we hold in personal space are called Static Balances. Can you discover a balance that gives you an uneven base (resulting in the tipping of the body; for example, knee and shoulder)?

2. Make different balances in which you are equally supported on corresponding parts of the body; that is, each arm and leg match the other. This is symmetrical balancing.
   — Now try different balances in which you use one side of your body to support you. Never be on two similar parts at the same time. This is called asymmetrical balancing.

3. Let's explore asymmetrical balances. Balance on your feet only. Keeping this base still, move the rest of your body by swaying, twisting, curling.
   — Balancing on one foot, change the position of your head; arms; seat; other foot.

4. **_Balance Sequence:_** Develop a "Balance Story" with a beginning, middle, and ending, changing from a one-body part balance to a two-body part balance, to a three-body part balance. Hold each balance for three seconds.

MA-29 MORE STATIC BALANCES—INVERTED POSITIONS

FOCUS: Body awareness; weight-bearing   **EQUIPMENT:** One mat per child

ORGANIZATION:
- Children explore different ways of taking their body into the inverted position using their hands. Emphasize placing the hands flat on the mat, palms down, fingers and thumbs pointing forward. Have them get a mat and place it on the floor in a free space.

DESCRIPTION OF ACTIVITY:

1. Place your hands in front of you on your mat. What parts of your body can you take higher than your hands? Who can take your body weight on just one hand? Can you raise your feet into the air? Practice and try to hold a little longer each time! Explore different head positions. Which way is best to keep your balance? (Head up, eyes looking forward!) When you take your body into an upside-down position, this is called being inverted.

2. How many different ways can you come down from your hands: a bridge; a roll; a twist; step one foot down, then the other. Make sure you come down safely!

3. Take your weight on your hands and forehead. Now try to curl your body up and lift your feet off the floor. Explore putting your hands near your head; further away. Which position is best? (Hands and head forming a triangle)

4. Place your mat near a wall. Kick your feet up to the wall, one leg at a time or both together. Can you hold your feet off the floor for five seconds, using only your hands to support you in an inverted position?

MA-30 STATIC BALANCES ON SMALL APPARATUS

FOCUS: Body awareness; weight-bearing   **EQUIPMENT:** One mat and chair per pair

ORGANIZATION:

- Children, working in pairs, further explore static balancing on chairs and mats. While one partner performs a balance task, the other partner holds the chair stable. Have children find partners about their size, collect a chair and a mat, and place the mat near the chair in a free space.

DESCRIPTION OF ACTIVITY:

1. Find a way of balancing on two body parts. Change roles.
   - Take turns balancing on three body parts; four parts; one point or surface.
   - Balance so that some part of your body is on the chair and some part is on the floor.
2. Balance on your chair in a wide shape; long shape; curled; twisted; with your top wide and your bottom curled; top long and your bottom twisted. Take turns.
3. Practice this sequence: Balance on the chair; roll onto the mat; hold a balance on the mat. Now create your own balance sequence.
4. ***Follow-the-Leader*** (Scatter all chairs and mats throughout the play area. Have each pair find another pair to form a group of four.) Take turns being the leader as your group travels on, over, under, and around the chairs and mats. Balance on chairs and mats.

MA-31 STATIC BALANCES ON LARGE APPARATUS

FOCUS: Body awareness; weight-bearing; suspending   **EQUIPMENT:** Benches; large mats; climbing ropes; frame; horizontal bar; beam

ORGANIZATION:

- In order to ensure proper supervision and good understanding of the movement challenge, have all children perform the tasks at one apparatus station before moving on to the next. Have children set up the apparatus under your instructions and supervision. Review safety procedures of handling the apparatus. Ensure that safety mats have been placed properly under and around the apparatus.

DESCRIPTION OF ACTIVITY:

1. ***Bench or Beam Balancing Tasks:***
   - Hold a four-point balance on the bench; three-point balance; two-point balance; one-point balance.
   - Balance on round body parts only; flat body parts; twisted body parts.
   - Balance with one body part on the bench and another on the floor.
   - Do any kind of balance, lifting different body parts to a high level.
   - Travel along the bench; balance; jump off and hold a balance.
   - One half of your group make "human bridges" using the bench. The other half explore ways of travelling over, under, around the bridges. Change roles.
2. ***Climbing Frame Balancing Tasks:***
   - Travel up the frame to your own height. Hold a balance on a rung using your hands and seat only; hands and stomach; hands and back; etc.
   - Hang (or suspend) from your hands only; knees only; one hand and one foot on the same side, on opposite sides; four body parts; three body parts; one body part.
   - Balance while supporting your weight on the floor as well as the frame.
3. ***Climbing Ropes, Horizontal Bar Balancing Tasks:***
   - Suspend yourself from one rope; two ropes.
   - Suspend yourself from the bar using different body parts. Hold different body parts high as you suspend from a rope or bar.
   - Try balancing or hanging while part of your weight is on the floor.

MA-32 STATIC PARTNER AND GROUP BALANCES

FOCUS: Body awareness; weight-bearing; partnerwork

EQUIPMENT: One large mat per pair; carpet squares

ORGANIZATION:

• Partners explore static balances on different body bases. Have children find a partner their own size. Then have each pair get a mat and place it in a home space.

DESCRIPTION OF ACTIVITY:

1. With your partner, find a way of balancing on a total of: two body parts (two-point balance); three body parts (three-point balance); four body parts (four-point balance); five body parts (five-point balance). Can you include symmetrical and asymmetrical balances and inverted balances? Try to hold all balances for a count of five!

2. **Bunches Game:** Run in general space. When I call a number, I want you to get into Bunches (groups) of that number; for example, "Two!" quickly get into bunches of two.
   — A Bunch, when called, is only allowed to have a limited number of body parts touching the floor. I will hold up fingers for the bunch size. Cooperate to hold your "bunch balance!" for five seconds.

   Suggestions:

Bunch Size	Body Part Base
2	2, 3, 4, 7
3	4, 5, 6, 8
4	6, 7, 9, 10

3. **Carpet Square Balance:** Form groups of three, get a carpet square and find a free space. Can you all fit inside the square so that only five body parts are touching the square? Four body parts? Three parts?
   — Form groups of four and repeat the above tasks. Which group can balance on the least number of total body parts?

MA-33 DYNAMIC BALANCES

FOCUS: Body awareness; weight-bearing

EQUIPMENT: Several benches; mats

ORGANIZATION:

• Children explore travelling while balancing symmetrically or asymmetrically (Dynamic Balances); stopping in balanced positions, and transferring weight from body part to body part. Emphasize controlled movements! Have them begin in their homes.

DESCRIPTION OF ACTIVITY:

1. Travel about in general space in different directions, pathways, or patterns. On signal "Freeze!" stop immediately in a balanced position on one body part. Can you hold your balance for three seconds? (Repeat several times, freezing on a two-body-part balance; three parts; four parts. Travel in a different way each time. Vary the levels of travel and balances.)

2. Hold a one-point balance and travel about in general space; a two-point balance; three-point balance; four-point balance. Is your balance symmetrical or asymmetrical? On the signal "Freeze!" hold your balance on your travelling base.

3. Put your weight on different points: elbows, knees, head, hands, feet. Now put your weight on different surfaces: back, tummy, side. Try to move from one surface to another; from one point to a surface (foot to back). How smoothly can you move from one position to another?
   — Travel on two points and one surface; one point and one surface.

4. Develop a Travelling Balance Story. Move smoothly from one balance to the next. Practice.
   — Take your "Travelling Balance Story" and perform it on a bench. End in a balanced position off your mat.

MA–34 STEP-LIKE ACTIONS

FOCUS: Body awareness; locomotion

EQUIPMENT: Benches; ropes; ladder; beam; chairs; one drum; mats; steps; climbing frame; hoops; plank; ropes

ORGANIZATION:

- Children explore travelling in general space and on apparatus using different step-like actions on the feet; then hands and feet, and hands only. Have them begin in a home space.

DESCRIPTION OF ACTIVITY:

1. **On Your Feet:** Travel into open space on your feet by skipping. When you hear my drum beat signal, change the way you are travelling on your feet (running, walking, hopping, galloping, side-stepping). Vary the direction and pathway/pattern.
   — Travel taking long steps; short steps; with one foot crossing in front of the other, then behind the other; with feet close together; wide apart; side-by-side; one in front of the other; stiff legs.
   — Travel on different parts of your feet: toes; heels; inside; outside; combination of heel and toe.
   — Using only your legs and feet, show excitement; fear; anger; sadness.
   — Show walking upstairs; waiting in line for a long time; tap-dancing.

2. **Travelling Feet Sequence:** Create a sequence with a beginning, middle, and ending. For example: Walk backwards on your toes in a winding pathway; side-step to the left in a wide shape; skip with big steps in a circular pattern. Can you reverse your sequence? Can you reorder your story?

3. **Bench Travelling:** Find different ways to travel along a bench using your feet only. Travel over, across, on, and off your bench using your feet only. Travel along the bench with one foot on the bench and the other foot on the floor.
   — Make a sequence of travelling actions along the bench using your legs.

4. **Equipment Travelling:** Travel in and out of hoops or a horizontal ladder; back and forth over ropes; on and off chairs; up and down steps or a plank; across a mat; onto, along, and off a beam using your legs.

5. **On Hands and Feet:** Travel with different body parts facing upward (tummy, back, side). Travel in different directions: forward, backwards; sideways; forward to sideways; sideways to backwards.
   — Travel on hands and feet while turning over continuously.
   — Travel on two feet and one hand; two hands and one foot; one hand and one foot on the same side of the body; then on opposite sides of the body.
   — Travel with hands and feet moving together; hands moving first, then feet; hand and foot on the same side moving together; hand and opposite foot moving together; with your hands far from your feet, and then near to your feet.
   — Fix your hands on the floor and move your feet only. Experiment with keeping your feet apart while moving; keeping them together while moving.

6. **On Hands Only:** Fix your feet and move your hands only. Now take your weight on your hands and lift your legs in the air. Can you come down with feet together; feet apart; make feet land in a new place? Find other ways of travelling on hands.
   — Create a Travelling Hand and Feet Sequence.

7. **Apparatus Travelling** (Scatter benches, hoops, ropes, hurdles, box horse, and mats, and set up climbing frame and ropes in the play area.) Travel safely around, over, under, along, in, and out of the apparatus using hands and feet; using hands only.

MA-35 ROCKING AND ROLLING ACTIONS

FOCUS: Body awareness; transference of weight

EQUIPMENT: One mat, hoop, ball and beanbag per child; benches; tables; box horse

ORGANIZATION:

- "Rocking" is the action of smoothly and gradually transferring from one body part to another. This action is best performed on a rounded body part, with arms, legs, and body movement helping to gain momentum. "Rolling" is a smooth and continuous transfer of weight, usually involving the spine, from one body part to another.
- Children explore rocking and rolling actions in personal and general space, with a partner, using manipulative equipment, and then on apparatus. Ensure that they have ample time to experiment. Have children get a mat each and take it to a home space.

DESCRIPTION OF ACTIVITY:

1. Show me how you can rock in standing position; sitting; lying on your back; lying on your stomach; lying on a side. Rock in different shapes: curled; stretched; twisted. Which shape rocks best? (curled)

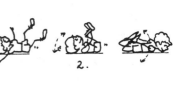

2. In back-lying position, try rocking with your hands and feet far from your body; near your body. Lie on your tummy and rock. How many different ways can you rock, holding your ankles?
   — Rock from one body part to another, then back to the first: seat–shoulders–seat; back–feet–back; side–front–side.

3. Show me how you can rock in different directions: forward; sideways; backwards. Rock as far as possible in one direction before starting back in the opposite direction.
   — Start with a small rocking motion and gradually make it bigger and bigger.
   — Rock slowly; rock quickly. Keep the action smooth!

4. **Partner Rocking:** Find a partner. Explore different ways of rocking together: feet interlocked; hands joined; back-to-back; hands and feet touching. Make up a rocking sequence.

5. **Using Equipment:** Get a hoop. Show me how you can rock inside your hoop on different body parts. Now hold your hoop with different body parts and rock.
   — Find a partner and together rock with one hoop in different ways.
   — Roll and catch a ball with your partner while rocking.
   — Can you throw and catch a beanbag while you rock with your partner?

6. Roll in a long stretched shape like a cylinder along your mat. Experiment with your arms overhead; at your sides; arms and legs crossed.

7. Roll in a curled shape in different directions: forward; sideways; backwards. Try to start your roll with a different body part on the mat: knees; hands; back; feet.
   — Can you start with a rocking action, move into a rolling action, and then back to a rocking action?

8. **Partner Rolling:** Find a partner your size. Take turns to find different ways of rolling with your partner: side-by-side; roll toward and away from each other.
   — Now use your partner as an obstacle and, without touching him or her, roll under your partner; roll while your partner jumps over you.
   — Roll through a hoop held upright by your partner.
   — Find ways to roll together: sideways with hands joined; sideways with feet interlocked.

9. With your partner, create a Rock and Roll Story with a beginning, middle, and ending. Perform your sequence for another pair, who in return will perform their sequence for you.

MA–36 NONLOCOMOTOR ACTIONS

FOCUS: Body awareness; transference of weight

EQUIPMENT: Mats; benches; box horse; hoops; climbing apparatus; scooters

ORGANIZATION:

- The following tasks explore "Nonlocomotor movements" (Stretching and Bending; Swinging, Swaying and Jiggling; Twisting and Turning; Pulling and Pushing) or how the body can move in specific patterns in one's personal space. Note that whereas twisting is a rotation of a body part around its own axis, turning is a rotation or circular movement of the whole body or body parts around in space. Discuss how these actions are used in our daily lives; for example, dialing a telephone, turning a door knob, pushing a lawn mower, pulling on a kite, etc. Ensure that children have ample time to explore these actions, and provide opportunity for them to watch each other. Have them begin by finding a home space.

DESCRIPTION OF ACTIVITY:

1. Find how many different parts of your body can bend (fingers; arms; legs; toes; whole body itself). Our body bends only at joints. Bend your body in different directions: forward, sideways, backwards. Can you bend then stretch these body parts? Bend and stretch while using different bases of support.
2. Keeping your feet fixed, sway until you almost lose your balance. Sway to the right; to the left; back and forth; slowly; quickly. Sway on different body bases such as your knees; seat.

   — Jiggle one body part; another; another. Jiggle two parts at the same time; two other parts. Repeat with three parts; four parts.
   — Swing your arms in different ways: back and forth; in full circles; to each side; in front of your body. Swing slowly; quickly.
   — Swing one leg; the other leg; arm and leg on the same side; arm and opposite leg. How can you swing both legs? Swing your upper body; your lower part.
3. Keeping your feet fixed, twist your body to the right, then to the left. Can you bend and twist it at the same time?

   — How can you twist a body part in one direction while twisting another body part in the opposite direction?
   — Keep one body part still while twisting another. Twist two or more body parts at the same time. Twist the upper half of your body without twisting the lower half.
4. Find how many different body parts you can turn on (seat, back, tummy, two feet, one foot). Put your weight on one foot and use the other foot to turn around. This is called pivoting. Turn CW; turn CCW. Travel and turn.

5. ***The Alphabet Twister*** (Make the "Alphabet Grids" on heavy posterboard [3 by 1 meter or 9 by 3 feet] as shown. Divide the class into groups of four and assign each group a set of words and a grid.) In your group take turns making the selected word (such as "work"; "play"; "stop") by placing different body parts in the squares.

6. Now find a partner about your size. Grasp right hands and try to pull the other across a line; repeat with left hands; two hands.
   — Sit back-to-back with your partner and try to move him or her.
   — From front-lying position, push yourself up with your hands.
   — Pull your sitting partner to his or her feet.
   — Push and pull your partner on a scooter.

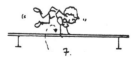

7. ***Using Apparatus:***
   — Twist and turn along the benches and mats.
   — Pull yourself along the bench; push yourself along it.
   — Jump off a box horse, turning in the air, land, and hold a twisted balance.
   — Push off with your hands as you jump back and forth over a beam.
   — Pull yourself up the climbing frame or rope. Twist your legs around the rope or part of the frame. Bend and stretch on the frame. Swing on the ropes; sway and jiggle on the frame.

MA-37 EXPLORING EFFORT—TIME

FOCUS: Effort awareness; body control

EQUIPMENT: Small and large apparatus

ORGANIZATION:

- The factors of Effort Awareness (or how the body moves) are *Time, Weight (force), Space,* and *Flow.* This activity focuses on the *Time* factor. Children explore the basic elements of speed or the rate at which the body moves: fast, medium, slow, acceleration, and deceleration. Have children begin by finding a home space.

DESCRIPTION OF ACTIVITY:

Floor Tasks:

1. Slowly stretch out in your personal space. Slowly curl up into a ball. Quickly stretch out; then quickly curl up again. (Repeat using other nonlocomotor actions such as swinging, bending, twisting, turning.)
   — Make a sequence of slow and quick nonlocomotor actions.
2. Run slowly; run at a medium speed; run quickly. On signal "Freeze!" stop immediately and hold a three-point balance. (Repeat, using other travelling actions such as skipping; side-stepping; walking; hopping; jumping; galloping.)
   — Travel in different directions and pathways/patterns, changing your speed. Use different body parts. Return home on signal.
3. Leave your home, moving slowly. Gradually increase your speed or accelerate, until you are moving quickly. Gradually slow down again, or decelerate, stopping in your home.
4. Make a slow sequence of three different movements; then make a quick sequence of three different movements.
5. Create a Change of Speed Sequence. Try the following: In personal space, turn quickly in place, curl up slowly into a ball; stretch out quickly making yourself as flat as possible.
   — In general space, roll sideways slowly; skip quickly in a winding pathway; decelerate to a slow crawl.
6. *Apparatus Tasks:* Travel around, over, under, on and off, across, and through the apparatus, changing speeds as you move. For example, approach and cross a bench quickly; then return over the bench slowly; run at medium speed along the bench, jump off, land, and walk away slowly.

MA-38 EXPLORING FORCE

EQUIPMENT: None

ORGANIZATION:

This segment focuses on the *Weight* factor. Children explore how the body moves in space with *force* (strong, medium, or weak actions; sudden or explosive movements; sustained or smooth movements). They explore creating force (quick starts, sustained powerful movements, held balances) and absorbing force (sudden controlled stops, gradual "give"). To begin, have them find a home space.

DESCRIPTION OF ACTIVITY:

1. Show me a strong action with your arms; with your legs. Now try to make this same action weak (use swinging and kicking actions).
2. Run lightly in general space; run heavily. Change your travelling action and repeat.
3. Stand still. Suddenly burst into speed. Then suddenly stop in control. Now explode, jumping up as high as you can, but landing softly in balance.
   — Dart into another space. Stop suddenly again. Explode again. Repeat this sequence: Dart–Freeze–Explode–Land.
   — Create a SUDDEN–SUSTAINED sequence of your own.

MA-39 EXPLORING TIME AND FORCE

FOCUS: Effort awareness; body control

EQUIPMENT: Chalkboard and chalk or posterboard and marker

ORGANIZATION:

- Children are introduced to basic effort action words. They explore different ways of creating these effort actions. Write the effort words on chalkboard or posterboard. Have children make up different sequences using these words.

DESCRIPTION OF ACTIVITY:

— *Slashing* actions are strong, quick, and flexible, such as swinging a bat; kicking a ball; shooting a puck; throwing overhand. Think of others (sword-fighting).
— *Punching* actions are strong, direct, and quick, such as heading a soccer ball; boxing; Tae Kwon Do.
— *Wringing* actions are strong, slow, and flexible, such as winding up to throw a ball; twisting the top off a jar; wrestling.
— *Pressing* actions are strong, direct, and slow, such as doing push-ups; shot-putting; pushing objects.
— *Dabbing* actions are gentle, direct, and quick, such as keystroking or typing; dribbling a ball; rope jumping lightly.
— *Flicking* actions are gentle, quick, but flexible, such as flicking your fingers; short soccer pass; jump shot in basketball; short badminton serve.
— *Floating* actions are gentle, flexible, and slow, such as easy breast-stroking; treading water; slow bicycling; a slow waltz in dance.

MA-40 EXPLORING FLOW

FOCUS: Effort awareness; body control

EQUIPMENT: Two box horses; benches; mats

ORGANIZATION:

- This segment focuses on the *Flow* factor or the continuity of movement. Flow of movement can be smooth or jerky and lacking in coordination. Children experiment, select and practice linking a series of actions in a sequence so that the movements flow together in smooth succession. Children learn that appropriate pauses (such as a balance) are quite acceptable in a sequence.

DESCRIPTION OF ACTIVITY:

1. Let's explore doing an action smoothly, and then doing the same action jerkily: swinging your arms; kicking your legs; running; turning; shaking your hands; etc.
2. Now let's explore creating different sequences of actions so that the movements flow smoothly together.
   — Travel by transferring your weight from feet to hands repeatedly. Find another way. Find a third way. Can you combine the three ways into a free-flowing sequence?
   — Run, jump, and turn in the air, land lightly, and finish in a low level.
   — From a squat position, roll in some way, jump to your feet quickly, and then run lightly in a curved pathway.
   — Roll forward, walk out; roll forward again and jump out; take your weight on your hands with your hips high, land, and roll.
3. Create your own sequence. This time add a pause by holding a balance to your sequence. Remember to link your actions together smoothly.
4. *Using Apparatus:*
   — Run to a low box, leap onto the box with one foot, step onto the other foot and jump, land softly, and roll. Repeat on the other box and mat.
   — Run and spring onto the box, landing on your hands and feet; push off with your feet, while your hands remain on the box until the feet have landed. Repeat on the other box and mat.
   — Combine three different ways of travelling on and off and along a bench. Include pauses in your sequence.

MA-41 EXPLORING PARTNER RELATIONSHIPS

FOCUS: Copying; mirroring; interacting; partnerwork

EQUIPMENT: Beanbags; benches; tables; deckrings; mats; box horse; hoops; chairs; climbing apparatus

ORGANIZATION:

- Children explore actions of *copying, leading, following, shadowing, meeting and parting,* and *mirroring.* Discuss the term "mirroring" (copying an action, but as if you were looking into a mirror). Have one pair demonstrate "mirroring." At first, allow children to choose their own partners. Later, arrange the children in pairs according to size. Encourage children to work with a variety of different partners, including boys with girls.

DESCRIPTION OF ACTIVITY:

1. One partner be the leader; the other partner be the follower who copies the leader's movements as he or she travels in different directions, pathways/patterns, levels, and speed. Change roles on signal. Follower, staying as close as possible to the leader is called shadowing.
2. *Partner Copying Story:* Create a sequence of three different movements. Show how you and your partner can start and finish together.
3. *Meeting and Parting:* Start together in a home space. Travel in the same way, moving apart from each other, and then meeting again. Continue in this way, watching out for others as you travel. On signal, find a new partner and repeat.
4. *Continuous Interchange:* First partner, make a shape for the second partner to go over, under, or through. Immediately upon landing, second partner make a shape for the first partner to do the same.
5. *Follow-the-Leader* (Set a variety of apparatus such as mats, benches, hoops, tables, chairs, box horse, climbing ropes and frame throughout the play area.) Partners, take turns being the Leader as you travel in the same way around, along, across, over, under, through, on, and off the apparatus.
6. *Face-to-Face Mirroring:* Stand, facing your partner. One partner be the leader; the other partner, copy the leader's actions: hand-clapping; foot-stamping; hopping in a circle; snapping fingers; swaying upper body; stretching, curling, or jiggling of or twisting body parts; making shapes; holding balances. Change roles, repeat.
   — Change to other body bases (sitting; kneeling; front-lying) and do face-to-face mirroring actions.
7. Explore face-to-face mirroring while travelling in general space, taking turns at leading and following: side-stepping; rolling; hopping; jumping; travelling on other body parts, with different parts leading.
8. *Side-by-Side Mirroring:* Travel in a variety of ways, such as walking backwards; skipping; galloping; leaping; rocking and rolling. Change directions, pathways, levels, speeds, and body parts.
   — Explore side-by-side mirroring in personal space: bending, stretching, twisting, turning.
9. *Equipment Mirroring:* Select a piece of equipment. Take turns being leader and follower. Copy your partner's actions while facing; while side-by-side. For example, toss a beanbag or deckring from hand to hand; roll a hoop along the floor; travel along the bench or mat side-by-side.

MA-42 WORKING IN SMALL GROUPS

FOCUS: Relationships; groupwork

EQUIPMENT: One drum

ORGANIZATION:

- Cooperating in groups of three or more, children perform matching movements of mirroring, copying, and shadowing. Form groups of three with a leader for each group.

DESCRIPTION OF ACTIVITY:

1. *Copy Cat Sequence:* Leader, lead your group in a sequence of movements. The rest of the group copies your movements as closely as possible. On signal (drum beat), the second member take over as leader, moving in a different sequence. On signal, the third member leads the group in yet another sequence of movements.
2. *Group Mirroring* (Form groups of four or five with a leader for each group and have each group stand in a circular formation in a free space.) Create a sequence using nonlocomotor actions and balances on different bases. Each member should contribute in the development of the sequence. Practice so that your group can together perform the sequence while other groups mirror the actions.

MA-43 CREATIVE MOVEMENTS 1

FOCUS: Space awareness; imitating

EQUIPMENT: None

ORGANIZATION:

- Creativity can be developed by children taking on the identity of a familiar creature, character or object and then interpreting its movements. For example: *Animals*—dogs, snakes, seals, frogs; *Mythical creatures*—dwarfs, fairies, giants, witches; *People*—boxers, cowboys, firefighters, ballet dancers; *Play objects*—balls, spinning tops, robots, swings; *Machines*—planes, trains, racing cars, lawn mowers; *Circus*—clowns, tightrope walkers, jugglers, lion tamers; *Nature*—sunsets and sunrises, rain, wind, clouds, leaves.
- The following tasks provide a variety of movement experiences from the above categories and can be used throughout this section at your discretion. Let half the class observe the other half from time to time. Have children begin in their homes.

DESCRIPTION OF ACTIVITY:

1. *Scamper* like a frisky puppy. Oh-oh, you have a sore paw. How can you move now? What sounds would you make?
2. *Slither* like a snake, making "hissing" sounds. *Wriggle* like an earthworm.
3. *Waddle* like a duck, making "quacking" sounds. *Strut* like a proud rooster. What sounds will you make?
4. *Leap* like a frog trying to "zap" a fly. How does a frog sound? *Jump* like a kangaroo, moving in and out of each other. *Spring* like a cat about to pounce on a mouse.
5. *Drag* yourself like a seal just coming out of the water. How do you move on land? What sounds do you make? Now be a crab coming out of the water and travelling along the sand.
6. *Kick* like a wild horse. How will you sound?
7. *Glide* like a butterfly, landing on a flower, flapping your wings, and then moving on to another flower. *Stretch* ever so slowly like a sleepy cat waking up.
8. *Animal Charades:* Get into groups of four. Take turns imitating different animals. The other members of your group must guess what you are.

MA-44 CREATIVE MOVEMENTS 2

FOCUS: Locomotion; space and effort awareness **EQUIPMENT:** None

ORGANIZATION:

- Children explore various travelling, step-like actions and nonlocomotor actions. Remind children to look for open spaces. Encourage and praise.

DESCRIPTION OF ACTIVITY:

1. You are a **Boeing 747** about to take off. Travel down the runway, gathering speed. Now you are flying high in the sky, moving in a straight pathway. Zoom with your arms out, swoop, turn, and glide. Come in for a landing in a spiral pathway, slowing down and landing softly on your front. Repeat, flying a different flight path.
2. Roll like a **pig in mud.** Rock like a **rocking chair,** slowly at first, and then quickly. Crawl like a **curious baby,** changing directions often. Creep like a **mouse** past a big sleeping cat.
3. Skate like your favorite **hockey player.** Make quick starts and stops, changes of direction, pathways, and speeds. Now you are a **star figure skater.** Turn around on one skate; change body shapes and levels.
4. Travel like an **angry giant;** a **frightened dwarf;** a **cackling witch** on her broom; lightly on your tippy-toes as a **fairy.** Be a **tightrope walker.** Move with tiny steps; move sideways; sway to the right, to the left; jump-turn.
5. Twirl like a **helicopter blade.** Twist about in a **washing machine,** and then stretch out and curl up in the **dryer** as you spin around and around. Jump like **popping corn;** sizzle like **bacon** in a frying pan.

MA-45 CREATIVE MOVEMENTS 3

FOCUS: Body and effort awareness **EQUIPMENT:** None

ORGANIZATION:

- Children explore different body actions as they imitate play objects, machines, and people. Have children scatter and find a home.

DESCRIPTION OF ACTIVITY:

1. Be a **Rag Doll.** Be a **Jack-in-the-Box.** Be a **Robot,** programmed to vacuum the rug. Be a pair of **Scissors** cutting paper.
2. Be a **Boxer.** How will your arms and feet move? Show me your best **karate kicks.** Be a **Sword Fighter** making jabs and slashes through the air.
3. You are a **Balloon** slowly being blown up—get bigger and bigger. Now I let you go! Then I will blow you up again. Oh-oh, I blew you up so much that you burst! Be a **Spinning Top.** When will you come to a stop? Now be a **yo-yo.** How will you go-go?
4. Be a **Speed Boat** travelling through rough water. Watch those turns! Look out for others! Be a **Rocketship** blasting off to the moon. Land on the moon with a crash. Be a **Moon Machine.**
5. **Invention Game:** Get into groups of three. Think of all the different machines that we use daily. Can your group become one of these machines? Let's see if the other groups can guess what machine you are! Now invent a "wacky machine" of your own!

FOCUS: Space awareness; dramatization   **EQUIPMENT:** None

ORGANIZATION:

- The following ideas stimulate the imagination, enhance creative expression, and foster good listening skills. Provide opportunity for children to observe each other. Offer constant encouragement and praise good effort. Have children scatter and find a home space to start.

DESCRIPTION OF ACTIVITY:

1. You are **Baby Chick** inside its shell and are trying to hatch out. You finally hatch! Explore your new world. Try to walk on your wobbly legs.

2. Take your large **Pet Dog** for a walk. Suddenly your dog spies a cat and the chase is on! Now you are a little **Fly** buzzing around. Land on a piece of sticky bubble gum. Oh-oh! You are stuck!

3. You are **Lion Hunters** moving about in a dark, thick scary jungle looking for the lions who prowl around in the shadows. Show me what happens when you meet each other! Oh-Oh! you fall into a trap! Struggle and struggle to get out of the trap. Finally you free yourself, but are covered from head to foot with ants! Shake and shake every part of you to get rid of the bugs.

4. You are a **Firefighter.** The fire alarm sounds. Quickly put on your coat, boots, and firefighter hat. Jump onto the fire engine and hang on. You arrive at the scene of the fire. Grab the hose and climb the ladder, aiming your hose at the flames. Rescue someone who is trapped.

5. **Summertime Fun:** Let's go fishing! Put a worm on your hook, and throw out your line. Give the line a tug; feel the line pull. Looks like you've got a big one. Reel it in! Don't let it get away.

6. **Wintertime Fun:** Find a partner and make a snowman together. Now show me how you can toboggan together. Throw imaginary snowballs at each other and show me how you would dodge them. Play follow-the-leader as you skate on ice.

7. **Circus Fun:** Balance like a tightrope walker, taking tiny steps, moving sideways, turning, swaying to right or left. Crack a whip like a lion tamer. Walk over a bed of hot coals. Lift a heavy weight. Do a clown act. Add some circus acts of your own!

8. **Quiet Halloween** (Divide the class into four groups: the Ghosts, the Witches, the Monsters, and the Scary Bats. Assign each group to a corner of the play area.) Listen for the name of your group; then show me how you would travel toward the center of the play area. Move in the center area near to each other but without touching each other or making a sound. Quickly and ever so quietly disappear to your corner as I call another group's name.

9. Act out different fairy tale stories such as "Jack and the Beanstalk"; "Billy Goats Gruff"; "Wizard of Oz."

Rhythms and Dance

The Rhythms and Dance activities are meant to develop creative expression, rhythmic movement, musical appreciation, and active listening skills. They improve muscular growth and coordination; space, body, and effort awareness; and social skills in an atmosphere of fun. Specific music suggestions are provided through the dance section. Lively popular music is suggested otherwise.

This section presents 48 Rhythms and Dance activities, including:

RHYTHM DEVELOPMENT

RD–1   Fundamental Rhythms
RD–2   Even Rhythms
RD–3   Uneven Rhythms
RD–4   Body Part Rhythms
RD–5   Rhythms and Body Shapes
RD–6   Spatial Rhythms
RD–7   Even/Uneven Rhythms and Tempo
RD–8   Light and Strong Rhythms
RD–9   Sudden and Sustained Rhythms
RD–10 Exploring Time and Energy
RD–11 The Underwater World
RD–12 Leading and Following
RD–13 Meeting, Travelling Together, and Retreating
RD–14 Group Rhythms (in Canon)
RD–15 Movement Conversations

NOVELTY, FOLK, AND SQUARE DANCES

RD–16 Bird Dance
RD–17 Hand-Jiving
RD–18 Bunny Hop
RD–19 Bridge of Avignon

NOVELTY, FOLK, AND SQUARE DANCES (*Continued*)

RD–20 Come Let Us Be Joyful
RD–21 Polly-Wolly-Doodle
RD–22 Bingo
RD–23 Crested Hen
RD–24 Pop! Goes the Weasel
RD–25 Paw-Paw Patch
RD–26 Bleking
RD–27 Cshebogar
RD–28 Jingle Bells
RD–29 Grand March
RD–30 Patty-Cake Polka
RD–31 Alley Cat
RD–32 Grapevine-Step
RD–33 Hava Nagila (the Hora)
RD–34 Longways Set, Casting Off, Sashays
RD–35 Bow Belinda
RD–36 Square Dance Signals
RD–37 Stars and Circles
RD–38 Basic Square Dance Formation
RD–39 Oh Johnny
RD–40 Gustaf's Skoal

RHYTHMICS

RD–41 The Orchestra

RD–42 Aerobic Shakers

RD–43 Rhythm Sticks

RD–44 Tinikling

RD–45 Rhythm Ribbons

RD–46 Rhythm Hoops

RD–47 Rhythm Balls—Elementary Ball Bouncing

RD–48 Rhythm Balls—Throwing, Rolling, Routines

RD-1 FUNDAMENTAL RHYTHMS

FOCUS: Teacher guidelines

EQUIPMENT: Drum or tambourine

ORGANIZATION:

- In this section, the four basic themes of "Movement Awareness"—Space Awareness, Body Awareness, Effort Awareness, and Relationships—are rhythmically developed. Children explore the fundamental even and uneven rhythms; create rhythmic movement sequences; interact in singing movement songs, folk, novelty, and square dances; and use manipulative equipment to develop rhythm patterns. Rhythmic movements can be accompanied by your voice; percussion instruments such as drums, tambourines, lummi sticks, maracas, castinettes, bells, and cymbals, etc.; children's voices; selected contact sounds (snapping fingers, clapping hands, stamping feet); visual stimuli (pictures, toys, balloons, elastic bands, ice cubes, candles, playdough, tools, live animals, colors, etc.); language stimuli (action words, action poems, dramatic stories and folk tales); nature stimuli (clouds, rain, lightning, fire, sun rising–setting, egg hatching, seed growing, etc.).

RD-2 EVEN RHYTHMS

EQUIPMENT: Drum or Tambourine

ORGANIZATION:

- In this activity, the Fundamental Even Rhythms of walking, marching, stamping, and running, jumping, hopping, bounding, and leaping are explored. To begin, have children find a home space and stand facing you.

DESCRIPTION OF ACTIVITY:

1. Listen to my drum beat (steady, strong beats 1-2-3-4). Clap your hands in time. Clap and stamp your feet in place to the drum. Walk in general space, keeping in time to my drum. Move in and out of others, but don't touch anyone. On two loud drum beats, stop, stamp your feet in place, and snap your fingers to the beat.
   - March, making sharp direction changes every eight counts; every four counts.
   - Change pathways every eight counts: walk forward in a zig-zag pattern, backwards in a circular pattern, sideways in a diagonal pattern, and then forward in a winding pathway back to your home.

2. Now listen to my drum (quick, steady beats). Keep in time with light running steps in place. Show me how you can run in general space, changing directions every eight counts; changing pathways every eight counts.
3. Can you clap your hands and jump in place to the drum? Jump from side-to-side; forward and back; wide apart and together; alternating one foot in front of the other. Do a quarter-turn jump each drum beat; half-turn.
4. Now hop in time with my drum, in general space, changing your hopping foot every four hops; every two hops. Hop on one foot, while touching the heel; then the toe of the other foot to the floor in four counts. Reverse foot roles and repeat.
   - Step and then hop on one foot; step and then hop on the other foot. Continue these step-hops in a straight pathway; step-hop in a circular pathway.
5. Run–run–leap to my drum beats (1-2-3-4). Repeat.
6. ***Even Rhythm Dance:*** Stamp in place for four steps; run forward for eight steps; leap in the air (1-2) and land (3-4). Half jump-turn (1-2); then jump from side-to-side (3-4-5-6); half jump-turn (6-8); stamp in place for four steps. Create your own dance.
   - With a partner: Run backwards for eight steps; hop in a circle for eight steps; march forward in a figure-eight for eight steps; stamp (1-2-3-4). Create your own dance.

RD–3 UNEVEN RHYTHMS

FOCUS: Fundamental rhythms; partner- and groupwork

EQUIPMENT: Drum or tambourine; music with an uneven rhythm; tape or record player; colored sheets of paper

ORGANIZATION:

- In this activity, the uneven rhythms of skipping, galloping, and side-stepping are explored. To begin, have children scatter and find a free space.

DESCRIPTION OF ACTIVITY:

1. Listen carefully to the rhythm of the drum (1-and-2-and-3-and-4-and). Clap this rhythm. Now show me how you can skip to this rhythm in general space. Skip in different directions and pathways: skip forward, backwards; skip in a winding pathway; circular; figure-eight; rectangular.

2. Still keeping the rhythm, gallop and change directions and leading foot every eight counts. Gallop in different pathways: rectangular, figure-eight, winding, spiral.
   — Change your gallop to a sideways direction. Show me how you can side-step in general space to the rhythm of the drum. Change direction every eight beats.

3. Let's create an **Uneven Rhythm Dance** using these basic uneven steps we have just explored: Skip forward for eight counts; skip backwards for eight counts; gallop in a circle for 16 counts, changing your leading foot every four counts; side-step for eight counts to the right, then side-step for eight counts to the left. Repeat.
   — Now create your own Uneven Rhythm Dance using these fundamental uneven rhythms.

4. Find a partner and, together, explore ways of skipping, galloping, and side-stepping (face-to-face, side-by-side, in a line, back-to-back). Create an Uneven Rhythm Dance with your partner.

5. **Uneven Rhythm Group Dance:** Listen to the music being played and clap to its rhythm. Skip freely in general space to the music.
   — On two loud drum beats, skip toward another dancer, pair up, and continue to skip together. Are you keeping in time to the music?
   — On three loud drum beats, form a circle of three dancers, all join hands, and side-step in a CCW direction around the circle.
   — On four loud drum beats, gallop in a line of four dancers. Change your leading foot every four counts.
   — On one loud beat, skip off from your group in general space, once again by yourself.

6. **Sniggles:** I have a friend to introduce to you. His name is Sniggles. Sniggles is going to be part of our class today. Sometimes Sniggles is happy. Sometimes he is sad. He gets angry and tired, too. Show me how Sniggles moves when he is happy; tired; angry; scared; excited.
   — How do you think Sniggles feels when he sees different colors? (Hold up one of the colored sheets of paper, such as red.) What does this color make him want to do? (Repeat with other colors—blue, yellow, green, black, etc.)
   — Show me how Sniggles moves when he hears different sounds: hand-clapping; knee-slapping; foot-stomping; tambourine or drum; lively music; relaxing music. (Use even and uneven rhythms.)
   — Can you make up a Sniggles Dance using even and uneven rhythms?

VARIATIONS:

a. Return to the classroom to follow up the Sniggles idea by having children draw their own Sniggles.
b. Talk about Sniggles being a "warm fuzzie" and not a "cold prickly."

RD-4 BODY PART RHYTHMS

FOCUS: Body awareness   **EQUIPMENT:** Drum or tambourine

ORGANIZATION:

- Children explore moving different body parts to even and uneven rhythms, and moving rhythmically on different body bases, in personal and general space. To begin, have dancers find a home space.

DESCRIPTION OF ACTIVITY:

1. Listen to my drum (use even rhythm 1-2-3-4 or uneven rhythm 1a-2a-3a-4a). In your personal space, show me how you can move different body parts to the rhythm: *Hands*—clap, shake, slap knees, punch; *Fingers*—snap, flick, squeeze and open; *Elbows*—point, jab; *Heads*—shake, nod; *Feet*—stamp, kick; *Arms*—circle, move up and down; *Hips*—circle, swing from side to side; *Knees*—bend and straighten, poke; *Shoulders*—shrug.

2. Show me how you can move your feet in rhythm, and at the same time, move another body part of your choice. Repeat, using other body parts with your feet. Can you move three different body parts at the same time to the drum beats? four different parts?

3. Now clap your hands and move on your feet in general space in different directions and pathways: Walk, run, skip, gallop, side-step, jump, hop, leap, and stamp. Show me how you can move a different body part each time you change the way your feet are moving, every eight counts.

4. ***Silly Willy:***

   Chorus: I know a little boy. His name is Silly Willy.
   He is so very nice. But he acts so silly.

   Verse 1: And so goes his *finger,* And his finger goes so,
   And his finger it goes . . . always so-o-o!

   Move an index finger in this pattern: up-in-out-in-up.

   Chorus: (Substitute the following body parts and actions.)
   Verse 2: Arm (*swing opposite arm across body to and fro*)
   Verse 3: Leg (*swing leg on the same side as arm, sideways*)
   Verse 4: Seat (*wiggle*)
   Verse 5: Head (*turn from side to side*)
   Verse 6: Eyes (*blink*)
   Verse 7: Tongue (*move in and out*)

5. Move to each of the body bases on my drum beats: Sit–Kneel–Lie down–Stand. (Repeat, changing order.)
   — Create a "Sitting Dance" by exploring movements in your personal space, such as rocking, spinning, swinging legs, and travelling movements.
   — Create a Lying-Down Dance.

6. Travel in general space to the rhythm of the drum, letting a body part lead you for eight counts; freeze on a surface (large base) for four counts; then change the way you are travelling with a new body part leading, for another eight counts; freeze on three-point base for four counts. Continue in this way, changing your travelling and freezing bases.

7. ***The Car Ride:*** Let's pretend that your elbows are the headlights of your car. Shine your headlights on the ceiling, a wall, the floor, another pair of headlights. Show me how you can use different bases as you "drive" your car in general space, with your headlights leading (feet, seat, knees, front, etc.). Show me how the wheels on your car spin around and around (sitting base). Be windshield wipers swishing from side to side (standing base). Be the door that opens and closes (lying-on-side base). Create another car part on a different base.

RD-5 RHYTHMS AND BODY SHAPES

FOCUS: Body and space awareness; creative expression

EQUIPMENT: Drum or tambourine; elastic band

ORGANIZATION:

- Children explore moving rhythmically in different body shapes that are symmetrical and asymmetrical. To begin, have dancers find a home space.

DESCRIPTION OF ACTIVITY:

1. Travel to the rhythm of my drum in general space. Freeze in a shape (wide, narrow, round, twisted, flat, pointed) for four counts. Travel in a different way when you hear the sound of the drum. Use different body bases and freezing shapes. (Repeat several times.)

2. In your home space, show me how you can change shape each time you hear a drum beat: shape-shape-shape-shape. Hold each shape for four counts.
   — Show me how you can move in a round shape; in a flat shape; in a pointed shape. Try this sequence: round-flat-pointed-flat.

3. Create a Travelling Shape Dance, moving from a large shape to a small shape to a large shape. Try these action words: STRETCH-SINK-CURL-EXPLODE!

4. **The Elastic Band** (Use an actual elastic band to illustrate the stretching-snapping qualities.)
   — STRETCH-STRETCH-STRETCH-SNAP! Stretch in a different way each time: funny shape, an upside-down shape, high stretch, low stretch; then snap.
   — BEND in as many different ways as possible using different body parts: to the front, sideways, backwards, kneeling, sitting, lying.
   — TWIST your body in different ways; twist an arm, a leg, other body parts. Use different body bases; twist at different levels.
   — Travel for eight counts, freeze, do four stretches (two counts each); travel for another eight counts, freeze, do four bends; travel for eight more counts, freeze, do four twists. Then SNAP!

5. **Puzzle Shapes** (Form groups of three and find a free space.)
   — Make a "Curl Puzzle" by fitting together in curled shapes. No touching!
   — Now make a "Stretch Puzzle." Are you using different levels?
   — Move from a Stretch Puzzle to a Curl Puzzle, and then back to a Stretch Puzzle.
   — Now remake your puzzle using twisted shapes!

6. Curl in a tight ball; then, responding to the rhythm of my tambourine, slowly open wide. Close again. When you move both sides of your body identically, your shape is symmetrical.
   — Curl into a tight shape again. Responding to the rhythm of my tambourine, slowly open one side of your body; the other side stays tightly closed. When you move both sides of your body differently, your shape is asymmetrical.

7. Now take four counts to push one side open. Then take four counts to pull that side closed. Repeat, taking three counts; two counts; then one count. Show me the strength in your feet, elbows, and shoulders as you quicken your push and pull. Which part of your body comes back first? Change sides and repeat. (Accompany with a tambourine.)

8. **Machine Talk:** Pretend that you are machines. Some of your machine parts move; others are stationary. Some parts push and pull; others open and close. Create a "Machine Talk Dance"!

1.

3.

STRETCH!

BEND!

4.

TWIST!

5.

RD-6 SPATIAL RHYTHMS

FOCUS: Space awareness; partnerwork

EQUIPMENT: Drum or tambourine;
directional signs;
pattern designs;
one large piece of drawing paper per pair;
one crayon marker per pair;
masking tape or "fun tack";
music in 4/4 time;
tape or record player

ORGANIZATION:

- Children explore moving rhythmically in space: in different directions, pathways and patterns, at different levels and ranges, individually and in pairs. Tape directional signs and pattern designs on the wall for dancers to see. Have them begin in a home space.

DESCRIPTION OF ACTIVITY:

1. Show me how you can skip in different pathways to the drum beats. Change your pathway every eight counts: straight, curvy, zig-zag, circular, figure-eight.
   - Now change the way you are travelling in different pathways, every eight counts: walk in a zig-zag pathway, run in a curvy pathway, jump a square pattern, hop in a straight pathway, side-step in a circular pathway, gallop in a figure-eight pattern, crawl in a triangular pattern, roll in a straight pathway.
   - Look at the directional signs and pattern designs on the wall. Show me how you can change direction, the way you are travelling, and your pathway every eight counts as you follow these wall designs.

2. In your personal space, show me how you can make a Square Design by running forward eight steps; side-stepping CW eight steps; skipping backwards eight steps; and sideways stepping again. Can you always look forward as you move in your square pattern?
   - Can you make a triangle design by changing directions three times?
   - Make a square by changing directions four times. Decide on a focus.

3. Take eight counts to change from a high level to a low level; eight counts to go from low to high. Travel for eight counts at a high level; then eight counts at a low level, eight counts at a high level, etc. Change your direction or pathway each time.

4. Stand tall in your home. Take eight counts to slowly shrink until you are small. Now take another eight counts to grow and grow until you are big again. Shrink again. For another eight counts, slowly spread until you take up as much space as possible. Now most of your body parts are far from each other. Take eight counts to curl into a tight ball, tucking all parts in close to you. Now in eight counts grow and grow until you are big. SHRINK-SPREAD-CURL-GROW!

5. Find a partner and, together, create a Design Dance. Decide where your dance will begin: in the middle of the play area, at the front, back, or a side. Include four different directions, pathways or patterns, levels, ranges, even and uneven rhythms, and tempo changes. Draw your design on a large piece of paper and tape it to the wall for you to follow.

RD–7 EVEN/UNEVEN RHYTHMS AND TEMPO

FOCUS: Differentiating rhythms; tempo; creative expression   **EQUIPMENT:** Tambourine or drum

ORGANIZATION:

- Children further explore Even and Uneven Rhythms in personal and general space and react to tempo changes. To begin, have children find a home.

DESCRIPTION OF ACTIVITY:

1. Listen to the even rhythm of my drum (1-2-3-4). Echo-clap this rhythm using your hands. Repeat several times, echo-clapping with other body parts in your personal space. Repeat with uneven rhythms. Can you hear the difference between the two rhythms?

2. Tempo is the speed at which the rhythm moves. It can be slow, constant or steady, or fast. Listen to the drum speak. Echo-clap to the quick, light beats of my drum. Move other body parts. Echo-clap to the slow, heavy rhythm of my drum. Move other body parts.

3. As you hear the different tempos and rhythms, show me how you will travel in general space. (Change from slow, steady, or fast movements, even and uneven rhythms.) Move in different directions, pathways and patterns, and on different body parts. (*Example:* Roll for eight slow, even beats; skip for eight quick uneven beats; jump for eight steady, even beats.)

4. ***Dance of the Toys:***
   — ***Ragdoll Dance*** (slow uneven beats): arms hang, legs bend and wobble, heads bob.
   — ***Toy Soldiers*** (steady even beats): march right, left, right, left; arms swing at sides; eyes focus straight ahead.
   — ***Ballerina Dolls or Karate Kids*** (quick uneven beats): side-step lightly over the floor, twirling, swishing, kicking.
   — ***Bouncing Balls*** (slow-quick even beats): dance high, dance low, roll and bounce.
   — Create another "Dancing Toy" of your own.

SPECIAL ACTIONS:

1. Show me how you can open your whole body as if it were a door or a book. How can you close it? Try again on different body bases. Open slowly, then quickly; open quickly, then close slowly. Now open and close different body parts: eyes, mouth, fingers, legs.

2. ***Rising and Sinking:*** Who can name some objects that rise or sink? (Kite in the sky; airplane taking off and landing; plant growing and withering; sun rising and setting.) ***Sunrise, Sunset:*** You are the sun slowly rising and spreading your yellow and pink light over the earth. Rise higher and higher in the sky. Show me how your "sunbeams" reach out and touch the grass; the tree tops; the sparkling water. How do the sunbeams make you feel? (warm, cozy, content) The day is almost over. You begin to drop slowly from the sky. Gather in all the light as you sink lower and lower. Disappear, bringing on the night.

3. Spin around four times in your home space (tambourine shaking) on different body parts. Spin slowly; spin quickly. Travel and turn; slowly; quickly. Jump and turn CW in the air; jump and turn CCW. Land softly. Travel-jump and turn-spin.

4. ***Focal Point and Gesturing:*** Fix your eyes on a certain point and, as you move in your home, never let your eyes move from that spot. Change levels and body bases. Stare at a spot in the room; creep toward it. "Freeze!" Now slowly gaze around the room, moving only your head. "Freeze!" Each time you hear the drum beat, look—high, low, behind, between your leg. Let your hands be your "eyes" as they gaze and look.
   — *Talking Hands:* Let one hand say a big action; the other hand reply with a small action. One hand say something quickly; the other hand reply in slow motion.

RD-8 LIGHT AND STRONG RHYTHMS

FOCUS: Effort, space, and body awareness   **EQUIPMENT:** Tambourine or drum

ORGANIZATION:

- Children explore the element of *Energy* through light and heavy (fine and firm) actions in personal and general space. To begin, have dancers find a home space and sit down.

DESCRIPTION OF ACTIVITY:

1. In your home space, click your fingers up high, along the floor, behind you, in close, far away from you. Now travel lightly on your feet and click your fingers as they lead you dancing up high, dancing low, dancing backwards, sideways, turning around and around.
2. Let your fingers lead you to your home. Sit and lightly tap the floor. Gently stroke the floor as if you were moving your hands over a soft kitten. Knock firmly on the floor. Smack the floor, stronger and stronger. Faster, slower. Let me hear the thunder. Now tap your feet on the floor. Make your taps stronger and stronger. Stamp your feet. Faster, slower. Listen to the thunder!
3. Show me how an arm can flutter (shake gently) and then drift down; flutter and drift up. Repeat with the other arm; both arms. Repeat with your legs. Flutter your whole self; then drift to a new spot. Flutter and drift. Flutter and drift.
4. Show me how your hand can slash through the air. Use your other hand to rip your space with a slash. Use both hands. Slash with a leg; with the other leg. Rip your space apart with your hands and legs.
5. Now listen to my drum speak (vary a heavy–light pattern). Is it saying to travel loud and strong, or to travel light and easy? Can you create a dance to the sounds you are hearing?

RD-9 SUDDEN AND SUSTAINED RHYTHMS

EQUIPMENT: None

ORGANIZATION:

- Dancers explore the element of *Flow* through sudden and sustained action words using the whole body and body parts in personal and general space. Review the movement terms "sudden" and "sustained."

DESCRIPTION OF ACTIVITY:

1. What does the word "sudden" mean to you? (fast, quick, swift, percussive) What kinds of things move suddenly and take you by surprise? (a door slamming shut, alarm clock ringing, balloon bursting) Let's explore some sudden (or jerky) movements with different parts of the body in your home space: punch, poke, jab, kick, explode, jump, slash, jerk.
2. Now try some sudden travelling movements in general space: run, dash, dart, scurry.
3. What does the word "sustained" mean? (slow, to keep going, to hold, smooth) What kinds of things move in a slow, sustained way? (a snail, a plant growing, syrup or molasses, slow motion on television)
4. Let's explore some sustained (or smooth) movements with different body parts in your home space: hands, feet, arms, changing body base, changing from one level to another. Now try some slow and sustained movements while travelling through space: float, glide, moonwalk (walking in slow motion).
5. *Matador!:* Hold an imaginary cape in front of you. Quickly move your cape from side to side. Turn slowly as the "Bull" passes. Advance slowly, waving your cape. Suddenly retreat, frantically waving your cape.
   - Find a partner. One partner be the Matador; the other, the "charging bull." Make a routine of light and heavy, sustained and sudden movements. Reverse roles.

RD–10 EXPLORING TIME AND ENERGY

FOCUS: Effort, body, and space awareness

EQUIPMENT: Drum; cymbals

ORGANIZATION:

- Children explore strong, sudden actions; strong, slow actions; light, sudden actions; and light, slow actions in personal and general space. To begin, have everyone find a home space.

DESCRIPTION OF ACTIVITY:

1. Find a free space. When you hear the quick, strong beat of my drum, shoot away to another spot. Freeze in a strong shape when the drum beat stops. Make sure you have a good base of support. Now grip your hands tightly together. Try to slowly pull them apart. Stick your elbow to your thigh. Slowly pull it away.
2. When you hear the sound of the cymbal, flit quickly about. Now slowly glide up, up high in the sky; flit-flit-glide-glide to a low level.
3. Curl up tight. Poke out your elbow; poke your knees; your head. Poke out a different body part each time you hear a drum beat. This is a strong, sudden action. Now flick your elbow, your fingers, your knees. This is a light, sudden action. (Accompany with cymbal.)
4. ***Eggshell Dance:*** Curl up tight inside your shell. Begin to poke, trying to break out. You are out, but you feel so jerky. Flick out your wings, your feet, your beak. Pick the air. Now test your wings as you glide up in the sky. Flit from tree to tree. Shoot up and up. Glide to land lightly on a branch. Curl up tight. Sleep.

RD–11 THE UNDERWATER WORLD

FOCUS: Effort, body, and space awareness

EQUIPMENT: Tambourine; quiet background music; tape or record player

ORGANIZATION:

- Children move rhythmically in personal and general space as they explore sudden and sustained movements through the action words *glide, dart, scurry, float, hover, coil,* and *sway.* To begin, have children find a home space.

DESCRIPTION OF ACTIVITY:

1. Have you ever gone snorkeling? What equipment do you need for this activity? Let's put on our masks, snorkels, and fins and explore the colorful underwater world!
2. Let's be brightly colored fish gliding to the gentle shaking of my tambourine. On the loud beats, dart here and there and everywhere. Glide when you hear the shaking sound again.
3. Now we are crabs scurrying along the bottom of the sea. Scurry when you hear the shaking sounds; stop quickly when the sound stops.
   — Can you be an octopus floating around your supper, the fish? Coil your tentacles around your prey.
   — Show me seaweed swaying gently to and fro.
4. ***Underwater World:*** I will divide you into five groups and locate you in one area of the play room:
   — *Group 1:* giant turtles that lazily glide
   — *Group 2:* seahorses that scurry here and there
   — *Group 3:* sharks that dart here and there
   — *Group 4:* whales that float and hover
   — *Group 5:* sea urchins that sway and drift

RD-12 LEADING AND FOLLOWING

FOCUS: Partner relationships; listening

EQUIPMENT: Variety of instruments such as drum, tambourine, cymbal, sticks, tone blocks

ORGANIZATION:

- Partners explore the skill of mirroring each other and experience the responsibilities of leading and following in personal and general space. Have the dancers choose a partner, find a home space, and decide who will lead first.

DESCRIPTION OF ACTIVITY:

1. **Mirroring:** Partners, stand and face each other in your home space. Listen to the music being played. Leader, move to the music in your personal space, while your partner copies your movements, as if looking into a mirror. Change roles every time you hear a loud cymbal sound. New leader, try to move in a very different way, changing your base of support, level, direction, and range.

2. New Leader, travel in any way you choose in general space. Follower, copy the leader. Switch roles on the loud drum beat. New leader, travel in a different way. (Repeat several times, pointing out interesting ways.) For example, skip forward in a winding pathway; walk backwards in a circular pathway; creep slowly in a zig-zag pathway; run quickly in a spiral pathway.

3. Choose a new partner. Decide who will be the leader first. Each partner, take turns leading and following, as you travel for 16 counts:
   — in a low way, in a high way
   — in a slow way, in a quick way
   — on a large base (surface), on small bases (points)
   — in a turning way

4. Can you and your partner create a **Leading and Following Dance** to the sound and speed of the four different instruments I will play? *drum* (quick light beats); *cymbal* (slow beats); *tambourine* (shaky steady beats); *sticks* (sharp strong beats) First listen to the sound pattern of each instrument. Decide how you will move to each sound. Does the way you choose to travel fit the sound and speed of the instrument? As you perform your dance, change the leader each time I change the instrument.

RD-13 MEETING, TRAVELLING TOGETHER, AND RETREATING

FOCUS: Partner relationships; space awareness

EQUIPMENT: Drum or tambourine

ORGANIZATION:

- Partners interact as they explore different ways of meeting, travelling together, and parting in general space. Have dancers choose a partner and find a free space.

DESCRIPTION OF ACTIVITY:

1. To begin, space yourselves about 5 meters (15 feet) apart. Listen to the sound of my tambourine. Very slowly, creep toward each other. When you meet, scurry back to your home.
2. This time, move toward your partner in another way. Try to move in a different way than your partner (feet first, on your tummy, elbows leading, tip-toes) Can you scurry back home in a different way? (all-fours, quick pitter-patter of your feet, on your back squirming)
3. Now with your partner, choose a way of quickly travelling together and then parting in slow motion.
4. Choose your own meeting, travelling together, and parting action words and create a dance with your partner. Think about meeting in a special way, gesturing with your hands, mirroring an action, travelling in a certain pathway, and moving at different levels.

RD-14 GROUP RHYTHMS (IN CANON)

FOCUS: Group relationships

EQUIPMENT: Drum;   music in 4/4 time;
cymbal;   tape or record player

ORGANIZATION:

- Dancers move together "in canon" or one after the other, as they explore the travelling actions of sliding and spinning. They then interact with each other in their group to create a sequence. Have dancers get into groups of three and order themselves first, second, and third; then space themselves arm's length apart. If there are one or two children without a group, make groups of four, but have two dancers in those groups travel at the same time.

DESCRIPTION OF ACTIVITY:

1. With the drum, the first dancer slide into an open space and freeze on the loud beat at any level you wish. Now the second dancer, slide toward the first dancer. When you arrive, freeze at a different level. Third dancer, slide toward the other dancers in your group and freeze in yet a different level. Can your group finish in a close interesting shape?
2. Now with the cymbal, the first dancer spin away and freeze. Then second dancer spin away and freeze in a different space. Finally, the third dancer spin away and freeze in yet another space. Is each dancer in your group frozen apart from the others?
3. Now dancers in each group, change your order. Let's perform this sequence again: Slide-freeze; spin away-freeze. (Let groups observe each other. Comment on group shapes created.)
4. **The Safari:** Your group is going on an imaginary journey into the Jungle. You will have to travel over some obstacles: climbing up a mountain; wading through a river, jumping over an alligator; crawling through tall grass; squirming through a narrow tunnel; rolling down a hill; sliding through a narrow gap; squeezing between two giant trees. Move in canon, or one after the other. Change the order in which you travel, often. (Accompany the story with suitable background music.)

RD-15 MOVEMENT CONVERSATIONS

FOCUS: Group relationships

EQUIPMENT: Same as activity RD-14.

ORGANIZATION:

- Discuss the term "Conversation." Have children think about a conversation with a friend and how the conversation can be very agreeable, change to another topic, or turn into an argument. Have Dancers interact in their group of three as they perform a Movement Conversation. Each member of the group must decide whether to follow the movement idea or change it to create a new situation.

DESCRIPTION OF ACTIVITY:

1. Can your group create a "Stretching Conversation"? While one member stretches at a high level, the other two stay still in a starting shape. As soon as the first dancer is still, the second dancer take over. Decide whether you will use the same or different base of support and stretching direction.
2. Now listen to the sharp sounds of my drum. Show me how you can poke with your elbow into a different space for each drum beat. Now try to poke with a different body part such as your feet; your knees; at a high level; at a low level. Create a "Poking Conversation." Decide who will go first, second, or third, and how you will "poke" with your group.
3. Dancers, leave your personal space and show me how you can leap and spin in the air to the sound of my cymbal. Decide on a body shape as you soar (or fly like an eagle) through space and try to land in that shape. Repeat several times. Create a "soaring conversation" with your group of three.
4. Your group has created a conversation with each of the three action words: stretch, poke, and soar. Now in your group of three, decide who will stretch, poke, or soar, what your starting shape will be, and in what order you will dance. Let your actions speak to the others in your group in a movement conversation. Finish by all dancing together; then return to your starting shape.

RD-16 BIRD DANCE

FOCUS: Novelty dance

EQUIPMENT: "Bird Dance" from K-Tel's *Dance, Dance, Dance Album* with the Emeralds; tape or record player

ORGANIZATION:

- This popular novelty dance involves the basic steps of skipping and elbow-swinging. Have dancers pair off and then scatter around the play area, with partners facing.

DESCRIPTION OF ACTIVITY:

1. **Part A:** Cheep, cheep, cheep, cheep.
   Make "pecking" actions with your fingers.
   — Flap, flap, flap, flap.
   Hook your thumbs under your arms, and make flapping movements.
   — Wiggle, wiggle, wiggle, wiggle.
   Sway hips from side to side.
   — Clap, clap, clap, clap.
   Clap your hands.
   — *Repeat Part A, three more times.*
2. **Part B:** Circle R-2-3-4-5-6-7-8.
   Hook right elbows with your partner and skip CW in a circle for eight counts.
   — Circle L-2-3-4-5-6-7-8.
   Hook left elbows with your partner and skip CCW in a circle for another eight counts.
   — *Repeat Part B once more. But on the last four counts of the left elbow swing, everyone quickly find a new partner and face each other ready to begin the dance again.*

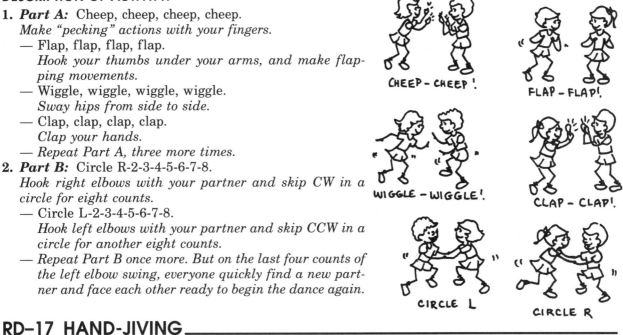

CHEEP - CHEEP!

FLAP - FLAP!

WIGGLE - WIGGLE!

CLAP - CLAP!

CIRCLE L

CIRCLE R

RD-17 HAND-JIVING

FOCUS: Novelty dance

EQUIPMENT: Any lively, popular tune; tape or record player

ORGANIZATION:

- This "Clap Rhythm" routine is an enjoyable "ice-breaker" to get your class into "action." The children are not required to memorize or learn the routine; rather they can just follow as you talk through and demonstrate without the music. Begin at a slow tempo at first; then gradually pick up the tempo until they can perform the routine to the music being used. Have dancers scatter around the play area and stand or sit cross-legged.

DESCRIPTION OF ACTIVITY:

1. Pat thighs. Clap hands.
   Pat thighs twice. Clap hands twice.
2. Cross right; cross left.
   Turn your palms down and cross right hand over left twice. Then cross left hand over right twice.
3. Hit right fist on left; hit left fist on right.
   Make two fists; hit right fist on top of left twice; then hit left fist on top of right twice.
4. Touch right elbow and shake right pointer. Touch left elbow and shake left pointer.
   Touch right elbow with left hand, and with right elbow bent, shake left pointer finger twice. Reverse and repeat.
5. Crawl-2-3-4; Crawl-2-3-4;
   Breaststroke-2-3-4; Breaststroke-2-3-4.
   Do a front crawl swimming motion with left arm and hand; then with right hand and arm. Repeat. Do a breaststroke swimming motion with both hands and arms. Repeat.
6. Lasso-2-3-4; Lasso-2-3-4.
   Circle right arm overhead four times. Repeat with left arm.
7. Hitchhike-3-4; Hitchhike-3-4.
   Point thumb over right shoulder four times. Repeat four times with left thumb.
8. Grab a fly, put it in your hand, squish it, flick it away, and stamp on it.
   Reach up in the air and catch an imaginary bug, put it in your palm, squish it, flick it away, then stamp on it.

RD–18 BUNNY HOP

FOCUS: Novelty dance

EQUIPMENT: Music in 4/4 time;
tape or record player

ORGANIZATION:

- This American line dance uses kicking and hopping steps. At first have dancers scatter and teach them the basic steps of the dance. Then have dancers form groups of six to eight. Each group scatters and stands in single-file formation, with members placing hands on the hips of the dancer in front.

DESCRIPTION OF ACTIVITY:

1. Kick right, kick right.
   Hop on the left foot and kick right foot twice to the right.
   — Kick left, kick left.
     Hop on the right foot and kick left foot twice to the left.
   — Hop forward, hop back. *Hop forward, then hop backward.*
   — Hop forward 3-4. *Hop forward four steps.*
2. Repeat this pattern around the play area.

RD–19 BRIDGE OF AVIGNON

FOCUS: Folk dance

EQUIPMENT: Music reference—Folkraft 1191;
tape or record player

ORGANIZATION:

- This French folk circle dance in pairs involves the basic steps of "skipping," "bowing," and "pantomiming." Teach children the words of the dance in English and, if possible, in French. Encourage them to sing along while performing the dance. Have them locate Avignon (France) on a map. Have dancers pair off and form a large circle; couples standing side-by-side, with inside hands joined, and facing CCW.

DESCRIPTION OF ACTIVITY:

1. *Chorus:*
   On the Bridge of Avignon, they are dancing, they are dancing;
   On the Bridge of Avignon, they are dancing in a ring.
   All skip CCW 16 steps, singing.
2. *Verses* (Repeat the Chorus after each pantomime. Encourage lots of exaggeration on each pantomime.)
   — Gentlemen all do this way; then they all do this way.
     Partners face and bow; then move to the right one place and bow to new partner; and skip . . .
   — Ladies all do this way; then they all do this way.
     Partners face and curtsy; then move to the right one place and curtsy to new partner; skip . . .
   — Soldiers all do this way; then they all do this way.
     Partners face and salute; then move to the right one place to salute a new partner; skip . . .
   — Angels all do this way; then they all do this way.
     Partners "pray" or "fly"; then move to the right one place to meet new partner; skip . . .
   — Street boys all do this way; then they all do this way.
     Waggle your fingers at your nose ("pied de nez"); then move one place to meet new partner; and skip . . .
   — Good friends all do this way; then they all do this way.
     Partners shake hands; then move one place to the right and shake hands with a new partner; skip . . .

RD-20 COME LET US BE JOYFUL

FOCUS: German folk dance

EQUIPMENT: Music reference—*Folk Dances for All Ages,* EPA-4135; tape or record player

ORGANIZATION:
- This dance involves the steps of walking, skipping, and elbow-swinging. Arrange groups of three dancers in a large circle. Each trio joins hands, stands side-by-side, and faces another trio, about two meters (seven feet) apart.

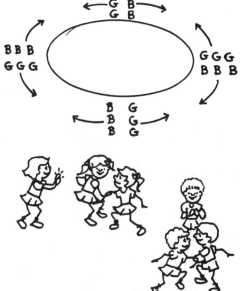

DESCRIPTION OF ACTIVITY:

1. Forward 2-3, bow; Back 2-3-4. Forward 2-3, bow; Back 2-3-4.

   Walk forward three steps, bow to the opposite trio; walk four steps back to place. Repeat.

2. Swing 2-3-4, swing 2-3-4; Swing 2-3-4, swing 2-3-4.

   Middle dancer of trio, link right elbows with the dancer on your right and turn in place with four skipping steps; repeat with the dancer on your left. Repeat both skipping turns.

3. Turn and forward 2-3, bow; Back 2-3-4. Forward 2-3-4- . . . -8.

   All turn to face the opposite trio. Walk forward three steps, bow, then walk four steps back to place. Now walk forward eight steps, passing shoulders with the opposite group, and on to face the next trio. Change positions in your trio and repeat the dance from the beginning.

RD-21 POLLY-WOLLY-DOODLE

FOCUS: American mixer

EQUIPMENT: Music reference—Merit *Audio Visual Folk Dance Fundamentals;* tape or record player

ORGANIZATION:
- This mixer uses the basic steps of side-stepping, skipping, turning, swinging, and bowing. Encourage dancers to sing along while performing the dance. Have dancers form a double circle, facing with both hands joined.

DESCRIPTION OF ACTIVITY:

1. *Verse 1:* Oh, I went down south for to see My Sal
   Inside partners take four side-steps to the left; outside partners take four side-steps to the right.
   — Singing Polly-Wolly-Doodle all day.
     Drop hands and each turn around once for four counts; stamping one foot on "polly," the other foot on "doodle," and three quick stamps on the word "day."
   — My Sally am a spunky gal, *Inside partners take four side-steps to the right; outside partners, take four side-steps to the left.*
   — Singing Polly-Wolly-Doodle all day. *Again turn around for four counts, stamping feet.*

2. *Verse 2* (Repeat the same actions as for Verse 1.)
   — Oh, my Sal she am a maiden fair, Singing Polly-Wolly-Doodle all day,
     With laughing eyes and curly hair, Singing Polly-Wolly-Doodle all day.

3. *Chorus:* Fare thee well, fare thee well. Fare thee well, my fairy fay. *First partners bow, then the second partners bow. Take four skipping steps away from each other.*
   — For I'm going to Louisiana for to see my Susie Anna. *Both take four skipping steps diagonally forward to your left to meet a new partner.*
   — Singing Polly-Wolly-Doodle all day.
     In place, right-elbow swing your new partner using four skipping steps.
   — *Repeat the dance from the beginning with your new partner.*

RD-22 BINGO

FOCUS: American folk dance

EQUIPMENT: Music reference—Folkraft 1189; tape or record player

ORGANIZATION:

- This popular dance is in three parts and involves the basic steps of walking and a right-and-left grand. Teach children the words to the dance and encourage them to sing along! Have dancers form a single circle, partners side-by-side; all facing CCW and joining hands.

DESCRIPTION OF ACTIVITY:

1. A big black dog sat on the back porch and Bingo was his name. A big black dog sat on the back porch and Bingo was his name. *Walk CCW around the circle singing the words.*
2. B-I-N-G-O; B-I-N-G-O *Walk four steps toward the center, bringing arms up. Walk back four steps, lowering arms.* B-I-N-G-O; And Bingo was his name. *Walk four steps forward again. Walk back four steps, drop hands, and face your partner.*
3. B-I-N-G-O! *Shake right hands with your partner, singing "B"; then walk forward, passing your partner, to meet the next oncoming dancer and shake left hands, singing out "I." Continue walking forward to meet the third dancer, shake right hands and sing out "N"; move on to the fourth dancer and shake left hands, singing out "G." Instead of shaking hands with the fifth dancer, swing right elbows while singing a drawn-out "O . . ." This dancer is your new partner, and the dance is repeated.*

RD-23 CRESTED HEN

FOCUS: Danish folk dance

EQUIPMENT: Music reference—Folkraft 1154; tape or record player

ORGANIZATION:

- This dance involves the step-hop step and turning-under skills. The name is derived from a man's traditional red toque, which resembles a hen's comb or crest. Dancers form sets of three: two girls and a boy, or two boys and a girl, or all the same sex. Each set joins hands, forms a circle facing CW, and designates one dancer to be the center dancer.

DESCRIPTION OF ACTIVITY:

1. Stamp-hop, step-hop, 3-4-5-6-7, turn; Stamp-hop, step-hop, 3-4-5-6-7, open. *Moving left (CW), stamp left foot and step-hop seven steps; turn on the eighth count, reverse direction. Now do eight step-hops, CCW. Then outside dancers, quickly break handhold, to form a line of three dancers side-by-side. Outside dancers place outside hands on hips, keeping inside handhold with center dancer.*
2. Arch 2-3-4-5-6-7-8; Arch 2-3-4-5-6-7-8. *Center and right dancer raise joined hands and form an arch; left dancer, take six step-hops turning under the arch. Center dancer follow under the arch of your own arm with two step-hops. Both arch dancers step-hop in place.*
   — *Repeat with center and left dancer forming an arch and the right dancer turning under for eight step-hops.*
3. Join hands and step-hop. *Each set join hands again and repeat dance from the beginning, choosing a new center dancer from your group.*

RD–24 POP! GOES THE WEASEL

FOCUS: Round dance

EQUIPMENT: Music reference—Folkraft 1329; tape or record player

ORGANIZATION:

- This American round dance involves walking, skipping, and turning-under steps. Dancers form a circle of "sets of four," with couple 1 CW facing couple 2 and couple 2 CCW facing couple 1 as shown. Teach the words and encourage dancers to sing along!

DESCRIPTION OF ACTIVITY:

1. All around the cobbler's bench; The monkey chased the weasel,
   All join hands in your set of four and circle left, once around, with eight skipping steps.
2. In and out and 'round about
   Each set walk two steps forward, raising your joined hands; then walk back two steps, lowering your hands.
3. Pop! goes the weasel!
   Couple 1 raise inside hands to form an arch; couple 2 join inside hands, and skip under the arch. All walk forward to meet a new couple.
4. A penny for a spool of thread; Another for a needle,
   That's the way the money goes—Pop! goes the weasel!
   Repeat dance sequence in steps 1, 2, and 3, and sing the words.

VARIATION: Have each set of four create their own dance to "Pop! Goes the Weasel."

RD–25 PAW-PAW PATCH

FOCUS: Folk dance

EQUIPMENT: Music reference—Folkraft 1189; tape or record player

ORGANIZATION:

- This American folk dance uses the basic steps of skipping, side-stepping, casting-off, and pantomiming. Have dancers pair off and form longways sets of six couples, facing up the set. Call the lines 1 and 2, as shown. The couple at the front of the set is called the head couple. (Note: A paw-paw is the fruit of the custard-apple tree.)

DESCRIPTION OF ACTIVITY:

1. Where oh where is sweet little Nellie, Where oh where is sweet little Nellie,
   Where oh where is sweet little Nellie, Way down yonder in the paw-paw patch.
   First partner of line 1 cast off to the right and skip around the entire set back to place. (You could substitute each dancer's name for "Nellie.")
2. Come on boys let's go find her; Come on boys let's go find her,
   Come on boys let's go find her; Way down yonder in the paw-paw patch.
   First partner of line 2, lead your entire file around line 1, and home, while using a beckoning arm motion.
3. Pickin' up paw-paws, put 'em in a pocket, Pickin' up paw-paws, put 'em in your pocket,
   Pickin' up paw-paws, put 'em in your pocket,
   Couples join inside hands and pick up imaginary paw-paws with outside hands.
4. Way down yonder in the paw-paw patch.
   Head couple, holding hands, side-step down the center of the set to the foot of the set; then make an arch holding hands high; while other couples side-step, in turn, under the arch, pretending to pick paw-paws, and side-step into place in your respective lines. Everyone else clap and stamp a foot to the music. Dance begins again with a new head couple.

RD–26 BLEKING

FOCUS: Folk dance; bleking step

EQUIPMENT: Music reference—Folkraft 1188; tape or record player

ORGANIZATION:

- This Swedish folk dance in pairs uses the Bleking Step (hop and heel-touch), "seesaw arm action," and Step-hops. For the dance, have dancers pair off and form a single circle, with partners facing each other and joining both hands. To learn the Bleking and Step-hop Steps, have dancers scatter and face you.

DESCRIPTION OF ACTIVITY:

1. **Bleking Step:** Placing your hands on your hips, hop lightly on the left foot, extending the right heel forward to touch the floor; then hop lightly on the right foot, extending the left heel forward. Practice several times.
   - Now repeat the Bleking steps and add the "seesaw arm action": Thrust the right arm forward at the same time as you extend the right heel forward; then thrust the left arm forward as you extend the left heel forward.
   - Now repeat the Bleking step with your partner. Face each other and join both hands.

2. **Step-Hop Step:** With hands on hips, step on the right foot and hop on that foot; then step on the left foot and hop on the left foot. Practice in your home space; then move in general space.
3. **The Bleking Dance:**
   - The Bleking Step: Slow-slow; fast-fast-fast.
     Join hands and face your partner. Do two slow Bleking steps, followed by three fast Bleking steps. At the same time, move your arms in a "seesaw" motion. Repeat three times.
   - The Step-Hops: Step-hop in place; step-hop in place.
     With hands on hips, do four step-hops in place.
   - Step-hop to the right; step-hop to the right.
     Do four step-hops turning to the right to change places with your partner.
   - Step-hop in place; step-hop in place.
     Do four step-hops in partner's place.
   - Step-hop to the right; step-hop to the right.
     Do four step-hops, turning to the right, back to your place.

VARIATIONS:

a. In Part 3, have partners join hands and turn "windmills" in the same direction while step-hopping.

b. In Part 3, have partners do 12 step-hops in general space; then find a partner to do the last four step-hops, facing together.

RD-27 CSHEBOGAR

FOCUS: Folk dance

EQUIPMENT: Music reference—*Folk Dances for All Ages*, EPA-4135; tape or record player

ORGANIZATION:

- This Hungarian folk dance (pronounced "Shay-bo-gar") involves the basic steps of skipping, side-stepping, stamping, elbow-swinging, and draw step. Have dancers form a single circle of partners, all joining hands and facing the center.

DESCRIPTION OF ACTIVITY:

1. Side-step right-3-4- . . . -8; Side-step left-3-4- . . . -8.
   Take eight side-steps CCW; then eight side-steps CW.
2. Skip forward-2-3 and Stamp; Skip back-2-3 and Stamp.
   Skip three steps forward into circle center, stamp once; skip three steps back to place, stamp once.
3. Right elbow swing-3-4- . . . -8.
   Hook right elbows with partner and skip around twice in place for eight counts. Finish facing each other in a single circle with hands joined.
4. Step-close (four times); Step-close (four times); Step-close (four more times).
   Take four draw steps (step, close) toward the center; then take four draw steps back to place. Now take two draw steps toward the circle center; then take two draw steps back to place.
5. Right elbow swing-3-4- . . . -8.
   Hook right elbows with partner and skip around twice in place. Finish facing the center of the circle in starting position.

RD-28 JINGLE BELLS

FOCUS: Dutch folk dance

EQUIPMENT: Music reference—Folkraft 1080; tape or record player

ORGANIZATION:

- This Dutch variation uses skipping and side-stepping steps, elbow-swinging, and the skaters' position (hands are crossed in front with right hands joined over left). Have pairs of dancers form a circle, everyone facing CCW; girl on the boy's right. Encourage dancers to sing along!

DESCRIPTION OF ACTIVITY:

1. Dashing through the snow, in a one-horse open sleigh.
   With hands joined in skaters' position, take four skips forward then four skips backward, starting with the right foot.
   — O'er the fields we go, laughing all the way. *Repeat Part 1.*
2. Bells on bob-tail ring, making spirits bright;
   Take four "skating steps" (side-steps) to the right, away from the circle center; then take four skating steps left, toward the center.
   — What fun it is to ride and sing a sleighing song tonight.
   In skater's position, do eight skips CCW around the circle. Finish in a double circle, facing your partner (with the boys' backs to center).
3. *CHORUS:* Jingle Bells, Jingle Bells, Jingle all the way!
   Clap your hands three times; then clap both hands with your partner three times.
   Clap your hands four times; then clap both hands with partner once.
   — Oh, what fun it is to ride in a one-horse open sleigh.
   Partners hook right elbows and swing once around for eight skips.
   Repeat CHORUS. *Repeat clapping sequence, then left-elbow swing with partner for eight skips. Finish in original starting position, ready to repeat entire dance.*

FOCUS: Novelty mixer

EQUIPMENT: Marching music;
tape or record player

ORGANIZATION:

- Dancers learn controlled walking or marching rhythm and marching patterns.
- Have all the boys stand in a line along one side of the play area, while all the girls stand in a line along the other side of the play area. Everyone in the lines faces the "foot" of the play area. You stand in the middle of the endline (the "head") of the play area, facing the lines.

DESCRIPTION OF ACTIVITY:

1. ***March down the middle in two's.***

   Each line march forward to the foot of the play area, turn the corner, and continue toward the center of the foot. Meet a partner there, join inside hands, and march down the middle toward me, girls on boys' right.

2. ***Two to the left and two to the right.***

   When you reach me, the first couple go left; second couple go right; third couple go left; fourth couple go right; and so on. March to the foot of the play area and turn the corner.

3. ***March down the middle in four's.***

   Each couple meet another couple, join hands, and, as a group of four, march side-by-side down the middle toward me.

4. ***Four left and four right.***

   The first group of four, turn and march right; second group of four, turn and march left; and so on.

5. ***March down the middle in eight's.***

   Groups of four meet at the foot, join hands, and, as a group of eight, march side-by-side down the middle toward me.

6. ***Four left and four right.***

   Reverse the pattern. Groups of eight, divide in half when you reach me. One group of four march to the left; while the other group, march right to the foot, turn the corner, and at center a group of four, alternating sides, turn down the middle.

7. ***March down the middle in four's; two left and two right.***

   March down the middle in groups of four abreast. When you reach me, one pair go to the right; the other pair, to the left. March to the foot of the play area and turn the corner.

8. ***March down the middle in four's; one to the left and one to the right.***

   March down the middle in two's toward me. When you reach me, one dancer to the left; the other to the right. March in place when you return to your original starting position.

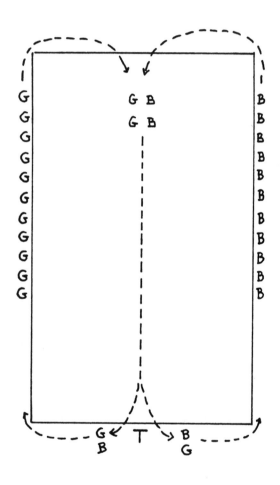

RD–30 PATTY-CAKE POLKA

FOCUS: Folk dance mixer

EQUIPMENT: Music reference—Folkraft 1260; tape or record player

ORGANIZATION:

- This American mixer uses a heel-toe step and side-step. Arrange dancers in a double circle; partners facing and both hands joined. Directions are for inside circle partners; reverse for outside partners.

DESCRIPTION OF ACTIVITY:

1. Heel-toe, heel-toe, Side-step (four times); Heel-toe, heel-toe, Side-step (four times).
   Touch your left heel to the floor in front; then touch your left toe to the right instep. Repeat. Take four side-steps to the left. Now touch right heel to floor in front; then touch right toe to left instep. Repeat. Take four side-steps to the right.
2. Clap hands; clap right; clap hands; clap left; clap hands; clap partner's; clap hands; slap knees.
   Clap your hands together; clap partner's right hand; clap your hands together; clap your partner's left hand; clap hands together; then clap both partner's hands; clap your hands together; then slap knees.
3. Hook right elbows and walk.
   Hook right elbows with partner and walk once around partner, taking six steps. Inside partner walk two steps forward to meet a new partner. Repeat entire dance with your new partner.

VARIATIONS:

a. In step 2, have dancers clap this way: partner's right hand three times; partner's left hand three times; both partner's hands three times; then slap knees three times.
b. At Christmas do the Patty-Cake Polka to the song "Jingle Bells."

RD–31 ALLEY CAT

FOCUS: Novelty dance

EQUIPMENT: Music reference—Dancecraft 73304 or Kimbo Records KIM 503-A; tape or record player

ORGANIZATION:

- This American dance uses step-touch and jump-turn steps. Have dancers scatter around the play area and face you. Make sure everyone can see you.

DESCRIPTION OF ACTIVITY:

1. Right, touch; right, touch. Left, touch; left, touch.
   Step right foot to the right; then close right to left instep. Repeat. Step left foot to left; then close left foot to right instep. Repeat.
2. Right, back; right, back. Left, back; left, back.
   Reach back with right foot and touch floor behind. Touch right foot to left heel. Repeat. Do again with left foot.
3. Knee, knee; knee, knee. *Touch right knee to left knee; then touch floor. Repeat. Touch left knee to right; then touch floor. Repeat.*
4. Knee, knee, clap, and jump right. *Raise and lower right knee once. Repeat with left. With weight on both feet, clap hands together once; then do a quarter jump-turn to right as you say "Meow!"*
5. Repeat dance seven times, until you have turned completely around twice. On the last time through, repeat each step once only. End with a clap and jump.

RD–32 GRAPEVINE-STEP

FOCUS: Folk dance; grapevine-step

EQUIPMENT: Tambourine; Mediterranean music in 4/4 time; tape or record player

ORGANIZATION:

- The "Grapevine-Step" is basic to many Mediterranean folk dances. At first, have dancers practice the step individually, then in a line formation, and finally in a circle, with hands joined. Use a tambourine to beat out the rhythm; then have dancers move to the music. Have dancers perform the steps slowly at first, gradually accelerating to dance tempo.

DESCRIPTION OF ACTIVITY:

1. Step right, left in front; Step right, left in front.
   Step right foot right, cross left foot in front of right; step right foot right, and cross left foot in front. Practice this foot pattern.
2. Step right, left behind; Step right, left behind.
   Step right foot right; then cross left foot behind; step right foot right; then cross left foot behind. Practice this foot pattern.

3. Grapevine-Step (Combination of Steps 1 and 2)
   Step right, left in front; Step right, left behind.
   Step right foot right, cross left foot in front of right; step right foot right, and cross left foot behind. Practice this foot pattern.
4. **Line Dance:** Stand side-by-side and join hands to form a long line. Grapevine-step around the play area to the beat of my tambourine; then listen to the music and grapevine-step to its beat.
5. **Circle Dance:** Form a single circle, facing inward. Grapevine-step CW to the beat of the music; then grapevine-step CCW.

RD–33 HAVA NAGILA (THE HORA)

FOCUS: Folk line dance; grapevine-step

EQUIPMENT: Music reference—Folkraft 1110; tape or record player

ORGANIZATION:

- This Israeli line dance involves the Grapevine, swing, and hopping steps. At first have dancers practice these steps individually; with a partner; in groups of five or six in a line formation; and finally in a circle formation. Have dancers begin slowly; then gradually increase the tempo of the Hora step-pattern.

DESCRIPTION OF ACTIVITY:

1. Step left, right in front; Step left, right behind.
   Practice the Grapevine-step.
   — Step left, hop, swing right; Step right, hop, swing left.
     Practice the Swing-step: Step left, hop on left foot, and swing right foot across and in front of left foot. Step right, hop on right foot, and swing left foot across and in front of right foot. Repeat.
2. **Hora Step-Pattern:** Combine Steps 1 and 2. Alternate four grapevine-steps and two swing-steps. Practice this pattern slowly at first; then increase tempo.
3. **Partner Hora Dance:** Find a partner, stand side-by-side, facing in the same direction, and join arms at shoulder height. Together, repeat this step-pattern, gradually increasing tempo. Now listen to the music. Can you hear the tempo increasing? Perform this step-pattern with your partner to the music.
4. **Hora Line Dance:** Form groups of five or six, standing side-by-side, facing in the same direction, and joining arms at shoulder height. Perform the Hora step-pattern to the music.
   — **Hora Circle Dance:** Form circles of 10 to 12 dancers, joining arms at shoulder height. Perform the Hora step-pattern, moving in a CCW direction.

RD–34 LONGWAYS SET, CASTING OFF, SASHAYS

FOCUS: Folk dance formations

EQUIPMENT: Music in 4/4 time; tape or record player

ORGANIZATION:

- Have dancers each find a partner; then form a set of six pairs. In each set, partners face each other in separate lines about three meters (ten feet) apart. Dancers in each line space themselves arm's length apart. The couple nearest the music is the Head couple; the couple furthest away is at the "foot" of the set.

DESCRIPTION OF ACTIVITY:

1. *Weaving March:* While one line stays still, the leader of the other line, march your line of dancers in and out of the stationary line and back to place. Switch roles and repeat.
2. *Single Casting Off:* Head couple, turn away from your partner and skip outside your line to the foot of the set. Next couple, repeat.
3. *Double Casting Off:* Head couple, join inside hands, turn left, and skip outside the lines to the foot of the set. Next couple, repeat, but turn right. Alternate left and right casting off.
4. *Whole Line Casting Off:* Each Head partner turn to the outside and lead your line as you skip to the foot of the set. Meet your partner there, join hands, and skip up the set to your original places.
5. *Sashay Down:* Head couple, join both hands, and side-step between the two lines toward the foot of the set to join the end of your lines. Next couple, repeat.
   - *Sashay Up:* Couple at the foot of the set, join both hands and side-step between the two lines toward the head of the set to join the front of your lines. Next couple at foot of set, repeat.

RD–35 BOW BELINDA

FOCUS: American round dance

EQUIPMENT: Music reference—Folkraft 1189; tape or record player

ORGANIZATION:

- The steps of walking, skipping, do-si-do, and bowing are involved in this dance. Have dancers find a partner and form groups of six pairs in a longways set. Partners face each other, with lines about three meters (ten feet) apart.

DESCRIPTION OF ACTIVITY:

1. Bow, bow, O Belinda, Bow, bow, O Belinda.
   Partners walk forward four steps and bow (or curtsy).
   - Bow, bow, O Belinda, Won't you be my darling?
   Partners walk backward to place. Repeat above.
   - Right hand round, O Belinda . . . ; Left hand round, O Belinda . . .
   Partners walk forward, join right hands, and turn once in place with four steps. Then join left hands and turn once around with four steps.
   - Both hands round, O Belinda . . .
   Walk forward, join both hands, and turn once around with four steps.
2. Back to back, O Belinda . . .
   "Do-si-do" your partner: fold your arms, walk forward toward partner, pass right shoulders, back to back, left shoulders, and walk backwards to place.
   - Skip, skip, O Belinda . . .
   Partners cast off and skip around the outside of the set. Head couple, form an arch for dancers to skip under. Other couples, join hands and side-step up the set to place. Repeat dance with new Head couple.

RD-36 SQUARE DANCE SIGNALS

FOCUS: Basic calls; listening

EQUIPMENT: Square dance or country music; tape or record player

ORGANIZATION:

- Dancers learn the basic square dance calls and practice the movements. Teach the dancers to listen carefully to the call and to know what it means. Have dancers move with a shuffle step (a quick walk or half-glide step) rather than running or skipping. To begin, have dancers scatter around the play area.

DESCRIPTION OF ACTIVITY:

Move in time to the music by using the Shuffle Step. Each time you hear a square dance call, find a different partner; then together perform the movement.

— *Hit the Trail:* Shuffle step in time to the music, moving in different directions.
— *Stop, Clap, and Stomp:* Stop where you are and keep time to the music by clapping and foot stomping.
— *Honor Your Partner; Honor Your Corner:* Bow to a dancer; then bow to another.
— *Allemande Right (Left):* Join right (left) hands with a dancer and shuffle turn in place.
— *Go Forward and Back:* Shuffle step forward three steps and a touch toward a dancer who is moving toward you in the same way. Then move back to place with three shuffle steps and a touch.
— *Do-si-do:* Cross arms in front at chest level, pass a dancer right shoulder to right shoulder, back-to-back, and shuffle step back to place.
— *Right (Left) Elbow-Swing:* Hook right (left) elbows with a dancer and turn once around in place.
— *Two-Hand Swing:* Partners join both hands, lean away from each other, and circle CW once around.

RD-37 STARS AND CIRCLES

FOCUS: Square dance figures; listening

EQUIPMENT: Same as activity RD-36.

ORGANIZATION:

- Have dancers form groups of four and find a free space. Within each group, have dancers pair off and each pair face the other. Use the terms "right" partner and "left" partner, rather than "boy" and "girl." If mixed pairs, the girl should be on the boy's right.

DESCRIPTION OF ACTIVITY:

1. *Turns:* Practice the following turns with your partner: Allemande Left, Do-Si-Do, Right-elbow Swing.
2. *Circle to the (Right) Left:* All join hands and circle once around.
3. *Right-hand Star:* Hold right arms at the wrist, at shoulder level, of the dancer in front of you, and shuffle step CW once around.
   — *Left-hand Star:* Hold left wrist of the dancer in front of you and shuffle step CCW once around.
4. *Swing your opposite and swing your partner:* Left partner, walk toward the opposite right partner and right-elbow swing once around. Then both dancers, walk back to your partner and swing once around.
   — *Swing your partner and swing your opposite:* Do the reverse.
5. *Go to the middle and come back out; go to the middle and give a little shout:* Each group of four join hands and, raising arms upward, shuffle step toward center of circle. Lower arms as you shuffle step back to place. Repeat and add a shout "Ya-hoo!"

RD-38 BASIC SQUARE DANCE FORMATION_____

FOCUS: Positions; figures; group work

EQUIPMENT: Square dance or country music; tape or record player

ORGANIZATION:

- Introduce "Setting the Square," its positions, and a variety of common square dance figures; then practice patter calls and figures in a routine. Have dancers pair off and form groups of four couples.

DESCRIPTION OF ACTIVITY:

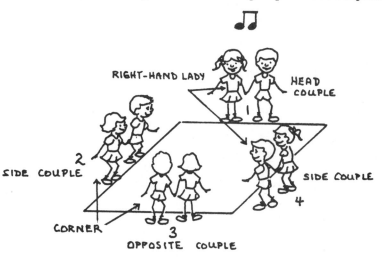

1. *Setting the Square:* Each couple of the group stand on one side of the square, facing inward, about three meters (ten feet) from the other pairs. The girl partner is always on the boy's right. *Head Couple,* with your backs to the music, is 1; the *Opposite Couple* is 3; *Side Couples* are 2 and 4. Couple 2 is to the right of the Head Couple.

2. *Positions:*

   — *Partner:* Each member of the pair.

   — *Corner, corner lady, or left-hand lady:* Dancer on the boy's left.

   — *Right-hand lady:* Dancer in the couple to the boy's right.

   — *Opposite or opposite lady:* Dancer directly across the set.

   — *Home:* Each couple's starting position.

3. *Square Dance Figures:*

   — **Honor your partner:** Bow to your partner.

   — **Honor your corner:** Bow to the corner who bows back to you.

   — **Swing your partner (corner):** Partner stand side-by-side, right hip to right hip. Each put your right arm around partner's opposite side at hip. Shuffle once around each other, leaning slightly away.

   — **Allemande left:** Boy partner face your corner, hook left elbows, and shuffle once around the corner, returning to your partner.

   — **Promenade:** Each couple join right hands over left joined hands (skater's position), and walk side-by-side in a CW direction once around; then return to home position.

4. *Practice the following Routine:* Honor your partner; Honor your corner; Circle right; Do-si-do partner; Swing your corner; Girls' Star left; Boys' Star right; Allemande left; and Promenade home; Head couples bow; Side couples bow.

RD–39 OH JOHNNY

FOCUS: American square dance

EQUIPMENT: Music reference—Folkraft 1037; tape or record player

ORGANIZATION:

- The shuffle step, waist-swing, allemande left, do-si-do, and promenade are involved in this dance. Have dancers form Square Dance Sets, with girls at boys' right.

DESCRIPTION OF ACTIVITY:

1. You all join hands and you circle in the ring.
   Four couples, join hands and shuffle step CCW for eight steps.
   Stop where you are and give your partner a swing.
   Stop, drop hands. Boys, hold partners at waist and swing.
2. Swing that little gal behind you.
   Boys, turn to your left and swing your corner girl.
   Now swing your own if she hasn't flown.
   Boys, swing your partner again.
3. Allemande left with the corner gal.
   Boys, turn to your corner, join left hands, shuffle step once around, and return to your partner.
   And you do-si-do with your own.
   Boys, do-si-do with your partner.
4. Now all promenade with the sweet corner maid singing, "Oh Johnny, Oh Johnny, Oh!"
   Boys, promenade CCW with your corner girl, who becomes your new partner for the next repetition.

RD–40 GUSTAF'S SKOAL

FOCUS: Swedish square dance

EQUIPMENT: Music reference—*Folk Dances for All Ages*, LPM 1622; tape or record player

ORGANIZATION:

- This dance involves Head and Side couple figures, and the shuffle, skipping, and turning steps. "Skoal" (pronounced "skol") is a toast that means "to your health." Have dancers pair off and form Square Dance Sets of four couples, girls on boys' right.

DESCRIPTION OF ACTIVITY:

1. Head couples forward 2-3 bow; back 2-3-bow;
   Side couples forward 2-3 bow; back 2-3-bow.
   Head couples, with inside hands joined, walk "stately" forward three steps, and bow to the opposite couple; then walk three steps backward to place and bow to each other. (Side couples remain in place.) Now side couples do the same, while head couples remain in place.
2. Side couples arch, head couples skip 2-3-4;
   Meet your opposite, skip under arch;
   Drop hands, head home, meet partner and swing.
   Side couples, join inside hands and form arches. Head couples, skip to middle. There meet your opposite, drop partner's hand, join inside hands with facing dancer, and skip under the nearest arch. After going under arch, drop hands and head home to original partner. Meet partner, join both hands, and skip once around in place.
3. Head couples form the arches while side couples repeat the sequence in part 2.

RD-41 THE ORCHESTRA

FOCUS: Rhythm sense; space awareness

EQUIPMENT: Variety of rhythm instruments; one whistle; one drum; music in 4/4 time; tape or record player; conductor's wand

ORGANIZATION:

- Children individually, then in small groups, explore even and uneven rhythms and rhythm patterns in personal and general space, while using different rhythm instruments. Give children each a rhythm instrument and have them find a home space.

DESCRIPTION OF ACTIVITY:

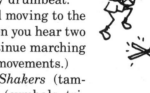

1. In your home space, explore the sound your instrument makes. Listen carefully to it. Listen to my drum beat (even and uneven). Can you echo this rhythm using your instrument? Freeze on the loud beat! Keep rhythm to my drum and explore moving your instrument into different spaces around you: to one side or the other; in front; behind; above. Try moving other body parts as well as your instrument in rhythm to my drumbeat.

2. *The Marching Band:* Keeping in time with your instrument and moving to the music, everyone march in and out of each other. March in place when you hear two whistle blows; then trade your instrument with someone else. Continue marching on one whistle blow. (Repeat several times, using other locomotor movements.)

3. Those with *Strikers* (drums, claps) form Group 1; those with *Shakers* (tambourines, wrist bells, maracas) form Group 2; those with *Ringers* (cymbals, triangles, tone blocks) form Group 3. You are an Orchestra: Group 1—your rhythm pattern is 1-2-3-4; Group 2—1&-2&-3&-4&; Group 3—1-2, 3-4; 1-2, 3-4. When I point with my "conductor's wand" to your group, sound this rhythm pattern with your instrument. Stop on my "cut" signal. (Have each group, in turn, perform their rhythm pattern; then bring in various combinations—Groups 1 and 2; Groups 2 and 3; Group 1 and 3, including all three groups at once.)

RD-42 AEROBIC SHAKERS

FOCUS: Aerobic routine; rhythm sense

EQUIPMENT: Two shakers per player; music with a strong 4/4 beat; tape or record player

ORGANIZATION:

- To make shakers, put 45 milliliters (3 tablespoons) of unpopped popcorn kernels into a small plastic food container. Punch two holes in the opposite sides of the container near the lid and thread 25 centimeters (10 inches) of elastic through the holes. Knot the ends of the elastic to make a handle that fits children's hands snugly. To begin, have players get two shakers, strap shaker over each hand, and stand in lines of six to eight players, all facing you.

DESCRIPTION OF ACTIVITY:

1. *Polka Step:* Pretend to strum a guitar while hopping on right foot and lifting left; then hopping on left foot and lifting right. Repeat eight times.

2. *Knee Slaps:* Hop on the left foot, raise right knee, and slap it with both hands. Repeat four times. Then hop on the right foot, raise left knee, and slap it four times.

3. *Diagonal Run:* Run four steps toward the right corner; pivot on the left foot once around while shaking right hand overhead; then run back to where you started. Now shake hands at sides while touching alternate heels to the floor eight times. Then repeat diagonal run to the left.

4. *Cross-Over Pattern:* Shake hands at sides as you step right, step left over right, step right, and kick left leg out to the side. Lean away from the kick. Repeat cross-over step to the left. Repeat pattern.

5. *Moon Shake:* With your legs pulsing in time to the music, shake your hands out from your sides upward and cross them in front of you to starting position. Repeat this four times. Repeat routine from the beginning each time, until the music stops.

RD-43 RHYTHM STICKS_____

FOCUS: Rhythm patterns; manipulation; partner and group work

EQUIPMENT: two lummi sticks per child; drum or tambourine; music in 4/4 time; tape or record player

ORGANIZATION:

- Rhythm or lummi sticks can be made from 25-millimeter (1-inch) dowelling, cut into 30-centimeter (12-inch) lengths. As an art project, these sticks can be painted, then hung to dry by using string tacked to one end of the stick. For manipulation skills development, see Lummi Stick Play in Section 6. Progressing from individual to partners to group work, children explore rhythmical patterns using lummi sticks. Have each child get two lummi sticks, find a home space, and sit cross-legged.

DESCRIPTION OF ACTIVITY:

1. Let's explore rhythm patterns using two sticks in your home space:
   - Tap the sticks on the floor in front of you four times; to the right side; to the left side; one stick on each side.
   - Tap the sticks together in the air four times;
   - Tap the ends of the stick on the floor four times; tap the ends of the sticks against each other four times, alternating palms up and down;
   - Cross hands and tap the upper ends to the floor;
   - Flip each stick, in turn, and catch it.

2. Try these simple sequences (in counts of four):
   - Tap sticks to front; together in air; flip and catch.
   - Tap sticks to right side; left side; cross hands and tap one stick to each side.
   - Tap ends on the floor; tap ends against each other; flip and catch; cross and tap.
   - Now create your own Tapping Routine, choosing any three tapping actions; for example, tap front, tap together, flip and catch; or tap ends, tap to each side, cross hands and tap to sides.

3. **Partner Rhythms:** Find a partner and sit cross-legged, facing each other. Listen to the music being played. Tap out this rhythm pattern in time to the beat:
   - Tap the floor in front four times; tap your partner's sticks; tap one stick to each side of you, then pass right sticks; tap the ends of your sticks in front of you; tap your partner's; tap one stick to each side of you, then pass left sticks. Now create a Partner Tapping Story with your partner.

4. **The Pow-Wow:** Everyone sit cross-legged with your group in a large circle, facing center and spaced arm's length apart. I will sit in the center as your Chief and start our "pow-wow" by tapping out different rhythm patterns; then you repeat it.

VARIATIONS:

a. **The Pow-Wow:** Form groups of six with members sitting cross-legged in a circle, all facing center and spaced arm's length apart. Each group has a different rhythm pattern to tap out with lummi sticks. As Chief, you point to a group who sounds out its pattern—sometimes alone or in combinations with other groups, or all at the same time!

b. Refer to Kimbo's *Lummi Sticks for Kids* (KIM 1014) or *Simplified Lummi Stick Activities* (KIM 2015) by Laura Johnson; Kimbo Educational, P.O. Box 4770, Long Branch, New Jersey, 07740.

FOCUS: Rhythmical footwork; groupwork

EQUIPMENT: Music in 3/4 time; tape or record player; two strikers per group; two crossbars per group

ORGANIZATION:

- This Philippine dance mimes the movements of a long-necked, long-legged bird as it steps from one rice paddy to another. Teach the Tinikling Strike Rhythm and Basic Step to music in 3/4 time; then introduce other steps. Have children form groups of four and scatter around the play area. Each group collects two strikers (2- to 3-meter [9-foot] bamboo poles or 4-centimeter [1.5-inch] diameter dowelling) and two crossbars (75-centimeter [30-inch] lengths of 5-centimeter by 10-centimeter [2-inch by 4-inch] lumber on which the poles rest). In each group, two dancers kneel at each end of the strikers and rest the poles about 37.5 centimeters (15 inches) apart on the crossbars that are located about 2.5 meters (7 feet) from each other.

DESCRIPTION OF ACTIVITY:

1. ***Tinikling Rhythm:*** On signal "Strike, Tap, Tap!" kneeling dancers, slide strikers together along crossbars and strike the poles together; then open strikers about 37.5 centimeters (15 inches) apart and lift about 2.5 centimeters (1 inch) from the crossbars, and tap twice on the crossbars.
   - Practice the Tinikling Rhythm several times.
   - All say the rhythm aloud. The two dancers, clap the rhythm by slapping your thighs once on "Strike" and clapping your hands twice on "Tap!" "Tap!"

2. ***Basic Tinikling Step*** (At first, have kneeling dancers hold strikers still while dancers learn the step; then add the tinikling striking rhythm. Have each dancer start with right side to the poles and practice in turn. Jump ropes or the lines on the floor can also be used as stationary objects.):
   - Left out, right in, left in, right out; left in, right in, left out . . .
      "*Strike*": step forward on left foot;
      "*Tap*: step right foot between strikers;
      "*Tap*": step left foot between strikers;
      "*Strike*": step right foot outside strikers to dancer's right;
      "*Tap*": step left foot between strikers;
      "*Tap*": step right foot between strikers;
      "*Strike*": step left foot outside to original position.

3. ***More Tinikling Steps*** (Have dancers practice the foot patterns with stationary poles before trying steps with the striking action. Ensure that strikers and dancers change roles frequently.):
   - *Side Jump:* Start on either side of the poles. Jump lightly in place on "Strike!"; jump twice between the poles on "Tap!" "Tap!"
   - *Front Jump:* Face the poles and jump forward and back.
   - *Straddle Step:* Dancer, begin by standing between the two poles. On "Strike!" jump feet apart outside the poles. On "Tap! Tap!" jump feet together inside the poles.
   - *Cross-Over Step:* Dancer, each time you step in and out, use a cross-over step. Begin with your right foot outside the poles. Cross left foot over the right as you step left foot inside; then step right foot inside.
   - *Rocker Step:* Dancer, face the poles. Choosing any foot, step in and out (forward and backward) in a "rocking action."
   - Invent a Tinikling step of your own!

VARIATIONS:

a. Have two dancers enter and leave toward the same side; enter near an opposite end to partner with right sides to poles.

b. Have two dancers face each other, join both hands, and perform the basic tinikling step; join inside hands and move side-by-side.

c. Have partners face each other and hold hands as they do the Straddle Step.

d. Have partners do the Rocker Step side-by-side, with inside hands joined.

RD-45 RHYTHM RIBBONS

FOCUS: Rhythmical movement; manipulation

EQUIPMENT: One rhythm ribbon per player; music with a strong 4/4 beat; tape or record player

ORGANIZATION:

- Make rhythm ribbons by attaching a 4- to 5-meter (12- to 15-foot) length of plastic, synthetic, or silk ribbon to a 50-centimeter (20-inch)-long dowel. Use a fishing line swivel and trace, screw-eye, and about 30 centimeters (12 inches) of fishing line between the two parts. Have each player get a ribbon and scatter facing you. Check for good spacing to avoid ribbons tangling. Challenge players to repeat movements while holding ribbon in nondominant hand. Add footwork that complements ribbon movement.

DESCRIPTION OF ACTIVITY:

1. **Windshield Washers:** Swing ribbon from side to side.
   Traffic Cops: Swing ribbon forward and back.
   Helicopters: Circle ribbon overhead.
   Propellers: Circle ribbon in front.
   Wheels: Circle ribbon at either side.
2. **Butterflies:** Make figure-eight's in front.
   Ribbons: Make figure-eight's overhead.
   Bows: Make figure-eight's on either side.
3. **Coils:** Make bigger and bigger circles; then smaller and smaller circles.
   Zingers: Make spirals from left to right and from right to left.
4. **Air Snakes:** Continuously raise and lower wrist to make snakes in the air.
   Floor Snakes: Lower arm so ribbon snakes along the floor.

RD-46 RHYTHM HOOPS

EQUIPMENT: One hoop per dancer; music in 4/4 time; tape or record player

ORGANIZATION:

- Children explore using a hoop to move rhythmically. Have each child get a hoop and stand in a home space. Check for good spacing.

DESCRIPTION OF ACTIVITY:

1. **Hoop Dancing:** Listen to the music. Show me what you can do with your hoop to keep in time with the music.
   — Swing hoop from side to side; twirl hoop around your arm; waist; neck; etc.
   — Hold it horizontally overhead in both hands and sway from side to side.
   — Skip with your hoop; step inside and hold at waist level, skip to the beat; walk backwards; run; gallop; side-step; step-hop; move in a zig-zag pattern; etc.
2. **Hoop Jumping:** Place your hoop on the floor. Let's explore jumping in and out of our hoops in time to the music in the following sequence: Jump out the front (1-2 counts); jump in (1-2); jump out the back (1-2); jump in (1-2).
   — Jump to the right side (1-2); jump in (1-2); jump out to the left (1-2); jump back in (1-2); jump in and out around your hoop CCW (eight counts).
   — **Hoop Hopping:** Repeat the above sequence while hopping.
3. **Hoop Tinikling:** Begin on your right foot on the right side of your hoop. Hop left foot inside; hop on right foot inside; hop on left foot outside to left; hop right foot inside; hop on left foot inside; hop on right foot outside to right. Repeat pattern. Step out pattern slowly; then gradually increase tempo.
4. **Hoop Tossing:** Toss a vertical hoop upward and catch it. As the hoop comes down, bend your knees and lower your body to catch it. Stretch your body upward when you toss it.

RD-47 RHYTHM BALLS—ELEMENTARY BALL BOUNCING_____

FOCUS: Rhythmical bouncing; hand-eye coordination

EQUIPMENT: One utility ball per child; popular music in 4/4 time; tape or record player

ORGANIZATION:

- Children explore moving rhythmically with a ball in personal and general space. Accompany movements by using music with a strong beat and a moderate tempo. Ensure that children have ample time to practice. To begin, each child gets a ball and finds a home space.

DESCRIPTION OF ACTIVITY:

1. *One-Hand Bounce:*
   —Standing in your home space, bounce the ball with your right hand; then bounce the ball with your left hand to the music being played.
   —Concentrate on coordinating your whole body with the ball.
   —Flex your knees rhythmically.
   —Press the ball to the floor with a hollowed hand that is adjusted to the ball size, firm wrist, relaxed hand action.
   —Keep contact for as long as possible in a flowing smooth movement.

2. *Alternate Hand Bounce:*
   —Bounce the ball with alternate hands (almost a cross bounce from side to side).
   —As ball comes upward, reach out, stretching the opposite side, contact the ball from above, turn it over in your palm as the ball rests in your hand, and send it downward to the floor.
   —Let your body flow with the bouncing rhythm.

3. *Body Wave Bounce:*
   —Stand with feet together and bounce your ball three times.
   —On third bounce, add a body wave with an arm circle.
   —Bounce the ball two more times; squat on the third count as the ball bounces upward and catch. Practice this sequence.

4. *Hi-Low Bounce:*
   —Stand with feet together and bounce ball four times.
   —Move down on one knee and do eight quick bounces (twice as fast).
   —On the eighth bounce, stand up and change hands. Repeat sequence.

5. *Cross-Legged Sit Bounce:*
   —Sitting cross-legged, bounce ball in front with two hands.
   —Bounce ball with right hand four times; repeat with other hand.
   —Bounce ball in a semicircle from your left side to the right eight times; then repeat from left to right.
   —Repeat, but change hands at center, after four bounces.

6. *Locomotion Bounces:*
   —Walk forward with a light springy step, with one bounce for each step, for eight bounces; walk backwards.
   —Skip forward with four bounces; turn 180 degrees to face the opposite direction; change hands and repeat.
   —Side-step to right, bouncing ball with left hand; repeat to left, bouncing ball with right hand.
   —Run and bounce ball using your right hand. The ball contacts floor each time your left foot touches. Repeat using your left hand.

7. Create a Ball Bounce Routine that has a definite beginning and closing. Select and practice five different ways of bouncing the ball from the above tasks.

RD–48 RHYTHM BALLS—THROWING, ROLLING, ROUTINES

FOCUS: Rhythmical throwing; rolling; sequence-making; partnerwork

EQUIPMENT: One utility ball per child; popular music in 4/4 time; tape or record player

ORGANIZATION:

• Have each child begin with a ball in a home space.

DESCRIPTION OF ACTIVITY:

1. **Two-Hand Ball Throw:** Stand with your feet together and the ball in both hands. Throw the ball diagonally forward and upward. Let your body follow the throw as you stretch your body and arms upward in the direction of the ball's flight, and keep your arms reaching upward. Let the ball roll off your fingertips on its way up; let the ball roll back onto your fingertips into the palms on the way down. Then drop your arms to original position. Catch the ball without a sound! Let your knees bend with the catch and straighten with the throw. Keep the whole movement smooth and rhythmical. Practice.

1.

2. **One-Hand Throw:** Repeat throwing action as above, using your right hand, then your left hand. Catch the ball in your throwing hand.

3.

3. **Diagonal Throw:** Stand with feet together and ball in your right hand. Step diagonally forward with your right foot (facing diagonally right) and throw the ball from right hand to left hand. Add a body wave with your throw.

4. **Ball Routine:** Stand with feet together and ball in your right hand. Do eight bounces in a semicircle from your right side to your left side. Throw the ball up, body wave, and catch it on the first bounce in both hands. With left hand, throw ball to right, catch with right hand. Repeat to left. Repeat this whole sequence again. Add your own throwing action here.

5.

5. **L-Sit Roll:** Begin in long-sit position and roll your ball CW around you. If unable to reach around the toes, roll your ball over your ankles, but do not bend knees. Repeat CCW.

6. **Hip Roll:** Begin in back-lying position, knees bent, and feet close to hips, with arms stretched to side and ball in right hand. Lift your hips off the floor and roll the ball under hips from side to side.

6.

7. **Side-to-Side Roll:** Begin in stride-standing position, with weight on your right foot; left leg and toe stretched; ball in your right hand. Bend down and roll the ball from right to left; left to right.

8. **Ball Roll Routine:** Begin in hook-sit position, ball on the floor under your right hand. Roll ball to the left under your lifted straight legs. Do a Hip Roll with ball to the right. In long-sit position do an L-Sit roll CCW. In cross-leg sit position, ball in left hand, do eight bounces in a semicircle to right; catch in right hand and do an arc throw to left. Repeat routine from beginning.

9. **Ball Bounce Routine** (Bounce-Bounce-Quick, Quick-Pass [1-2] [3-4] [1-2] [3-4]): Bounce and catch the ball with both hands for two counts. Repeat; then with your right hand, bounce the ball twice just in front of the right foot. On the second bounce, send the ball across to your left, catch in both hands, and repeat pattern.

   — *Partner Routine:* Stand, facing about two meters (six feet) apart. Repeat ball bouncing pattern, but on "Pass," the ball is bounced with right hand across to partner.

BOUNCE – BOUNCE

QUICK – QUICK – PASS
9.

Play Gymnastics

The Play Gymnastics activities progressively build muscular strength and endurance, flexibility, balance, and overall coordination. They also develop children's self-confidence and improve their posture and safety awareness.

This section provides 58 different activities organized into the following areas: Supporting and Balancing; Rotation Around the Body Axes; Springing and Landing; and Climbing, Hanging, and Swinging.

PG-1 ONE-LEG BALANCE CHALLENGES

FOCUS: Balancing; leg strength

EQUIPMENT: One photocopy of activity per pair

ORGANIZATION:

- Have players find a partner of equal size: one partner performs the activity; the other partner is the spotter and observes and "coaches" the performer. Give a photocopy of this activity to each pair and have them practice together. During practice, coach should lightly support performer by holding one hand and then releasing it when performer is in balance.

DESCRIPTION OF ACTIVITY:

Try each One-Leg Balance Challenge with your partner. Position yourself as shown, point toes, and focus eyes ahead to help balance. Hold each balance for five seconds. After you have tried all the balances, repeat them using the other leg.

1. *Front Scale:* Balance on one leg. Raise the other leg backwards until it is parallel to the floor. Bend forward, look ahead at your own height, and raise the arms sideways. Try to keep both knees straight. Change to balance on the other leg.

2. *Front Scale Reverse:* Start in the front Scale position. Swing your back leg downward and at the same time twist the upper body to finish facing in the opposite direction. Maintain your balance without moving your standing foot from the spot.

3. *Balance Jump:* Start in the Front Scale position. Fix your eyes on a distant focal point. With a quick jump, change standing legs without losing balance. Repeat.

4. *Leap and Balance:* Stand with your arms out sideways. Run forward to leap in the air off one foot. Reach forward with the other leg, land on that leg, and hold your balance without moving. Can you hold that balance for five seconds?

5. *Knee Dip:* Balance on the right foot. Grasp your left foot behind your back with your right hand. Bend to touch your bent knee to the mat, while holding the left foot. Hold your other arm out to maintain balance. Stand up, without any other part of your body touching the floor or losing your balance. Repeat, touching with the other knee.

6. More Balancing Challenges:

   — *Stork Stand*

   — *Stork Stand, One Leg Sideways*

   — *Bird Dog*

   — *High Splits, Legs Straight*

   — *Cloud Stand*

   — *Ankle Hold*

   — *Swan Balance, with Upward Turn*

7. Create your own One-Leg Balance.

STORK STAND

BIRD DOG

SWAN BALANCE

CLOUD STAND

ANKLE HOLD

HIGH SPLITS

FOCUS: Supporting and balancing

EQUIPMENT: One mat per pair (optional); one beanbag per pair

ORGANIZATION:

- Have players find a partner and scatter. One partner performs the activity; the other partner is the spotter and observes and "coaches" the performer.

DESCRIPTION OF ACTIVITY:

1. *Pecking Bird:* Place the beanbag about 30 centimeters (12 inches) in front of you. Kneel down and raise both arms behind. Try to touch your nose to the beanbag without losing your balance.

   — Repeat, balancing on one knee and foot, with arms out sideways. How far out can you go?

2. *Ostrich Balance:* Balance on one foot only. Pick up a beanbag off the floor with one hand and return to the standing position, without losing your balance. Only your foot may touch the floor. Use your other arm to maintain balance. How far out can you place the beanbag?

3. *Head Touch:* Stand on one foot. Place your hands on the floor and lift the raised leg backwards. Can you touch your forehead to the floor and return to your original position, without losing balance or moving your standing foot?

4. *One Leg Squat-Balance:* Stand with arms raised sideways for balance. Raise one leg in front keeping the knee straight. Squat down, keeping your weight over the supporting leg. Hold your balance. Return to the standing position. Can you squat using the other leg?

5. *V-Sit:* Sit, hold your ankles out in front, with your feet flat on the mat. Bring your knees up. Straighten your legs as you raise them to form a "V" with your body and legs. With ankles together and toes pointed, balance in this position on your seat. Can you hold this position with your arms raised sideways? Hold your ankles. Try the V-sit with knees bent.

6. *Shoulder Rest:* Lie on your back with your hands by your sides. Roll backwards so that your hips are above your shoulders and your feet are as high as possible. Support your hips by placing your hands under the hips against your back. The weight of the body should be taken on the shoulders, the neck, the upper arms, and elbows. Hold the balance for five seconds; roll back down to the mat and repeat. Point the toes throughout.

   — Move your legs as if "bicycling" in the air.

   — Lay the arms along the mat.

7. *Shoulder Rest in Pairs:* Find a partner. Lie on your backs with your heads about 45 centimeters (18 inches) apart. Do a Shoulder Rest, both at the same time. Can you touch feet and hold your balance?

PG-3 BACK BENDS

FOCUS: Supporting and balancing

EQUIPMENT: One mat per group

ORGANIZATION:

- Form groups of three players: one is the performer; the others are spotters. Each group gets a mat to share and places it against a wall. Performers should stretch lower back only as far as comfortable. Ensure that spotters do not lift and hyperextend performer's lower back.

DESCRIPTION OF ACTIVITY:

1. ***Wrestler's Bridge:*** Performer, lie on your back on the mat with knees bent and feet flat on the floor. Open knees, grasp ankles, and pull feet as close to your seat as possible. Point toes outward. Without losing foot position, release hands and stretch arms to side for support. Arch your body to balance on feet and top of head. Relax and repeat.

   — Spotter, observe and correct performer's technique. Does your partner's back arch? Place hands gently under performer's hips ready to help if necessary.

2. ***Climb Down the Walls:*** Performer, stand on mat with back to wall and heels 50 centimeters (20 inches) away from it. Stretch arms overhead, lean back to place palms on the wall, and focus eyes on the wall. Slowly walk hands down wall as far as possible; hold for three seconds and walk hands up again.

   — Spotters, join hands under performer's hips ready to help if necessary.

3. ***Assisted Back Bend:*** Performer, stand on the mat facing your spotter. Now stretch arms overhead and lean back as far as possible. Place palms on the mat and tilt head back to look at the mat. Bring your hands as close to your heels as you can.

   — Spotters, join hands behind the performer's waist ready to help if necessary.

4. ***Back Bend with One Leg Raised:*** Performer, lie on mat with knees bent and feet flat on floor. Make a High Wrestler's Bridge (refer to Variations); then straighten one leg overhead and point toe. Change legs and repeat. Can you raise both one hand and one leg?

   — Spotters, kneel on either side of performer and join hands under performer's back without touching performer.

VARIATIONS:

a. Have players do a Back Bend over a rolled mat; over a kneeling partner; without assistance.

b. ***High Wrestler's Bridge*** (Use only after players have improved back flexibility): Performer lies in Wrestler's Bridge position but places palms on either side of head. Performer then lifts trunk and straightens elbows to raise head from mat. Spotter places hands under performer's hips.

c. ***Walking Wrestler's Bridge:*** Challenge players to walk forward in High Wrestler's Bridge position, alternately stepping with hand and opposite foot.

PG–4 SQUAT BALANCES_____

FOCUS: Supporting and balancing   **EQUIPMENT:** One mat per player

ORGANIZATION:
- These balances are lead-ups to the headstand. Have each person get a mat and scatter around the play area.

DESCRIPTION OF ACTIVITY:

1. *Tripod Balance:* Squat and place hands on the mat shoulder-width apart with fingers spread and pointing forward. Bend the elbows and lower forehead to mat to form a triangle with the hands. Put weight equally on all three points; then lean forward to lift feet from the floor so that the right knee rests on the right elbow and the left knee rests on the left elbow. Hold balance for three seconds and return to the starting position.
2. *Frog Stand:* Squat in the Tripod Balance position with hands shoulder-width apart and pointing forward. Bend elbows, lean forward, and press knees against outside of elbows. Continue to lean forward until feet lift. Raise your head from the mat to look straight ahead. Hold balance for three seconds and return to starting position.

VARIATION:

Standing Tripod Balance: Have players stand, bend forward, and place hands on mat as in the Tripod Balance. Raise knees to rest on the elbows. Hold balance for three seconds and return to starting position.

PG–5 INVERTED BALANCES_____

FOCUS: Supporting and balancing   **EQUIPMENT:** One mat per pair

ORGANIZATION:
- In these Inverted Balances, children learn the progressions to the headstand, with the assistance of a spotter. Emphasize that performers return to starting position or roll forward if they overbalance. Have each find a partner of equal size, get a mat to share, and then scatter around the play area.

DESCRIPTION OF ACTIVITY:

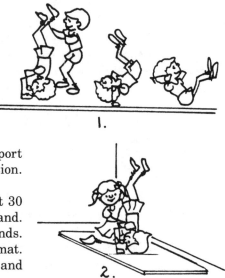

1. *Tucked Frog Stand:* Performer, squat and place hands on the mat shoulder-width apart, with fingers spread and pointing forward. Now, tip into a Frog Stand. Lower forehead to the mat to form a triangle with the hands. Bring the knees together, raise them overhead, and bend them, as if you are sitting upside down. Hold for five seconds; then tuck head under, lower weight to shoulders, and push off with hands to a Forward Roll.
   — Spotter, stand directly in front of performer. At first, support hips and then support ankles. Slowly raise legs to position. Remember to move to side when performer rolls forward.
2. *Wall Headstand:* Performer, place mat against wall. Squat 30 centimeters (12 inches) from wall and repeat Tucked Frog Stand. Straighten legs and rest feet against wall. Hold for five seconds. Arch back slightly and point toes; then slowly lower legs to mat.
   — Spotter, kneel at side and support performer at shoulders and just above the knee.

PG-6 HEADSTANDS

FOCUS: Supporting and balancing

EQUIPMENT: One mat per pair

ORGANIZATION:

- Have players find a partner of equal size, get a mat to share, and then scatter around the play area. For Kick-Up Headstand, form groups of three players. Remind players to return to starting position or roll forward if they overbalance.

DESCRIPTION OF ACTIVITY:

1. *Curl-Up Headstand:* Performer, squat in a Tripod Balance. Slowly raise legs until overhead. Point toes and hold feet together for five seconds; then slowly lower legs to mat.
   — Spotter, stand facing performer. At first support hips and then ankles.

2. *Kick-Up Headstand:* Performer, squat in a Tripod Balance and walk feet forward so that the front leg is bent and the rear leg is straight. Now, kick up rear leg and then your forward leg until both are overhead. Point toes and arch your back slightly. Hold for five seconds and return to starting position.
   — Spotters, stand to side and in front of performer. Place lower leg against performer's back. Catch front leg at ankle; then catch the second leg.

3. *Straddle Press to Headstand:* Start in the push-Up position. Draw legs toward your hands, keeping legs apart and straight. Tip your forehead down onto the mat. Keep toes pointed and hips high as you lift your straight legs overhead. Keep the back arched slightly as legs come together. Hold for five seconds. Spot as for Kick-Up Headstand.

PG-7 THE SPLITS

FOCUS: Supporting and balancing

EQUIPMENT: One mat per pair; several benches

ORGANIZATION:

- As children perform their "Splits," emphasize that they should stretch to a comfortable position. If pain is felt, they should ease off. Advise them not to "bounce." Have them hold each split for ten seconds, rest, then repeat. To begin, each child finds a spot alone, facing you.

DESCRIPTION OF ACTIVITY:

1. *The Middle Splits:* Sit with legs astride and as close to in-line as you can. Point the toes, keep your back straight, and look straight ahead. Lean forward with the hands to touch as far out as possible, hold for ten seconds, then repeat.
   — Try this with your back against a wall.

2. *Stride Splits with Support:* Support yourself between two benches. Gradually lower yourself to sit with one leg forward and the other back. Keep your hips square, with both legs turned out. Point the toes. Lower yourself to a comfortable position, hold, then stand. Repeat, with the other leg forward.

3. *Stride Splits:* Sit on the floor with one leg forward and the other back, with the hips square and toes pointed. Support yourself on each side with your hands on the floor.

PG–8 PARTNER BALANCES—EXPLORATION

FOCUS: Balancing and supporting; partnerwork   **EQUIPMENT:** One mat per pair

ORGANIZATION:

• Have players find a partner of equal size. Partners get mat and scatter. Encourage players to balance on different body parts; at different levels; in different shapes. Encourage players to help each other and to make suggestions.

DESCRIPTION OF ACTIVITY:

1. *Copy Your Partner:* Do any kind of balance. Have your partner copy your balance. Take turns. Hold all balances for five seconds.

2. *Mirror Your Partner:* Decide on a balance. Perform your balance facing each other; alongside each other; and back to back.

3. *Siamese Twins:* Balance close to each other so that the same body parts are touching.

4. *Make Bridges:* Invent bridges, with one partner balancing on some part of the other partner. Balance on different body parts: head, hands, knees, back, seat, tummy, elbows, feet, shoulders.

5. *Sequences:* Partners, select any three balances that you have done and perform them together, one after the other, mirroring each other.

PG–9 BALANCE EXPLORATION WITH EQUIPMENT AND APPARATUS

FOCUS: Balancing and supporting

EQUIPMENT: Several mats;   hoops;
box horse;   beanbags;
chairs;   deckrings;
several balance benches;   balls
several wands;

ORGANIZATION:

• Have players find a partner of equal size. Each pair collects any two pieces of equipment and then scatters around play area. Set up several balance benches with wide surface up.

DESCRIPTION OF ACTIVITY:

1. Collect a beanbag, deckring, ball, wand, or hoop. With your partner, explore different ways to use your equipment while holding a balance on: knees; one knee and one hand; back; tummy; seat; one foot only; etc.
   — Exchange equipment with another pair and repeat.

2. Now move to any piece of apparatus and hold a balance on it. Can you move while you balance on the apparatus? Run to another piece of apparatus to balance and move on it.
   — Hold a balance with your partner on the apparatus. Explore different balances on different apparatus.

3. Create a routine with your partner that uses three different balances and your equipment.
   — Create a partner-balancing routine on the apparatus.

PG-10 COFFEE CAN STILTS

FOCUS: Static and dynamic balancing

EQUIPMENT: One pair of coffee can stilts per player;
one beanbag per player;
one rope per player;
one ball per player;
high jump standards and crossbar

ORGANIZATION:

- As a class project ahead of time, have each player make a pair of coffee can stilts out of cans and rope. Provide ample time for them to get used to moving on their stilts. Remind players to look ahead at their own height, always watching where they are going. Explain that if they overbalance, they should jump to the floor and start again. Set up the equipment around the play area. Have each player collect a pair of stilts and move to a free space.

DESCRIPTION OF ACTIVITY:

1. Walk forward with small steps. Look ahead, not down.

2. Walk sideways; walk backwards.

3. Step over objects: lines on the floor, beanbags, ropes.

4. Go under objects: high jump crossbar, ropes.

5. Balance on one foot, hop on one foot; then on the other foot. Hop on alternate feet.

6. Jump into the air. Jump and quarter-turn; half-turn.

7. Two-foot jump forward; backwards; sideways.

8. Walk at different levels: low, medium, high.

9. Move objects forward with your feet while walking: beanbags, small balls, etc.

10. Walk along a line, placing the can on the line each step.

11. Move through an obstacle course made up of the above equipment and activities.

12. Invent your own activity.

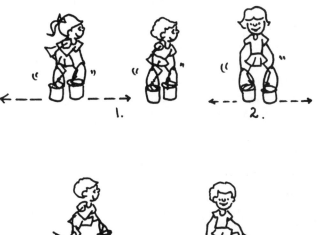

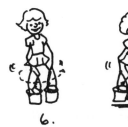

FOCUS: Supporting and balancing

EQUIPMENT: One mat per pair (optional); several cone markers; two bricks or wooden blocks (optional); two chairs (optional)

ORGANIZATION:

• Have players find a partner about their own size and then find a free space.

DESCRIPTION OF ACTIVITY:

1. **Teeter-Totter:** Sit on each other's feet, facing each other. Hold each other's upper arms. Rock back and forth while in this position, lifting off the floor as you rock. As one partner lifts his or her seat, the other partner raises his or her feet. Continue rocking up and down in this way.

2. **Scooter:** Start as for Teeter-Totter, except that as a seat is raised off the mat, that partner moves backwards about 15 centimeters (6 inches), while the other moves the feet forward with his or her seat, in a scooting motion. Bend and straighten the knees as you go. Continue.

3. **Hitchhike:** Stand facing each other with hands on each other's shoulders. First player, stand on partner's insteps, and then try to walk together. Change roles and repeat.

4. **The Wheelbarrow:** Stand one behind the other. Front player go down into the push-up position. Support your weight on your arms and spread your legs. Rear player, grasp the front player's legs above the knees and lift them to your waist. Walk forward like a wheelbarrow, while the front player walks on hands. Change positions and repeat.
   — Form teams for short relays. Change roles each time you turn to race back to the starting line.

5. **Front Seat Support:** Sit on the floor with legs straight out in front and toes pointing away from the body and ankles together. Place the hands flat on the floor, halfway between your hips and knees. Lean slightly forward and bend the elbows slightly. Straighten elbows to raise your seat and legs off the floor, while supporting your weight on your hands. Hold for three seconds. Spotter, hold your partner's ankles. Raise the ankles about 15 centimeters (6 inches) off the floor. If difficult, try from between two chairs; two bricks.

6. **Chinese Get-up:** Partners, stand back to back with elbows locked. Brace yourselves against each other's back; then lower yourself to the sitting position with the legs out. To do this, take short walking steps away from each other. To rise, bend the knees and draw the feet up close to the body. Push with the legs, brace against your partner's back, and rise to the standing position.

7. **The Cross-Over:** Partners, face each other and hold right hands in the handshake grip. One player steps over the other (who bends down) with the left leg, to face in the opposite direction astride his or her own arm. The partner stands up and steps over the first player, who bends down, to end up back-to-back. Have them unravel themselves without breaking the grip.

8. **Wring the Dishrag:** Face your partner and join hands. Both partners, raise your arms on one side, lowering your arms on the other side as you turn back to back. Continue turning the same direction; then repeat, turning in the opposite direction.

PG–12 PARTNER BALANCES

FOCUS: Cooperative supporting and balancing   **EQUIPMENT:** One photocopy of activity per group; one mat per group

ORGANIZATION:

- Have children find partners of equal size. Photocopy this activity for each pair; then have each pair collect a mat and find a home space. Check for good spacing. As pairs perform balances, circulate to offer assistance, praise, and encouragement. Advise players to balance only on stronger parts of the body such as shoulders, knees, and hips, not the neck or lower back. Have partners demonstrate an original balance.

DESCRIPTION OF ACTIVITY:

Take turns to balance with a partner. Hold each balance five seconds; then change roles.

1. Lean your feet together for ten seconds.

2. Try to rest your shoulders on your partner's feet.

3. Bending your knees, holding wrists, how low can you go?

4. Balance with your hands on your partner's shoulders and your knees on your partner's hips.

5. Lie face up while your partner supports you.

6. Find another way to balance with your partner.

PG–13 COUNTERBALANCES

FOCUS: Cooperative supporting and balancing   **EQUIPMENT:** See activity PG–12.

ORGANIZATION:

- A Counterbalance is a cooperative balance, using the other's weight to hold what would normally be an off-balance position. Have players find a partner of equal size. Give a photocopy of this activity to each pair; then have each pair collect a mat and find a home space. Check for good spacing.

DESCRIPTION OF ACTIVITY:

1. Holding wrists, lean back and move around in a circle.

2. Hold the wrist and lean out. Hold with the other arm and repeat.

3. Lean against each other on the way up and on the way down.

4. Sit down, knees bent, toes touching, holding each other's wrists. Pull each other up to the standing position.

5. Balance bumper-to-bumper (back-to-back).

6. Sit on an "air" chair.

7. Pushing against hands, lean as far away from each other as you can.

8. Create a counterbalance of your own!

PG–14 PARTNER SUPPORT-BALANCE STUNTS

FOCUS: Cooperative supporting and balancing

EQUIPMENT: One photocopy of activity per group; one mat per group

ORGANIZATION:

- Form groups of three players of equal size: two players perform together, the other is the spotter. Give a photocopy of this activity to each group and have them practice together. During practice, circulate to offer assistance, praise, and encouragement.

DESCRIPTION OF ACTIVITY:

Take turns to balance with a partner and have the third player observe and correct your technique. Hold each balance five seconds; then change roles.

1. *Ankle-Support Balance*
2. *Reverse-Ankle Support Balance*
3. *Mini-Centipede*
4. *Shoulder-Support Balance*
5. *Back-Support Balance*
6. *Hands- & Feet-Support Balance*
7. Create a support-balance of your own!

PG–15 SUPPORT-BALANCE STUNTS IN THREE'S

FOCUS: Cooperative supporting and balancing

EQUIPMENT: One photocopy of activity per group; one large mat per group

ORGANIZATION:

- Form groups of four players of equal size. Give a photocopy of this activity to each group and allow time for players to practice together. Emphasize the need for a solid base in each group balance.

DESCRIPTION OF ACTIVITY:

While three players form a balance, have the fourth player assist. Change roles frequently and hold each balance for five seconds.

1. *Platform Balance*
2. *W-Balance*
3. *Star Balance*
4. *Lazy-Chair Balance*
5. *Chariot Balance*
6. *On-Top-of-the-World*
7. *Trim-the-Hedge*
8. *Fan Balance*
9. Invent Your Own Balance

PG-16 INTRODUCING THE BODY AXES

FOCUS: Teaching and safety guidelines

EQUIPMENT: Chart paper and marking pens; one mat per player

ORGANIZATION:

- Discuss the terms "rotation," "axis," and "center of gravity" or "point of balance." Use a globe of the earth to show how our planet rotates on its axis. Make a chart with the names of the three body rotational axes: "lateral," "medial," and "longitudinal," so that players become familiar with them. Players should be able to identify each type of rotation. Have different children demonstrate the three types of rotations.

DESCRIPTION OF ACTIVITY:

1. We can rotate around our body's center of gravity in three ways:
   - ***Rotating Around Lateral Axis:*** Involves forward and backwards rotations along the floor or on apparatus; examples include forward and backwards rolls. Lateral rotations are the most common rotations in gymnastics.
   - ***Rotating Around Medial Axis:*** Involves rotation to the side; examples include cartwheels.
   - ***Rotating Around Longitudinal Axis:*** Involves rotation through the length of the body; examples include spins, half turns or full turns, pivots, pirouettes, and rolls such as log rolls. Longitudinal rotations are often combined with rotations around the other two axes to form more difficult gymnastic stunts.
2. You are going to learn to perform these different rotations. Let's begin with rotations around the Longitudinal Axis.

PG-17 LOG ROLLING

FOCUS: Longitudinal axis rotations; partnerwork

EQUIPMENT: One mat per pair

ORGANIZATION:

- Have children find a partner, get a mat, and find a home space. Arrange mats so that performers are always in view (circular formation). Check for good spacing.

DESCRIPTION OF ACTIVITY:

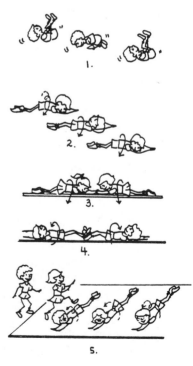

1. ***Egg Roll:*** Lie on your back. Hug your knees to your chest, elbows into your sides, chin tucked between your knees. Roll sideways so that you finish on your knees. Push with your elbows and knees as you roll. Then Egg Roll to the other side. One partner roll; the other, follow.
2. ***Log Roll:*** In front-lying position, arms extended overhead and hands clasped, make yourself as long as you can. Roll sideways over onto your back, onto your tummy again. Log Roll across your mat, followed by your partner; then roll back. Now Log Roll so that feet and hands do not touch the mat.
3. ***Log Roll in Pairs:*** Lie on your tummies facing each other on the mat. Link hands and roll in the same direction. How many times can you roll like this? Can you roll so that your feet do not touch the mat?
4. ***Log Roll with Feet Locked:*** Lie down on the mat on your backs so that your feet are touching; then lock your feet together. Now roll slowly in the same direction with your feet locked.
5. ***Leap the Log Roll*** (Form groups of six to eight players. Divide into two groups, the "Rollers" and the "Leapers"; each group stand in single file at each end of the mats, facing each other. Have one group demonstrate this activity.): On the signal "Roll," the Rollers, start log rolling down the mat, well spaced apart. At the same time the Leapers, leap over the approaching Rollers. Rollers, when you reach the end of the mat, you become Leapers; Leapers, you become the Rollers. Continue.

FOCUS: Asymmetrical, longitudinal rotations; partnerwork   **EQUIPMENT:** One mat per performer

ORGANIZATION:

- The Judo Roll is also called the Shoulder Roll and is used as a "safety roll" in gymnastics to learn how to fall and to prevent injury. Review the terms "symmetrical" and "asymmetrical." The Judo Roll and Churn-the-Butter are asymmetrical movements. Use these rolls as "breaks" in gymnastics. Have the players get two mats and place them in a free space; one on top of the other for extra thickness.

DESCRIPTION OF ACTIVITY:

1. ***Judo (Shoulder) Roll:*** Performer, squat down with your feet wide apart and one foot forward. Place one arm forward so the back of your hand is on the mat. The hand should be placed outside the front foot. Tuck your head to your chest, turning your head in the direction of the hand. Hold the other arm out sideways for balance. Roll forward, keeping your chin on your chest, to land on the back of your shoulder. Roll diagonally across your back to finish in the standing position, with one foot behind the other.

1.

2. ***Churn-the-Butter Roll:*** Start in the back-support position with legs, body, and arms straight, weight supported on the hands behind and fingers pointing forward. Lift one arm and one leg, reach up, and roll over into the front-support position. Lift other arm and leg, reach up, and roll over again to starting position. Continue rolling smoothly—or "churning-the-butter"—along your mat.

2.

3. Find a partner. Get into the back-support position with feet touching. On signal "Churn!" Churn-the-Butter in the same direction; then reverse direction.

4. Develop a rolling routine with your partner: Start side-by-side and churn away from each other; then log roll toward each other. Now Judo Roll away from each other; then Egg Roll toward each other.

   — Create your own rolling routine, which includes these rolls.

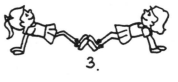

3.

VARIATIONS:

a. ***Judo Roll:*** Start in the standing position; two-foot take-off.

b. Walk into the Shoulder Roll.

c. Run into the Shoulder Roll.

d. Place mats end-to-end and do a series of Shoulder Rolls.

e. Form lines of four to six players. All Churn-the-Butter in line, rotating at the same time.

PG-19 FORWARD ROLL—TECHNIQUE

FOCUS: Lateral axis rotation; technique; spotting; partnerwork

EQUIPMENT: One mat per pair

ORGANIZATION:

- Have players find a partner, get a mat, and find a free space. Check for good spacing. Each partner learns to spot for the other. Advise children with long hair to tie it back so that their performance is not hindered.

DESCRIPTION OF ACTIVITY:

1. *Technique:* Begin in the crouch or squat position, with your weight on your toes. Place your hands on the mat slightly ahead of your toes, shoulder-width apart and fingers facing forward. Round your back by tucking your head between your knees. Your chin should be touching your chest. Push off from your toes, raising your seat as you roll forward, with your chin tucked to your chest. Land on the tops of your shoulders and push with your hands as you roll forward to the sitting position, keeping your heels wide and close to your seat. Hug your shins with your arms while rolling to your feet; then finish in starting position.

2. *Spotting for the Forward Roll:* Kneel on one knee alongside your partner. Place your leading hand on the back of your partner's neck and the other hand under the near ankle. As your partner rolls forward, assist by lifting with the leading hand and pushing gently forward with the back hand.

3. *Practice:* Take turns performing and spotting.

PG-20 FORWARD ROLL—PROGRESSIONS

FOCUS: Reinforcing technique; sequence-building

EQUIPMENT: One mat per pair

ORGANIZATION:

- Forward rolls are further explored and developed. Emphasize that the head should be well tucked out of the way and that the landing should be made on the tops of the shoulders and the back of the neck, not the head. Have children find a partner, collect a mat, and find a free space. Check for good spacing. They should take turns at performing and spotting.

DESCRIPTION OF ACTIVITY:

1. Squat with your arms folded across your chest. Without using your hands, do a forward roll, land on shoulder tops, and roll to feet, returning to the squat position.

2. Squat with your arms wrapped around your lower legs. Do a forward roll without using your hands. Land on the top of your shoulders. Make sure your head is well tucked under. It should not touch the mat.

3. Start in the standing position. Do a forward roll and finish in the standing position, standing still for three seconds. Now take a short run to the mat, forward roll to a squat. Repeat.

4. Forward roll to a squat position; rock backward onto your neck and shoulders, rock back, and push with your feet into another forward roll. Repeat.

5. Forward roll to a stand; forward roll to a stand; forward roll to a stand.

6. Stand, cross ankles, and forward roll with legs crossed. Finish in starting position. Can you do a series of these along the mats?

7. Create a rolling sequence of your own! Include all the rolls you have learned.

PG–21 FORWARD ROLLS USING APPARATUS

FOCUS: Rolling over, along, and off apparatus; stationwork

EQUIPMENT: Mats;
springboards;
benches;
tables;
box horse

ORGANIZATION:

- Set up the apparatus in Stations around the play area, spaced well apart. Place mats at sides and ends of apparatus. Form the class into as many groups as there are Stations, and assign each group to a piece of apparatus. While one member of the group performs, the others act as spotters. After about three minutes at each Station, have the groups rotate clockwise to the next Station.

- Choose the Station activities from the following, or include some previously taught activities.

DESCRIPTION OF ACTIVITY:

1. *Rolling Over a Low Object (Rolled Mat):* Collect a rolled mat and place it on the mat. Place your hands on the other side of the rolled mat, taking most of your weight on your arms. Tuck your chin to your chest. Remain tucked throughout the roll and stand to finish.

   — Use pillows, cushions, bench (with a mat wrapped around it) as low objects; roll over another player, or a series of players.

2. *Rolling Down an Incline (Springboard):* Place a mat over the springboard. Place both hands on the mat at the high end of the board. Spring high to get started. Remain in the tuck position during the roll down; then stand.

3. *Rolling Up an Incline (Springboard):* Place a mat over the board. Start at the low end of the board. Use a bigger push-off to roll up the springboard. You may have to use a run in.

4. *Rolling from a Height (Bench, Table or Low Box Horse):* Move up onto the box; then from a squat position, reach for the mat with your hands, and tuck into a Forward Roll; roll again on the mat to a stand.

5. *Roll Along a Height (Bench, Table, or Low Box Horse):* Spring onto the apparatus; then roll along and off the apparatus. When your feet touch the floor, roll again.

VARIATIONS:

a. As players become more capable, increase the challenge by raising the height of the apparatus.

b. Add a short running approach to each Station task.

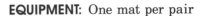

PG-22 BACKWARDS ROLL—TECHNIQUE

FOCUS: Lateral axis rotation; technique; spotting; partnerwork   **EQUIPMENT:** One mat per pair

ORGANIZATION:

- Have the players find a partner, and then get a mat and take it to a free space. Explain that the partners should take turns at performing and spotting.

DESCRIPTION OF ACTIVITY:

1. *Performer:* Start in the squat position with your back to the mat. Place your hands pointing back over your shoulders with the palms up and the thumbs near your neck. Tuck your chin down onto your chest. To start the roll, sit down on the mat and push backwards with your toes, keeping in the tucked position. As you roll, bring your knees to your chest and roll onto your back. Push off the mat with your hands to land in the squat position on your toes, not on your knees. Hold balance.

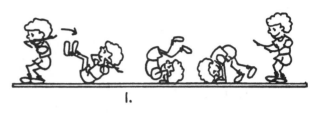

2. *Spotters:* Position yourself at the side of your partner and kneel on the knee away from him or her. Assist by placing one hand under the head at the back of the neck and the other under the hip. Gently push in the direction of the roll. Help your partner gain enough speed to get the body weight over the hands.
   — Gradually allow performer to roll without your help.

3. *Practice:* Take turns performing and spotting.

PG-23 BACKWARDS ROLL—PROGRESSIONS

FOCUS: Reinforcing technique   **EQUIPMENT:** One mat per pair

ORGANIZATION:

- Emphasize that weight be taken equally on both hands, not on the head. At the end of each roll, the feet should touch the mat first, not the knees. Advise children with long hair to tie it back so that their performance is not hindered.

DESCRIPTION OF ACTIVITY:

1. *Backwards Roll from Sit to Squat:* Start the Backwards Roll from the sitting position. To get speed, rock forward and then backwards into the roll, giving a very hard push with the feet.
   — Can you finish with your feet together in a squat? with your feet apart?

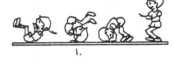

2. *Forward Roll—Backwards Roll:* Start with a forward roll to the squat position. Then do a backwards roll to finish in the squat position.
3. *Backwards Roll Series:* See how many backwards rolls you can do in a row and finish in the squat (tuck) position.

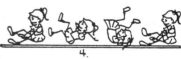

4. *Split-Leg Backwards Roll Series:* Standing with feet astride, roll backwards to finish in the same position.
5. *Backwards Roll with Legs Crossed:* Squat cross-legged, roll backwards, and finish in the cross-legged sit position.

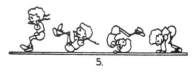

6. *Backwards Roll on One Foot:* Start in the squat position with your back to the mat. Raise one leg in front, bring hands to shoulders, and then roll backwards in the tuck position. Continue to roll; then land on one foot and stand tall on both feet.

PG–24 ROLL AND BALANCE COMBINATIONS

FOCUS: Lateral axis rotations; sequence-building

EQUIPMENT: One mat per player

ORGANIZATION:

- Overbalancing means shifting the body weight away from the base. Children learn how to roll out safely if they overbalance before attempting more difficult roll-balance combinations. As a warm-up to the following tasks, review the Forward Roll (activity PG–19), the Backwards Roll (activity PG–22), and the Frog Stand (activity PG–4). Have the players get a mat and then scatter around the play area. Check for good spacing.

DESCRIPTION OF ACTIVITY:

1. Show me a balance on one hand and one foot; then overbalance into a roll. Repeat using different "point" balances on small body parts (elbows, knees, hands, feet) and overbalance into a roll.

1.

2. Try these sequences:
   — Do a low balance, to a roll, to another low balance.
   — Do a high balance, roll, to a high balance, to a different roll.
   — Do a medium balance, roll, to a low balance, to a different roll.

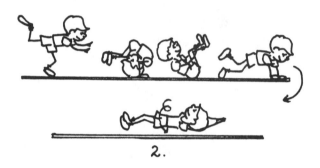

2.

3. Do one forward roll, stand and hold balance. Do two forward rolls and hold your balance. Stand, forward roll, to squat and balance on toes.

4. Squat; then do a backward roll to a squat. Repeat, finishing in a standing position. Repeat, doing two backward rolls.

5. Squat, forward roll, into a frog stand. Hold the frog stand for five seconds; then overbalance into another forward roll. Repeat.

6. Squat, forward roll, into a frog stand, overbalance into a forward roll, to the squat position, stand and do a stork stand (balance on one leg with arms out sideways).

6.

7. Squat, forward roll to a squat, hold balance; then do a backward roll to a squat, hold balance.

8. Squat, forward roll into a frog stand, hold balance, rock back to the squat position.

9. Squat, forward roll, to a frog stand. Hold the balance, tip forward to a forward roll, stand and then do a backward roll to a stand.

10. Squat, form a high bridge, tuck into a forward roll to a stand. Repeat.

10.

11. Create your own sequence of forward rolls, backwards rolls, frog stands, and other balances and demonstrate to the class.

PG–25 TANDEM ROLLS

FOCUS: Partner rolling; lateral axis rotations   **EQUIPMENT:** Two large mats per group

ORGANIZATION:

- Form groups of four. In each group have children pair off with a partner of equal size. Each group collects two large mats and places them end-to-end, securing them together with the Velcro® strips. Mats are arranged lengthwise throughout the play area as shown. Allow each pair ample space to experiment with Forward and Backwards Roll Combinations.

DESCRIPTION OF ACTIVITY:

1. *Tandem Forward Roll:* Squat side-by-side and face same direction. When one partner says "Roll," roll forward together, stand, and hold balance.
   — Can you tandem-roll from a standing position?
   — Can you and your partner do a series of tandem Forward Rolls?

1.

2. *Tandem Backwards Roll:* Squat side-by-side and face same direction. When one partner signals "Roll," roll backwards together, stand, and hold balance.
   — Can you tandem-roll backwards from a standing position?
   — Can you and your partner do a series of tandem Backwards Rolls?
3. Forward roll, stand, backwards roll, and stand.
   — Forward roll, stand, jump-turn to face opposite direction, and backwards roll. Perform both rolls while moving in the same direction.
4. Each pair create your own tandem roll together.

PG–26 CARTWHEEL—TECHNIQUE

FOCUS: Rotating around medial axis; technique; spotting; partnerwork   **EQUIPMENT:** Three mats per group

1.

ORGANIZATION:

- Arrange several mats end-to-end. Tape a line down the middle of each row of mats as a guide for performers. Form groups of three or four children and assign each group to a mat area. Have group members take turns as performers and spotters. When children can perform a cartwheel properly, have them practice on the lines on the floor.

DESCRIPTION OF ACTIVITY:

1. *Performer:* Stand sideways to the mat, feet astride and left side toward the mat. Raise left arm overhead and right arm out to the side. Bend to left side to place the left hand and then right hand in line on the mat. At the same time, throw the right leg overhead, followed by the left leg. The legs should be apart and straight as they pass overhead. Straighten arms and raise your head throughout the Cartwheel. Land on the mat; first with the right foot, then with the left, to stand upright with the feet apart.
2. *Spotter:* Stand behind performer. Hold performer's shorts at waist with a cross-arm grip. As performer cartwheels, the arms will uncross.
3. *Practice Cartwheel:* Try to move in a straight line along the mats with your legs as high as possible.
4. *Running Cartwheel—Progression:* Start with a short run. Just prior to take-off, add a little skip-step on the right foot, to take off on the left foot. Do the Cartwheel and finish with a controlled landing. Hold balance.

PG–27 SPRINGBOARD—RUNNING APPROACH

FOCUS: Approach; take-off; springing technique; landing

EQUIPMENT: Springboard, beatboard, or mini-tramp; several mats

ORGANIZATION:

- Review the safety guidelines, the technique of the Run-in, springing from the springboard, and landing correctly: Knees, hips, and ankles bend (give); arms are stretched upward and forward; eyes look straight ahead. Arrange the class in small groups if you have more than one springboard. Designate three spotters and have them demonstrate the equipment set-up and spotting technique.

DESCRIPTION OF ACTIVITY:

1. *Spotting Technique:* Always use three spotters: one on either side of the springboard and the third who stands in front, ready to assist players who overbalance.

   — Spotters, place mats at the sides and in front of the springboard.

   — Performers, have three turns at each task; then change roles with a spotter.

2. *Springing Technique:* Stand on the springboard with your toes slightly over the edge and look straight ahead. Bend at the knees, and take your arms back. Quickly throw your arms forward and upward, spring up, and push off. Cushion your landing by bending at the knees and using arms to balance you. Straighten legs and extend your arms and hands upward. Hold for three seconds.

3. *Approach Technique:* Approach the board with short quick running steps; change to a one-foot take-off from the first part of the board (similar to the long jump). Land on both feet at the far end of the board, bringing the arms down and back as you bend at the knees and hips. On the push-off, straighten your body out, stretching vigorously upward with the arms to gain height. Land softly on the mat on two feet, no more than one meter (three feet) ahead of the board: Bend at the hips and knees; take your arms down and back to a safe landing. Stand still and hold your arms out to the side.

4. Run in, spring, and land without overbalancing and hold your balance for three seconds.

5. Run in, spring, and land with your feet close together. Repeat, landing with your feet wide apart.

6. *Knee Slap:* Run in, spring on the end of the springboard, slap both knees while in the air, and finish with a safe landing. Can you slap your knees twice? Cross your arms, then slap your knees?

7. Run in, spring, and slap your heels behind you. Land softly.

8. Run in, spring, and "click" your heels in the air. Land properly.

PG-28 SPRINGBOARD—HIGH SPRINGS

FOCUS: Sequence-building

EQUIPMENT: Springboard, beatboard, or mini-tramp; several mats

ORGANIZATION:

- At first, teach all springboard activities without the rolls. As ability improves, add the rolls. Designate three spotters. Have them set up the springboard and mats with the long sides of the mats to the end of the springboard and then take up positions: one spotter on each side of the springboard and the third in front ready to assist performers who overbalance.
- Caution the performers to look ahead while in mid-air. Explain that if you "look up, you stay up; if you look down, you fall down." Remind performers to sweep arms upward to gain height as they spring.

DESCRIPTION OF ACTIVITY:

1. *High Spring:* Run in, spring from the board, throwing your arms upward to get as much height as you can. Land safely on the mat no more than one meter (three feet) ahead of the board; then go into a Forward Roll. Stand; hold balance for three seconds with arms out sideways.
   — Repeat. At the height of your jump, clap your hands overhead.
2. *Tuck:* Run in, spring high, "tuck" (clasp your knees to your chest), then whip the legs down quickly to land on the mat, and do a Forward Roll. Hold balance.
3. *Jackknife or Pike:* Run in, spring from the board high. Keep the legs astride and straight as you lean forward and bring your feet up to your hands to touch your toes. Whip the legs down quickly to land on both feet, Forward Roll, stand and hold balance.

PG-29 SPRINGBOARD—TURNS AND ROLLS

EQUIPMENT: See activity PG–28.

ORGANIZATION:

- Have children try these turns from floor level first and then from off the springboard.

DESCRIPTION OF ACTIVITY:

1. *Quarter-Turn:* Run in, spring from the board; as you do, raise your left arm overhead and throw your bent right arm across your body to the left. This will enable you to do a Quarter-Turn in the air. Land and stand still. Try turning a Quarter-Turn to the right side.
2. *Half-Turn:* Using the same technique as for the Quarter-Turn, do a Half-Turn (180 degrees) to finish facing the board. Try turning in the air, CW, then CCW. Land softly and hold balance.
   — Spring, clap hands and do a Half-Turn, land and do a Backwards Roll, stand.
3. *Full-Turn:* Using the same technique as for the Quarter-Turn, do a Full-Turn (360 degrees) to finish facing the mat. Land softly and hold balance.
   — Spring, clap hands, Full-Turn, do a Forward Roll, then stand.
   — Clap hands twice, three times, four times, etc.

PG-30 SPRINGBOARD SEQUENCES

FOCUS: Springing and tumbling; sequence-building

EQUIPMENT: Springboard;
several mats;
one large ball per group

ORGANIZATION:

- Designate three spotters. Have them set up the springboard with the short side of the mat to the end of the springboard and mats joined end-to-end; then take up positions: one spotter on each side of the springboard and the third in front ready to assist performers who overbalance. Teach all springboard activities without the rolls at first. As ability improves, add the rolls. Remind performers to look ahead at their own height while in the air. Caution the performers to land first, count "1, 2, 3," then proceed with the next stunt; otherwise they may go into their next stunt directly from the board.

DESCRIPTION OF ACTIVITY:

1. ***Run in, Spring, Land, Bunny Hop, Forward Roll:***
   Run in, spring to land on the mat, do a Bunny Hop, then a Forward Roll. Hold balance.
   — Spring, land, two Bunny Hops, Forward Roll, hold balance.
2. ***Run in, Spring, Seat Kick, Bunny Hop:*** Run in, spring from the board to do a Seat Kick, land, then squat down to do a Bunny Hop, stand and hold balance.
   — Do a Forward Roll after the Bunny Hop, and hold balance.
   — Throw your arms overhead as you do the Seat Kick.
3. ***Run in, Spring, Clap Hands Under Leg:*** Run in, spring from the board to clap hands under your left leg, land, do a Forward Roll, stand and hold balance.
   — Repeat, clapping hands under your right leg.
4. ***Run in, Spring, Clap Hands in Front and Back:*** While in the air, clap hands in front and behind your body, land, do two Forward Rolls, stand and hold balance.
5. ***Run in, Spring, Catch a Ball:*** While at the height of your spring, catch a ball thrown by your partner, land, do two Forward Rolls, stand and hold balance.
   — Land, do two Forward Rolls, and one Backwards Roll.

PG-31 BACKWARDS SPRINGS SEQUENCES

DESCRIPTION OF ACTIVITY:

1. ***Backwards Tuck:*** Stand on the board with your back to the mat. Spring back to a Tuck (hug your knees to chest); then whip legs down quickly to land on the mat. Do a Backwards Roll and stand.
2. ***Backwards Pike, Touch Knees:*** Stand on the board with your back to the mat. Spring back to a Pike (touch knees with hands). Land, do a Backwards Roll, and then stand.
3. ***Turn, Backwards Pike, Touch Knees:*** Face the mats, spring, half-turn, do a Backwards Pike to touch knees. Land, do a Backwards Roll, and stand.
4. ***Turn, Backwards Pike, Touch Toes:*** Face the mats, spring, half-turn, do a Backwards Pike to touch the toes. Land, do a Backwards Roll, and stand.
5. Create your own spring–roll sequence.

PG—32 INTRODUCTION TO THE BALANCE BENCH _____

FOCUS: Teaching and safety guidelines; balance and control

EQUIPMENT: Balance benches; mats

ORGANIZATION:

- During balance bench activities, have players use bare feet; curl fingers around the edges to grip the bench for mounts and dismounts; move along the bench in one direction only unless you state otherwise; focus eyes ahead and hold arms out at sides for balance; step off the bench if they lose balance rather than wait to fall off; bend at hips, knees, and ankles to land softly after dismounting. Have one group demonstrate the correct lifting, carrying, and anchoring of the bench. Emphasize the importance of safety at all times.
- These activities should be attempted on the wide surface of the bench first and then on the balance beam.

DESCRIPTION OF ACTIVITY:

1. *Lifting and Carrying the Bench:* Use five carriers for each balance bench. Carry the bench this way: two players at each end and three on the sides, all facing the same direction.
   - Bend knees and lift together; hold the back flat and the head up as you straighten the knees.
   - Walk in step, moving quickly and quietly; then bend the knees, hold the back flat and head up, as you lower the bench to the floor.

2. *Safety Mats:* Use four mats per bench; one at each end and one on each side.

3. *Anchoring the Bench:* For stability, have two players anchor each bench: one player at each end sitting facing the middle. When working in pairs only, one player straddle-sits the bench while the other performs the task.

4. *Bench Exploration:* Form groups of four to six players. Arrange the benches alongside each other, with mats at both ends and sides. Have each group stand in a line at one end of the bench. As soon as a player reaches halfway on the bench, the next player may begin. When a player reaches the opposite end of the bench, he or she jumps off, landing lightly, and then joins the line again. Players should take turns being the anchors for the bench. Here are some suggestions:
   - Walk forward along the bench to the other end; next time walk backwards along the bench.
   - Run forward along the bench to the other end; next time jump your way to the other end.
   - Gallop forward with the right foot forward to the opposite end; next time gallop with the left foot forward. Repeat skipping.
   - Can you keep one foot on the floor and the other on the bench and move along the bench? Next time travel with the opposite foot on the bench.
   - Let me see you explore ways of getting on and off the bench, over the bench, under the bench, across the bench, from one end to the other.
   - Starting at one end, jump up on the bench, jump forward off the bench and to one side, jump up again, then off to the other side. Can you move along to the end of the bench this way?
   - Show me another way of moving along the bench.

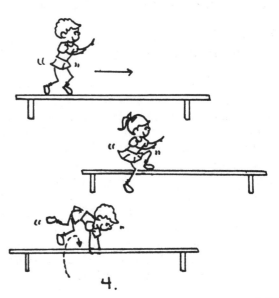

PG-33 BENCH WALKS

FOCUS: Travelling; body positioning; balance

EQUIPMENT: Balance benches; mats; beanbags

ORGANIZATION:

- Form groups of four to six players. Arrange the benches with mats at both ends and sides. Review the procedure for anchoring the benches and appoint anchors for each bench. Perform these tasks on the wide surface of the bench and then on the narrow side. Performers should remove shoes and socks for a better feel as they travel along the bench. Emphasize that performers hold their arms out to the side for balance and look ahead at their own height (not look down). Stress good body position and a steady balance while walking. Have the spotter walk alongside the performer with arm raised and palm up, under the hand of the performer.

DESCRIPTION OF ACTIVITY:

1. Walk forward carefully with small steps; toe touching heel as you go. Walk backwards, heel to toe.

2. Walk sideways, on the balls of the feet.

3. Walk forward, turn around, and walk backwards to the end. Walk forward, turning as you go.

4. Walk forward. Bend your knees to touch your hand to the bench. Walk forward and repeat. Can you pick up three beanbags along the bench as you go? It helps to look straight ahead all the time.

5. Walk in a crouch position, turn around, and walk backwards. Jump off using your hands.

6. Walk forward. At about halfway, balance on one foot, walk forward, stop, balance on the other foot, and walk to the end. Jump off with a light landing.

7. Create your own way of walking on the balance bench.

PG-34 BENCH TRAVELS

EQUIPMENT: Balance benches; mats

ORGANIZATION:

- Form groups of four to six players. If possible, arrange two benches alongside each other for each group. Use the wide surface of the bench only.

DESCRIPTION OF ACTIVITY:

1. Lie on your tummy along the bench. Show me how you can pull yourself along the bench. Lie on your back along the bench. Can you push yourself along using your hands and feet? using your feet only?

2. Move along the bench on body part points: hands and feet; seat and feet; knees; etc. Let a different part lead: head, seat, feet, hand, elbow.

3. Start in a stretched-out position. Can you move along the bench being stretched, then curled, then stretched . . . right to the end?

4. Travel along the bench by twisting and turning to the end; first on your tummy, then on your side, on your back. Show me another way of travelling along the bench.

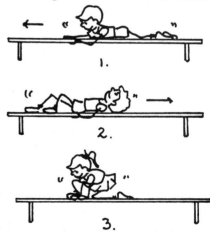

PG–35 BENCH TRAVEL STUNTS

FOCUS: Body control; strength

EQUIPMENT: Balance benches; mats

ORGANIZATION:

- These activities should be performed on the wide surface of the bench. Form groups of four to six players. Arrange the benches alongside each other, with mats at both ends and sides. Review the procedure for anchoring the benches, and appoint anchors for each bench. As soon as one player reaches halfway on the bench, the next player may begin. Remind the players to take turns at being a performer and an anchor.

DESCRIPTION OF ACTIVITY:

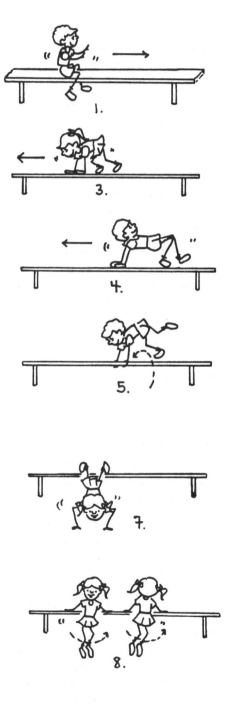

1. *Sit Walk:* Straddle-sit on the bench at one end with your feet touching the floor. Face the opposite end of the bench. Can you move along the bench from one end to the other without using your hands? Now try this again, but travel backwards.

2. *Duck Walk:* In squatting position, "waddle" your way to the end of the bench. Can you sound like a duck as you move?

3. *Cat Walk:* In all-fours position, walk like "a cat on a fence" to the other end.

4. *Crab Walk:* While in the back-support position with hands on the floor, feet on the bench and tummy facing up, Crab Walk to the end of the bench.

5. *Bunny Hop:* Grip both sides of the bench. Push off with one foot, jump over the bench, with the opposite foot landing first, and then the other. Move your hands forward and hop back over the bench to the other side. Continue to the end. Can you straighten your legs out as you jump? How high can you get your legs?

6. *Over and Under:* Lie on your tummy along the bench. Roll sideways to alternately go underneath and up the other side without touching the floor, or the underneath part of the bench.

7. *Pencil Walk:* Place your hands on the bench and your feet on the floor. Keep you body stiff and straight. Move sideways along the bench, taking your weight on your hands and feet.

   — Repeat, but this time travel with your hands on the floor and your feet on the bench.

8. *The Windmill:* Start with both hands on the bench and both feet on the floor in the front support position. Roll over and over along the bench, taking the weight on your hands and feet as you turn over and over to the end of the bench. It helps to keep your body and elbows straight.

9. Invent a Bench Walk Stunt of your own!

FOCUS: Travelling; body control; partnerwork

EQUIPMENT: Balance benches;
mats;
one wand per bench group;
two balls per bench group

ORGANIZATION:

- Place balance benches around play area with wide surface up and position mats around benches. Have players find a partner of equal size and group with two other pairs at a bench. One pair straddle-sits the bench to anchor it while the other pairs practice. Have pairs change roles frequently. These activities may also be practiced using the Station Method.

DESCRIPTION OF ACTIVITY:

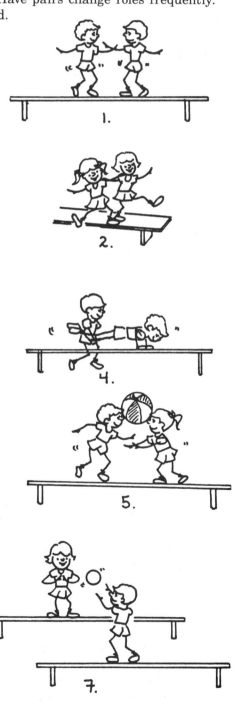

1. **Pass Your Partner:** Partners, start at opposite ends of the bench and walk toward each other, passing at the wide middle support. You may hold each other as you pass.
   — Repeat with hands on head or behind back, without falling off.

2. **Partner Counterbalance:** Partners, stand at one end of the bench on opposite sides, facing same direction. Rest foot on bench beside partner's foot, join inside wrists, and raise opposite arm to side. Rise up to balance each other on the bench. How long can you hold the balance? How far can you walk while holding the balance?

3. **Run and Jump:** One partner, stand at the end of the bench. Run forward to other end; then jump over a rope or wand to land softly on mat with knees bent. Other partner, hold rope or wand lightly so it can easily be knocked from your hands if partner bumps it.

4. **Wheelbarrow:** Take turns walking your partner in "wheelbarrow" position along the bench to the other end to do a Forward Roll off onto the mat. Change places and repeat.

5. **Ball Balance:** Squat facing partner, with arms raised sideways. Try to hold a ball between you without using hands (head-to-head, side-to-side, stomach-to-stomach, and so on). Can you move up and down, or along the bench while holding the ball in balance?

6. **Line Passing:** Form groups of five or six players. Each group, walk along the bench in single-file formation and, at the same time, pass the ball overhead to the next player behind. Each player, when you reach the end, step off, run to the end of the file, get back on the bench, and continue passing the ball. Can you do this without falling off?

7. **Pass the Ball** (Join another group and place benches opposite each other, about two meters [six feet] apart to start.) Get a ball to share and stand on opposite benches facing each other. Pass the ball back and forth without losing balance. Repeat, moving sideways along the bench.

8. **Partner-Supported Walk** (Turn benches narrow side up, and position about one meter [three feet] apart.) Stand on opposite benches facing each other. Join both hands and walk sideways to end of bench without losing balance.

9. Invent a partner Balance Bench Stunt and teach it to the other pairs in your group.

PG-37 BENCH WALK TASKS WITH SMALL EQUIPMENT

FOCUS: Travelling; equipment manipulation; body control

EQUIPMENT: Balance benches and mats; two beanbags, two deckrings, two hoops and two balls per group

ORGANIZATION:

- Form groups of four to six players. Arrange the benches with mats at both ends and sides. Appoint anchors for each bench. Try all these activities first on the wide surface and then on the narrow beam. If necessary, have the spotter walk alongside the performer with arm raised and palm up to offer support.

DESCRIPTION OF ACTIVITY:

1. Walk forward along the bench, stepping through the hoop. Continue to end of bench. Walk backwards, stepping through the hoop.
2. Walk forward along the bench, tossing and catching a beanbag as you go. Try turning and tossing as you go. Can you walk backwards and still catch the beanbag? Try this with a deckring; with a ball. Repeat this task using other locomotor movements: skipping, galloping, side-stepping, running.
3. Walk forward, balancing a beanbag on your head. Walk backwards, balancing the beanbag on a different body part: shoulder, elbow, back.
4. Walk along the bench and bounce a ball on one side as you go. Can you alternate sides? Walk backwards and repeat this task. Now walk forward, bouncing a ball along the bench. Repeat task, using other locomotor movements.
5. Pass the ball to a partner, who is standing on the floor, as you move along the bench.

PG-38 BENCH DISMOUNTS

FOCUS: Dismounting/landing technique; springing technique; landing

EQUIPMENT: Balance benches; mats

ORGANIZATION:

- Place balance benches around play area and position mats around them.

DESCRIPTION OF ACTIVITY:

1. Working from either end of the bench, perform these dismounts:
   - Standing on both feet, jump off the bench and land on the mat. Do a backwards jump to land on the mat.
   - Jump as high as you can before landing.
   - Jump for distance. Go as far as you can.
   - Jump a quarter-turn and land; half-turn jump and land; full-turn.
   - Jump making a big shape; a pointed shape; a small shape.
2. Do a "Star Jump" from one end of the bench. Remember to bend at the hips, knees, and ankles when landing. Be in control on your landing; hold your balance for three seconds; then do a forward roll.
3. *Sequences:* Try the following:
   - Walk backwards along the bench to halfway; then walk sideways, and jump off the end in a big shape.
   - Skip forward along the bench, jump off backward landing on both feet, and roll backwards into a balance.
   - Gallop forward with one foot leading; do a pivot-turn at the opposite end; then gallop back with the other foot leading; dismount with a Heel Slap.
   - Crab Walk along bench to middle, sit and spin around twice, Cat Walk to end, push-off with hands to dismount facing the bench.
   - Now invent your own "travel and dismount" sequence!

PG–39 INTRODUCTION TO THE BALANCE BEAM_____

FOCUS: Teaching and safety guidelines

EQUIPMENT: Balance beam; masking tape; benches; beanbags; mats; utility balls; seatboard or low box;

ORGANIZATION:

- With masking tape, mark six practice lines on floor 30 centimeters (12 inches) apart. Arrange the balance beams, upturned benches, and practice line area around the play area. Choose six children to set up the equipment and demonstrate safety guidelines. Choose two spotters and have one spotter stand on each side of the beam. Spotters should change roles with performers every few minutes.
- Teach in three steps: individual beam movements; new movements combined with those already learned; and new movements combined with a mount or dismount.

DESCRIPTION OF ACTIVITY:

1. ***Lifting and Carrying the Beam:*** Five children carry the beam as you would a bench: two stand at each end and three stand at the sides; all face the same direction. Bend knees keeping back straight, lift together, and then walk in step. Bend knees again as you lower beam to floor.

2. ***Equipment Set-up:*** Use a beatboard or low box to mount the balance beam. Set it up at one side in middle of balance beam. Place mats on either side, under, and at ends of beam.

   — Practice beams (2 × 4-inch lumber studs) may be laid directly on the floor for some activities and anchored at each end. They may be covered with carpet for a softer surface.

3. ***Progressions:*** Always work on the beam in bare feet. First, practice all movements on lines taped to floor; then practice on the 2 × 4 practice beams. Next, practice on the beam itself.

4. ***Balance Beam Exploration*** (Form groups of four to six, each group with a balance beam or bench turned upside down and safety mats placed on sides and ends. Children take turns at performing and spotting.)

   — Walk forward along the beam. Keep your head up. Hold your arms in different positions as you move slowly: behind your back; one up, one down; both up; arms held sideways. Which way gives you the best balance?

   — Walk forward slowly along the beam to the middle. Turn on the balls of your feet and walk back. Keep your head up. Your partner may spot for you as you walk.

   — Shuffle-step sideways along the beam, balancing on the balls of the feet. Shuffle one foot up to the other. Look ahead as you go.

   — Show me how you can balance on the beam in the "push-up" position, on the toes and hands. Look up as you hold the balance. Now walk forward on all fours. Move smoothly.

   — Walk backwards while balancing a beanbag on the back of each hand. Can you turn around in the middle without dropping the beanbag?

   — Walk forward slowly along the beam, carrying a ball out and away from your body. Try this walking backwards, sideways.

   — Find another way to move or balance on the beam.

PG-40 BALANCE BEAM MOUNTS

FOCUS: Mounting technique; balancing

EQUIPMENT: Balance beams; benches; mats; beatboard

ORGANIZATION:

- Have players set up balance beam and beatboard (or benches upturned), placing mats on either side, under, and at ends of beam. Designate two spotters to stand one on each side of beam, facing the performer.

DESCRIPTION OF ACTIVITY:

1. **Front-Support Mount:** Stand at side of beam and place hands on beam shoulder-width apart. Spring up to the front-support position, keeping arms straight and thighs pressed against beam. Hold head high, arch back, and point toes. Repeat, taking two or three short running steps.

2. **Straddle Seat Mount:** Spring to Front Support Mount. Swing left leg over the beam with toe pointed; turn your body so that you sit astride (straddle) the beam. Place hands behind body and sit tall with head up and toes pointed.

3. **Knee Mount:** Spring to a Front Support Mount. Lift one knee to kneel on beam and support weight on hands and knee. Raise other leg behind, hold head high to arch back, and point toes.

4. **Squat Mount:** Stand to face side of beam and place both hands on it, shoulder-width apart. Spring up, draw knees to chest, and place toes on the beam between hands. Squat on beam and hold head high.

PG-41 BALANCE BEAM DISMOUNTS

FOCUS: Springing; landing and balancing

EQUIPMENT: See activity PG-40.

ORGANIZATION:

- Dismounts include springs from hands and feet, rolls, and twists. All dismounts should be executed without wavering or overbalancing on the landing. Have each group set up their balance beam, placing mats on either side, under, and at each end of beam. Use extra mats in the landing area. Have a group working at both ends of beam. One spotter stands at each end of the beam and faces the performer.

DESCRIPTION OF ACTIVITY:

1. **Forward Jump Dismount:** Stand with knees and hips slightly bent. Jump and stretch forward and upward with back arched. Swing the arms upward and out, keeping the legs together and extended. Land smoothly with feet together, looking straight ahead.

2. **Backwards Jump Dismount:** Similar to the Forward Jump Dismount, but with your back to the end of the beam. Look straight ahead. Do not try to see where you will land.

3. **Side Dismount:** Similar to the Forward Jump Dismount, except that it is done to the side of the beam.

4. **Half-Pirouette Dismount:** Similar to the Forward Jump Dismount. While in mid-air, half-turn left to land on mat, facing the end of the beam with the left hand on the end of the beam. Raise the right hand overhead, and hold balance.

5. **Front Dismount:** From the push-up position on the beam, on hands and toes, kick one leg upward and to one side, and at the same time swing the other leg up to meet it in the air. Drop to the mat and land with both feet together and one hand on the beam.

PG–42 BALANCE BEAM BALANCES

FOCUS: Balancing on apparatus

EQUIPMENT: Balance beam or balance bench;
mats;
two beanbags per group

ORGANIZATION:

• These activities may be performed on the balance beam, the narrow side of the balance bench, or the climbing frame beam. Place mats at the sides and ends of the beam. Form groups of four to six and have members take turns at being a performer and a spotter. Spotters, when necessary, walk alongside the performer with extended hand under that of the performer.

DESCRIPTION OF ACTIVITY:

1. *Pick Up:* Space two beanbags along the bench. Walk to the first, kneel on one knee, pick up the beanbag, place it behind you, rise and do the same with the second one. Walk to the end. Keep your head up.

2. *Kneel and Point:* Walk to middle; kneel on one knee. Raise the arms sideways; raise the other leg straight out in front to place heel on the beam, with toes pointed. Hold balance five seconds; stand, and walk to end of beam.

3. *Dips:* Walk along the beam slowly. Sweep the foot of each free leg below the beam as you walk forward. Bend the knee of the standing leg, but straighten the knee of the free leg and point toes as you "dip."

4. *Squat Balance:* Walk forward with Dips to the middle. Hold arms sideways, squat on your toes, and raise your arms sideways. Look straight ahead while holding this balance for five seconds. Then walk to the other end.

5. *Kneeling Balance:* Walk to the middle, stop, balance on one foot and one knee. Raise arms sideways, look straight ahead, and hold balance. Can you raise your rear toes off the beam and still hold the balance? Kneel on the other knee and repeat.

PG–43 BALANCE BEAM WALKS

FOCUS: Balancing; travelling; sequence-making

EQUIPMENT: Balance beam;
mats

ORGANIZATION:

• Remind performers to hold arms out sideways for balance and to look ahead at their own height as they move along beam. Advise them that if they look down, they will fall down.

DESCRIPTION OF ACTIVITY:

1. *Cross-Over Step:* Stand sideways on beam. Now move sideways: step left foot left; then step right foot across in front of supporting left leg. Repeat.
   — *Cross-Behind Step:* Step left foot left; step right foot behind supporting left leg to move sideways. Repeat.

2. *Alternating-Cross Step:* Stand sideways on beam. Step left foot left, step right foot in front of supporting left leg, step left foot left, and step right foot behind supporting left leg. Repeat.

3. *Toe-Walking Step:* Stand on your toes and walk along the beam. Walk backwards on your toes. Can you hop instead of step? Hop to middle of beam, turn on ball of foot, and hop back to end on other foot.

4. *Dip Step:* Stand at end of beam. Bend knee of supporting leg and, with each step, swing other leg forward so that the foot is just below the beam. Keep the leg straight and toe pointed. Move arms gracefully as you step forward.

PG-44 BALANCE BEAM TURNS

FOCUS: Balancing on apparatus; turning

EQUIPMENT: Balance beam or balance benches; mats

ORGANIZATION:

- Have each group set up balance beam and place mats on either side, under, and at end of beam. One spotter stands at each end of the beam and faces performer. Two children could perform on the beam at the same time. Suggest that performers use a different mount and dismount each time.

DESCRIPTION OF ACTIVITY:

1. **Quarter-Turn:** Stand on toes of right foot. Quickly turn to face right by throwing left arm across your body toward your right arm. Repeat, turning to face left by throwing right arm toward left.

2. **Half-Turn:** Rise on toes of right foot and quickly turn right to face opposite direction. Repeat turn to left.

3. **Full-Turn:** Rise on toes and quickly turn right all the way around to face forward again. Repeat turn to left.

4. **Pivot-Turn:** Stand with one foot ahead of the other. Rise on balls of feet and, without lifting feet from beam, turn to face opposite direction; then lower heels to beam again.

 — **Squat-Turn:** Performer squats and repeats Pivot-Turn.

5. **Sequence-Making:** Create a sequence that combines a balance beam walk with a balance and with a turn. Add a mount and a dismount to your routine.

PG-45 BALANCE BEAM ROUTINES

FOCUS: Routine-building; groupwork

EQUIPMENT: Chart paper and marking pens; paper and pen per group; balance beam or benches; mats

ORGANIZATION:

- Print the routine below on chart paper and post it so that players can see it while on the beam. Suggest that spotters call out each step for performers. Have players set up the beam and mats. Form groups of three players: one player is the performer; the other two are the spotters and stand on either side of the beam, facing the performer. Have players change roles every few minutes.

DESCRIPTION OF ACTIVITY:

1. **Routine:**
 — Run to beam and Squat-mount in the middle of the beam.
 — Pivot-turn right and stand with right foot in front of left, right arm overhead, and left arm sideways. Rise on balls of feet. Lower heels and lower right arm to side at the same time.
 — Run forward four steps: Left, right, left, right.
 — Dip on left side; dip on right side. Pivot-turn to face opposite direction.
 — Squat on beam; then turn to face opposite end of beam again. Stand and walk to end of beam.
 — Front Dismount.

2. **Routine-Building:** Each group, create your own routine with a mount and dismount and add movements, balances, and stunts of your own or ones that you have learned. Record your routine on paper. Each group member should contribute to creating your routine.

PG-46 EXPLORING THE CLIMBING APPARATUS_____

FOCUS: Grips; travelling; hanging

EQUIPMENT: Climbing frame;
horizontal or parallel bars;
several folding mats

ORGANIZATION:

- Divide the class into groups of four or five (ideally) and have groups sit on the floor in lines, each group facing its climbing frame "station" (or mini-frame). Review the parts of the frame. Train children in the technique of moving and erecting the frame and attachments, and discuss the safety procedures involved. Children should be in bare feet or gym shoes, and pockets should be empty. Do not permit them to storm the frame, and caution them not to interfere with others. Stand so that you can see all groups at the same time. Skill is impaired by fatigue—watch for the signs. Permit groups to work at stations for a *maximum* of four minutes. Once set up, check the frame, making sure it is safe and secure at the top and bottom. Use mats under the frame. Explain some of the activities that may be done on the frame: climbing, hanging, swinging, sliding, crawling, pulling, balancing, twisting, turning, jumping, and landing. Demonstrate the two safety grips: Over Grip and Under Grip. Teach these grips first.

DESCRIPTION OF ACTIVITY:

1. **The Over Grip:** When hanging from the bar, place the thumb underneath and the fingers on top. You should be able to see your knuckles.

   — **The Under Grip:** Grasp the bar with fingers and thumb pointing toward you.

   — Move to the bar. Practice hanging using either grip.

   — Practice swinging using the Over Grip.

   — Try pulling yourself upward using either grip.

OVER GRIP   1.   UNDER GRIP

2. Now explore your station, moving in different directions: climb, crawl through or over, hang, pull.

3. Can you travel up one side and down the other? Climb in and out of the rungs as you travel upward; climb downward the same way. Can you leave the apparatus with your hands touching the mats first?

4. Climb diagonally up the frame and come straight down, jump off with a safe landing. As you climb, move only one body part at a time: a hand, then the other hand; a foot, then the other foot; or a hand, then a foot. As you climb, keep three out of the four body parts in contact with the frame.

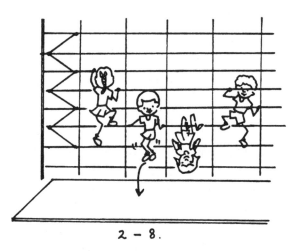

2 – 8.

5. How many different ways can you hang from the apparatus? Change smoothly from one hanging position to another.

6. Can you stand on your hands on the floor with your legs resting on the frame? Now try walking your feet up the rungs as far as you can go!

7. **Bridges:** Stand with your back to the frame, heels about 45 centimeters (18 inches) away. Bend backwards to grasp a bar behind your head. Can you go hand-under-hand down the bars until you touch the floor? Can you come back up the same way? Help each other.

8. Climb up and find a spot. Hang from both hands facing the bars. Can you slowly lift both feet up, hook knees over a rung, and hang with hands?

FOCUS: Climbing; hanging; swinging

EQUIPMENT: Climbing frame; several mats

ORGANIZATION:

• Divide the class into groups of four or five children and assign two groups to work at the climbing frame, one group on each side. Have other groups involved in other "stationwork," and rotate groups every four or five minutes so that all stations are visited.

DESCRIPTION OF ACTIVITY:

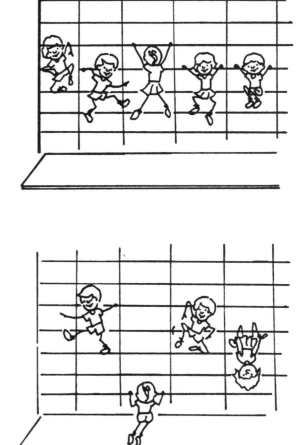

1. Travel horizontally across the frame, twisting in and out as you go.

2. Climb up, following a zig-zag path. Come down following a curved path. Climb up in a diagonal pathway from one corner to the opposite. Climb straight down, and then repeat travelling from that corner to the diagonal opposite corner.

3. Can you make a wide shape, and then move to a new space and make a narrow shape? Continue making a curled shape; a twisted shape.

4. Can you travel in a square pattern as you move up, across, down, and across again? Travel in a triangular pattern; rectangular.

5. Climb up; find a place to hang. Swing your legs sideways with both legs together. Show me how you can safely land on the mat, bending at the knees.

6. Climb as high as you can using one leg only. Can you climb with both legs stiff?

7. Find a spot on the frame. Raise as many body parts as you can above your head.

8. Stand with your back to the bars. Can you grasp a bar so that your feet don't touch the floor? Hang and raise your knees up to touch your chest, and then lower. Repeat.

9. With a partner, move over, around, and under each other.

10. **Star Hang:** Climb up, hold on with one hand and one foot. Raise the other arm and leg out sideways. Make a star by hanging from your hands only. This may be done by facing the bars or sideways to the bars.

11. **Push-Ups:** Place your hands on a bar and lean at about 45 degrees to the floor. How many times can you touch your head to the bar?

12. **Circle the Bar:** Climb to find a spot. Circle your body completely around the bar. Move to another spot and repeat. Can you circle the bar backwards?

13. **Corkscrew:** Twist your way up the frame, in and out, moving sideways through the frame. Return the same way.

14. Invent your own way of hanging or swinging on the frame; of travelling. Put these movements together in a sequence.

FOCUS: Safety guidelines; climbing and hanging

EQUIPMENT: Climbing ropes; safety mats

ORGANIZATION:

• Review how to arrange the ropes and the mats underneath, ready for activity. Demonstrate and provide practice time for this. Discuss the safety guidelines, and teach the correct procedures for climbing and descending the rope. Number the children from one to (number of climbing ropes). Number each of the ropes; then have children sit in a line facing their climbing rope at a safe distance away.

DESCRIPTION OF ACTIVITY:

1. **Safety Guidelines:**
   — Use the ropes only when told to do so by your teacher.
   — Stand well away from the ropes when others are using them, unless spotting.
   — Do not tie knots in the ropes.
   — Do not climb a swinging rope.
   — Climb, hand-over-hand going up and hand-under-hand coming down. Do not slide down the rope as this causes rope burns.
   — Do not interfere with others who are using the ropes.
   — When climbing, look up and hold tight.
   — Always place mats under the climbing ropes when in use.
   — Do not leave a rope swinging after a dismount; stop it from swinging first!

2. **Sitting Pull-Up:** Sit and hold rope high. Brace feet against mat. Raise yourself hand-over-hand, with body straight, to the standing position. Lower yourself and repeat.

3. **Standing Pull-Up:** Stand and hold rope high. Without moving feet, lower yourself hand-under-hand until you are lying on the mat. Keeping your body stiff, can you raise yourself slowly back up? Remember to raise yourself hand-over-hand!

4. **Chin the Rope:** Lie on the mat under the rope. Reach up; grasp the rope as high as you can. Move feet around in a big circle; then pull up so that your chin touches your hands. Try this with only one arm pulling; use the other arm to push off the mat.

5. **The Snail:** Again lie on the mat under the rope. Grasp the rope a little lower; curl your knees up to your chest. Continue to curl so that the feet touch the mat behind your head. Uncurl and start again. Can you curl and touch by bringing your feet over on the same side of the rope?

6. **The Clutch:** Stand near your rope. Jump upward, grasping your rope as high as you can. Grip the rope with your feet and hang for ten seconds. (Everyone in your group can count with you!)

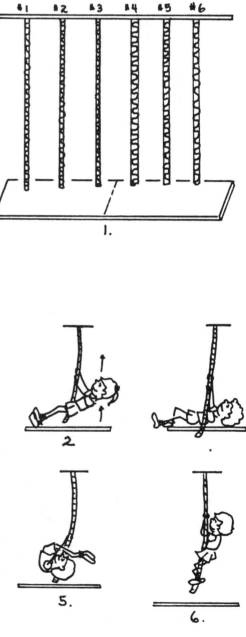

PG–49 CLIMBING AND HANGING TASKS

FOCUS: Climbing techniques; hanging

EQUIPMENT: Climbing ropes; safety mats

ORGANIZATION:

- Three climbing methods are introduced: Stirrup, Foot-Leg Lock, and Scissors methods. Have different children demonstrate the techniques. Climbers may then choose the method that they find the most comfortable to climb and descend the rope.

DESCRIPTION OF ACTIVITY:

1. *Climbing Methods:*
   — *Stirrup:* Rope should hang outside left leg, under left foot, and over top of right foot. Stand on rope with left foot to lock feet in position.
   — *Foot-Leg Lock:* Rope should hang in front of body and between legs. Hook right leg around rope so that it passes over top of right foot. Stand on rope with left foot to lock rope in position.
   — *Scissors:* Rope should hang inside right knee and outside right foot. Cross left foot behind right foot. Press rope between inside of left foot and outside of right foot to lock it in position.

2. *The Climber:* Pull up with hand-over-hand, allowing the rope to slide through your feet and knees. Lock feet on the rope after each pull, straighten legs, and reach hands up for another pull. Practice locking feet after each pull.
   — To descend, lock feet in position, move hands down rope hand-under-hand. Lock feet into new position and lower hands again. Do not slide down the rope. Practice three hand-over-hands; four hand-over-hands; five hand-over-hands; etc.

3. *The Clock:* Sit on the mat. Grasp the rope as high up as possible. Pull up to raise your seat off the mat. Using tiny steps, shuffle your feet around to the 9 o'clock position; 3 o'clock; 12 o'clock; 6 o'clock.

4. *Rope Dancer:* Sit, holding the rope as high as possible. Pull up so that your seat is off the mat. Hanging on to the rope kick your legs, one at a time, out in front.

5. *Clappers:* Reach up to hang on the rope. Can you raise your legs off the mat, lift them straight out in front, and clap your feet together?

6. *Leg Lifts:* Stand and grasp the rope up high, push off to lift your knees up to your chest and hold them there. Can you grip the rope with your toes from this position?

7. *L-Sit:* Stand, hold rope high, and raise legs parallel to the floor. Can you hold this sitting position for three seconds?

8. Invent a climbing or hanging stunt of your own!

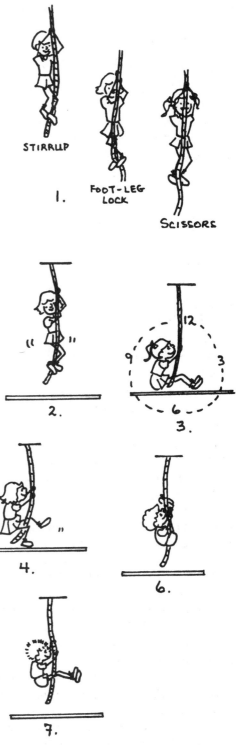

STIRRUP

FOOT-LEG LOCK

SCISSORS

1.

2.

3.

4.

6.

7.

FOCUS: Hanging; swinging; and turning

EQUIPMENT: Climbing ropes; safety mats; four benches; one hoop per group; box horses or tables; beanbags

ORGANIZATION:

• Place mats under ropes. Divide the class into equal groups based on the number of available ropes. Assign each group to a climbing rope and a mat-covered bench. Teach the basic swing first from the floor level; then have children swing from a bench, and then a box horse.

DESCRIPTION OF ACTIVITY:

1. ***Basic Swing:*** Grasp the rope up high and push back to gather speed. Hang on to the rope, grip with your feet, and swing back and forth four times across the mat. Gently let go of the rope as you land on the mat, bending at the knees, and stop the rope from swinging. (If needed, give the performer a gentle push to get a swinging action.)

2. ***Bench Swing*** (Position benches about one meter [three feet] behind the climbing ropes as shown.) Stand on the bench, grasp the rope high, get a firm grip with your hands and feet, and swing out across the mats and back to land on the bench. Can you swing back and forth four times and then land on the mat? Remember to stop the swinging rope!

3. ***Hoop Landing*** (Place a hoop about one meter [three feet] in front of the rope and safety mat.) Swing from the bench, across the mat, and land in a hoop. Can you swing from the hoop back to the bench?

   — Now hold a beanbag between your feet; swing and drop the beanbag in the hoop; then return to land on the bench.

   — Now swing toward the hoop, try to grab the beanbag from the hoop with your feet, and then swing back to your bench to place the beanbag on it.

4. ***Sitting-Swing Challenge:*** Swing from the bench. Hang freely in the sitting position. Do not knot the rope.

5. ***L-Swing Challenge:*** Hold the legs in the "L" position as you swing.

6. ***The Whip Kick*** (Position the box horse about one meter [three feet] behind climbing rope.) Push back to gather speed at take-off. On the forward swing, whip the legs forward and upward to increase speed. Land softly on the box. Repeat, swinging back and forth three times, whip-kicking each time.

7. ***Swing and Turn:*** Swing out from the box, do a half-turn at the end of the forward swing, and return to stand on the box.

   — Do a full-turn at the end of the forward swing.

   — Return to sit on the box.

   — Can you do all these using different leg positions?

8. ***Circle Swing:*** Stand on the box. Push out sideways at take-off to swing in a circle to return to the box.

BASIC SWING 1.

BENCH SWING 2.

3. HOOP LANDING

4.

5.

6.

PG–51 SWINGING GAMES

FOCUS: Hanging; swinging; and turning

EQUIPMENT: Climbing ropes and mats; ten hoops; six beanbags per group; three bowling pins (bleach bottles) per group; one small utility ball per group; two box horses or tables; one bucket

ORGANIZATION:

- Children work in groups of three to five as they try these fun, challenging climbing rope games. For large groups, set up three or four rope stations as well as three or four other gymnastic stations, and have groups rotate every four to five minutes.

DESCRIPTION OF ACTIVITY:

1. *Stepping Stones* (Four hoops are positioned in a wide circle around rope station.) Stand in one hoop and hold rope high. Swing from your hoop to land in each of the other three hoops and back again. Tuck knees to chest as you swing. Land only in the hoops.

   — How many times can you go around the four hoops without stopping?

   — Spread the hoops farther apart and repeat.

2. *Beanbag Pick-Up* (Place five hoops around the rope area and place a beanbag in each of four hoops.) Stand in the vacant hoop, then swing out to pick up a beanbag from each hoop with your feet, in turn, and return it to your starting hoop. Repeat until all four beanbags are in your hoop.

3. *Rope Bowling* (Place three bowling pins about 3 meters [ten feet] away from the rope and give each group a ball.) Hold the rope high, place the ball between your feet, and swing forward toward the pins. At the end of forward swing, release ball and try to bowl over the pins.

4. *Tarzan Swing:* Place a small ball between your ankles, swing across the mat, and then release the ball so that it drops into a bucket. Return to the box horse.

5. Invent a "swinging game" of your own in your group. Make sure your game is a safe one!

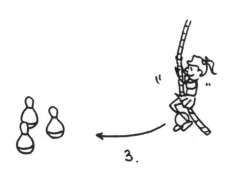

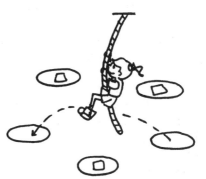

FOCUS: Hanging and swinging

EQUIPMENT: Climbing ropes; safety mats

ORGANIZATION:

• For eight climbing ropes, divide the class into four equal groups. Assign each group two climbing ropes and have each group place a mat directly under the climbing rope. Each performer should have a spotter positioned on each side. To begin, each group sits in a line behind the climbing ropes.

DESCRIPTION OF ACTIVITY:

1. How many different ways can you hang from the two ropes?

2. What shapes can you make as you hang from the ropes?

3. Can you climb from one rope to the other, and then to the floor?

4. Can you hang on to the two ropes and let your feet "run in the air"?

5. *The Twister:* Twist yourself into different positions while hanging on to the two ropes.

6. *Hula:* Stand, jump up to grasp the ropes as high as you can. Pull up so that your arms are bent. Can you swing your hips around in a circle to do the "Hula"? Swing your hips the other way.

7. *Still Rope Swing:* Stand holding both ropes as high as you can so that your feet do not touch the mat. Pull up so that your arms are bent and your legs straight. Can you swing your legs forward and backwards without swinging the ropes?

8. *The Grasshopper:* Stand; jump up to grasp the ropes as high as you can. Spring off your feet; place one foot forward and the other foot back. Continue to alternate feet in this way.

9. *L-Sit Hang:* Grasp the ropes as high as you can. Can you raise your legs in the "L" position as you hang?

10. *Inverted Hang:* Grasp the ropes as high as you can, push off, and swing yourself upside down, hooking your feet around the rope. Can you hold this inverted position for five seconds?

11. Invent your own "Two-Rope Hanging Stunt"!

12. Invent a "Two-Rope Hanging Game"!

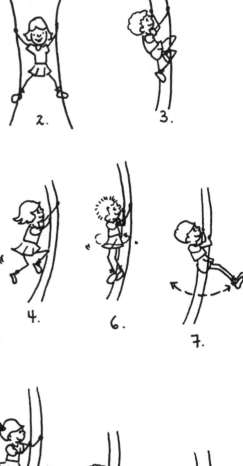

PG-53 INTRODUCTION TO THE BOX HORSE_____

FOCUS: Springing and landing
from a height

EQUIPMENT: Box horses;
benches;
tables;
mats;
beanbag;
hoop;
crash pad;
climbing rope

ORGANIZATION:

• Set up five different stations using box horses, benches, tables, crash pad, and climbing rope. Place mats under all landing areas. Make sure apparatus is well spaced apart and stable: Anchor the benches by having a player sit on each end; prevent table from moving by having a player on each side holding it securely. Rotate groups through the stations every four minutes. Emphasize safe landings: Bend at the hips, knees, and ankles, and look straight ahead while dismounting. Appoint three spotters: one on either side, and one on the mat facing the performer.

DESCRIPTION OF ACTIVITY:

Station 1: Low box horse and landing mat.
Place your hands flat on the top of the box and spring onto it with a two-foot jump. Get your balance and control; then spring off the box high into the air with arms raised upward to a safe landing, and then forward roll.

Station 2: Bench and landing mat.
Explore springing off the bench, getting as much height as you can. Land correctly and safely; then do a roll: forward roll, log roll, shoulder roll.
— Do a Forward Roll from the bench.

Station 3: Table and landing mat. Ensure that table is secure.
Explore springing off the table and doing a stunt while in the air: Click your heels together; slap your heels behind you; touch your toes; hug your knees. Remember to land correctly, bending at the knees.

Station 4: Box horse and crash pad.
Explore springing off the box horse, making a wide shape in the air, landing and rolling. Now try making a narrow shape; a twisted shape. Can you spring off and do a half-turn in the air? do a full-turn?

Station 5: Box horse, climbing rope, safety mat.
Explore different ways of swinging out from the box horse and swinging back to land on box horse. Can you hold a beanbag between your ankles, swing out from the box horse, drop the beanbag into a hoop in the center of the safety mat, and then return back to the box horse?

STATION I

STATION 2

STATION 3

STATION 4

FOCUS: Grip technique; hanging

EQUIPMENT: Horizontal bar or even or uneven parallel bars; several mats

ORGANIZATION:

• Explain and demonstrate the procedure for carrying, setting up, and using the bars. Divide the class into groups of four or five. Set up as many hanging stations as there is equipment available and incorporate these stations with other gymnastic stations. Rotate groups every four to five minutes. For each performer, there should be two spotters who stand on either side of the performer. Explain and have children demonstrate the following five basic grips. When moving backwards, use the Over Grip; when moving forward, use the Under Grip. Have the children use a low bar at first to gain confidence. Mats should always be used under the horizontal bars. Remind children to always use a safe landing: bending at knees, hips, and ankles to absorb the shock.

DESCRIPTION OF ACTIVITY:

1. *Over Grip:* When hanging from the bar, place the thumb underneath and the fingers on top. You should be able to see your knuckles.

2. *Under Grip:* Grasp the bar with fingers and thumb pointing toward you.

3. *Mixed Grip:* This is a combination grip. One hand holds the bar with the Over Grip; the other with the Under Grip.

4. *Cross Grip:* Hold the bar with both hands using the Over Grip, but the arms are crossed.

5. *Eagle Grip:* Hang with the arms spread wide and your back to the bar. Your knuckles should be on top of the bar and your thumbs under.

6. *Practice:* Stand by your bar. When I call out the names of the five Grips, I want you to show your group how to do them. They will help you if you have problems.

PG–55 HORIZONTAL BAR—HANGS

DESCRIPTION OF ACTIVITY:

1. Stand facing the bar. Jump forward to hang on the bar. Use the Over Grip; use the Under Grip. Swing back and forth each time.

2. *Long Hang or Pencil Hang:* Jump up to grasp the bar with the Over Grip. Hang as straight as a pencil and look ahead. Dismount by dropping straight down to the floor to a safe landing. Finish with arms overhead.
   — Hold your hang for ten seconds.

3. *Inverted Hang in the Tucked Position:* Start in Long Hang position. Draw knees up to chest as you lean backwards and hold this position.
   — Spotters, hold the upper arm and give support under the shoulder with the other hand.

4. *Inverted Hang in the Piked Position:* Start in Long Hang position. Draw legs up straight so that they finish parallel to the floor.
   — Can you get your legs close to your face and still hold them straight with toes pointed?

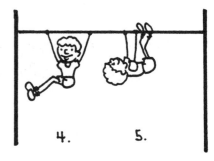

5. Invent your own hanging position on the bars.

PG–56 HORIZONTAL BAR—SWINGS AND INVERTED HANGS

FOCUS: Swinging; inverted hanging; dismounting

EQUIPMENT: Horizontal bar or even or uneven parallel bars; safety mats

ORGANIZATION:

- Swings, dismount, and inverted hangs are introduced. Review the Safety Grips: the Over Grip and the Under Grip (activity PG–54). Review the procedure for carrying, setting up, and using the bars. Use children to demonstrate the following tasks. Have spotters stand on either side and support the arm and under the shoulder or back. Insist that all performers be spotted during inverted hangs.

DESCRIPTION OF ACTIVITY:

1. **Swing and Arch:** Grasp the bar with the Over Grip while your feet are still on the floor. Push off with one foot as you throw the other forward and upward. Swing under the bar and at the same time pull in with the arms and throw your head back. Stretch the whole body to a slightly arched position with tummy forward. Dismount by releasing the bar at the height of the forward swing to a safe landing.

2. **Dismounts:** Swing, gradually come to a still hang, release the bar, and drop gently to a safe landing on the mat.
   — Swing, bend slightly at the hips, and release the grasp at the height of the backswing. Drop straight down onto both feet to a safe landing.

3. Jump up to a Long Hang. Swing forward and backwards five times under control.
   — Dismount at the height of the backswing.
   — Dismount at the height of the frontswing.

4. **Ankles to the Bar:** Hang by the Over Grip. Kick your feet up by bringing your knees up to your chest and tilting your head back. Touch the bar with your ankles. Curl down to the mat.

5. **Knee Hang:** Hang by the Over Grip. Bring the feet up through the hands; hook the knees over the bar. Hang by the knees without using the hands. Return to hold the bar, and then dismount.
   — Spotters, support performers as they hang upside down.

6. **Skin the Cat:** Hang from the bar using the Over Grip. Kick your feet up by bringing your knees to your chest. Bring your feet between your arms. Slowly lower your feet as far as possible. Release the bar and drop to the floor. Can you return to your starting position, then dismount?
   — Spotters, hold arm with one hand and support under the shoulder with other hand.

7. **Forward Circle:** Hold the bar with the Over Grip. Spring up to the "Front Support" position on the bar. Overbalance forward and bend forward at the waist to turn around the bar. Pull the bar in close to your tummy. As you roll over, drop to the mat while still holding the bar.

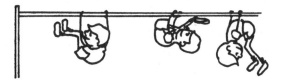

6.

7.

FOCUS: Station method; groupwork

EQUIPMENT: Mats; springboard; climbing ropes; climbing benches; two beanbags; two hoops; one utility ball; bucket; horizontal bar; box horse; crash pad; music; tape or record player

ORGANIZATION:

- This method is very useful when reviewing previously learned skills; when teaching large groups of children; when only enough equipment for a small group is available; when you want to individualize instruction and work with small numbers; and to provide opportunities for leadership. Any of the activities in this section may be taught by this method. Station tasks may be selected from the same area; for example, bench work; or from different areas (see below). Select five previously learned tasks and introduce one or two new tasks. Closely supervise the new tasks but try to circulate to all stations. Form the same number of groups as there are stations, and assign each group to a station. Have leaders, co-leaders, or other children demonstrate the skills involved at each station. Also have each group set up a station, arranging equipment and apparatus as required. Use music to start and stop activity. Allow two or three minutes at each station. On the stop signal, have groups rotate CW to next station, with the leader in front.

DESCRIPTION OF ACTIVITY:

Station 1. Tucked Frog Stand. Mats needed. (See activity PG–4.)

Station 2. Run in, Spring, Land, Bunny Hop, Forward Roll. Springboard needed. (See activity PG–24.)

Station 3. Tarzan Swing. Climbing ropes and bench needed. (See activity PG–51.)

Station 4. Skin the Cat. Horizontal bar and mats needed. (See activity PG–56.)

Station 5. Running Cartwheel. Mats needed. (See activity PG–26.)

Station 6. Jackknife. Springboard and mats needed. (See activity PG–28.)

Station 7. Rope Bowling. Climbing ropes, bowling pins, and utility balls needed. (See activity PG–51.)

Station 8. Forward Circle. Horizontal bar and mats needed. (See activity PG–56.)

PG-58 GYMNASTIC OBSTACLE COURSE _____

FOCUS: Review of skills

EQUIPMENT: Mats;
two chairs;
one table;
one box horse;
one balance bench;
two hoops;
one crash pad;
one climbing rope;
one high jump bar;
one horizontal bar;
one springboard

ORGANIZATION:

- Set up name cards and equipment at stations around the play area. Start with about eight stations: the number of stations should equal at least half the number of children in the class. Each station should be a safe distance apart and take about the same time to complete.

- Select a mixture of travelling; rolling; springing and landing; swinging; and climbing activities. Select a variety of apparatus and equipment. Use previously learned skills only. Begin by "walking" players through the obstacle course so that they know what to do at each station. Encourage children to move quickly, but safely, through the course. Try to avoid "bottlenecks" or places where the activity slows down; keep everyone moving! Provide duplicate equipment at some stations to allow more players to work at the same time. Have players repeat the course two or three times. Have players pair off and go through the Obstacle Course in 15-second intervals.

DESCRIPTION OF ACTIVITY:

Station 1. **Log Roll Under a Low Bar, Forward Roll, Bunny Hop.**

Station 2. **Spring onto long Box Horse, Forward Roll Along, Forward Roll onto Mat.**

Station 3. **Shoulder Roll Over Crash Pad.**

Station 4. **Crawl Under Two Chairs.**

Station 5. **Bunny Hop Along Bench, Jump into Hoop.**

Station 6. **Spring to Table, Tarzan Swing, Land on Bench.**

Station 7. **Stand on Bench, Swing Across Mat, Land in Hoop.**

Station 8. **Spring onto Box Horse, Tuck Jump, Forward Roll along Mat.**

Station 9. **Spring the Board, Half-Turn, Land, Backwards Roll.**

Station 10. **Cartwheel-Cartwheel, Cross-ankle Forward Roll.**

1.

2.

5.

6.

9.

Game Skills

Game Skills activities develop the abilities children need to participate in most traditional games, such as soccer, volleyball, softball, hockey, and football as well as more innovative games, such as parachute play, scooter play, Frisbee™ play, and juggling.

The 177 Game Skills activities in this section are arranged in units which you might teach over a two- or three-week period.

GS-1 HOOP SIGNALS

FOCUS: Locomotion; weight-bearing; listening

EQUIPMENT: One hoop per child; banners; beanbags

ORGANIZATION:

- Have each child get a hoop, find a home space, lay the hoop flat on the floor, and then stand inside of it. Check for good spacing.

DESCRIPTION OF ACTIVITY:

1. **Hoop Signals:** Listen carefully. I will call out a Movement Signal, followed by a Stillness Signal to be performed in the hoop. How quickly can you respond to each of these signals as I call them?

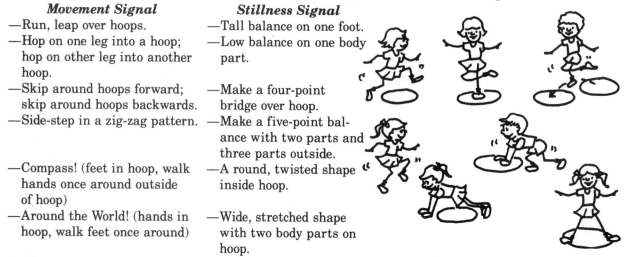

Movement Signal	Stillness Signal
—Run, leap over hoops.	—Tall balance on one foot.
—Hop on one leg into a hoop; hop on other leg into another hoop.	—Low balance on one body part.
—Skip around hoops forward; skip around hoops backwards.	—Make a four-point bridge over hoop.
—Side-step in a zig-zag pattern.	—Make a five-point balance with two parts and three parts outside.
—Compass! (feet in hoop, walk hands once around outside of hoop)	—A round, twisted shape inside hoop.
—Around the World! (hands in hoop, walk feet once around)	—Wide, stretched shape with two body parts on hoop.

2. **Frozen Hoop Tag** (Choose two or three players to be IT and have them wear banners and each hold a beanbag; everyone else scatters.): On signal "Go!" IT players chase the free players, who may move around or over the hoops, and try to tag them with your beanbag. A tagged player must form a four-point bridge over a hoop. A free player can unfreeze a frozen player by crawling under that player's bridge. IT, after you have tagged five players, the fifth player becomes the new IT.

GS-2 HOOP TRICKS

FOCUS: Manipulation; weight-bearing; balancing

EQUIPMENT: One hoop per child

ORGANIZATION:

- Have each child get a hoop and find a home space. Check for good spacing.

DESCRIPTION OF ACTIVITY:

1. Stand your hoop on edge in the upright position. Can you step through your hoop head first? feet first? Can you jump in and out of your hoop while holding it? Find another way to go through your hoop.
2. Place your hoop flat on the floor; then step into it. Now using only your feet, show me how you can get the hoop back over your head and away from you.
3. Show me how you can balance your hoop on as many body parts as you can! Balance your hoop on just one body part; another body part.
4. In your home space, show me how you can use your hoop like a jump rope. Try turning it forward and jump. Can you turn your hoop backwards and jump it?
   - Try using Single jumps; Double jumps; Rocker step; Jogger step.
   - Let me see you travel forward while jumping your hoop. Can you change direction? Think of another way to hoop-jump.
5. Invent another hoop trick!

GS–3 HOOP JUMPING FUN

FOCUS: Jumping; take-offs and landings

EQUIPMENT: One hoop per player;
two traffic cones per pair

ORGANIZATION:

- Children explore moving in and out of their hoops in different directions, with different take-offs and landings. Have each player get a hoop, find a free space, and start by standing inside the hoop.

DESCRIPTION OF ACTIVITY:

1. ***Stepping Stones Warm-Up:*** Lay your hoop on the floor within stepping distance of each other. On signal "Stepping Stones!" step from one hoop into another. If someone is in the hoop ahead of you, wait until it is empty. Now try to jump with both feet together from one hoop into another.

2. ***Hoop-Jumping Routine:***
   — Jump forward out of your hoop; jump backwards into hoop.
   — Jump backwards out of hoop; jump forward into hoop.
   — Jump sideways to right out of hoop; jump sideways into hoop.
   — Jump sideways to left out of hoop; jump sideways into hoop.
   — Jump in and out of hoop, all the way around it!
   — Repeat this hoop-jumping sequence.

3. ***Hoop-Hopping Routine:*** Repeat sequence above using double hops on your right foot; then double hops on your left foot.
   — Hop on one foot in and out of your hoop, all the way around it; then repeat in the opposite direction with your other foot.

4. ***Hoop Jump-Turns:*** Let me see you . . .
   — Do four quarter jump-turns inside your hoop.
   — Do two half jump-turns; then one full jump-turn.
   — Do a half jump-turn sideways out of your hoop.

5. ***Hoop Long Jumping:***
   — How far can you jump forward out of your hoop? Turn around and long jump back into your hoop. Land softly!
   — Now run toward your hoop, take off on one foot inside your hoop, and land softly on two feet. Repeat, taking off on the other foot.

6. ***Hoop Jumps:*** Find a partner and a free space; share a hoop.
   — One partner, in kneeling position, hold the hoop out in front, horizontal to the floor and about knee height off the floor.
   — Other partner, jump into the hoop, landing on both feet. Can you quickly spring out again? How can you use your arms to help you jump? Did you remember to land softly? Take turns.
   — Now run toward the hoop, take off on one foot, and land with two feet in the hoop. Can you take off with one foot and land on the other foot in the hoop?
   — What other ways can you safely jump into the hoop? (Each pair rest a hoop on two cones. Pairs then jump in and out of the hoop in different ways without knocking the hoop off the cones.)

7. ***Hoop Pattern Jumping*** (Form groups of six to eight, each player with a hoop. Assign each group to a certain area. Ensure that groups are well spaced apart.)
   — Groups, place hoops flat on the floor to make a pattern; for example, straight, zig-zag, snake, by two's, circle.
   — How many different ways can you travel through this pattern: jumping feet together, hopping on one foot, stepping, moving on hands and feet.
   — Design a new hoop pattern and explore different ways of travelling through it.
   — Visit another group's hoop pattern and travel through it. Continue until you have visited each group's hoop.

GS-4 HOOP ROLLING FUN

FOCUS: Manipulation; rolling technique

EQUIPMENT: One hoop per player; several cone markers

ORGANIZATION:

- Explain and demonstrate the Forward rolling technique and introduce the Back-spin technique. Have each player get a hoop, take it to a free space, and hold the hoop vertically. Check for good spacing.

DESCRIPTION OF ACTIVITY:

1. *Rolling Technique:*
   — Stand so that your hoop is on your right side with your left hand on top of the hoop to hold it upright.
   — Place your right hand behind on the hoop with the palm against the hoop, and your fingers pointing slightly downward.
   — Push the hoop forward so that it rolls upright. Run after your hoop as you roll it in a straight pattern along the floor.
   — Now change sides so that the hoop is on your left side; your right hand is on top holding it upright; and your left hand pushes the hoop forward.

2. *Rolling Tasks:* Can you . . .
   — Roll it in a circle; in a figure-eight; in and around markers and other players?
   — Roll your hoop forward, then circle it two or three times before it stops?
   — Roll your hoop forward, allow it to fall, and then jump in and out until it stops moving, without touching your hoop?

3. *Back-Spin Technique:*
   — Stand behind your upright hoop with one hand holding the top, the palm facing down, and fingers around the hoop.
   — Bring your hoop backwards and to the side. Throw the hoop forward quickly, flicking your wrist upward to create a backwards spin and pull the hoop downward toward the floor as you let go. The hoop should roll forward and then return to you. Practice!

4. *Rolling Hoop Relay:* Form teams of four. Have each team set up in shuttle formation, spaced 10 meters (30 feet) apart. Each leader holds a hoop. Each player, in turn, rolls a hoop to the opposite player and then joins the end of that line. Repeat until everyone has gone twice.

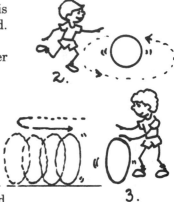

GS-5 HOOP ROLLING STUNTS

EQUIPMENT: One hoop per player

1. Roll your hoop with alternate hands by changing quickly from one side to the other side of the hoop as you roll it.
2. Roll your hoop; then jump through it without touching the hoop. Can you jump back through it before it falls to the floor?
3. Roll your hoop with a back-spin. As it returns, lift it up with your right foot. Repeat the stunt, lifting it with your left foot.
4. Roll your hoop with a back-spin and try to straddle-jump over it.
5. *Partners:* Roll one hoop back and forth to your partner. Then each roll a hoop back and forth to each other, so that they cross in the middle! Hold both hoops: Can you roll both hoops at once?
6. As you roll your hoop alongside your partner, call "Change!" and then quickly change hoops without allowing them to stop. Find a new partner, run alongside each other, and change again. Continue.
7. Invent a rolling stunt of your own! Invent a stunt with your partner!

GS-6 HOOP SPINNING FUN

FOCUS: Manipulation; spinning; rolling; partnerwork

EQUIPMENT: One hoop per player

ORGANIZATION:

- Have players get a hoop and take it to a home space.

DESCRIPTION OF ACTIVITY:

1. Show me how you can make your hoop spin! Begin by holding your hoop with both hands so that the hoop is standing upright. Place your favorite hand on top of the hoop, grasping it between your thumb and forefinger. Spin the hoop by a quick flick of your wrist in a circular motion.
2. Can you spin your hoop like a top, touch a wall, and then return to grab your hoop before it drops to the floor? Who can spin it and touch two walls? Touch three walls?
3. Show me how to spin it CW; CCW; with your right hand; with your left hand. Who can keep the hoop spinning the longest?
4. See if you can spin your hoop like an eggbeater, and then run around it once and catch it before it falls to the floor. Repeat, running around it in the other direction. How many times can you run around it before it falls?
5. Find a partner. In a free space, stand and face your partner, about three meters (10 feet) apart. Spin your hoop in your own space. Can you catch your partner's hoop before it stops spinning?

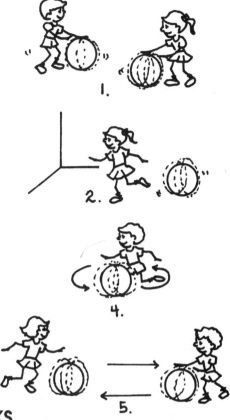

GS-7 PARTNER HOOP ROLLS AND SPIN TASKS

1. Roll your hoop to your partner while your partner rolls his or her hoop to you. Catch and repeat. Can you do this without moving from your spot?
2. Move across the play area with your partner while rolling hoops back and forth between you.
3. Spin your hoop, and then run around your partner's spinning hoop and return to catch your own hoop with your right hand. Repeat, catching with your left hand. Who can make two trips around?
4. Stand 4 meters (12 feet) apart. Spin your hoops at the same time and then run figure-eight's around the two hoops. How many times can you pass your hoop before both hoops stop spinning?
5. Roll your hoops toward each other, and then run to change places so that you catch your hoop before it stops rolling.
6. Back-spin your hoop and straddle-jump over it as the hoop comes toward you; then run and grab your partner's hoop.
7. **Ali-Oop:** Form groups of three and return one of the hoops. Outside players stand facing each other about 5 meters (15 feet) apart. Roll the hoop back and forth to each other while the middle player straddle-jumps it. Change roles after every five jumps. Continue until everyone has had a turn in the middle.

GS–8 HOOP TOSS AND TWIRL FUN

FOCUS: Tossing and catching; rotations; partnerwork

EQUIPMENT: One hoop per player; one large cone marker or chair

ORGANIZATION:

- Have each child get a hoop, take it to a free space, and hold the hoop vertically. Check for good spacing.

DESCRIPTION OF ACTIVITY:

1. *Hoop Toss-and-Catch Technique:* Hold your hoop in your favorite hand. Use an underhand toss to send the hoop into the air. By flicking your wrist as you let go, the hoop should spin backwards. Keep watching the hoop while it is in flight. Catch it with both hands.

2. *Hoop Tossing Tasks:*
   — Toss the hoop with your favorite hand and catch it with both hands ten times.
   — Toss the hoop with your other hand and catch it with both hands ten times.
   — Toss and catch the hoop with your right hand ten times.
   — Toss and catch the hoop with your left hand ten times.
   — Toss the hoop with one hand and catch it in the other hand.
   — Toss and catch your hoop while walking; while skipping.
   — Toss, clap hands, catch hoop; toss, slap hands to floor, catch hoop.
   — Toss your hoop in the air, spin around, and catch it.
   — From a low position, toss hoop overhead. Jump up to catch it in the air.
   — Toss hoop overhead; let hoop drop over your head and shoulders as it lands.
   — Find another way to toss and catch your hoop.

3. *Partner Hoop Toss:* Find a partner and stand three meters (ten feet) apart, facing each other. (As their ability and accuracy improve, have partners step back to increase throwing distance between them.)
   — Using one hoop, can you toss the hoop back and forth to each other and catch?
   — Can you each toss your hoop to the other at the same time and catch?
   — One partner toss the hoop, while the other partner rolls it. Change roles after ten tries.
   — Toss high while your partner tosses low.
   — Catch both hoops and toss them back at the same time.
   — Raise your arm in front and have your partner toss hoop over your arm within three tries. Change roles and repeat.
   — Collect a cone marker or a chair (turned upside down). How many times can you toss the hoops over the marker or one of the chair's legs in five tries?
   — Invent a partner tossing trick of your own!

4. *Hula-Hoop Challenge:* Step inside your hoop and hold it around your waist. Show me how you can spin your hoop around your waist. How long can you keep it going? Now try to do the hula-hoop spin in the other direction. Can you walk while doing the hula-hoop spin?

5. *Arm Spinner:* Show me how you can spin your hoop around your right arm. Can you spin it CW? then CCW? Now spin it on the other arm.
   — While rotating the hoop on one arm (wrist), try to move it to the other arm without breaking the rhythm. Try to spin the hoop on your arm while walking around.
   — Share your hoop with a partner. Join hands and keep the hoop spinning on your arms. Which pair can keep two hoops spinning on your arms at the same time?
   — What other body parts can you rotate your hoop around? neck; fingers, legs; ankles.

6. *Hoop-Hop Challenge:* Try to spin your hoop around the ankle of one foot and hop over it with the other foot!

GS-9 PARTNER HOOP FUN

FOCUS: Cooperation; manipulation; locomotion

EQUIPMENT: One hoop per pair

ORGANIZATION:

• Have children pair up; one partner of each pair gets a hoop, then each pair finds a free space.

DESCRIPTION OF ACTIVITY:

1. *Horse and Buggy:* One partner, step inside the hoop and hold it on either side at waist level. You are the "Horse." The second partner, hold onto the hoop from behind. You are the "Driver." Together gallop around the play area. On signal "Switch!" change roles and continue to gallop.

2. *Wring the Dishrag:* Face your partner on opposite sides of the hoop, which you hold with both hands horizontally and chest high. Twist the hoop under to one side, turning back-to-back, then facing each other again. Try it slowly; quickly; around in the other direction; on the run.

3. *Row the Boat:* Partners, face each other, hook-sitting with feet touching under the hoop, which is held in both hands between you; then rock gently back and forth to create a rowing action.

4. *Saw the Wood:* Partners, stand facing each other with right feet forward, and hold the hoop vertically between you in both hands. As arms straighten and bend, the front foot also changes to create a sawing action.

GS-10 HOOP RELAYS

FOCUS: Team work; agility

EQUIPMENT: Several cone markers; five hoops per team

ORGANIZATION:

• Divide the class into teams of four or five players per team. Use cones to mark out a starting line. Have each team stand in single-file formation behind the starting line facing a row of five hoops that are equally spaced two meters (six feet) apart. Ensure teams are well spaced apart.

DESCRIPTION OF ACTIVITY:

1. *Hoop Caper Relay:* Run to the first hoop and put it over your body; leap over the second hoop; go through the third hoop; leap over the fourth; and so on. When you reach the end, run back to your team to tag the next player, who does the same.

2. *Hoop Combo Relay* (Use only four hoops for this relay.): Hop to the first hoop and do two half jump-turns inside; run to the second hoop, put it over your body; leap over the third hoop to land with both feet in the fourth hoop. Run back to the starting line by zig-zagging in and out between the hoops. Repeat until all players on your team have had a turn.

3. *Hoop Tunnel Relay* (Have each team form a circle, with players well spaced apart.): Each player, hold a hoop vertically in front of your body with the bottom of the hoop touching the floor. On the signal "Go!" first player, drop your hoop, and then crawl through all the other hoops. As soon as you pick up your own hoop and hold it upright, the second player may go. When everyone on the team has had a turn and each player is sitting cross-legged inside his or her hoop, the relay ends. Which team will be the quickest?

4. *Space Shuttle Relay:* First and second players, run together inside the hoop, around a turning cone, and then return to your team. The first player drop out and join the end of the line. The second player pick up the third player and run together to the turning cone, around it, and back. The second player drop out and the third and fourth players run together. Continue in this way until you have made ten round trips.

FOCUS: Familiarization; manipulation

EQUIPMENT: One beanbag per player;
one hoop per player;
music;
tape or record player;
whiffle balls;
basket

ORGANIZATION:

- Beanbag Play is an excellent lead-up to Ball Play. In this activity, children review and develop the fundamentals of underhand and overhand throwing and catching. Introduce "Beanie" to the class: Draw a happy face on a beanbag with a marking pen. Throughout the activity, several dispersal and collection ideas will be given; use your own ideas as well! For starters, have the boys get their beanbags first; then the girls. Reverse the order when collecting the beanbags at the end. Challenge the players to take Beanie to a home space in a creative way.

DESCRIPTION OF ACTIVITY:

1. Say "Hello!" to your Beanie. Stand with Beanie on your head. Can you kneel down without having Beanie fall off? Can you sit, and squat, then try to stand up without touching Beanie with your hands? Can you turn around in your home space without Beanie falling off your head?
2. Show me how many different ways you can travel in general space with Beanie on different body parts. Move in different directions and at different levels.
3. Build a bridge using four body parts over your Beanie. Make a different bridge using four body parts. Make a three-point bridge over Beanie. Can you touch your belly button on Beanie?
4. Now put Beanie on one foot. Can you toss Beanie into the air with that foot and catch it? Try this with the other foot.
5. Let me see you run toward your Beanie, jump up and click your heels over the top of it, and land softly. What other tricks can you do with your Beanie?
6. ***Steal the Hats:*** Get a hoop and lay it flat in a home space and stand inside the hoop. Now put Beanie (the Hat) on your head. When you hear the music, walk or run about the play area. Try to steal other players' hats and put them in your hoop. If your hat is stolen, you cannot get it back, but you can still try to steal other hats. You are not allowed to touch the hat on your head or steal hats from other homes. If your hat falls off, quickly pick it up and put it back on your head. Who will collect the most number of hats?
7. ***Frozen Beanbag Line Tag*** (Choose three players to be IT. Give them each a whiffle ball to hold. Have IT players stand on lines in the middle of the play area; everyone else scatters and stands on a line in the play area. All players have a Beanie on their heads.): To play this game, everyone must stay on the lines of the floor. On signal "Tag!" IT players try to tag free players with the ball. Tagged player, you become the new IT, take the ball, and give chase. If the Beanie falls off your head while being chased, you become "frozen" to the spot until another free player comes along, picks up the Beanie, and puts it back on your head. If an IT player loses the Beanie, quickly place it back on your head and continue the chase. (After a certain time, change the body part on which the Beanie is placed and continue the game.)
8. It is time to put Beanie away. Pick Beanie up, give it a gentle pat, and then put it on your head. Walk around the play area. As you pass the beanbag basket in the middle, nod your head forward so that Beanie drops in. Return to the Listening Circle.

GS-12 BEANBAG UNDERHAND TOSSING AND CATCHING_____

FOCUS: Technique; visual tracking; right–left dexterity   **EQUIPMENT:** One beanbag per player

ORGANIZATION:
- Children review and practice the underhand toss-and-catch technique using their dominant hand, then their nondominant hand in personal space, as later, in general space. Number the players off by four's; then call each group in turn to get a beanbag each, and find a home space.

DESCRIPTION OF ACTIVITY:

1. *Underhand Toss Technique* (A toss is a one-hand underhand throw.)
   — Hold Beanie in the palm of your tossing hand and grip your fingers around it. Don't hold it by the corners!
   — Put the foot opposite your throwing hand, forward.
   — Swing your throwing hand down and back, as you take your weight on your back foot. Then swing the throwing hand forward and upward, as you step forward onto your front foot.
   — When you let your Beanie go, your hand follows Beanie in the line of direction. Let your eyes follow the toss, too!
2. *Two-handed Catch Technique:*
   — Watch the Beanie as it comes toward you. Don't take your eyes off of it until you feel it in your hands! Line yourself up so that you are directly in front of the beanbag.
   — If Beanie is coming toward you, below your belly button, then make a "basket" with your hands, palms up, so that the little fingers are touching.
   — If Beanie is coming toward you, above your belly button, then make your basket with the thumbs touching.
   — Reach forward with your basket and keep your fingers relaxed.
   — Let the Beanie fall softly into your hands; then close your fingers over it. Bring your arms in toward you, "giving" to make a soft catch.

3. *Practice:* Toss Beanie upward with your throwing hand and catch it in two hands. How quietly can you catch Beanie? Toss Beanie up with your other hand and catch it softly in two hands.

GS-13 BEANBAG UNDERHAND TOSSING AND CATCHING TASKS_____

EQUIPMENT: One beanbag per player

ORGANIZATION:
- Have the children get a beanbag in alphabetical order from A to Z. Beanbags are returned to their storage container in the reverse alphabetical order.

DESCRIPTION OF ACTIVITY:
1. Toss Beanie up, touch your shoulder, and catch it in two hands. Toss Beanie up, touch your other shoulder, catch. Toss Beanie up, touch your knees, catch. Toss Beanie up, touch . . . , catch.
   — Who can toss Beanie up, touch the floor, and catch it?
   — Can you toss Beanie up, turn right around, and catch it?
2. Toss Beanie up, clap once, and catch it in two hands. Toss Beanie up, clap two times, catch; toss, clap three times, catch; etc. Keep going! Repeat with your other hand.
3. Let me see you toss and catch Beanie with your right hand ten times. Repeat with your left hand.
   — Can you toss Beanie with one hand and catch with the other?
   — How high can you toss Beanie and still catch it in two hands? one hand? other hand?
4. Who can toss the Beanie straight up, kneel down and catch it; then toss it up from the kneeling position, stand up, and catch it? Toss, sit down, and catch it. Toss from sitting position, stand up, and catch it.
5. Show me another way you can toss and catch your Beanie using your favorite hand; using your other hand.

GS-14 BEANBAG STUNTS

FOCUS: Visual tracking; manual dexterity

EQUIPMENT: One beanbag per player (or deckrings)

ORGANIZATION:

- Have all children wearing a certain color get a beanbag and find a free space. Continue calling out colors until everyone has a beanbag. Call out colors again to return beanbags to the storage container.

DESCRIPTION OF ACTIVITY:

1. Hold your Beanie as high as you can with your right hand. Drop it, and catch it in two hands. Do this again, but this time try to catch it below your belly button!
   — Can you clap once before you catch it? Can you catch it in just your right hand? left hand?
   — Hold Beanie in your left hand and catch it in your left. Hold it in your right hand and catch it in your right. Catch it just before it hits the floor.
2. Put Beanie on your head, nod Beanie off your head forward, and catch it in your hands. Try this again, but catch on a foot!
   — Toss your Beanie above your head. Can you catch it on top of your head?
   — Can you toss your Beanie upward and catch it on your back?
3. Toss Beanie high into the air. Jump up and catch it in both hands at its highest point. Can you time it so that your feet are completely off the floor when you make the catch?
4. Find a partner and stand back-to-back. Pass the Beanie overhead, and then through your legs to each other. Pass the Beanie from one side to the other side. Pass in the opposite direction.
5. Invent another stunt that you can do with your Beanie! Invent a partner beanbag stunt.

GS-15 BEANBAG SIGNALS

FOCUS: Tossing and catching while moving; listening

EQUIPMENT: One beanbag per player

ORGANIZATION:

- Have children get a beanbag and take it to a free space according to their favorite sport; for example, swimming, soccer, hockey, gymnastics, basketball, etc. This game can be played using deckrings, too.

DESCRIPTION OF ACTIVITY:

1. On signal "Toss and Walk!" walk around in general space, tossing Beanie upward with your favorite hand and catching it in two hands. (Repeat, using other locomotor movements such as running, skipping, galloping, side-stepping.)
2. On signal "Freeze!" let your Beanie fall to the floor and stand on it holding a balance. On signal "Leap!" run and leap over as many beanbags as you can before the next signal is called.
3. The game continues in this way, but I will call a new moving signal each time:
   — "Jump!" Jump sideways back and forth over your beanbag.
   — "Hop!" Hop around the beanbags; change hopping leg often.
   — "Bridge!" Make a bridge over a beanbag.
   — "Roll!" Roll over the beanbags on the floor.
4. Pick up Beanie; toss and catch it as you run once around the play area. As you pass the basket, drop your beanbag in.

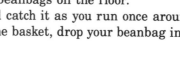

GS-16 BEANBAG CHALLENGES

FOCUS: Developmental tasks; partnerwork

EQUIPMENT: One beanbag per player

ORGANIZATION:
- Have each player get a beanbag and find a free space.

DESCRIPTION OF ACTIVITY:

1. *Beanbag Dive:* Stand with your feet apart and beanbag on your head. Allow the beanbag to slowly slide backwards. Now, reach between your legs to catch it with both hands before it touches the floor. Repeat.

2. *Jump and Catch:* Place the beanbag between your feet. Jump up and flick it upward into your hands.

3. *Head Catch:* Toss the beanbag just above your head. Who can catch it on top of your head?

4. *Reach Under and Catch:* Toss the beanbag straight up on one side of you. Lift your leg on that side, reach between your legs with the other hand, and catch the beanbag just outside that leg.

5. *Beanbag Exchange:* Find a partner and a free space. Alternate passing the beanbag overhead and between legs. Invent another passing activity while standing back-to-back.

6. *Reflexes:* Pair off and stand at arm's length from your partner, facing each other. One partner, hold the beanbag lightly at shoulder height. Other partner, hold your hand above your partner's hand. First partner, drop the beanbag without warning. Your partner will try to catch it before it touches the floor. Catch with right hand; then with left. Take turns.

7. *Blind Throw:* Partners, stand facing each other about three meters (ten feet) apart. The player with the beanbag, turn your back to your partner and toss it behind you with an underhand throw. After partner catches beanbag, change roles and repeat.

8. *Blind Receiver:* Position as for "Blind Throw," except the player without the beanbag, turn your back to your partner. Tossing partner, toss the beanbag toward the receiver and, at the same time, call out your partner's name. This is the signal for the receiving partner to quickly turn around and try to catch the beanbag. Switch roles after every three tries.

9. *Travelling Beanbag Toss:* Partners, toss your beanbag back and forth to each other while walking (jogging, skipping, galloping, side-stepping) around the play area. If you drop the beanbag, stop and do ten jumping jacks on the spot; then continue.

10. *Exploration:* Can you and your partner invent another way to throw and catch the beanbag?

VARIATIONS:

a. *Running Circle Catch:* Form circles of six to eight players and have one player stand in the center and hold a beanbag. As circle players run in a CW direction, the middle player tosses the beanbag back and forth to each player. On signal, switch directions and middle player.

b. Use deckrings or utility balls instead of beanbags.

GS-17 BEANBAG TARGET TOSSING

FOCUS: Accurate throwing

EQUIPMENT: One beanbag per player; one wall target per player; one large plastic garbage pail

ORGANIZATION:

- Children, working in pairs, practice the underhand throw for accuracy. Emphasize to step forward with the foot opposite the throwing hand as the beanbag is tossed. Make wall targets by taping 50-centimeter (20-inch) squares about 1.5 meters (5 feet) from the floor. If possible, "Happy Faces" could be painted on the walls and used as targets. Have the taller partner get a beanbag first, then get a hoop; while the shorter partner gets a hoop first, then a beanbag.

DESCRIPTION OF ACTIVITY:

1. ***Beanbag Egg Toss:*** Stand back-to-back with your partner and walk three giant steps away from each other, turn and face. Receiving partner make a "target" with your hands. Toss your Beanie back and forth to each other. If no one drops the Beanie after five tosses, then both players take one step back; otherwise, continue passing and catching until you make five catches. Which pair can toss and catch the furthest?
   - *Game 1:* Toss with favorite hand, catch two hands.
   - *Game 2:* Toss with other hand, catch two hands.
   - *Game 3:* Toss with one hand, catch in same hand.
   - *Game 4:* Toss with one hand, catch in other hand.
   - *Challenge 1:* If one player drops the Beanie, the pair must begin again!
   - *Challenge 2:* On first miss, go down on one knee; two misses, go down on both knees; three misses, sit down; four misses, start again!
2. ***Wall Target Tossing:*** Find a partner and stand two giant steps away from a wall target. Take turns, tossing your Beanie at the target. Remember to step into your throw! Make five tosses with your right hand; then five tosses with your left hand. Take one step back away from your target and toss again. How many times can you hit your target?
3. ***Toss Away*** (Place a large plastic garbage pail in the middle of the play area and have the class form a large circle about 3 meters [10 feet] around it.) Toss your beanbag into the pail. If you miss, do three jumping jacks; then try again, until your Beanie lands in the pail.

GS-18 BEANBAG TOSSING GAMES

FOCUS: Visual tracking; dodging

EQUIPMENT: Two beanbags per group; cone markers

ORGANIZATION:

- These games further develop underhand tossing and catching skills. Check for good technique and spacing.

DESCRIPTION OF ACTIVITY:

1. ***Dodge the Beanbag*** (Form groups of three. Number off 1, 2, and 3 in each group; then have the first player get a beanbag. Scatter in your groups throughout the play area. Have each group mark out a confined area in which they will play the game. Increase the size of this area as ability improves.): The first and second players stand about 5 meters (15 feet) apart, facing each other; the third player stand between them. The two outside players, use an underhand toss with either hand, to try to hit the middle player below the waist. Middle player, try to dodge the beanbag. If hit, you must exchange places with the player who made the hit. Remember to stay in your area and not interfere with any of the other groups.
2. ***Beanbag Pattern Passing*** (Form groups of six to eight players, with each group in circle formation, and players spaced arm's length apart.): Leader with the beanbag, begin the passing pattern. Using a one-handed underhand toss and a two-handed catch, pass to a player across the circle, who is not on either side of you. Now repeat this pattern; for example, pass from Jonathan to Ryan to Stacey to Scott to Nikki to Abby to Jonathan. As the passing ability improves, add another beanbag!
   - Repeat, using deckrings; using small utility balls.
   - *Challenge:* Which group can go through the passing pattern five times, the quickest?

GS–19 BEANBAG RELAYS

FOCUS: Tossing and catching; balancing; cooperation

EQUIPMENT: One beanbag per team; cone markers; popular music; tape or record player

ORGANIZATION:

- Four beanbag relays are suggested below. Refer to Section 7, "Relays," for other relays using beanbags. Encourage fair play and cooperation. Use music to start and stop the activity.

DESCRIPTION OF ACTIVITY:

1. **Shuttle Pass Relay** (Use cones to mark two lines about 5 meters [15 feet] apart and parallel to each other. Form teams of four, with two players behind one line facing the other two behind the other line.): When you hear the music, the first player pass the beanbag with an underhand toss to the first player on the other file; then join the end of the other file. Continue passing back and forth. If you drop the beanbag, you cannot count the pass. The first team to make 30 passes, wins. Keep your score aloud.
   — Pass with one hand; catch with both hands.
   — Pass with one hand; catch in one hand.
   — If you drop the beanbag, start the count again from zero!
   — Use deckrings; use small utility balls.

2. **Line Pass Relay** (Divide the class into teams of four players. Have each team line up, side-by-side, spaced arm's length apart from each other. The first player holds the beanbag.): On signal "Pass!" the first player pass the beanbag to the second player, who passes the beanbag to the third, who passes it to the fourth. The fourth player carries the beanbag to the front of the line to stand alongside the first player, and the passing continues down the line. If the beanbag is dropped, the passing must start from the first player again. When the beanbag has been passed twice down the line, the relay ends. The first team to sit cross-legged, in order, is the winner.

3. **Beanbag Balancing Relay** (Form teams of four; each team in single-file formation behind a starting line, and facing a turning cone 10 meters [30 feet] away; the leader of each team with a beanbag.): When you hear the music, begin. Each player, in turn, balance Beanie on your head as you walk to a turning cone, around it, and back. If Beanie falls off, quickly put it back on your head and continue. As you cross the starting line, nod Beanie off your head into the hands of the next player. (Repeat relay with players balancing Beanie on other body parts.)

4. **Pass and Duck Relay** (Form teams of four or five players. The leader of each team holds a beanbag and stands 3 meters [10 feet] from and facing the other team members in single-file formation.): On signal "Pass!" leader, toss the beanbag to each player, in turn, who passes the beanbag back to you. Each file player squat down after tossing beanbag back. Leader, when you have received the bag from the last player, hand it to the front player of the file, who becomes the new leader, and go to the end of the file. Everyone stands again. Relay continues until everyone has had a turn at being leader, and the team is in its original starting position, sitting cross-legged.

GS–20 DECKRING PLAY

FOCUS: Familiarization; manipulation   **EQUIPMENT:** One deckring per player

ORGANIZATION:

- Deckring activities help develop hand-eye coordination and object control. Most of the beanbag tasks can be repeated using deckrings. Through the following tasks children will explore and discover other ways of manipulating their deckrings. Introduce "Deckie" to the class; then roll them out on the floor for the children to capture and take to a home space.

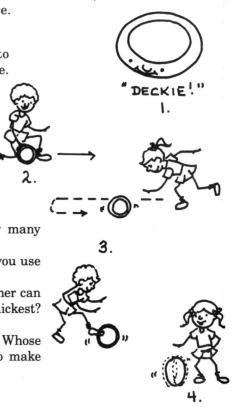

"DECKIE!"
1.

DESCRIPTION OF ACTIVITY:

1. As I roll the Deckies toward you, capture one and take it to your home space. Show me what you can do with your Deckie.
2. How can you make your Deckie roll along the floor? Remember to roll it into open spaces. To roll Deckie forward, place the palm and fingers of your favorite hand behind the deckring, pointing downward, and push Deckie away with your pointer finger. Practice with your best hand; then try to roll Deckie with your other hand.
3. Roll Deckie forward and show me how you can:
   — Run in front of your Deckie and pick it up with one hand. Can you pick it up with the other hand?
   — Jump over your Deckie as it rolls along the floor. How many times can you jump over Deckie before it stops rolling?
   — Run alongside Deckie and scoop it up with one foot. Can you use your other foot to do this?
   — Have a rolling competition with your partner. Which partner can roll the Deckie the farthest? in the straightest path? the quickest?
   — What other tricks can you do?
4. Make Deckie spin in place, like you did with your hoops. Whose Deckie will spin the longest? Now show me another way to make Deckie spin.

GS–21 DECKRING TOSSING CHALLENGES

FOCUS: Visual tracking; manual dexterity   **EQUIPMENT:** One deckring per player

ORGANIZATION:

- Children explore different ways of tossing and catching a deckring, while stationary and while moving. To begin, scatter the deckrings on the floor around the play area. As a warm-up, do "Beanbag Signals," activity GS–15, using the deckrings.

DESCRIPTION OF ACTIVITY:

Find a Deckie and pick it up. This will be your home space. Let me see you do the following challenges:

- Toss Deckie up with right hand and catch right hand; toss left, catch left.
- Toss Deckie up with one hand and catch it with the other.
- Toss Deckie into the air, clap once, and then catch it. Toss it again, clap two times, and catch it. Repeat the toss-clap-catch pattern.
- How high can you toss your Deckie and still catch it? How low can you catch?
- Toss Deckie up in the air and catch it in kneeling position; toss from knee-sit position and stand up to catch Deckie. Repeat in sitting position.
- Toss Deckie up, turn right around, and catch it. Can you turn around twice and catch it?
- Toss and catch your Deckie while walking; running; skipping; side-stepping; galloping; walking backwards; etc. Watch where you are going!

GS-22 MORE DECKRING CHALLENGES

FOCUS: Visual tracking; manual dexterity   **EQUIPMENT:** Two deckrings per player

ORGANIZATION:

• Have each player get a deckring and find a free space.

DESCRIPTION OF ACTIVITY:

1. *Deckring Reaction:* Hold Deckie up with one hand, let it go, and catch it with both hands. Try this with your other hand. How low can you catch your Deckie? Can you clap before you catch it?
   — Hold Deckie up with right hand, let it go, and catch with right. Do this again, using your left hand. Can you catch it below your knees?
   — Repeat the above task, holding with right hand, catching with left.
2. *Deckring Flips:* Try to flip your deckring in the air and catch in two hands. Try this with the other hand. How many times can you make it flip and still catch it?
3. *Deckring Tricks:*
   — Put Deckie between your feet; jump up and catch it.
   — Toss Deckie up, step forward, and catch it behind your back.
   — Toss Deckie up high and catch it, facing the other way.
   — Toss Deckie flat into air and catch it over a foot.
   — Toss Deckie into the air, reach under one leg and catch it.
   — Try to juggle two deckrings with one hand.
   — Hold a deckring in each hand and toss and catch at same time.
   — Invent a trick of your own.

GS-23 DECKRING PARTNER STUNTS

FOCUS: Visual tracking; manual dexterity; partnerwork   **EQUIPMENT:** One deckring per pair

ORGANIZATION:

• These partner stunts can be performed with a beanbag. Have players pair up. One partner gets a beanbag, while the other partner finds a free space.

DESCRIPTION OF ACTIVITY:

1. *Partner Overhead Pass:* Partners, lie on your backs with heads touching. One partner, hold the deckring between your feet. Grasp your partner's wrists, swing your legs overhead, and pass the deckring to your partner's feet. Continue passing back and forth.
2. *Deckring Flip:* Stand facing your partner. Hold your deckring between your feet; then flip it forward for your partner to catch.
   — Can you flip it sideways to your partner? flip it backwards?
   — Try flipping it over your head.
   — Support your weight on your hands and use your feet to flip it backwards.
3. *Deckring Rebound:* Partners, stand facing about 4 meters (12 feet) away from each other. One partner, toss the deckring high in the air toward the other partner. Receiving partner, jump up and catch the deckring at its highest point. Time it so that your feet are completely off the floor when you make the catch. Land softly, bending at the knees. Take turns.
4. *Double Deckring Pass:* Stand 3 to 4 meters (10 to 12 feet) apart and toss one deckring to each other: toss with right hand, catch with both; toss left, catch with both; toss right, catch left; toss left, catch right. Repeat, but each partner toss a deckring to the other at the same time. Which pair can pass three deckrings to each other?

GS-24 BEANBAG-DECKRING GAMES_____

FOCUS: Visual tracking; throwing and catching; partnerwork

EQUIPMENT: One deckring per player; one beanbag per player

ORGANIZATION:

• Have players pair up: the taller partner gets a beanbag, while the shorter partner gets a deckring; then each pair finds a free space. Check for good spacing.

DESCRIPTION OF ACTIVITY:

1. *Beanbag Basketball:* Partners, stand facing about five giant steps away from each other. One partner hold the deckring horizontally while the other partner toss the beanbag toward the deckring. Try to catch the beanbag through the deckring. Switch roles after every five tosses.

   — Gradually increase the tossing distance as the task becomes too easy!

2. *Beanbag Horseshoes:* Each partner will need a beanbag for this game. Now partners, stand facing each other 10 meters (30 feet) apart. Place the deckring in the middle between you. Using an underhand toss, see which partner can toss the beanbag closer to the deckring. Play to five points; then trade partners and play a new game.

3. *Snake Pit:* For this game, each player will need a deckring and a beanbag; then scatter around the play area. The deckring is the "Snake!" Everyone, roll your Snake forward along the floor. On signal "Hit!" hit as many Snakes as you can with your beanbag. If you miss, quickly retrieve your beanbag and try again. Continue until all the Snakes are still. Repeat.

4. *Deckring Spear:* One partner toss the deckring up and toward the other partner. Receiving partner, reach out with one arm and try to "spear" the deckring by catching it over your hand. Take turns.

   — Try to spear the deckring with the other hand.

   — One partner, flip the deckring in the air; other partner, try to spear it through one hand.

5. *Partner Deckring Egg Toss:* Partners, stand back-to-back, then step two giant steps away from each other, turn and face. Using just your Deckie, toss it back and forth to each other. Toss with one hand, then with the other; catch with two hands, then one hand.

   — Every time you make five catches in a row, each partner may take another step back! How far away from each other can you toss and catch your Deckie?

   — One partner starts with a beanbag; the other, with a deckring. Toss the objects back and forth to each other at the same time.

6. Invent your own partner beanbag-deckring game!

GS-25 LUMMI STICK FUN

FOCUS: Familiarization; manipulation

EQUIPMENT: One lummi stick per player

ORGANIZATION:
- Lummi sticks can be made from 25-millimeter (1-inch) dowelling, cut into 30-centimeter (12-inch) lengths. As an art project, the sticks could be painted and then hung to dry. Children work individually with one lummi stick, and then later two sticks, in personal and general space. Have each team leader collect sticks for the team.

DESCRIPTION OF ACTIVITY:

1. Let's explore different ways of using "Lummi." Put your Lummi on the floor. Show me how many different ways you can jump over it: forward and back; side-to-side; end-to-end.
   — Hop over Lummi from one side to the other side, ten times. Change hopping leg and repeat. Can you put your stick between your feet, jump up, and catch it?
2. Let me see you balance Lummi on some body part and walk around in general space. Find a different way to balance Lummi and move.
3. Hold the Lummi vertically in one hand and pass it back and forth to the other hand. Pass the lummi stick around your waist; knees; ankles. Pass the Lummi in a figure-eight pattern around your legs. Reverse the direction.
4. Show me how you can make your fingers climb the stick; climb back down! Try this with your other hand.
5. Now hold the Lummi horizontally with one hand, like this. Roll it forward with your thumb and fingers; backwards. Try this with your other hand. Twirl the lummi stick like a baton. What other tricks can you do?

GS-26 TWO-LUMMI STICK CHALLENGES

FOCUS: Manipulation; visual tracking

EQUIPMENT: Two lummi sticks per player

ORGANIZATION:
- Have each player get two lummi sticks and find a free space.

DESCRIPTION OF ACTIVITY:

1. Place one stick on the floor near you. Try to balance the other lummi stick on one finger of one hand; then use the other hand. Can you balance one lummi stick in each hand? Try to balance sticks on two different body parts and walk around.
   — Create another balancing trick.
2. Hold one lummi stick in your favorite hand, drop it, let it bounce once, and catch it in the same hand. Repeat using the other hand. Now drop the stick with one hand, and catch with the other. Who can hold a stick in each hand, drop them at the same time, and catch?
3. Hold one end of the stick. With your right hand, flip the Lummi over once and catch it at the same end, with your right hand. Repeat with your left hand.
   — Flip the lummi stick once with one hand and catch it in the other hand.
   — Who can make the lummi stick flip several times over and still catch it?
   — Hold a stick in each hand, flip them over once, and catch.

4. Hold a lummi stick vertically in each hand. Toss one lummi stick upward, spin once around, and catch it. Toss the other lummi stick up, spin in the opposite direction, and catch it.
   — Invent a trick of your own, using two lummi sticks.

GS–27 LUMMI STICK PARTNER CHALLENGES

FOCUS: Manipulation; visual tracking; partnerwork

EQUIPMENT: Two lummi sticks per player; one deckring per player; one bowling pin per player; music with a steady beat; tape or record player

ORGANIZATION:

- Have children get a lummi stick each; then pair up and find a free space. Check for good spacing.

DESCRIPTION OF ACTIVITY:

1. **Lummi Stick Partner Toss:** Toss one stick back and forth to your partner. At first, stand near each other; then gradually step further away.

   — Can you each toss your Lummi at the same time and catch the other's?

2. **Lummi Stick Tugs:** Each hold one end of the lummi stick and try to pull it away from your partner. Change hands and repeat.

   — Grip the stick with both hands so that one of your hands is between your partner's. Try to pull your partner across a line. Hold the stick vertically; then hold it horizontally.

3. **Lummi Stick Hockey:** One partner get a deckring and a pin. Partners, face each other in squat position, about 6 meters (20 feet) apart, with the pin placed between you. Use your lummi stick to send the deckring toward the pin and knock it over. Use right hand; use left hand.

4. **Ring Toss:** One partner hold the lummi stick vertically in one hand; other partner hold the deckring. Stand facing each other about two giant steps apart to start. Try to "ring the deckring on the stick." Change tossing and stick-holding hands after every five tries. Change roles after ten tosses.

5. **Dancing Sticks:** Each partner hold a lummi stick in each hand. Listen to the music I am playing. Copy your partner as you tap the floor in time to the music.

6. **Flipping Sticks:** Challenge each other to see who can flip their lummi stick the most number of times and still catch it. Then see who can hold a stick in each hand, flip them at the same time, and make the catch.

7. Create a trick with your partner using one lummi stick. Create another trick using two lummi sticks.

GS–28 WAND STUNTS

FOCUS: Familiarization; manipulation; balancing; dexterity　　**EQUIPMENT:** One wand per player

ORGANIZATION:

- Wands are inexpensive manipulative equipment that can be cut from 12.5 to 16 millimeter (½ to ⅝ inch) dowelling or from PVC plastic piping, in lengths of 60 to 80 centimeters (24 to 32 inches), adjusting to ability level. Discuss the importance of handling the wands safely. Then hand out the wands and have children take them to a free space.

DESCRIPTION OF ACTIVITY:

1. **Wand Signals:** Place your wand on the floor. Check for good spacing. Show me how you can . . .
   — Leap over ten different wands; then return to your own and make a low bridge across your wand. Who can make a bridge so that four body parts are on one side and three are on the other?
   — Stand on one side of your wand. Jump sideways over it, from one end to the other end. Repeat, hopping on your right foot; then hop back on your left foot.
   — Straddle your wand. Let me see you do a half jump-turn to land facing in the opposite direction in the straddle position. Repeat jump-turning in the opposite direction.
   — Stand just behind your wand. Show me how far forward you can jump from a standing position. Use your arms and bend at the knees to help you spring forward.
   — Show me another way of travelling over your wand.

2. **Wand Balancing:** How many different ways can you balance your wand horizontally? (Palm of your hand, back of your hand, two fingers, other hand, shoulder, knee, other knee, elbow)
   — Balancing your wand on the back of your hand, try to kneel, sit down, and then stand up again.
   — Who can place the wand horizontally on your foot, flip it up, and catch it?
   — Can you balance your wand vertically on the palm of your hand? Who can keep it balancing the longest? Try this with your other hand. Then balance it on the back of your hand. Balance the wand vertically on two fingers; one finger!
   — Try to transfer the wand from one body part to another.
   — Can you show me another way to balance your wand?

3. **Thread the Needle:** Hold your wand horizontally with both hands, in front of you. Show me how you can step over it; then step back over without letting go with your hands. Now hold the wand overhead; move it down your back, and then step over it.

4. **Falling Wand:** Use your right hand to stand your wand upright on one end; then let it go, spin around once, and catch it in your right hand. Repeat, using your left hand and spinning in the opposite direction.
   — Find a partner. Each stand your wand upright on one end. Can you grab your partner's wand before it falls?

5. **Dropping Wand:** Hold your wand at the bottom with your right hand, let it go, and grab it at the very top with your right hand before it hits the floor. Try this again, using your left hand.

6. **Bouncing Wand:** Hold your wand vertically in front of you with your right hand. Let it drop and bounce once; then catch it in your right hand. Try this with your left hand. Can you drop it with one hand and catch it in the other hand?

7. **Wand Tugs:** Find a partner. Grip a wand with both hands so that one of your hands is between your partner's. Try to pull your partner across a line behind you. Hold the stick horizontally; then hold it vertically.

8. **Creative Wands:** In your home space, show me how you can use your wand to do different activities. For example, let your wand be a walking cane; paddle; flute; telescope; sword; conductor's wand; baton; baseball bat; guitar.

GS–29 INTRODUCING JUGGLING SCARVES

FOCUS: Visual tracking; manual dexterity; concentration

EQUIPMENT: Two different-colored scarves per player

ORGANIZATION:

- Begin to teach juggling skills with lightweight nylon scarves, 45 centimeter to 60 centimeter (16 inch to 24 inch) square. Scarves float in the air almost in slow motion, allowing players to follow them more easily. Buy inexpensive nylon scarves from any department store, choosing a wide variety of colors. As players' skills improve, have them progress to juggling beanbags and then balls.

DESCRIPTION OF ACTIVITY:

1. Get two scarves of different colors and find a free space. Place one scarf on the floor and experiment tossing and catching the other scarf:
   — Toss your scarf into the air and wait as long as you can to grab it before it touches the floor.
   — Toss your scarf into the air and catch it with a different body part each time: head, knee, back, foot, elbow, and face.
   — Can you toss your scarf up and turn around as many times as you can and still catch it?
   — Toss the scarf up and catch it under one leg.
   — Toss the scarf up and catch it behind your back.

2. Pick up the other scarf. Holding a scarf in each hand, show me how you can toss both scarves in the air and then catch them at the same time.
   — Try to juggle two scarves with one hand!
   — What other stunts can you perform with two scarves?
   — Find a partner and explore ways of tossing scarves to each other.

3. *Juggling with two scarves. Progression:*
   — *One-Scarf Toss and Catch:* Place one scarf on the floor near you, and hold the other scarf in your best hand in the "ghost position" (grab the middle of the scarf with thumb, pointer, and middle finger). Raise your arm as high as you can across your body toward the opposite shoulder. At the height of the toss, let it go upward with a flick of the wrist. Watch the scarf as it floats down and grab it (with a "clawing action"), about waist level, with the other hand. Now toss the scarf with the other hand and catch it in your favorite hand. Practice this pattern saying "Toss-catch, toss-catch!"

   — *Two-Scarf Toss and Catch:* Hold the first scarf in your favorite hand; the second, in your other hand in the "ghost position," about waist level. Raise your right arm across your body and at the height of the toss, let the scarf go with a flick of your wrist. Watch this scarf closely. When it is at the highest point, toss the scarf in your left hand toward the opposite shoulder. Your arms will make an "X" pattern across your chest. Let the scarves float down to the floor. Pick them up and repeat. Remember to watch the scarves, not your hands. Do not cross your arms when catching the two scarves. The first scarf tossed is the first scarf to be caught. Now catch the scarves at waist level in this way: Catch the first scarf in your other hand with a "clawing action"; catch the second scarf with your favorite hand. Practice the pattern, saying "Toss, toss, catch, catch!" (or use the colors of the scarves as the cues).

TWO SCARVES

GS-30 JUGGLING WITH THREE SCARVES

FOCUS: Visual tracking; dexterity; concentration

EQUIPMENT: Three juggling scarves of different colors per player; background music; tape or record player

ORGANIZATION:

- Through the following progression, children should successfully be able to juggle three scarves in a cascade or figure-eight pattern. Ensure that they have mastered each stage before moving onto the next. Background music could be used to help establish the juggling rhythm. Emphasize that the scarves are thrown across the body in an "X" pattern and are released with a flick of the wrist as high as possible. Remind players that you cannot have two scarves in a hand at the same time; one scarf must be tossed. Have players select three scarves of different colors and scatter in free space. Check for good spacing.

DESCRIPTION OF ACTIVITY:

1. **Holding Three Scarves:** Hold the first scarf between the thumb, pointer, and middle fingers of your dominant hand. Hold the second scarf in the same way in your non-dominant hand. Then hold the third scarf with the bottom two fingers of your dominant hand. Do not stick the scarf between your fingers. Now you're set to juggle!

2. **Three Scarves—Two Throws:** Begin with the hand that holds two scarves. Throw the first scarf across your body. When it gets to the top of the toss, throw the second scarf from your other hand. (*Cues:* "One and Two" or "Pink and Yellow.") Remember to reach under the first throw when coming across the body. Let both scarves fall to the floor. Did they land on opposite sides of your body?

3. **Three Scarves—Three Throws:** Repeat for Two Throws. When the second scarf reaches the height of the toss, throw the third scarf across your body as you did the first scarf. (*Cues:* "One, Two, Three!" or "Pink, Yellow, Orange.") Let all three scarves float to the floor.

4. **Throw Three Scarves—Catch Three:** Hold the scarves in the starting position. Throw the first scarf across. When it reaches the top of the toss, throw the second scarf from your other hand, under the first and across your body. As that hand lowers, use it to catch the first scarf. When the second scarf reaches the top of the toss, throw the third scarf under the second and across the body. Use that hand to catch the second scarf; then throw the first scarf again, and use that hand to catch the third. Practice!

FOCUS: Visual tracking; manual dexterity; concentration

EQUIPMENT: Three beanbags of different colors per player; music with a steady 4/4 beat; tape or record player

ORGANIZATION:

- Explain that the basic juggling skill is performed by sending the beanbags in a figure-eight pattern between the waist and the top of the head. Emphasize that players toss with a scooping action from the inside and catch on the outside. Emphasize that players keep their hands and shoulders down and throw with their fingers and wrists. For less distraction, have players face a wall. Have players collect three beanbags of different colors, and find a free space in the play area. Use music with a steady 4/4 beat to help establish juggling rhythm.

DESCRIPTION OF ACTIVITY:

1. **One-Bag Toss:**

   — Hold the beanbag in your dominant hand between your thumb and second and middle fingers.
   — Toss your beanbag from hand to hand with underhand tosses in a figure-eight pattern.
   — To catch the beanbag, scoop it toward the middle of your body and throw it again. Catch it toward the outside of your body and carry it back to the middle of your body to toss it again.
   — Keep your hands down and throw with your wrists and fingers.

2. **Two-Bag Toss:**

   — Hold a beanbag in each hand. First toss the beanbag in your dominant hand and count "One!" When that bag gets to its peak, throw the other beanbag under the first beanbag toward your dominant hand and count "Two!" The first beanbag should go above the opposite shoulder, but no higher than head height, and land in the palm of your nondominant hand. Meanwhile, the second beanbag will land in your dominant hand.
   — Practice until you can exchange the beanbags ten times in a row without dropping them.

3. **Three-Bag Toss:**

   — Hold the first and third beanbags in your dominant hand and the second beanbag in your other hand.
   — Begin as you did when tossing two beanbags: Toss the first beanbag toward the opposite shoulder and count "One!" and then toss the second beanbag toward the other shoulder and count "Two!" Just as the second beanbag reaches its peak, toss the third beanbag under the second and count "Three!"
   — Catch the first beanbag in your nondominant hand. The second beanbag will go over the third and land in your dominant hand, while the third beanbag lands in your other hand.
   — Toss the first beanbag from your nondominant hand and count "Four!" just as the third beanbag reaches its peak.
   — The third beanbag goes over the first and lands in your nondominant hand, while the first beanbag lands in your dominant hand.
   — Practice this pattern, using the cues "1, 2, 3, 4!"

GS–32 BALLOON PLAY

FOCUS: Striking; visual tracking; manual dexterity   **EQUIPMENT:** One balloon per player

ORGANIZATION:

- Balloons, with their floating quality, are great fun for all ages! They can be used to introduce and develop many of the skills required for major sports such as volleyball, basketball, soccer, and baseball. Since balloons are inexpensive, purchase the more durable ones in bulk. The children will enjoy blowing up the balloons in class before their P.E. session. Knot the balloons and store them in a large garbage bag until you are ready to use them. Have extras on hand for those that pop. Check for good spacing.

DESCRIPTION OF ACTIVITY:

1. Take your balloon to a home space. Show me how you can keep it up by tapping it gently with just your right hand; just your left hand.
   — Who can tap the balloon from one hand to the other hand?
   — Can you keep the balloon in the air while kneeling; while sitting?
   — Tap the balloon up, let it fall, and then hit it just before it touches the floor.
   — Tap the balloon up, turn once around, tap it up again, turn once around in the other direction, tap it up again. Try this in the sitting position.
2. Now show me how you can keep the balloon in the air as long as possible, without touching it with your hands. Use your feet, head, elbows, shoulders, seat, knees, chest, back, etc.
3. Can you use just your knees to keep the balloon in the air like a soccer player? Use just your elbows to keep the balloon up. Use your feet. Use your head.
4. Keeping your thumbs near each other and your palms up, try to bat the balloon with both hands from your forehead. This is called volleying and is a volleyball skill. Now interlock your fingers and keep your arms long in front of you. Bat the balloon upward with your arms in this position. This is called bumping, another volleyball skill.
5. Tap your balloon up, jump up, and grab it out of the air like a rebounder in basketball. Can you do a jump-shot with your balloon?
6. Bat the balloon as if your hand was a tennis racquet. How else can you strike your balloon?
7. ***Balloon Balance:*** Each partner show me how you balance your balloon on the back of your hand; on two fingers; on your pointer finger; on your nose; etc.
   — With your partner, can you hold a balloon between your heads without using your hands? Try to move around the play area this way with one player leading and the other following. Move around the play area with the balloon between your chests; sides; backs; seats; etc.
8. ***Partner Balloon Volley:*** Find a partner. Can you volley the balloon back and forth to each other without it touching the floor? Try to tap the balloon near your forehead, with the thumbs and fingers of both hands. Which pair can keep two balloons going at the same time?
9. ***Partner Feet Volley:*** Can you and your partner keep one balloon in the air using only your feet? Volley the balloon back and forth using only your heads.
   — Which pair can keep the balloon by using only your knees? Try to keep two balloons afloat using only your elbows! With your partner invent another balloon trick!
10. ***All Popped Out!*** (Divide the class into two teams and have one team wear banners.): Each player tie a one-meter (one-yard) length string to your balloon and then loosely around your ankle. On the signal "Pop!" each team try to pop all the balloons on the other team!

GS–33 MANIPULATIVE EQUIPMENT STATION PLAY

FOCUS: Accurate tossing; visual tracking; manual dexterity; partnerwork and groupwork

EQUIPMENT: Five or six hoops;
one beanbag per group member;
three or four plastic garbage or cardboard containers;
one deckring per group member;
one lummi stick per group member;
15 bowling pins per group member;
9 to 12 juggling scarves;
six or eight wands;
eight to ten cone markers;
several balloons (blown up);
station signs;
floor and masking tape;
music;
tape or record player

ORGANIZATION:

• Set up six Stations using the manipulative equipment the children have worked with in this section. The station tasks should reinforce the skills learned yet challenge them with new tasks. Divide the class into six groups and assign each group to a starting station: Group 1 to Station 1; Group 2 to Station 2; all the way to Group 6 to Station 6. Have groups rotate to the next station every four or five minutes. Use music to start and stop the activity. Circulate around to each of the groups, observing and offering guidance as needed. Some Station ideas are suggested below.

DESCRIPTION OF ACTIVITY:

1. **Hoop Play:** Roll hoops in and out of the cone markers. Practice the back spin.

2. **Beanbag Play:** Toss beanbags into the plastic garbage containers that are placed at different distances from a throwing line. Take turns throwing. Toss with right hand; toss with left hand.

3. **Deckring-Lummi Stick Play:** Use your lummi stick to send the deckring at the plastic bottle and knock it over. There should be one target for every two players. Use right hand; use left hand.

   — Flip the deckring in the air and spear it with your lummi stick.

4. **Scarf Play:** Practice juggling with three scarves. Explore different ways of tossing and catching three scarves with a partner.

5. **Wand Balance:** Explore different ways of balancing your wand on different body parts. Try to transfer your wand from one part to another!

6. **Balloon Challenge:** Set up five bowling pins (or plastic bottles) in a circular formation. Set up a second identical station. One player hold a balloon and stand in the middle to start the challenge. Tap the balloon upward; then quickly knock over a pin before the balloon can touch the floor. Tap the balloon upward again, knock over another pin; continue in this way. Can you knock over all the pins without the balloon touching the floor?

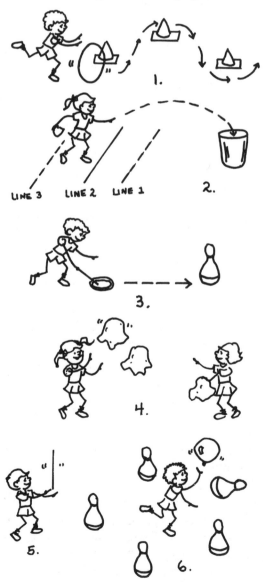

GS-34 BALL MANIPULATION

FOCUS: Manipulation; control

EQUIPMENT: One utility ball per player; four large storage containers

ORGANIZATION:

- Children explore different ways of handling the ball in personal space. One ball per player is ideal; however, it may be necessary to use a variety of different types and sizes of balls to ensure that each child will have a ball. Several suggestions are given for dispersing and collecting the balls. Place a container of balls in each corner of the play area. Divide the class into four even teams and assign each team a "ball corner" where players can get a ball, then take it to a home space.

DESCRIPTION OF ACTIVITY:

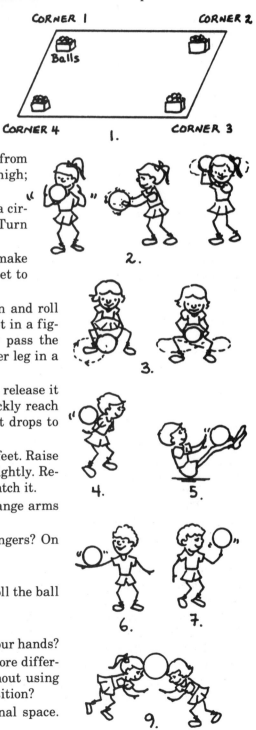

1. On signal "Ball Corner!" go to your ball container, get a ball, and take it to a home space. Show me how you can cooperate and be considerate of others when getting a ball. Remember which is your corner so that you can return the ball when I give the signal.

2. Let's explore different ways of handling your ball in personal space:
   — Keeping your hands near each other, pass the ball from one hand to the other hand. Pass with your hands high; medium level; low. Keep your eyes on the ball!
   — Hold the ball in both hands. Feel it. Make it travel in a circle path in your hands. Make it travel the other way. Turn it slowly at first; then faster and faster.
   — Stand tall in your home space. Show me how you can make the ball travel around you from head to feet; from feet to head.

3. Stand with your feet shoulder-width apart. Lean down and roll the ball around one foot, and then around the other foot in a figure-eight pattern. Can you reverse the pattern? Now pass the ball around one leg, between your legs, around the other leg in a figure-eight pattern. Try this in reverse.

4. Lean forward at the waist, raise the ball overhead, and release it behind your head so that it rolls down your back. Quickly reach your hands behind your hips to catch the ball before it drops to the floor.

5. Sit in a long-sit position. Balance the ball between your feet. Raise your legs and body to sit in a V-shape; then lean back slightly. Release the ball and allow it to roll down your legs, and catch it.

6. Who can roll the ball down your arm and catch it? Change arms and repeat.

7. Can you balance the ball on five fingers? On three fingers? On one finger?

8. Can you:
   — hold both arms out so that your wrists touch, then roll the ball up and down both arms?
   — bounce the ball up and down on both arms?
   — throw the ball up; then bounce it from your head to your hands?

9. Find a partner about your size. With your partner, explore different ways of holding the ball between both bodies without using your hands. Can you move in general space in this position?

10. Find another way of manipulating your ball in personal space.

GS–35 ROLLING AND FIELDING A BALL

FOCUS: Technique; visual tracking; right–left dexterity   **EQUIPMENT:** One 15-centimeter (6-inch) utility ball per player

ORGANIZATION:

- Review the technique for the one-hand roll and two-hand fielding, using the dominant and then the nondominant hand. Have players pair off. One partner gets a ball, while the other partner finds a free space. Check for good spacing.

DESCRIPTION OF ACTIVITY:

1. ***One-Hand Roll:*** Begin by holding the ball in two hands.
   - Keep your eyes on the target; line the ball up with the target.
   - Swing your rolling arm back beside your body.
   - Step forward with the opposite leg.
   - Bend at the knees and swing your rolling arm forward to release the ball close to the floor.
   - Follow through with your rolling hand pointing straight at the target.

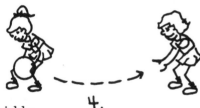

2. ***Fielding with Two Hands:***
   - Front the ball coming toward you and keep your eyes on it.
   - Bend at the knees. Lower your hands, cupping them so that your fingers are pointing down. Keep your fingers relaxed.
   - Watch the ball as it rolls into your hands and "give" with ball. When you feel the ball in your hands, grip it firmly.

3. ***Partner Practice:*** Stand about four giant steps apart to start.
   - Roll the ball back and forth to your partner. Roll with your favorite hand, five times; then with your other hand. Field the ball in two hands.
   - Take one step away from each other and repeat.
   - Take two steps forward; then let the ball roll.

4. ***Rolling Challenges:*** Stand four giant steps apart.
   - Each partner roll a ball at the same time. Roll slowly; roll quickly.
   - Turn your backs to each other and roll your ball through your legs to your partner, who tries to field the ball through his or her legs.
   - Invent a rolling trick of your own with your partner!

5. ***One-Hand Pick-Up:***
   - Keep your eyes on the ball as you run alongside it and catch up with the ball. When you are even with the ball, reach down by bending at the knees. Put the palm of one hand in front of the ball and scoop the ball into the other hand. *Practice:* Roll the ball with one hand and use your other hand for the pick-up.

6. Again roll your ball with your favorite hand into an open space. Can you jump over it once; then pick it up before the ball stops? Try this again using your other hand. Who can jump over the ball two times, then field it? Try to jump over it three times and field it.

7. Find a partner and scatter to a free space. Put one ball aside. Roll the other ball back and forth to your partner. This time try to pick up the ball with the toes of your feet: When the ball rolls over your toes, flip it upward quickly to catch in two hands.

8. ***Agility Pick-Up:*** Partners, stand facing each other about three giant steps apart and each hold a ball. One partner step one giant step to the right of your other partner. Roll your ball directly ahead, slowly at first. Each partner quickly move to pick up the other partner's ball and roll it directly ahead. How long can you keep this rolling pattern going?

GS-36 ONE-HANDED TARGET ROLLING CHALLENGES

FOCUS: Accurate rolling; right–left dexterity; teamwork

EQUIPMENT: One utility ball per pair;
two cone markers per pair;
one bowling pin, tin can, or bleach bottle per pair;
one cardboard box per pair;
one chair per pair;
floor tape

ORGANIZATION:

- In this activity, a variety of tasks are presented to help children develop accuracy in rolling. To start, have children pair off. While one partner gets a ball, the other partner gets a target; then they find a free space. Let pairs develop their own system for setting up targets and retrieving the ball. Check for good spacing.

DESCRIPTION OF ACTIVITY:

1. **Target Rolling:** Using your favorite hand, and then your other hand, take turns rolling the ball at the following targets:
   — an "X" or "Box" marked on the lowest part of the wall. Roll from three giant steps away; then after every five rolls back up one giant step.
   — a bleach bottle, tin can, or bowling pin placed 1 meter (3 feet) from a wall and 4 meters (12 feet) from a rolling line.
   — an open box positioned against a wall, on its side so that the open end faces the roller, 4 meters (12 feet) away.
   — between two cone markers, placed 1 meter (3 feet) apart, side-by-side, in the middle between the two rollers.
   — through the legs of a chair, placed in the middle between the two rollers, spaced 5 meters (15 feet) apart.

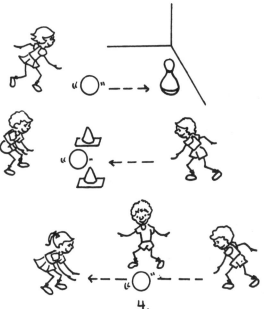

2. **Team Target Roll** (Form teams of six players who split into two groups of three. Each group stands in a line, spaced 2 meters [6 feet] away from the other groups and 5 meters [15 feet] from a low wall target. See diagram.): Using your favorite hand, Leader of Group A, roll the ball to the wall target so that the ball rebounds to the Leader of Group B. Group B Leader, field the ball with two hands; then roll the ball back to the wall to be fielded by the second player of Group A. Continue in this way. After each turn, go to the end of the opposite file. How many times can you hit the target in two minutes?

3. **Tunnel Ball** (Using floor tape or two long ropes, mark off a starting line and parallel back line, spaced 10 meters [30 feet] apart, or use the sidelines of the play area.): Each group of six to eight players, stand with your feet wide apart in a single-file formation behind a starting line. The last player must stand just behind a back line. The leader at the front holds a ball to start. On signal "Go!" leader, using both hands, roll the ball back through your legs to the player behind you, who keeps the ball rolling through his or her legs to the next player, and so on. Last player, pick up the ball behind the back line when it rolls to you; then run to the front of the line, while everyone shuffles back one place. As the new leader, pass the ball back between your legs. The game continues in this way until the original leader is back in his or her starting position. The first team to finish and sit cross-legged wins.

4. **Jump the Ball:** Form groups of three, get one ball, and find a free space. Check for good spacing. Players A and C stand about 5 meters (15 feet) apart; Player B stand in the middle between the other two players. Players A and C roll the ball toward Player B, trying to hit B below the knees with the ball. Player B, escape being hit by jumping the ball. If hit, change places with the player who hit you. If Player B is not hit after ten rolls, players should change places to ensure that each one gets a turn in the middle.

FOCUS: Hand-eye coordination;
visual tracking;

EQUIPMENT: Several large balls (six basketballs, six volleyballs, six utility balls);

six medium-sized balls;

several small balls (six rubber balls, six whiffle balls, six tennis balls);

six beanbags;

six deckrings

ORGANIZATION:

- Children explore tossing and catching a variety of types and sizes of balls and other small manipulative equipment (beanbags and deckrings), in personal and general space. Scatter the balls throughout the play area. Have each child pick up a ball, beanbag, or deckring and stand facing you in a free space.

DESCRIPTION OF ACTIVITY:

1. Toss the ball up and catch first in two hands, then in one hand. Can you toss with one hand and catch with the other? Toss and catch with the same hand.

2. How many times can you clap before catching a tossed ball? Now throw your ball in one direction and catch it. Can you catch it if you throw it in another direction?

3. How many different parts of your body can you touch and still catch the ball?

4. Who can toss and catch the ball using different levels? Catch it high; catch it low; catch it at waist height. How high can you throw your object and still catch it?

5. Can you toss your ball up, make a quarter-turn and still catch it? Try a half-turn? Who can turn all the way around? Repeat these turns in the opposite direction.

6. In your home space, let me see you toss and catch the ball while walking in place; marching in place; jogging in place; jumping in place; hopping in place; turning slowly around in place; turning in the opposite direction; dancing in place.

7. Now sit down in your home space. Toss your ball into the air. Can you stand up and catch it before it hits the floor? Now toss the ball from a standing position; then quickly kneel down and try to catch the ball.

8. Toss the ball into the air. Can you jump up and catch the ball before you land? Can you toss the ball up, "click" your heels together, and catch it?

9. How many different ways can you move and still toss and catch your ball: walking forward; walking backwards; galloping; side-stepping; skipping. On signal "Toss Home!" toss and travel to a home space. (Have players exchange balls, beanbags, or deckrings and repeat the above tasks.)

10. Invent a tossing and catching stunt of your own.

GS-38 UNDERHAND THROWING AND CATCHING

FOCUS: Throwing and catching technique; partnerwork

EQUIPMENT: One small utility ball per pair

ORGANIZATION:

- Review and demonstrate the underhand throw and catch; then have children practice throwing and catching, using either hand, at a wall, with a partner. Have partners act as "coach" for each other to help with technique.

DESCRIPTION OF ACTIVITY:

1. *Technique:* Toss the ball to a wall. Let it bounce once then catch it in two hands. Repeat five times, while partner watches and checks for good throwing technique; then exchange roles. Partner, check that throwing partner:
   — constantly watches the target; steps forward with the foot opposite the throwing hand;
   — on the back swing, shifts the weight to the back foot; swings the throwing arm forward and upward and shifts weight to the front foot; continues to swing arm forward after releasing the ball; lets hand follow the ball's path to the wall.
   — receives ball by reaching out to it with both hands, fingers relaxed; cups hands and bends wrists and elbows to absorb the ball's impact; tracks the ball right into hands!

2. *Partner Throwing-Catching Tasks* (Stand facing a partner about three giant steps apart from each other.):

— Find ways of underhand passing the ball to your partner while staying in your personal space. Use your favorite hand to throw; then your other hand; catch in two hands; in one hand.
— Throw the ball at different levels; throw the ball at different speeds.
— Catch the ball while standing, kneeling, sitting, and squatting.
— Balance on one body part and pass the ball to your partner. Balance on two body parts and pass the ball to your partner. Then try a three-point balance.
— How can you make a twisted shape with your body, your partner, and the ball?
— One partner, throw the ball to the other partner any way you can think of. Receiving partner, return the ball in the same way.
— Throw the ball under one leg to your partner.
— Turn your back to your partner and toss the ball backwards so that your partner can catch it.
— Place the ball on the floor between your feet. Lean forward and, with both hands, send the ball backwards to your partner, who is behind you.
— Can you toss the ball back and forth to each other while moving in general space? (walking, jogging, side-stepping, skipping, etc.)

3. *Stepping Game:* After you and your partner have thrown and caught the ball three times in a row, take a step backwards. Continue to take one step backwards after every three catches. If one partner misses a catch, then that partner must kneel on one knee and try to catch the ball again before being allowed to stand. Continue penalties as follows: Two misses, kneel on both knees; three misses, sit; four misses, lie down; five misses, start over again.

4. *Double Throwing-Catching:* Can you and your partner underhand throw a ball to each other at the same time, without the balls hitting each other?
— Throw to your partner's right; to your partner's left.
— Throw the ball high; throw the ball to chest level; throw the ball to waist level.
— Let the ball bounce once before catching it.

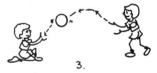

GS–39 TOSSING AND CATCHING GAMES

FOCUS: Visual tracking; throwing; catching; groupwork

EQUIPMENT: One utility ball per group; music; tape or record player

ORGANIZATION:

- The skills of one-hand underhand throwing and two- and one-handed catching are reinforced through these small group games.

DESCRIPTION OF ACTIVITY:

1. *Sky Ball:* Form groups of three players. Each group find a free space and stand in a triangle formation. Check for good spacing. One player get a ball and start the game by throwing it up high, over the heads of the other two players, using the one-hand underhand throw. Whoever is nearest, call out "Mine!" and at the same time try to catch the ball in both hands. Continue the game in this way, so that everyone gets a chance to throw and catch the ball. *Challenge:* Score one point for every good catch. Who will get to five first?

2. *Triple Pass* (Form groups of three and have each group scatter throughout the play area.): Players 1 and 3 stand on one side facing Player 2 standing 4 meter (12 feet) away. Player 1, hold the ball; then underhand pass to Player 2; then run forward to take Player 2's place. Player 2, pass the ball to Player 3; then run to take 3's place. Continue in this way. How many passes can you make without dropping the ball?

— Repeat passing pattern with players in a square formation.

— Vary the type and size of ball used.

3. *Hot Potato* (Divide the class into teams of six or eight players. Have each team form a circle, with players spaced arm's length apart and everyone facing inward. Each team leader holds a ball to begin.): When you hear the music, leader, begin passing the ball CW around your circle, from player to player, as if it were a "hot potato!" When the music stops, immediately stop the passing. The player "caught" holding the ball receives the first letter of the word "H-O-T!" When the music starts, continue the passing. The challenge is to NOT be the first player to receive all three letters of the word "H-O-T!"

VARIATIONS:

a. Pass the ball CCW around the circle.

b. Vary the size and type of object being passed: beanbag, large utility ball, basketball, volleyball, tennis ball, beach ball.

c. The player who is "H-O-T!" must perform a ball-handling task and then may re-enter the game.

d. To increase the challenge, pass two balls around the circle.

GS-40 ONE-HAND UNDERHAND TARGET THROWING

FOCUS: Accurate throwing;
visual tracking;
manual dexterity

EQUIPMENT: One target per pair: hoops, cardboard boxes, plastic garbage pails, cone markers, plastic bleach bottles or pins, two benches, wall targets made with floor tape; balls of various types and sizes

ORGANIZATION:

- Set up sufficient targets throughout the play area. Alternate high and low targets and ensure that the targets are evenly spaced apart. Have players pair off and each get a ball. Assign each pair to a starting target. Allow time at each target for partners to each have ten throws at the target, using the dominant hand and then the nondominant hand. On your signal, have pairs rotate in a CW direction to the next target. For a large class, form groups of three or four and assign each group to a starting target. Circulate around the play area, checking for correct throwing technique. Make note of the weaker throwers and provide opportunity for additional help and practice. Gradually increase the underhand throwing distance as ability level improves.

DESCRIPTION OF ACTIVITY:

1. **Low Target Suggestions:**
   - hoops on floor
   - cardboard boxes against wall
   - three bleach bottles or pins evenly spaced on a bench
   - three cone markers in a pyramid
   - plastic garbage pail near wall

2. **High Target Suggestions:**
   - hoops taped to wall with floor tape
   - geometric shapes (squares, rectangles, triangles, circles, etc.) marked on wall with floor tape
   - happy faces painted on the wall
   - different-colored posterboard taped to wall

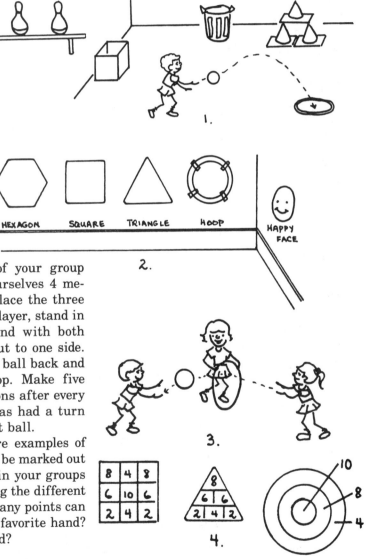

3. **Hoop Target Throw:** Two players of your group stand facing each other and space yourselves 4 meters (12 feet) apart. One end player, place the three balls near you on the floor. The third player, stand in the middle between the other two, and with both hands hold a hoop vertically up and out to one side. End players, try to underhand-throw a ball back and forth to each other through the hoop. Make five throws with each hand. Change positions after every ten throws. Continue until everyone has had a turn in the middle. Repeat using a different ball.

4. **Wall Target Grids** (The following are examples of three different types of grids that could be marked out on the wall using floor tape.): Players in your groups of three, take turns underhand-throwing the different balls at the grid to score points. How many points can you earn after three throws with your favorite hand? after three throws with your other hand?

VARIATIONS:

a. Vary the type and size of ball used; the size of the target; and the throwing distance.

b. **Performance Checking:** In pairs, have each partner take ten underhand throws at the wall target with each hand. The other partner records the scores out of ten and retrieves the ball each time.

GS–41 TENNIS BALLS AND TENNIS CANS PLAY _____

FOCUS: Visual tracking; hand-eye coordination; manual dexterity

EQUIPMENT: One tennis ball per player; one tennis can per player

ORGANIZATION:

• To further develop visual tracking and refine hand-eye coordination, children are challenged to toss a tennis ball upward and catch the ball in the can by themselves, and then with a partner. Emphasize keeping eyes on the ball until it is in the tennis can and "giving" with the ball as it lands in the can. Have each player collect a tennis ball and can and then find a free space. Check for good spacing.

DESCRIPTION OF ACTIVITY:

1. Show me how you can toss your tennis ball upward with one hand, let it bounce once, and then catch it in the can held by your other hand. Try this trick several times. Switch hands and repeat the task.

   — Can you catch the ball in the can without letting it bounce off the floor? Try several times; then switch hands and repeat.

2. Go to a wall. Toss your tennis ball up onto the wall. Let it bounce once off the floor, and then try to catch it in the can. Practice five times. Switch hands and try again.

3. Who can toss the ball up, spin around once, and then catch it in the tennis can on the first bounce? Do this trick again, but turn in the opposite direction. Switch hands and try again.

4. Let me see you toss the ball up, kneel down, and catch the ball in the tennis can on the first bounce. Do this trick again, but this time sit down. Switch hands and repeat the trick.

5. Hold the tennis can upside down and rest the tennis ball on the bottom of the can. Show me how you can balance the ball in this way while walking; jogging; galloping; skipping; side-stepping.

   — Now try to send the ball upward, quickly flip the can over in your hand, and catch the ball in the can on the first bounce. Can you catch the ball in the can before it bounces?

6. Who can toss the tennis ball under one leg and catch it in the can? Can you toss the ball from behind your back and catch it in the can?

7. Find a partner. Can you underhand-toss a tennis ball to each other and catch it in your tennis cans on the first bounce? on no bounces?

8. Invent a trick of your own. Invent a partner trick.

GS-42 OVERHAND THROWING

FOCUS: Technique; throwing for accuracy

EQUIPMENT: One utility ball per person; one beanbag per pair

ORGANIZATION:

- Have the children pantomime the Overhand Throw at first; then practice the skill at a wall using small balls; then later with a partner. To begin, have players get a small ball, take it to a home space, and face you. Ensure that they can all see you clearly. Check for good spacing.

DESCRIPTION OF ACTIVITY:

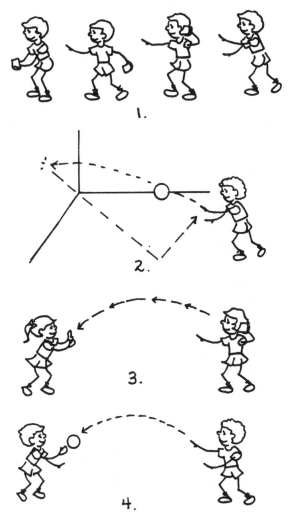

1. Put your ball on the floor for now. Let's pantomime the overthrow action first:
   — Turn sideways to the wall you are facing, with your feet shoulder-width apart.
   — Keep your eyes on your target (the wall). Let your nonthrowing arm point to the target.
   — Swing your throwing arm back and take your weight on your back foot. Your elbow is bent and level with your shoulder; your throwing hand is near and behind your ear.
   — Whip your throwing hand forward and, at the same time, step onto your front foot. Your wrist should quickly snap forward and downward as you release the ball.
   — Follow through with your throwing arm pointing toward the target, and shift your weight from the back foot to the front foot.
   — Practice! Throw with your favorite hand; throw with your other hand.
2. **Wall Overhand Throw:** Aim for an imaginary target. Throw with your favorite hand; then use your other hand. Catch the ball in both hands on the first bounce as it comes off the wall. After five Overhand Throws with each hand, back up one step and repeat. Remember to catch the ball in "soft" hands with fingers relaxed!
3. **Partner Beanbag Overhand Throw:** Overhand throw a beanbag back and forth to your partner. Use your partner as the "target" and keep your eyes on the target throughout your throw. Receiving partner, watch the beanbag coming toward you and catch in both hands, keeping fingers relaxed and "giving" with your arms to make a "soft" catch. After ten throws, switch throwing hand.
4. Now try these Overhand Throwing patterns with your partner:
   — Throw with right hand, catch with right hand.
   — Throw with right hand, catch with left hand.
   — Throw with left hand, catch with left hand.
   — Throw with left hand, catch with right hand.
   — Each overhand-throw a beanbag to your partner at the same time.
5. **One Step:** Overhand-throw the beanbag to your partner so that your partner can make the catch without having to take more than one step. If a catch is dropped, both of you must stay in your spot. If you both make good catches, then you may both back up one step.
6. Repeat the above partner tasks using a small ball.

FOCUS: Accurate throwing; visual tracking; catching; right–left dexterity

EQUIPMENT: One small ball per player; one small button per pair

ORGANIZATION:

- Refer to activity GS–40 for a variety of high and low target suggestions. More ideas are presented below. Have players pair off, get a ball between them, and in a free space pass it back and forth to each other using the Overhand Throw. They should throw with the dominant hand first; then with the nondominant hand.

DESCRIPTION OF ACTIVITY:

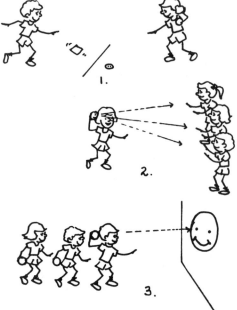

1. *Hit the Button Challenge:* Get a button and place it on a line between you and your partner. Each stand on one side of the button, about three giant steps away from the line. Try to hit the button and make it move over to your partner's side by overhand-throwing a beanbag at it.

2. *Free Ball* (Form groups of four players. Choose one player to be IT, who stands about 3 to 4 meters [10 to 12 feet] away and faces the other players spaced an arm's length apart.): IT, overhand-throw the ball to any player in any order. Receiving player, return the ball to IT using the Overhand Throw. Whenever IT throws the ball high into the air and calls "Free Ball!" any player may make the catch by calling "Mine!" The player who fields the ball becomes the new IT.

3. *Happy Face Relay* (Have each team of four players stand in single-file formation just behind a throwing line, facing a "happy face" wall target 3 meters [10 feet] away. Each player holds a tennis ball.): On signal "Throw!" the relay starts. Each player, in turn, overhand-throw the ball at the target, catch the ball in both hands after the first bounce, and then go to the end of the file. How many times can your team hit the target in two minutes? Leaders, keep score! Repeat the relay throwing with your other hand.
   — Increase the throwing distance to 4 meters (12 feet) and repeat relay.

4. *Performance Checking:* In pairs, each partner takes ten Overhand Throws at the wall target with the best hand; then ten throws with the other hand. The other partner records the scores out of ten and retrieves the ball each time. Vary the size of the ball; size of the target; and throwing distance.

GS–44 OVERHAND THROWING FOR DISTANCE

FOCUS: Distance throwing; visual tracking; catching; teamwork

EQUIPMENT: One small ball per player; one beanbag per player; two small balls per game; five cone markers per team

DESCRIPTION OF ACTIVITY:

1. *Partner Distance Throws* (Have players pair up. Each pair collect a beanbag and a small ball; then stand at one end of the field, well spaced apart.): One partner make three Overhand Throws to throw as far as you can. Other partner, use a beanbag to mark the spot where the ball lands (not rolls); then fetch the ball and return it to the throwing partner. Exchange roles and repeat.

2. *Butterfingers* (Divide the class into two equal teams. Have each team collect a ball and take up positions on opposite sides of a Neutral Zone.): Try to throw the ball over the neutral zone into the opposition's zone so that it touches the floor. Score one point for your team each time the opposing team allows the ball to touch the floor in its court; throws the ball out of bounds; or throws the ball into the neutral zone. Score two points for catching an air ball.

GS-45 OVERHAND THROWING ON THE RUN

FOCUS: Accurate throwing; visual tracking; catching; alertness

EQUIPMENT: One utility ball per group

ORGANIZATION:

- Players practice passing and catching the ball while moving in general space through small and large group play.

DESCRIPTION OF ACTIVITY:

1. *Partner Pass on the Run:* Find a partner, get a ball to share, and find a free space. Show me how you can pass the ball to your partner while moving in general space. Use the Underhand and Overhand Pass and catch with two hands. Stay alongside each other about three meters (ten feet) apart as you move. Watch out for others! If you drop the ball, quickly pick it up and continue the run.

   — Travel further apart and overhand pass to each other.

2. *Monkey in the Middle:* Form groups of three, get one ball for your group, and find a free space. Check for good spacing. The two outside players, try to keep the ball away from the middle player, who is the "Monkey." Monkey, you cannot touch the other two players when they have control of the ball; but if you intercept a loose ball, you change places with the thrower. Play the game in your own area.

3. *Line Passing* (Form groups of three players. Have each group get three balls and stand side-by-side. One of the outside players holds the ball.): All three players, start running in step with each other. Use the underhand throw to pass the ball down the line and back. How many times can you pass the ball in two minutes?

4. *The Canuck Run:* Stop and rearrange yourselves in single-file formation at arm's length apart. First player in file, hold the ball; then all start running forward together. Toss the ball overhead to the player behind you. Continue until the ball reaches the last player. That player sprints to the head of the file and continues to overhead pass. How many players can run to the head of the file in two minutes?

VARIATIONS:

a. Increase the size of the groups to four or five players.

b. Have players move farther apart for each run.

c. Have players throw deckrings or beanbags.

GS-46 OVERHAND THROWING AT MOVING TARGETS_____

FOCUS: Accurate throwing; catching; dodging

EQUIPMENT: 30 small sponge balls per game; one hoop per game; one beanbag per group of four; one utility or Nerf™ ball per group of three

ORGANIZATION:

- Accuracy in throwing at moving targets, catching, and dodging skills are developed through challenging games. Review the term "dodging": to move quickly aside.

DESCRIPTION OF ACTIVITY:

1. **Scramble Warm-Up** (Place about 30 sponge balls inside a hoop in the center of the play area. Choose three players to be the Throwers. They must stand with one foot inside the hoop and one foot out. Have the rest of the class form a large circle around the center hoop, with players spaced arm's length apart and facing CW.): On signal "Scramble!" circle players, begin to run CW around the circle. Throwers, try to hit these moving targets below the waist with your sponge balls. Remember, one foot must stay inside the hoop and one foot out! You are allowed to throw only one ball at a time. Circle player, if you are hit, hold the spot where you were hit and keep moving! See how brave you are. Can you run close to the Throwers? The game ends when all the balls have been thrown. Three new Throwers are chosen and the game begins again.

2. **Dodger in the Middle** (Form groups of three. Two players stand about 6 meters [20 feet] apart, with the third player, the Dodger, anywhere in between.): Throwers, try to hit the Dodger below the waist with the ball. Use Underhand or Overhand Throws. Have your hands in the "Ready" position to field the ball. Dodger, dodge the ball thrown at you by the outside players. If you are hit, exchange places with the thrower who hit you.

3. **Beanbag Keep Away** (Have players find a partner and then have each pair join another pair. Establish an area for each group to play the game.): One pair, get a beanbag and start the game by trying to pass it between yourselves; the other pair try to intercept the beanbag. If you succeed, pairs change roles. Remember to stay within your area.

4. **Fishbowl Dodgeball** (Form groups of six to eight players. Two players stand opposite each other outside a 4-meter [13-foot]-diameter circle. All other players stand inside the circle.): Outside players, try to hit the inside players below the waist with the ball. Hit players, join and assist the outside players until only two players are left in the middle. Those two players are the outside players for the next game.

VARIATIONS:

a. In **Scramble Warm-Up,** set up two or three circles of throwers, with about six to eight circle players for each game. Vary the locomotor movement of the circle players. Have them skip, gallop, sidestep, walk backwards.

b. Play "Throwing Tag Games" and "Snowball Tag" from Section 1; "Spaceships," "Battlestar Galactica," and "King's Court" from Section 7.

GS-47 OVERHAND THROWING AND DODGING GAMES_____

FOCUS: Throwing and catching; dodging; team play

EQUIPMENT: Two Nerf™ or sponge balls per game; one deckring; floor tape or one long rope

ORGANIZATION:

- Accurate throwing, catching, and dodging are further developed through these large group circle games. Use an existing floor circle, or use floor tape or a long rope to mark out an 8-meter (24-foot) large circle.

DESCRIPTION OF ACTIVITY:

1. *Dodgeball* (Divide the class into two equal teams. Have one team form a large circle, with players spaced arm's length apart and facing inwards. The other team stands inside the circle.): On signal "Go!" circle players, try to hit the inside players below the waist with the ball. You may throw underhand or overhand, but the ball must hit directly, not bounce on the floor. All throws must be made from outside the circle. Circle players, you may pass to another circle player for a better shot. Inside players, if you are hit, change places with the thrower. The game continues in this way.

2. *Donkey Dodge* (Have players form groups of three. Each group of three makes a Donkey: The front player is the "Head"; middle player, the "Body"; and the end player, the "Tail." The Donkey moves together by players holding onto the waist of the player in front. Choose two players to be ITs, give them each a ball, and have them start in the middle of the play area. The Donkeys scatter throughout the play area.): On signal "Donkey Dodge!" ITs run after the Donkeys and try to hit the "Tail" (end player) of any Donkey. The ball must hit the Tail below the waist and be a direct hit. "Head" and "Body," move and use your arms to protect your Tail. When a Tail is hit, IT becomes the Head; the Head becomes the Body; and the Body becomes the new Tail. The old Tail becomes the new IT.

3. *Battle Royal* (Form four equal teams. Have each team stand on one side of a 10-meter by 10-meter [30-foot by 30-foot]-square play area. Then have players evenly space themselves along their home sideline and number off consecutively. Center a ball in a deckring in front of each team.): Listen carefully for your number. When you hear it, quickly run out, grab a ball, and try to hit an opposing player below the waist with your ball. The hit must be a direct hit, and you can only throw one ball at a time! Sideline players, you may retrieve balls and pass them to your inside team player; but you may not throw them at opposing players. Inside players, you may block thrown balls with the ball that you are holding, or catch a thrown ball. If you are hit, then go to your sideline. The last player left earns a point for his or her team.

VARIATIONS:

a. For the above games, use two balls and watch the action increase!

b. Play "Team Dodgeball," "Line Dodgeball," "Cross-Over Dodgeball," and "Everyone for Yourself" from Section 7.

GS–48 ONE-HANDED BOUNCING TASKS

FOCUS: Technique; right–left dexterity; control   **EQUIPMENT:** One large ball per player

ORGANIZATION:

- Review correct bouncing technique: Finger pads are used to push the ball downward as the arms straighten and bend in a "pumping-like" action. Check for any slapping of the ball. Any type of large ball that bounces well can be used: volleyballs, basketballs, utility balls, plastic play balls. Have each player get a ball and bounce it to a free space.

DESCRIPTION OF ACTIVITY:

1. Bounce your ball in front of you; on one side; on the other side. Bounce your ball slowly; quickly; in slow motion. Use your favorite hand; then your other hand.
2. Bounce your ball high. Bounce it at waist height. Bounce it as low as you can. At which level is it easier to control? Bounce your ball from high to low; from low to high. Repeat these tasks using your other hand.
3. How close to you can you bounce your ball while standing? How far away? Can you kneel on one knee and bounce your ball? Kneel on both knees. Can you sit down and still keep your ball bouncing? Try wide-sitting and bouncing your ball; long-sitting; hook-sitting. Now try to stand up again! Switch hands and repeat.
4. Walk in a circle around your ball as you bounce it with your favorite hand. Change hands and bounce it in the opposite direction. Can you skip around in a circle while bouncing your ball? Try side-stepping. Change hands and direction, and repeat.
5. Show me how you can bounce your ball without looking at it directly. Look up and tell me how many fingers I am holding up. Now how many fingers? Who can bounce the ball while keeping their eyes closed? Now try this using your other hand to bounce the ball.
6. Try to bounce your ball as high off the floor as you can. Let it come down and catch it in two hands. How high can you catch it? How low?
7. Walk forward while bouncing the ball. Change hands and direction on the signal "Change!" and continue to walk forward bouncing the ball. Try this while side-stepping. Show me how you bounce the ball while running; in a figure-eight pattern; while galloping in a curvy pathway and bouncing the ball. Let me see you skip in a circular path and bounce the ball. How else can you move and still keep your ball bouncing?
8. Now in your home space, show me how you can bounce your ball from one hand to the other hand. Bounce at medium height; bounce low and quickly; high and slowly. Can you walk in general space and bounce your ball from one hand to the other? Run slowly?
9. Let me see you bounce the ball all around you without moving from your spot. Bounce the ball in the other direction. Stand with your legs wide apart. Can you bounce your ball through your legs, around one leg, back through, and around the other leg in a figure-eight pattern?
10. Who can roll the ball down the back, catch it behind your back, and then bounce it through your legs to catch it in front of you? Try again.
11. Invent a bouncing stunt of your own!

GS-49 BOUNCING GAMES

FOCUS: Ball control; left–right dexterity; groupwork

EQUIPMENT: One large ball per player;
one 15-centimeter (6-inch) utility ball per player;
one hoop per player;
four or more benches;
chart paper;
marking pen

ORGANIZATION:
- Have each player get a ball and bounce it using alternate hands to a free space.

DESCRIPTION OF ACTIVITY:

1. **O'Leary:** Bounce your ball with one hand, while chanting:
   "One, two, three, O'Leary, Four, five, six, O'Leary,
   Seven, eight, nine, O'Leary, Ten O'Learys in a row!"
   — Each time you say "O'Leary," swing your right leg over the ball.
   — Repeat chant, swinging your left leg over. Make up your own O'Leary stunts.

2. **In, Around, and Over:** Bounce your ball to get a hoop; then roll the hoop back to your home. Lay it flat on the floor. Bounce the ball inside your hoop. On the signal "Change!" bounce the ball to another hoop and continue to bounce your ball inside that hoop with your other hand. On the signal "Around!" bounce the ball around as many hoops as you can. Change hands each time you go around a different hoop. On the signal "Over!" bounce your ball over the hoops changing bouncing hands each time you go over another hoop.

3. **Hoop Bounce:** Get into groups of four. One player of each group get a hoop and a ball. Place the hoop flat on the floor and form a square around it. You should stand about 3 meters (10 feet) from the hoop. Use a soft Overhand Throw to bounce the ball into the hoop to another player. Use either hand to make the throw. How many times in a row can you bounce the ball into the hoop and make a good catch?

4. **Seven-Up Tasks** (Post two or three charts with the following seven tasks on the walls of the play area, or call out the tasks to the players in order.):
   — Throw the ball to the wall. Let it bounce once, clap twice, and then catch it. Repeat seven times.
   — Throw the ball to the wall. Catch it without a bounce. Repeat six times.
   — Throw the ball to the floor first; then catch it off the wall. Repeat five times.
   — Bounce the ball four times with your favorite hand, keeping your eyes closed.
   — Throw the ball high into the air, let it bounce once while you touch the floor with both hands, and then catch it. Repeat three times.
   — Bounce the ball. Turn around and catch it. Repeat two times.
   — Throw the ball under one raised leg to the wall and catch it. Repeat once.

5. **Bench Bounce** (Divide into four groups; then place four or more benches in the center of the play area. Ensure that benches are secure.):
   — Bounce and catch the ball with two hands while standing on the bench.
   — Toss and catch the ball with two hands while standing on bench. Toss with one hand, catch with two hands. Toss from one hand to the other hand.
   — Toss and catch the ball while walking forward along the bench.
   — Dribble the ball on the floor while walking along the bench. Turn around and dribble back with your other hand.
   — Invent a Bench Bounce trick of your own!

GS–50 WALL BOUNCING CHALLENGES

FOCUS: Throwing; catching; visual tracking; right–left dexterity   **EQUIPMENT:** One ball per player

ORGANIZATION:

- Children explore bouncing different types and sizes of balls off a wall. Collect a variety of balls such as large and small utility balls, volleyballs, rubber basketballs, soccer-type balls, sponge balls, small rubber balls, tennis balls, whiffle balls, etc. Have each player get a ball and stand facing a wall. Check for good spacing.

DESCRIPTION OF ACTIVITY: Let's explore bouncing different balls off a wall:

1. *Underhand Throw to the Wall:* Throw your ball to the wall, let it bounce once off the wall, and catch it in two hands. Try this again. Now throw with your other hand.

2. *Overhand Throw to the Wall:* Throw your ball to the wall and catch it after the first bounce. Throw with your favorite hand; throw with your other hand. Throw the ball high, catch it on the first bounce. Throw it at medium height; throw it low. Use your favorite hand; use your other hand.
   — Change balls with someone near you and repeat.
   — Repeat these tasks, catching the ball without a bounce.
   — Change so that you are using a different ball again. Take one step back and try these wall bounce tasks again.

3. *Overhand Throw and Bounce:* Throw the ball so that it bounces to the floor first, then to the wall. Can you catch the ball as it comes off the wall, without letting the ball bounce?
   — Try to clap your hands in front and behind you before making the catch.
   — Can you turn around once and still make the catch? Touch the floor; then catch the ball. Clap your hands under one leg. Combine two tricks together.
   — Who can jump up to catch the ball high before your feet land?
   — Change to a different ball and try these tricks again.

4. *Invent a Wall Bounce:* Invent a trick of your own. Teach your trick to another player near you.

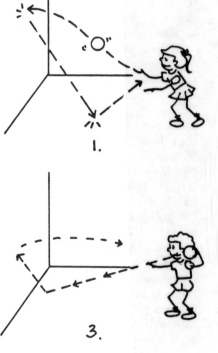

GS–51 PARTNER BOUNCING CHALLENGES

FOCUS: Visual tracking; right–left dexterity; cooperation   **EQUIPMENT:** One utility ball per partner

ORGANIZATION:

- Have players each collect a ball, find a partner, and then bounce the ball to a free space. Stand, facing each other, about 4 meters (12 feet) away.

DESCRIPTION OF ACTIVITY:

1. Bounce one ball back and forth to your partner. Catch in two hands. Use either hand to make the throw. After every five throws, back up one step.
   — Now each of you try to bounce a ball to your partner at the same time.
   — One partner bounce the ball to the other partner who throws the ball back. Switch after five throws.

2. *Partner Wall Bounce:* Stand one behind the other, about 4 meters (12 feet) from a wall. The front partner has a ball. Front partner, throw the ball at the wall; then quickly go behind the second partner, who lets the ball bounce once and then makes the catch. Continue in this way.
   — Throw the ball so that it bounces off the floor, then the wall, and make the catch.
   — Invent a partner bouncing trick of your own! Teach your trick to another pair.

GS-52 SHORT ROPE FUN

FOCUS: Teaching and safety guidelines; manipulation

EQUIPMENT: One short rope per skipper; music; tape or record player

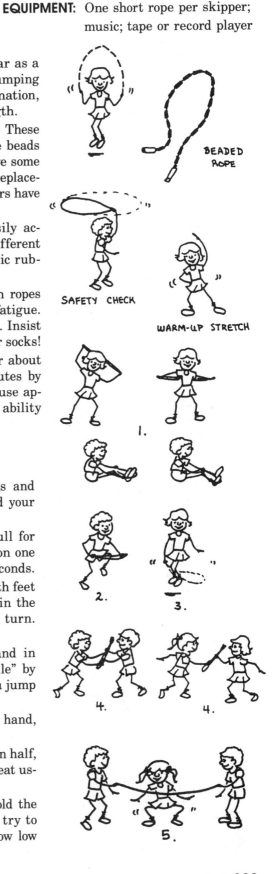

ORGANIZATION:

- Rope Jumping should be taught throughout the school year as a fitness activity or as the main focus of the lesson. Rope Jumping contributes significantly to the development of coordination, rhythm, timing, agility, aerobic endurance, and leg strength.
- Beaded Ropes should be used for skipping, if possible. These weighted ropes make turning easier, and the sound of the beads hitting the floor helps children pick up the rhythm. Remove some of the beads for a faster turning rope. Save extra beads for replacement purposes. Speed Ropes can be introduced when skippers have mastered the Basic Skipping Tricks.
- Store ropes by hanging them on hooks that can be easily accessed. Use colored tape on the handles to code the different lengths. Wooden floors, indoor/outdoor carpeting, or acrylic rubberized flooring are best as skipping surfaces.
- *Safety:* Ensure that skippers have enough space to turn ropes easily and safely. During activity, watch carefully for fatigue. Gradually increase activity time as fitness levels improve. Insist that skippers wear sneakers while skipping; no bare feet or socks!
- Warm-Up skippers by stretching arm and leg muscles for about five to eight minutes; Cool-Down for three to five minutes by walking and stretching. To develop rhythmical jumping, use appropriate music with a steady beat, increasing tempo as ability improves.

DESCRIPTION OF ACTIVITY:

1. *Rope Stretching Warm-Ups:*
   — Hold a folded rope overhead and taut in both hands and stretch from side-to-side. Repeat, holding rope behind your head; in front.
   — Now put your folded rope behind your waist and pull for five seconds; then relax. Show me how you can step on one end of your rope and pull upward for another five seconds.
   — In the long-sit position, put a doubled rope around both feet and gently pull toward you for ten seconds. Repeat in the wide-sit position, with the rope around each foot, in turn. How else can you stretch with your rope?

2. *Thread the Needle:* Holding your folded rope low and in front of you with both hands apart, "thread the needle" by stepping over it one foot at a time; then reverse. Can you jump over the rope? Careful!

3. *Swing and Jump:* Holding the folded rope with one hand, show me how you can swing it and jump over it.

4. *Rope Tugs:* Find a partner about your size. Fold a rope in half, and have a one-handed tug-o-war with your partner. Repeat using the other hand. Repeat using both hands.

5. *Limbo the Rope:* Form groups of three. While two hold the rope at waist level taut between you, the third member try to move under the rope with your body facing upward. How low can you go? Take turns.

GS-53 ROPE PATTERNS

FOCUS: Rope and body manipulation; listening   **EQUIPMENT:** One short rope per skipper

ORGANIZATION:

- Have children get a short rope, take it to a home space, and stretch it out along the floor.

DESCRIPTION OF ACTIVITY:

1. *Straight Pattern:*
   - Zig-zag jump over your rope from end to the other end; zig-zag jump backwards to your starting place. Repeat, facing rope sideways.
   - Hop back and forth across your rope, moving from one end to the other. Hop back on other foot. Repeat, facing sideways, and hopping sideways.
   - Straddle your rope. Show me how you can jump alternately crossing and uncrossing your feet, so that the rope is between your feet each time.
   - Keep your hands on the floor and jump back and forth as you move along the rope. What other ways can you move on or over your rope?
2. *Circle Pattern:* On the floor make a circle with your rope; then stand inside your circle. Make a one-foot balance; a low balance; a tall balance. Make yourself as small as you can; as big as you can. Make a bridge with three parts inside, one part outside. Make a different bridge.
   - Place one hand in the circle and legs straight out. Move like a Grinder once around the circle. Repeat, using the other hand in the opposite direction.
   - Begin in the center of your home circle. Show me how you can move in and out of your rope: forward, backwards, sideways; two feet together; one foot.
   - Make a quarter jump-turn in your circle; half jump-turn; full jump-turn.
   - Leap over your circle. Explore different ways of taking off and landing.
3. *Partner Circle Tag:* Find a partner and use two ropes and make one circle pattern on the floor. Play a game of tag with one partner trying to catch the other as you move around the outside of the circle.
4. *Geometric Rope Patterns:*
   - Rope Shape Warm-Up (Divide the class into six different groups and give each group a name: Group 1, Squares; Group 2, Rectangles; Group 3, Triangles; Group 4, Circles; Group 5, Diamonds; and Group 6, Figure-eight's. Make sure children know their group number and name; then have them scatter around the play area. Check for good spacing.):
   - Make a shape with your rope. What is your shape called?
   - How many different ways can you hop in and out of your shape?
   - Make a bridge over your shape; curl up inside.
   - Leap over as many different shapes as you can. Watch where you are going!
   - All Squares, do quarter jump-turns; Rectangles, be Grinders; Triangles, form three-point Bridges; Circles, be Stepping Stones; Diamonds, be Tap Dancers; Figure-eight's, be Skiers. (Have children trade shapes and repeat the tasks.)
5. *Letter Shapes:* Make the first letter of your name; last letter of your name. Can you make the fifth letter of the alphabet? eighth? tenth?
6. *Partner Rope Drawing:* Join with a partner and use your ropes to make your favorite giant number; make a two-digit number.
   - Draw an Eskimo's home; an Indian's home; a home of your choice using your ropes; the world's largest bowtie; coolest mustache; longest braid.
   - Add 8 and 7 together and draw the answer; 9 and 5.
   - Can you make a five-sided figure? What is it called?
   - Make a two-lettered word using one rope and your bodies. Make a three-lettered word; four-lettered word (using two ropes).
7. *Group Patterns:* Form groups of five or six, each member with a rope; then find a free space. Arrange ropes on the floor to create hopping and jumping patterns. Visit another group's pattern and explore different ways of moving through it.

GS–54 SHORT ROPE JUMPING

FOCUS: Turning and jumping technique

EQUIPMENT: One short rope per skipper; music with a steady 4/4 beat; tape or record player

ORGANIZATION:

- Skippers review sizing the rope for correct length, basic skipping form, and basic jump. Review single- and double-jump technique. Use lively music with a strong, steady beat to provide a jumping rhythm as skippers perform the following jumping patterns, turning rope forward and backwards. To begin, have skippers find a free space.

DESCRIPTION OF ACTIVITY:

1. ***Skipping Warm-Up:***
   — Arm Circles (gently forward, crossing in front)
   — Wrist Circles; Knee Circles; Ankle Circles
   — Wrist Stretches; Leg Lunges
   — Keeping knees and feet together, bounce lightly on the balls of your feet to the music. Jump forward, jump backwards. Jump on one foot four times; then on the other foot. Pantomime rope turning as you jump.
2. ***Size the Rope:*** Get a rope and check it for proper length by standing in the middle of it and drawing the ends up to your shoulders. The rope ends should just reach your arm pits. (If the rope is too long, undo knots at handles, remove some beads, adjust the length, and double-knot ends.)

3. ***Check the Spacing:*** Take your rope anywhere in the play area and check that you have enough space to turn it easily without touching anyone.
4. ***Basic Skipping Form:*** Stand tall, knees slightly bent and head up. Hold the rope behind your heels, handles held loosely. Keep your elbows close to the sides; point forearms and hands slightly forward and away from your body. Keep your knees and feet together. Turn the rope using small, circular wrist movements.
   — ***Toe Catch:*** Start with rope behind you. Swing it overhead and forward, and catch it under your toes.
   — ***Heel Catch:*** Start with rope in front of you. Swing it overhead and backward, catching it under your heels.
   — Repeat, but jump once, and then catch the rope.

5. ***Basic Jump Technique:*** Keeping feet together, make low jumps that are only three to five centimeters (one to two inches) from the floor; relax as you jump; bend knees slightly as you land softly on the balls of your feet and lower heels to floor, rather than flat-footed; keep turning rhythm constant, using your wrists rather than your arms to supply the power; jump smoothly.
   — ***Single or Pogo Jump:*** Turn the rope once, jump once. Practice.
   — ***Double Jump:*** Turn rope once; jump lightly when rope is overhead; then jump when rope passes underneath. Practice.

6. ***Short Rope Patterns*** (Jump in time to the music.):
   — Double-jump, turning rope forward for eight beats; turning rope backwards. Single-jump, turning rope forward for eight beats; turning rope backwards. Repeat.
   — Double-jump with feet together, turning rope forward, four times. Then jump rope four times on the right foot; four times on the left foot. Jump feet together four more times. Repeat pattern, jumping three times; then two times. Try this pattern, turning rope backwards.
   — Single-jump with feet together, turning rope forward, while moving to the right four times; to the left four times; forward four times; backwards to place four times. Repeat pattern, turning rope backwards.
   — Make a double-jump pattern of your own. Create a single-jump pattern of your own.

7. ***Hot-Pepper:*** How many times can you single-jump in 30 seconds? in 45 seconds? in one minute?

FOCUS: Mastering rope jumping basics; coordination

EQUIPMENT: One short rope per skipper; music with a strong 4/4 beat; tape or record player

ORGANIZATION:

- Skippers should practice these jump rope tricks first without a rope and then with a rope, using double jumps and then single jumps. Challenge skippers to repeat tricks while turning the rope backwards. Encourage jumping in time with the music. Have skippers get a rope, check that it is the correct length, and then scatter around the play area.

DESCRIPTION OF ACTIVITY:

1. ***Double-Side Swing:*** Hold one rope handle in each hand. Swing the rope to the right two times; then open it and jump over it. Do not cross your hands. Repeat to the left side. Practice this "swing right, swing right–jump–swing left, swing left–jump" pattern.

2. ***Single-Side Swing:*** Swing the rope on only one side of your body; then open it and jump over it. Swing and jump on the other side. Practice this "swing right–jump, swing left–jump" pattern.

3. ***Figure-Eight Side Swing:*** Side swing right; side swing left; side swing right; continue for eight swings.
   —***Figure-Eight Jump:*** Swing rope to right side of body; swing rope to left side of body; swing rope to right side of body; open it and jump over. Repeat pattern.

4. ***Easy Rocker:*** Place one foot ahead of the other. Jump with weight on the front foot, leaning forward slightly. Shift weight to back foot and jump again, leaning backwards slightly. Practice with the rope turning slowly at first; then turn the rope faster as the rocker movement becomes easier for you.

5. ***Boxer:*** Jump twice with your right foot and then twice with your left foot. Continue to jump twice on each foot.

6. ***Jogger:*** Using a running step, step over the rope with first the right foot and then the left foot. Continue to alternate footwork, taking one jump for each step. Repeat, stepping over rope with first the left foot, then the right.

7. ***Skier:*** Place rope stretched out along the floor and jump with feet together, from side to side, over it. Now add the rope. On the first turn, jump sideways to the right; on the second turn, jump sideways to the left. Imagine you are jumping side-to-side across a line each time you jump the rope.

8. ***Bells:*** Practice jumping forward and backwards with feet together over your rope. Now add the rope. On the first turn, jump forward; on the second turn, jump backwards. Remember, keep your feet together!

9. ***Rocker:*** Start with one foot forward. Jump, taking your weight on the front foot and leaning slightly forward. Then jump, shifting weight to back foot and leaning on it. Repeat Rocker step with the other foot forward.

10. ***Elevator:*** Jumping with feet together, bend knees more and more each time you jump until you are crouched as low as possible.

11. Challenge skippers to combine steps as follows: two Skiers, then two Bells; three Boxers, then one Elevator; two Rockers, then four Joggers.

GS-56 STRADDLE JUMPING TRICKS

FOCUS: Straddle jumping; coordination

EQUIPMENT: One short rope per skipper; music with a strong 4/4 beat; tape or record player

ORGANIZATION:

- Have skippers get a rope, check that it is the correct length, and then scatter around the play area. Skippers should practice these tricks first without and then with the rope, landing with double jumps and then single jumps. Challenge skippers to repeat Straddle Jumps while turning the rope backwards.

DESCRIPTION OF ACTIVITY:

1. *Side Straddle:* Start with feet together. On the first turn of the rope, jump your feet shoulder-width apart. On the second turn of the rope, jump your feet together again. Say to yourself, "Apart," "Together."

2. *Forward Straddle:* Start with feet together. On the first turn of the rope, jump your feet apart so that your right foot is in front of your left. On the second turn of the rope, jump your left foot in front of the right. Continue to switch feet on each turn of the rope.

3. *Double Straddle:* Practice the Double Straddle without the rope at first. Start with feet together. Now combine the Side and Forward Straddles without the feet ever returning to the basic together position.

4. Create a Straddle-Jumping Routine using the three straddle rope tricks you have learned.

5. *The "X":* As the rope passes under your feet, jump your legs apart in the side straddle position and jump. Then as the rope passes under your feet on the next turn, jump and cross your feet, one in front of the other. Return to the side straddle position for the next turn; then cross with the other foot in front.

6. *Bird Hops:* Set the rope aside and practice Pigeon-toed Hops (toes together and heels apart) and Duck Hops (heels together and toes apart). Alternate Pigeon-toed Hops and Duck Hops as you jump the rope.

7. *Twister:* Jump with feet together to do a quarter-turn to the left, moving only the hips and legs while your upper body faces forward; return to face front and jump; then twist to the right and jump; return to front and jump.

8. *Criss-Cross:* Start in standing position, feet together, with rope at the back of your heels. Bring the rope slowly overhead, crossing your arms at the elbows. Jump through the loop, open arms, and single-jump. As the rope swings overhead, criss-cross your arms again.

VARIATION: Challenge skippers to combine Straddle Jumping tricks with Basic Rope tricks learned earlier; for example: four Twister Jumps and two Bell Jumps; four Cross-Legged Jumps and four Boxer Jumps; four Bird Hops, two Skier Jumps, and two Jogger Jumps.

GS–57 PARTNER ROPE JUMPING

FOCUS: Cooperative rope jumping; coordination

EQUIPMENT: One short rope per skipper; music with a strong beat; tape or record player

ORGANIZATION:

- Have skippers pair up with a partner about the same size and get a rope to share. To check that the rope is the correct length, have partners stand side-by-side on the rope; the ends should extend to their outer armpits. Pairs then scatter around the play area.

DESCRIPTION OF ACTIVITY:

1. **Side-by-Side:** Partners, stand side-by-side, facing forward, with each partner holding one handle of the rope. You may wish to join inside hands or place an arm around your partner's waist or shoulders. In unison, turn rope forward with your free hands and jump; backwards and jump together. Now try the following tricks:
   — Skip forward; skip backwards; skip sideways together.
   — One partner, move out and back into position while continuing to turn the rope. Other partner, repeat; then both partners move out together and back into position again.
   — One partner, circle the other partner while continuing to turn the rope.

2. **Face-to-Face:** Start by standing face to face. One partner, turn the rope and both jump in unison. Take turns being the rope turner. One partner, run in, face your partner, and match steps. Run out; then run in again and jump in step with your partner. How many different tricks can you perform?
   — Jump-turn on the spot until you face your partner again.
   — Try to touch the floor with your hands, jump up, and then jump in unison.
   — While jumping in unison, nonturning partner try to take over the job of rope turning by placing your hands on the handles to get control. "Steal" the rope, turning back and forth from each other in this way.

3. **Two Ropes Side-by-Side:** Stand beside your partner, facing the same direction. Each partner's inside hand turn the other partner's rope, while your outer hands turn your own rope. Practice forward-turning both ropes at the same time and jumping in unison. Turn ropes backwards and jump together.
   — Jump the Basic Rope Tricks in this position.
   — Repeat tasks in side-by-side position, facing in the opposite direction.
   — Show me how you can travel around the play area while turning and jumping your ropes together.

4. **Two Ropes Face-to-Face:** Face each other, with one partner holding his or her rope behind and the other partner holding his or her rope in front. Turning both ropes at the same time, forward for one partner and backwards for the other, jump over both ropes at once. Now turn the ropes alternately, jumping each one in turn.

VARIATIONS:

a. **Invent-a-Trick:** Provide opportunity for pairs to create a new trick in the Side-by-Side and Face-to-Face positions.
b. **Show-Off Time!:** Provide opportunity for pairs to perform their tricks for the rest of the class.
c. Repeat Side-by-Side sequence with both partners facing opposite directions.
d. In *Two Ropes Side-by-Side* have skippers form groups of four, stand in the side-by-side position, and turn and jump ropes at the same time. Challenge groups to join up with another group of four and perform the stunt with eight skippers; twelve skippers.

GS–58 LONG ROPE JUMPING

FOCUS: Turning and jumping technique; groupwork

EQUIPMENT: One long rope per group; one deckring per group; music with a steady 4/4 beat; tape or record player

ORGANIZATION:

- Form groups of four skippers: two turners and two jumpers. Change roles frequently so that everyone has a turn at jumping and turning. Ensure that groups are well spaced around the play area. Use ropes that are 3 to 4 meters (10 to 12 feet) long. The rope length should suit the turners' ability. Using music will encourage skippers to turn the rope rhythmically and smoothly.

DESCRIPTION OF ACTIVITY:

1. **Ocean Waves:** Turners, ripple the long rope up and down along the floor. Each jumper, in turn, jump the rope once, travelling in a figure-eight pattern until you have made five jumps. Turners, gradually make the waves bigger. Can you still jump the waves?
2. **Snake Jump:** Turners, wiggle your long rope from side-to-side along the floor. Each jumper, in turn, jump the rope once, travelling in a figure-eight pattern, until you have made five jumps.
3. **Mountain Climb:** One turner, while knee-sitting, hold the rope on the floor; other turner, stand holding the rope at waist height. The rope should be taut between you. Each jumper, in turn, jump the rope once at the low end, travel in a figure-eight pattern, and jump again higher up. Continue until you have jumped as high as you can go!
4. **Blue Bells:** Turners, gently swing the long rope from side-to-side. Each jumper, in turn, jump in place over the rope. How long can you keep jumping before you stop the rope?
5. **Spoke Jumping:** Form groups of four pairs of turners and four jumpers. Turners, position as shown in the diagram: First pair of turners do Ocean Waves; second pair, Snake Jump; third pair, Mountain Climb; and fourth pair, Blue Bells. Jumpers, jump from rope to rope in a CW pattern, completing the circuit twice.
6. **Turning Technique:** Turners, holding a rope handle each, let the rope dangle between you. With elbow at your side, turn the rope with your forearm, in toward the body. Let the rope touch the floor at the bottom of each swing. Listen to the rhythm of the rope as it hits the floor each time. Turn rope with a high arch. Switch hands after every ten rotations. Repeat four times. Change turners and repeat above.
   — *Challenge:* Can one pair take over the rope turning without stopping the rope's rhythm?
7. **Easy Over:** Jumper, stand in the center of the rope. Turners, gently swing long rope for four Blue Bells; then turn the rope overhead of the Jumper. Keep repeating this pattern. Turners, watch the jumper's feet. Jumper, jump this pattern of five Blue Bells and one Easy Over until you miss; then another jumper performs the task. Continue until everyone has had a turn.
8. **Jump the Shot** (Have each group stand in a circle with the leader in the center, holding a rope with a deckring securely attached to one end.): Leader, gently swing the rope CW around the circle along the floor. Jumpers, try to jump the ring as it comes near you. If you are hit, do five repetitions of an exercise the leader commands; then rejoin the game. Change turners every eight swings. Continue game until everyone in your group has been a turner. Repeat game, with rope turning CCW.

GS-59 FRONT DOOR PATTERNS

FOCUS: Entering, exiting, and jumping; groupwork

EQUIPMENT: One long rope per group; music with a steady 4/4 beat; tape or record player

ORGANIZATION:

- Form groups of four skippers: two turners and two jumpers. Have each group get a long rope and scatter around the play area. Review and demonstrate the basic front door entry and exit, in which case the rope is turned toward the incoming jumper. Emphasize smooth rhythmical rope turning and that turners watch the feet of the jumper.

DESCRIPTION OF ACTIVITY:

1. *Blue Bells Warm-Up:* Turners, swing the rope back and forth like a pendulum. Jumpers, in turn, jump over the rope in different ways: both feet together, feet apart; one foot, then the other foot; a turn in mid-air. Rotate positions so that everyone has a turn at jumping and turning.

2. *Front Door Entry–Exit Pattern:* Turners, turn rope toward incoming jumper. Each jumper stand near left turner's right shoulder. Watch the rope as turners turn it toward you, down, and away. As rope passes your nose, enter and run through to exit near the right turner's right shoulder. Re-enter front door near right turner's left shoulder. Remember, run through—do not jump the rope! Repeat this pattern until each skipper has had four turns.

3. *Front Door Figure-Eight Pattern:* Start near left turner's right shoulder; run through the "open window"; exit near the right turner's right shoulder; around that turner; then re-enter front door near right turner's left shoulder; run through again, exiting near left turner's left shoulder; ready to do the circuit again. Repeat pattern until each skipper has gone twice. Reverse the figure-eight pattern by having the Jumper start near right turner's left shoulder.

4. *Front Door-Jump-Exit:* Jumper, enter Front Door, jump the rope once; then exit. Then repeat in a figure-eight pattern four times.

   — Now each jumper jump four times in the middle; then exit.
   — Run in Front Door, jump the letters in your first and last name. Run out the same side you entered.
   — Run in Front Door, jump on one foot four times, and then on the other foot. Repeat pattern three times; then exit.
   — Run in Front Door, jump quarter-turns in one direction; then in the reverse direction. Exit on opposite side that you entered.
   — Run in Front Door. Jump and exit any way you choose.

5. *Rope Exchange Game:* Begin with one jumper near each turner. Left Jumper, change places with the right turner after you jump. Try not to stop the rhythm of the rope's turning. Right Jumper, change places with the left turner. Continue this pattern of opposite jumpers and turners exchanging places.

GS–60 BACK DOOR PATTERNS

FOCUS: Entering and exiting technique; jumping; groupwork

EQUIPMENT: One long rope per group; one hoop per group; music with a strong 4/4 beat; tape or record player

ORGANIZATION:

- Form groups of four or five skippers and have each group get a long rope before scattering around the play area. Review and demonstrate the basic Back Door technique of turning the rope away from the incoming jumper. Emphasize smooth, rhythmical rope turning and that turners watch the feet of the jumper.

DESCRIPTION OF ACTIVITY:

1. **Call-In Warm-Up:** Turners, turn rope toward jumpers in the Front Door Pattern; then first jumper, run in the Front Door and begin jumping. At random, call the name of another jumper who will run in and join hands with you so that you jump together three times. First jumper, run out, and second jumper, call another jumper's name at random. Hold hands and jump together three times. Continue until all skippers have called in another jumper. Change rope turners and repeat.

2. **Back Door Entry:** Jumper, stand near the left turner's right shoulder. Watch the rope as it hits the floor and rises upward, away from you. When the rope is at the top, run through the open window; exit near the right turner's left shoulder. Re-enter near right turner's left shoulder; then run through again, exiting near left turner's left shoulder; around that turner, ready to do figure-eight again. Remember to run through; do not jump the rope! Repeat this pattern until each skipper has gone twice.

   — Reverse the figure-eight pattern by having Jumper start near right turner's left shoulder.

3. **Back Door-Jump-Exit Pattern:** Each jumper, repeat Back Door Entry. Remember to watch the rope as it hits the floor and rises upward, away from you. When the rope is at the top, run in and jump the rope once as it hits the floor; then exit. Repeat in a figure-eight pattern until each skipper has gone four times.

   — Repeat, jumping five times in the middle before exiting.

4. **Hoop Capture** (Have each group stand in a circle, with the leader in the center, holding a long rope with a hoop securely attached to one end.): Leader, gently swing the outstretched rope CW around the circle and along the floor. Jumpers, try to jump in the hoop as it comes near you. If successful, you become the new turner. Repeat, with turner swinging the rope in a CCW direction.

GS–61 LONG ROPE CHALLENGES

FOCUS: Jumping stunts; cooperation

EQUIPMENT: One long rope per group;
one 10-meter (30-foot) long rope per large group;
music with a strong 4/4 beat;
tape or record player

ORGANIZATION:

- Form groups of four to five skippers. Have leaders get a long rope; then groups scatter around the play area. Check for good spacing.

DESCRIPTION OF ACTIVITY:

1. *Copy-Cat Jumping Warm-Up:* Turners, rhythmically turn the rope front door. Jumpers, stand in single-file formation behind one rope turner, with the leader at the head of the line. Leader, run in front door and jump the rope any way you choose. Other jumpers, in turn, copy the leader's action. If the leader stops the rope, the next jumper becomes the new leader, and the old leader goes to the end of the line. Change turners after each jumper has had a turn at being leader, and repeat warm-up.

2. *Hot Pepper Challenge:* Turners, begin by turning the rope slowly. Jumper, enter front door and jump the rope; on your signal "Pepper," turners will turn the rope quickly. How many times can you jump without stopping the rope? Repeat until everyone has had a turn at jumping. Who in your group will be the "Hot Pepper Champ"? Challenge another group's "Champ!"

3. *High-Lo Water Challenge:* Turners, at first turn the rope so that it hits the floor; jumper, enter front door and jump in the middle. Now turners, gradually turn the rope higher, until quite high; then gradually turn the rope lower, until it touches the floor. Jumper, can you keep jumping without stopping the rope? Repeat until everyone has had a turn.

4. *Revolving Doors:* Each jumper, in turn, run in Front Door, jump on one foot four times, jump on the other foot four times; then run out Front Door again.

   — Run in Back Door, jump-turn four times; then exit Back Door.

   — Run in Front Door, jump a different way; then exit Back Door.

   — Run in Back Door, jump another way; then exit Front Door.

5. *Partner Stunts:* Two jumpers, enter front door together, and later exit together. Explore different ways of jumping together: Jump and clap partner's hands; jump-turn away from each other; jump and touch the floor; invent a partner stunt of your own!

GS-62 LONG ROPE STUNTS

FOCUS: Jumping coordination; rhythmical jumping; groupwork

EQUIPMENT: One long rope per group; one beanbag (or deckring) per group; one large utility ball per group; one short rope per group; music with a strong 4/4 beat; tape or record player

ORGANIZATION:

- Form groups of four or five skippers. Have each group collect a long rope, short rope, beanbag (or deckring), ball, and hoop, and scatter around the play area. Ensure that groups are well spaced.

DESCRIPTION OF ACTIVITY:

1. **Basic Tricks in a Long Rope:** Jumpers, in turn, run in Front Door and perform a short rope trick, then run out Back Door or Front Door.
   — Rocker; Jogger; Boxer; Bell; Quarter Jump-Turns; and Skiers
   — Forward, Side, and Double Straddle Jumps
   — Elevator; Cross-legged; Bird Hops; and Twister

2. **Travelling Rope Stunt:** Turners, turn a long rope in place while a Jumper jumps, in turn. On signal "Travel!" Turners, move sideways as you continue to turn rope. Jumper inside rope, jump sideways with the rope. Repeat for eight jumps; then reverse direction for another eight jumps.

3. **Spinning Wheel:** Each jumper, in turn, jump in the center of the rope as the Turners turn the long rope while travelling CW. Repeat for eight jumps, then reverse direction for another eight jumps. Turners, try to keep jumper centered.

4. **Beanbag Toss and Jump Stunt:** While jumping in the middle, each jumper, in turn, toss and catch a beanbag with a skipper standing just out of range of the turning long rope. Continue, until everyone has had a turn.

5. **Ball Bounce and Jump Stunt:** While jumping in the middle, each jumper, in turn, bounce a large ball.

6. **Long and Short Stunt:** Each jumper, start in the middle with a short rope held behind your heels and face one of the turners. As the turners turn the rope at a constant speed, turn your short rope at the same speed and jump inside the long rope. Repeat, but run in Front Door and jump sideways to turners.

7. **Jumping Jingles:**
   — **Papa, Papa:** Three jumpers, in turn, run in the Front Door until you are all jumping the rope together; then each jumper in turn, run out the Back Door, chanting: "Papa, papa, I am ill. Call for the doctor over the hill. First came the doctor; then came the nurse; Then came the woman with the alligator purse. Out went the doctor; out went the nurse; Out went the woman with the alligator purse."
   — **Creative Jingles:** Each group create a Jumping Jingle of your own; then demonstrate it to the other groups.

FOCUS: Cooperation; rhythm sense

EQUIPMENT: Four long ropes per group; music with a strong 4/4 beat; tape or record player

ORGANIZATION:

- Divide the class into groups of six to eight skippers. Have each group collect four long ropes and find a free space. Ensure that groups are well spaced.

DESCRIPTION OF ACTIVITY:

1. *File Jump:* Jumpers, stand in single-file formation behind one rope turner. First jumper, run in the Front Door, jump once, and then run out the Back Door. Stand behind the opposite rope turner. As soon as the first jumper exits, next jumper, run in the front door, repeat the action, and exit the Back Door, standing behind the first player. When all jumpers have had a turn, repeat. Change turners, and repeat once more.

2. *Triangle:* Three rope turners, hold the handles of two ropes, one handle in each hand. Turn the three ropes up and away from the center in unison. Three jumpers, run in Front Door and jump several times; then run out the same side you entered. Jumpers and turners, change roles and repeat.

3. *Wheel Jump* (Combine two groups for this stunt.): Four pairs of turners, each pair with a long rope, position in a wheel formation as shown. Jumpers, stand in single-file formation, facing one of the turning ropes. On signal, 'Turn!" rope turners turn the long ropes in unison. Each jumper, run in Front Door, jump once; then exit toward the next long rope. As soon as the jumper just ahead of you has entered the next rope, you may go. Continue in a CCW direction around the "wheel." Change roles and repeat in a CW direction.

4. *Loop Run* (Combine two groups for this stunt; four pairs of turners stand in a file. Each pair faces inward and holds a long rope between them.): Jumpers, stand in a file near one end turner. On signal "Turn!" turners turn long ropes. Each jumper, in turn, run a loop pattern as shown, until all have completed the Loop Run. As soon as the Jumper ahead of you has entered the next rope, you may go. Change roles and repeat "Loop Run."

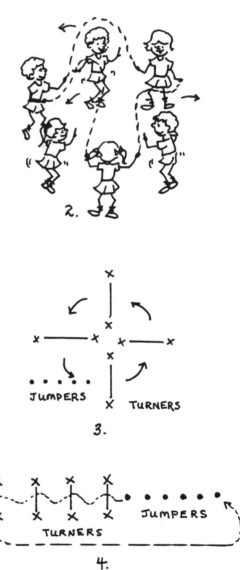

2.

3.

4.

1.

GS–64 ROPE JUMPING STATIONS

FOCUS: Long and short rope jumping skills; stationwork

EQUIPMENT: Several short ropes;
several long ropes;
two hoops;
four utility balls, beanbags, or deckrings;
recording paper and one pencil per group;
posterboard;
marking pen;
masking tape;
lively music with a strong 4/4 beat;
tape or record player

ORGANIZATION:

• Set up six to eight skipping stations around the play area in a circuit. Post signs (and posters, if available) to designate each station. Put strong and weak skippers together in groups of four to promote peer-teaching. Every four to six minutes, have skippers rotate from station to station in a CW direction. Write to your State or National Heart Foundation for jump rope posters. Following are suggestions for jump rope stations.

DESCRIPTION OF ACTIVITY:

1. **Short Rope Routine:** Create a short rope routine using the tricks you have learned. Work in counts of four or eight.

2. **Partner Skipping:** Practice rope jumping with a partner using one rope; then using two ropes.

3. **Skill-Builder Idea:** Using the tricks you have learned, combine them to create new tricks. Give your new trick a name!

4. **Long Rope Tricks:** How many different Short Rope Tricks can you perform in a long rope? Practice!

5. **Long Rope Stunts:** Using equipment such as balls, beanbags or deckrings, hoops, short ropes, and long ropes, invent long rope stunts. Teach them to other members of your group.

6. **Jumping Jingles:** Can your group create a short rope-jumping jingle (poem) that will involve everyone making up a part of the jingle, a recorder writing up the jingle, and each skipper in your group, in turn, jumping in a long rope while your group recites the jingle in unison?

7. **Rope Challenger** (Post posters of tricks the skippers have not as yet learned.): Choose a trick, read the description or helpful hints to go with the illustration, and try to learn it. You may get help from other skippers in your group and from me.

VARIATION:

Provide opportunity for skippers to "show off" the routines they have developed, the new tricks they have learned or created, and the group jumping jingle they have put together.

GS-65 INTRODUCING PARACHUTES

FOCUS: Teaching and safety guidelines; arm strength; cooperation

EQUIPMENT: One parachute per group

ORGANIZATION:

- Use parachutes indoors or outdoors, on play days, or as part of a lesson. Parachutes are great at any time because they require all players, regardless of skill or strength, to cooperate and to be vigorously and continuously involved throughout the activity. Parachutes of 7 meters (24 feet) in diameter are suitable for a class of 25 to 30 children. Smaller classes could use a 5-meter (16-foot)-diameter parachute, while larger classes could use either one 7-meter (24-foot)-diameter parachute or two 5-meter (16-foot) chutes. Have players stand around the edge of the parachute and grip the canopy at the seams.

DESCRIPTION OF ACTIVITY:

1. Hold the chute with both hands and roll the edge toward the center two or three times so that you get a better grip. If you have long fingernails, try not to pull too hard. Grip the edge of the chute at all times until you are told to let go.

OVERHAND GRIP

2. Use any of the following grips:
   — *Overhand Grip:* Grip the edge of the chute with the palms facing down. The Overhand Grip is the most common parachute grip.
   — *Underhand Grip:* Grip the edge of the chute with palms up.
   — *Cross-Over Grip:* Cross the arms and grip the edge of the chute with the Overhand Grip.
   — *Alternating Grip:* Use the Overhand Grip with one hand and the Underhand Grip with the other hand.

UNDERHAND GRIP

3. *Parachute Warm-Up* (Have children evenly space themselves around the parachute and hold onto the edge at waist level, using the Overhand Grip.) This warm-up is called *Ripples and Waves.* Shake the parachute gently, making only ripples. Gradually, let your ripples get bigger, making little waves. Now let those waves get bigger and bigger. Show me how hard you can shake the parachute! "Freeze!"

CROSS-OVER GRIP

4. *Merry-Go-Round Activities:* Hold the parachute with your right hand only and rest your left hand on your hip. Walk forward in a CW direction. Walk normally, holding the parachute as high as you can. Walk quickly. Walk backwards. Walk forward, gently raising and lowering the parachute on the signals "Up!" and "Down!"
   — Change to a left Overhand grip and jog forward CCW. On signal, "Switch!" quickly grip the parachute with your other hand and jog in the opposite direction. (Repeat several times.)
   — Grip the parachute in your right hand again and skip forward in a CW direction, gently shaking the parachute. "Switch!" to your left hand grip and gallop forward in a CCW direction.
   — Using a right Overhand Grip and changing your hopping foot with every four hops, travel in a CW direction.
   — Hold the edge of the parachute with both hands, using the Underhand Grip, and sidestep to the right; to the left. On signal, "Jump!" stop in place and gently bounce up and down.

GS-66 INFLATION FUN

FOCUS: Inflation technique and activities; groupwork

EQUIPMENT: One parachute per group; easy listening music (background); tape or record player

ORGANIZATION:

- Review parachute grips; then demonstrate and explain inflation action, before practice. The inflation action is basic to most parachute activities. Establish definite signals such as "Ready–Begin," or "1, 2, 3,—Stretch!" so that everyone responds at the same time.

DESCRIPTION OF ACTIVITY:

2.

4.

7.

8.

1. *Inflation:* Hold the canopy at waist level using the overhand grip. On the signal "Ready–Down!" squat and hold parachute to the floor. On signal "1, 2, 3,—Up!" stand and thrust arms overhead to allow as much air under the chute as possible. When the center of the canopy touches the floor, repeat to get an even better inflation.

2. *Tenting:* Inflate parachute; then on the signal "In—1, 2, 3!" walk forward three steps. As the chute settles, on signal "Out—1, 2, 3!" walk backwards three steps.

3. *Tent Run:* Players, inflate the chute as for Tenting, quickly let go of the chute with your right hands, and then run CCW around it. Challenge players to return to their starting positions before the chute touches the floor. Try to skip instead of run.

4. *Mushroom:* Inflate chute; then quickly pull the edge to the floor to seal in the escaping air and make a mushroom shape. Continue to hold the edges down until the canopy settles to the floor. Try walking forward three steps before sealing parachute to the floor.

5. *Inflation Challenge:* Using two chutes, challenge the other group to try to keep its chute inflated the longest time.

6. *Sunflower:* Inflate the parachute. Now quickly lower it to the floor and kneel on the outside edge to seal in the air. Raise arms sideways, join hands, and on the signal "In!" lean forward; on signal "Out!" lean backwards. Pretend to be a sunflower closing and opening.

7. *Fly Away:* Inflate the chute until it is totally inflated; then, on signal "Fly Away!" everyone let go at the same time. The chute should remain in the air for a few seconds before it settles down on top of you, but don't move off your spot!

8. *Igloo* (Explain that you are now going to make the whole class disappear.): Hold the parachute using the cross-over grip, inflate it, and walk forward three steps. On signal "Turn!" quickly turn and duck under the parachute. Re-grasp the inside edge, kneel (or sit), and seal edge to floor. Return to the outside and try again.

9. *Peek-a-Boo Igloo:* Make an Igloo and seal it to the floor, leaving only your heads outside. Make another Igloo, seal it to the floor, and then lie on your backs poking only your feet outside!

10. *Igloo Crawl:* Number off 1, 2, 1, 2 around the chute. Listen to the number I call. If it is your number, then crawl carefully under the chute across to the other side.

FOCUS: Conditioning activities for arms and legs

EQUIPMENT: One parachute per group; music with a steady 4/4 beat; tape or record player

ORGANIZATION:

• Have all players stand around the parachute and hold it at waist level using the overhand grip.

DESCRIPTION OF ACTIVITY:

1.

4.

7.

1. **Ocean Waves:** On signal "Ocean Waves!" slowly shake the parachute up and down: then shake a little faster . . . and faster (the wind is getting stronger and stronger . . . it's a hurricane!). Now make gentle waves as the wind is dying down . . . to a soft breeze! (Create Ocean Waves in the kneeling position.)

2. **Row Boat:** Sit with your legs outstretched under the chute. Hold the edge using the overhand grip with arms bent and the chute taut as you pull it to your chest. On signal "Row!" players on one side, reach forward to touch toes, while players on the other side lean backwards. Return to the starting position, pulling your arms backwards in a rowing motion, keeping the chute taut as you do.

3. **Firefighter's Pull:** Holding the chute using the underhand grip, step one leg forward, plant both feet firmly, lean back, and straighten your arms. On signal "1, 2, 3—Pull!" pull the chute toward you without moving your feet or jerking the chute. Pull as hard as you can for ten seconds. Change to the overhand grip, kneel and repeat; then sit and repeat.

4. **Wild-Horse Pull:** Turn your back to the parachute and hold it using the overhand grip. With one foot forward and the other back, plant your feet firmly and lean forward. On signal, "1, 2, 3—Pull!" pull as hard as you can for ten seconds. Repeat in the kneeling and sitting positions.

5. **Crab-Walk:** In crab-walk position, grip the chute with your right hand in the underhand grip. On signal "1, 2, 3—Pull!" crab-walk away from the middle, pulling the chute with you; then change hands and crab-walk in the opposite direction.

6. **Forward Straddle Jumps:** On signal "Jump!" jump one foot forward and the other back. Jump again, landing with opposite leg forward. Repeat for 30 seconds or more.

7. **Jumping Jacks:** Turn left side to the parachute and hold the edge in your left hand at the waist, using the overhand grip. On the signal "Apart!" jump the legs apart and raise both arms overhead. On the signal "Together!" jump the legs together and lower the arms. Repeat ten times. Repeat, holding the chute with the right hand.

8. **Wrist Roll:** Hold parachute at waist level using the overhand grip with arms fully extended. On signal "Go!" stretch the chute until it is tight and slowly roll the edge toward the middle. When the parachute is completely rolled, it is ready to put away.

GS-68 MORE PARACHUTE WORKOUT

FOCUS: Conditioning for tummy, arms, and legs

EQUIPMENT: One parachute per group; lively music; tape or record player

ORGANIZATION:
- Have players gather around the parachute.

DESCRIPTION OF ACTIVITY:

1. *Curl-Ups:* Lie on your back in the hook-lying position with your body under the parachute. Hold the edge of the canopy using the overhand grip. On signal, tighten the grip and curl up. Lower your back to the floor and repeat ten times.

2. *Modified V-Sit:* Lie on your back with your head to the chute. Reach arms overhead and hold the edge using the underhand grip. Pull the parachute tight. At the same time raise the chest and lift the bent legs. Hold the legs off the floor for ten seconds and relax. Repeat.

3. *Sprinters:* Inflate the parachute and form a mushroom by sealing the edges tightly to the floor. Hold the edge in the front-support position; alternately extend and bend legs ten times before the canopy touches the floor; then relax.

GS-69 PARACHUTE STRETCHES

FOCUS: Stretching activities

EQUIPMENT: See activity GS-68.

ORGANIZATION:
- Have all players squat around the parachute and hold it taut at floor level using the overhand grip.

DESCRIPTION OF ACTIVITY:

1. *Elevator:* On signal "Elevator up!" pull the parachute tight and slowly raise the chute high overhead keeping it tightly stretched. On signal "Elevator Down!" slowly lower the chute to the starting position. Continue raising and lowering the chute nine more times.
   — Hold the parachute at different levels: eyes, thighs, knees, ankles.

2. *Sky-High Pulls:* Stand with feet shoulder-width apart and hold the parachute at waist level using overhand grip. On signal "1, 2, 3—Up!" slowly raise the chute until your arms are straight overhead. Using only your arms and shoulders, and without moving your feet, pull back and hold the chute tight for ten seconds. Repeat using the overhand grip.

3. *Side Stretches:* Kneel and turn left side to the parachute. Hold the edge with the left hand. Now extend the right leg to the side, rest the right hand on the right thigh, and support the weight on the left knee. On signal, pull the chute toward the right side for ten seconds. Relax and change sides.

4. *Rhythmic Breather* (As for Elevator, except that players straighten arms overhead and take a deep breath in.): Exhale as you slowly lower arms. Repeat slowly several times.

GS-70 PARACHUTE SHAKE GAMES

FOCUS: Cooperation; alertness; arm strength

EQUIPMENT: One parachute per group;
one beachball per group;
one playground ball per group;
one whiffle or tennis ball per group;
ten to twelve beanbags per group;
six to eight skipping ropes per group;
one volleyball per group

ORGANIZATION:

• Have players evenly space themselves around the parachute and hold the seam using the Overhand Grip.

DESCRIPTION OF ACTIVITY:

1. **Ball Shake:** I will put different types of balls on the parachute, starting with a beachball. How many times can you make the beachball bounce up into the air? (Repeat using a playground ball, and then a whiffle or tennis ball.) Which one bounces the best?

2. **Snake Shake** (Place the skipping ropes on the chute.): How long will it take to shake all the "poisonous snakes" off the parachute? Don't let a snake touch you; otherwise, you must jog once around the play area, holding your poisoned part, and then rejoin the game.

3. **Popcorn** (Place all the beanbags on the chute.): How long will it take to "pop" all the popcorn (beanbags) off the chute? Try again. Can you beat your best score?

4. **Parachute Volleyball** (Divide the players into two even groups who stand on opposite sides of the chute facing each other.): When I throw the volleyball into the center of the chute, try to shake it off to touch the floor on the opponent's side of the chute. Score one point each time. Play to five points.

GS-71 PARACHUTE NUMBER GAMES

FOCUS: Cooperation; listening; alertness

EQUIPMENT: One parachute per group

DESCRIPTION OF ACTIVITY:

1. **Number Chase:** Count off by four's around the chute. Remember your number! Begin by gripping the seam in the right hand and jogging in a CW direction. Listen to the number I call out. If your number is called, immediately release your grip on the chute and run toward the next vacated place. You will have to put on a burst of speed to reach the spot left by another player with that number. (Repeat game, travelling in a CCW direction.)

2. **Number Race** (Divide the class into two equal teams, and have each team number off consecutively 1, 2, 3, etc. Position each team around one half of the parachute.): On signal, inflate the chute and listen carefully to the number I call. The player on each team whose number is called, run as carefully and quickly as you can in a CCW direction around the outside of the chute. Can you return to your place before the center of the chute touches the floor? (Repeat game, but travel in a CW direction.)

— Repeat game, but call two numbers.

3. **Number Exchange** (Number off players by five as they stand around the chute.): On signal, inflate the chute. As it fills with air, I will call out a number. Listen carefully. Everyone with that number, leave your place on the chute, and move under the chute to another open place before the chute touches you.

GS-72 MORE PARACHUTE GAMES _____

FOCUS: Teamwork; listening; alertness; control

EQUIPMENT: One parachute per group;
two different-colored balls;
one long rope;
three short ropes

ORGANIZATION:

- Have players space themselves evenly around the parachute and hold it at waist level using the Overhand Grip.

DESCRIPTION OF ACTIVITY:

1. **Hole in One** (Divide the class into two equal teams with each team positioned around one half of the parachute. Assign each team a colored ball and roll the balls onto the chute.): On signal "Play!" each team try to shake your ball into the center pocket and keep the other team from putting its ball through the center. Score one point each time your team puts the ball in the hole.

2. **Moon Walk** (Number off the players by four's around the parachute. Then have them kneel on one knee with the other knee up and hold the chute taut at floor level.): You are going to take a walk on the moon! Be ready to leave your place and walk on the chute when your number is called. As the space-walkers move across the chute, the rest of the class, shake it up and down at a lower level, keeping the chute stretched. When I call a new number, space-walkers carefully return to your place and new space-walkers begin your turn.

3. **Mousetrap** (Select six to eight children to be the "mice."): On signal "Inflate!" chute players inflate the chute. Mice, try to run under the chute, across and out the other side, before the chute players can trap you. Chute players, wait patiently until you hear the signal "Trap!" before sealing the chute to the floor. The trapped Mice must join the chute players. The game continues until there is one Mouse left. Six new Mice are chosen and the game begins again. Mice, look carefully where you are going at all times!

4. **Speed-Away** (Place a volleyball on chute.): Raise and lower the chute to roll the ball in a large circle around the parachute. Try to keep the ball circling around the outer edge of the chute. How many times can we get the ball to roll past the same spot?

5. **Jaws** (Choose two players to be the Sharks, who position themselves under the middle of the canopy on all-fours.): On signal "Ocean Waves!" standing players, shake the chute gently to create waves while the Sharks swim around under the chute to gently grab the leg of a parachute player and pull that player under the chute. The two players change roles and repeat the game until everyone has been a Shark.

6. **Tug-of-War** (Roll the chute into a long rope and tie three skipping ropes around it: one rope in the middle and the other two ropes on either side, about one meter [three feet] from the middle rope. Form two teams, have them position themselves on either side of the parachute behind the outer ropes; then place the long rope cross-ways on the floor directly under the middle rope.): On signal "Pull!" tug the chute so that the outer rope on the opposite side moves over the long rope marker. Play for the best two out of three tugs.

FOCUS: Teamwork; listening; ball control

EQUIPMENT: One parachute per group; two cone markers per team; one basketball per player; music; tape or record player

ORGANIZATION:

- Have all players stand around the parachute and hold it taut at waist level using both hands in the Overhand Grip.

DESCRIPTION OF ACTIVITY:

1. ***Chute Crawl*** (Number off the children 1, 2, 1, 2 around the parachute.): Number one's, in kneeling position, stretch the chute out level with the floor. Number two's, crawl under the chute to the opposite side from your starting position. Switch roles and repeat.

2. ***Parachute Race*** (Divide the class into two teams, each team with a parachute. Place two cone markers about 16 meters [50 feet] apart from each other. Have each team center their parachute over a cone marker.): On the signal "Race!" each team try to center your parachute over your opposition's cone marker. The first team to complete the task is the winner.

3. ***Grecian Flurry*** (Form teams of 12 to 16 players. Arrange teams in shuttle formation: four lines of three or four players. Place two cones in front of each team: one at the starting point and one at the turning point, about 18 meters [60 feet] apart. Give each team a parachute.): First three players in line, hold the parachute high overhead using one hand at the leading edge. On the signal "Go!" run to the turning point, around it, and then back to the team to pass the chute to the second three players, who will do the same; then pass to the third three players and so on. Continue until your team has made a total of ten round trips with the chute. The first team finished, sitting cross-legged behind the starting cone, wins.

4. ***Circular Dribbling*** (Have each player get a basketball and stand with left side to the parachute. Players hold the edge of the canopy with the left hand using the overhand grip and hold the basketball in the right hand.): When the music starts or on the signal "Dribble!" dribble the ball with your right hand. Walk forward slowly dribbling the ball; then gradually increase speed to a run, continuing to dribble. Slow to a walk again; then on the signal "Change!" stop, change hands, and dribble in the opposite direction, increasing speed to a run again. If you lose the ball, recover it and rejoin the parachute at your original place.

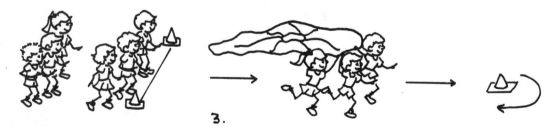

VARIATION:

Parachute Merry-Go-Round: As for the Grecian Flurry, except that players run in groups of six or eight. When the six players reach the turning point, they position the center of the chute over the turning cone and, holding it taut, run CW around it three times before returning to pass off to the next six players. Have the six players run around their starting cone three times first; then around the turning cone.

GS-74 INVENT A PARACHUTE GAME

FOCUS: Creativity using parachutes

EQUIPMENT: One parachute per group;
several jump ropes per group;
small and large playground balls per group;
four bowling pins (or cone markers) per group;
variety of other equipment

ORGANIZATION:

- Divide the class into four or five working groups. Have each group invent a game and teach it to the class. Several suggestions follow. Offer suggestions to groups having difficulty getting started. Encourage and offer praise. Have the other teams applaud the efforts of the performing group.

DESCRIPTION OF ACTIVITY:

1. Create a parachute game that uses no equipment.

2. Create a game that uses the parachute and several jump ropes. Decide how players will stand around the parachute to play your game.

3. Create a game that uses the parachute, four bowling pins or cone markers, and one ball.

4. Create a game that uses several small or large playground balls.

5. Create a game that uses a parachute and your own choice of equipment. Make sure that everyone participates.

RHYTHMICAL PARACHUTES

GS-75 RHYTHMICAL PARACHUTES

FOCUS: Rhythmical movements; sequence-building

EQUIPMENT: One parachute per group;
dance music of any type;
tape or record player

ORGANIZATION:

- Working together, the children and you develop simple routines and dances that use the parachute as the focal point for movement. Try to incorporate all basic locomotor skills, different directions and levels, moving forward, backwards, and sideways, the exchanging of positions, and known dance steps.

DESCRIPTION OF ACTIVITY:

1. Let's make up a routine in which you run, skip, and jump while holding the parachute. Let's do each movement eight times.

2. Now let's design a routine that includes a slide-step, a hop, and a change in both level and direction. Do each movement eight times.

3. Let's modify dances such as "Pop! Goes the Weasel," "Bingo," "Jingle Bells," "Cshebogar," "Bleking," "Hava Nagila" (Hora), or any other round dances from Section 4, "Rhythms and Dance," so that they can be performed around the parachute.

FOCUS: Teaching and safety guidelines; manipulation; control

EQUIPMENT: One scooter per player; one set of banners; one stopwatch

ORGANIZATION:

- Scooters are excellent equipment to use for indoor games. Relays and many other games can be adapted to scooter use if the size of the play area is reduced. One scooter per player is ideal; however, two players may share a scooter for many activities. Have each player get a scooter and sit on it in a home space.

DESCRIPTION OF ACTIVITY:

1. *Safety:*

   — Scooters are not skateboards; do not stand on them.

   — Scooters are not missiles; with or without passengers, do not send them crashing into each other.

   — Watch your fingers! Do not drag your hands along the floor.

   — Before using your scooter, check that its casters fit tightly.

2. *Practice:*

   — Sitting on your scooter, hold your feet off the floor, and push with your hands. Move forward and then backwards.

   — Sit upright, lift bent knees, and try to balance for ten seconds in a modified V-sit.

   — Now lower your feet to the floor. Try to propel yourself using only your feet. Move forward, then backwards.

   — Lie face down on your scooter, hold feet off the floor, and move forward using your hands only; feet only; then both. Roll onto your back and repeat.

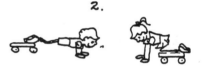

   — Lie face down on your scooter, holding your feet off the floor. Spin yourself around. Repeat in the opposite direction.

   — Kneel on your scooter and pull yourself forward; then push yourself backwards; around in a circle.

   — Place your toes on the scooter and then stretch out in full push-up position with hands on the floor. Move forward, backwards, and sideways.

3. Grip the edges of the scooter. Move forward, backwards, and sideways. Run while holding the edges of the scooter into free spaces. When you have gained speed, kneel on the scooter on both knees and glide as far as you can go.

   — Show me another way of moving on your scooter.

4. *Scooter Tag* (Choose three players to be IT, who each wear a banner. All other players, in sitting position on their scooters, scatter around the play area.): On signal "Go!" IT players try to tag the others. A tagged player must put on a banner and help to tag, until all players are tagged.

5. *Team Tag:* Form teams of five or six players. The leader of Team 1, give banners to your teammates. You are the IT team to start. Using a stopwatch, I will time each team in turn as they try to chase and tag all other players. Tagged players, wheel slowly around the outside of the play area until the next game starts. Everyone must stay on their scooters throughout the game. The team taking the shortest time to tag all the other players wins the game.

GS-77 DOUBLE SCOOTER TASKS

FOCUS: Partnerwork; manipulation; control   **EQUIPMENT:** One scooter per player

ORGANIZATION:

- Have players get a scooter and find a partner. Have each partner in turn try the following Double Scooter Tasks while the other partner watches for good technique and safety.

DESCRIPTION OF ACTIVITY:

1. Lie face down on both scooters and move in different directions.
2. On all-fours, place knees on one scooter and hands on the other. Find a way to move while in this position. How could your partner help you?
3. Now try to move with your feet on one scooter and your hands on the other.
4. Sit on one scooter and place your feet on the other. Can you move forward, backwards, and sideways?
5. Show me another way to move while using two scooters. Change roles with your partner and repeat these tasks.
6. *Scooter Caterpillar:* Sit on your scooters, one behind the other. The back partner, hold onto the hip area of the front partner. Using your legs, partners try to travel around the play area in this way. Can you link up with another pair and form a longer caterpillar? Keep linking up with yet another pair until your caterpillar is eight players long!

GS-78 PARTNER STUNTS

EQUIPMENT: Two scooters per pair

DESCRIPTION OF ACTIVITY:

1. *Footwork:* Sit on your scooter in the following ways and move forward, backwards, and sideways using your feet only:
   — Sit side-by-side with elbows linked.
   — Sit back-to-back with elbows linked.
   — Sit face-to-face with hands joined.
2. *Whirligig:* Face-to-face with your partner, sit on your scooter and place your feet on your partner's scooter. Find a way to move while in this position.
3. *Alligator Crawl:* Side-by-side with your partner, lie face down on your scooter and join inside hands. Move forward, backwards, and in circles using your feet and your free hand.
4. *Pushcarts:* One partner, sit on one scooter and place your feet on the other. Have your partner push you in all directions. Change roles and repeat.
5. *Wheelbarrows:* Return one scooter. Place hands on the scooter in push-up position; partner lifts your legs, holds them above the knees, and pushes you forward.
6. *Two Scooters:* Get your other scooter. Begin with scooters side-by-side. Kneel on your scooter on the inside knee and hold onto your partner's waist. Show me how you can use your outside feet to move in all directions.

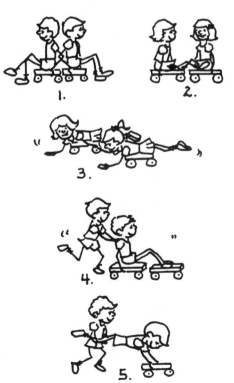

FOCUS: Teamwork; manipulation; control

EQUIPMENT: Two scooters per team;
four cone markers per team;
one baton;
one ball per team

ORGANIZATION:

- Form equal teams of four to six players. Have each team stand in single-file formation at one end of the play area. Each of the first two players in each team has a scooter. Place a cone marker 10 meters (30 feet) from each team as a turning point. On signal "Go!" each player in turn performs the following tasks as they move toward the cone marker, around it, and back to their team. As the first player crosses the starting line, the next player goes. The third player takes the first player's scooter and the first player goes to the end of the file.

DESCRIPTION OF ACTIVITY:

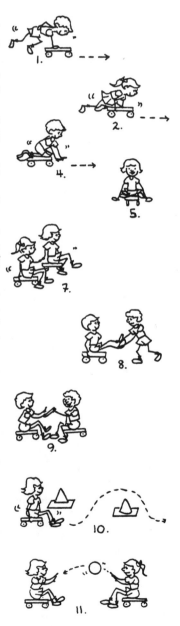

1. ***One-Hand Relay:*** Place one hand on the scooter, tuck the other hand behind your back, and run forward. Change hands as you pass the cone marker.

2. ***Two-Hand, One-Foot Relay:*** Place both hands and one foot on the scooter and push forward with your free foot. Change legs as you pass the cone marker.

3. ***One-Hand, One-Foot Relay:*** Place one hand and one foot on the scooter and push forward with your free foot. Change hands and feet as you pass the cone marker.

4. ***Kneeling Relay:*** Kneel on your scooter and move forward using your hands only.

5. ***Seat and Feet Relay:*** Sit with your feet on your scooter and move forward using your hands only.

6. ***Back-to-Back Relay:*** First two players, sit on the scooters back-to-back and link elbows. Move around the cone marker, and back to the team to give the scooters to the next pair and go to the end of the file. Continue until each pair has had two turns.

7. ***Link-Up Relay:*** Each player sit on a scooter. First player, move forward and around the cone marker, using your feet only. When you return to the team, grip wrist of the next player and repeat relay together; then link up with the third player. Continue adding a player until all players on team are linked.

8. ***Horse-and-Cart Relay:*** First player, sit on a scooter and have the second player pull you by the legs toward the cone marker. Change roles there and return to your team so the next pair can go. Continue until your team has had a total of six turns.

9. ***Shuttle-Scooter Relay*** (All players sit on scooters, half the team facing the other half 10 meters [30 feet] away in shuttle formation. Player at the front of one file gets a baton.): On signal "Go!" player with the baton, move forward, hand the baton to opposite teammate, and go to the end of that file. Player with the baton, repeat the relay. Continue until all team members have had a turn. Repeat.

10. ***Zig-Zag Relay*** (Place four cone markers in a row in front of each team, spacing them about 1 meter [3 feet] apart.): Each player in turn, zig-zag through the row of cone markers, circle the last cone in the row, and return directly to your team. Repeat.

11. ***Partner Ball-Pass Relay*** (Give a ball to each team.): First two players, pass the ball back and forth between you as you move toward the cone marker, around it and back to the team; then pass the ball to the next pair, who will repeat the relay. Continue until each pair has had two turns.

GS-80 SCOOTER TAG GAMES

FOCUS: Manipulation; alertness

EQUIPMENT: One scooter per player; several banners; one ball per game

ORGANIZATION:

- Have each player get a scooter and sit on it.

DESCRIPTION OF ACTIVITY:

1. *Frozen Tag* (Choose three or four players to be IT who wear banners and start in the middle of the play area. All other players scatter.): On signal "Go!" IT players, staying in the sitting position on your scooters, try to tag the free players. A tagged player is immediately "frozen" to the spot and must sit on his or her scooter, extending arms sideways. Another player can free the "frozen" player by passing under the extended arms. IT player, when you have made four tags, give your banner to the fourth player who becomes the new IT.
2. *Scooter Ball Tag* (Choose two or three players to be IT, have them start in the middle of the play area, and give them each a ball. All other players scatter around the play area.): On signal "Go!" IT player, try to tag a free player by touching him or her with the ball on the backside. Now tagged player, you are IT! Quickly retrieve the ball and begin the chase. Who can stay in the game the longest without being tagged?
3. *Scooter Team Ball Tag:* To start, one player, wearing a banner and holding a ball, is IT. All other players, scatter on your scooters. IT, try to tag a player by touching him or her with the ball. Tagged players, put on banners and help IT to tag others. IT team, you may pass the ball to each other as you attempt to close in on free players; however, an IT player may only hold onto the ball for five seconds before passing or tagging. Play the game until no free players remain.

GS-81 SCOOTER BALL GAMES

FOCUS: Ball control; manipulation; partnerwork and teamwork

EQUIPMENT: One scooter per player; one large utility ball per player; one cone marker per group

ORGANIZATION:

- Have players get a scooter and a ball before scattering around the play area.

DESCRIPTION OF ACTIVITY:

1. *Partner Ball Stunts:* Sit on a scooter and dribble the ball with one hand. Move forward while pushing with the other hand. Change hands and directions.
   — Sit on your scooter and find a partner. Put one ball away. Pass the ball back and forth while you and your partner move in all directions.
   — Can you and your partner create another stunt that uses two scooters and a ball?
2. *Follow-the-Leader:* In groups of four, copy and follow your leader as he or she moves in personal or general space while dribbling the ball. Change leader on my signal "Change!" How many different ways can you move?
3. *Scooter Dribble Relay* (Form groups of three or four players and have them sit on their scooters in single-file formation at one end of the play area. Place a cone marker 10 meters [30 feet] away from each group as the turning point.): First player, move forward using your feet while dribbling the ball. Move toward the cone marker, around it, and back to your group. Give the ball to the next player in the file; then continue until all players in your group have had a turn. The group that completes the relay and gets into starting position the quickest is the winner.

FOCUS: Passing and catching; positional play; teamwork

EQUIPMENT: One scooter per player; one utility ball per group; four cone markers per group; one set of pinnies per group

ORGANIZATION:

• To start, have each player get a scooter.

DESCRIPTION OF ACTIVITY:

1. *Passing Warm-Up:* Find a partner and collect a ball to share. Show me how you can pass a ball back and forth to each other. Try bouncing the ball to your partner; sending it through the air. Try short passes; long passes; quick passes; lob passes. Can you move on your scooters and still pass the ball to each other?

2. *In the Soup* (Form groups of three players and have one player sit on a scooter between the other two players, who are about 2 meters [6 feet] apart. Each group plays this game in a confined space.): Two outside players, pass the ball back and forth to each other, trying to keep it away from the middle player. Middle player, if you touch the ball, then change places with the outside player who threw the ball.

3. *Two-on-Two* (Form groups of four players. Use cones to mark the play area.): Two players in each group, pass to each other while trying to keep the ball away from the other two players.

4. *Three-on-Three:* Now form groups of six players. Three players on one team try to pass to each other, while trying to keep the ball away from the opposition three players. A player has three seconds to pass the ball; otherwise, the other team gets possession. Wheel to open spaces to receive passes. Each member of your team should "guard" a member of the opposition team. Score one point each time your team makes three consecutive passes (either an "air" or a bounce pass). Play game to five points; then challenge another team.

5. *Scooter Pin-Ball* (Each game consists of two teams of six to eight players, played in a 10-meter [30-foot] square area. One team wears the pinnies. Set up a cone marker as a goal at each end of the play area. To begin the game and to restart it after a goal is scored, roll the ball between two opposing players in the middle of the play area.): Pass or roll the ball among the players on your team and try to hit the cone marker. Three players must handle the ball before it hits the cone. A player has three seconds to make the pass; otherwise, the other team gets possession.

GS–83 SCOOTER BALL

FOCUS: Cooperation; team play

EQUIPMENT: One scooter per player;
one utility ball per game;
one set of banners per game;
one plastic garbage can per game;
several cone markers;
floor tape;
coin

ORGANIZATION:

- For each game, use cones to mark out a 10-meter (30-foot) square play area. Place a goal (a large plastic garbage can or cardboard box) on the middle of opposite sides of the play area. Using floor tape, mark out a 2-meter (6-foot) diameter circle around the garbage can. A team consists of four to six players. One team must wear banners. Toss a coin to see which team will get possession of the ball.

DESCRIPTION OF ACTIVITY:

1. The object of the game is to score a goal by throwing the ball into the opposition's container.

2. Players, you may carry the ball for five seconds as you travel on your scooter; then you must either pass it or try for a goal. Everyone must stay in contact with the scooter throughout the game.

3. A pass can be made by kicking the ball, rolling it, batting it, or by throwing it. A goal can only be made by throwing the ball into the container from outside the marked circle.

4. The walls of the play area can be used to help you pass the ball or score a goal!

VARIATION: Players score a point by hitting the opposition's container with the ball.

GS–84 SCOOTER HAND HOCKEY

FOCUS: Manipulation; control; team play

EQUIPMENT: Several cone markers;
one scooter per player;
pinnies;
large ball

ORGANIZATION:

- For each game, use four cones to mark out a 10-meter by 10-meter (30-feet by 30-feet) play area; use two cones, spaced 2 meters (6 feet) apart, to mark out a goal area at each end of the play area. Then form two teams of five or six players, with each team starting in its own half, sitting on scooters, and one team wearing pinnies. One player from each team is the goalie. Place a large ball in the middle of the play area between two opposing players.

DESCRIPTION OF ACTIVITY:

1. The object of the game is to bat the ball through the opposition's goal to score.

2. On signal "Hand Hockey!" the game begins by two opposing players at center batting the ball to a teammate. This face-off is repeated every time a goal is scored. Everyone, including the goalie, stay on your scooter throughout the game.

3. The ball must be batted, not picked up and carried or thrown. No body contact is allowed. Move into open spaces to look for a pass rather than crowding around the ball.

GS–85 INTRODUCING VOLLEYBALL

FOCUS: Ball handling; familiarization

EQUIPMENT: One volleyball (or utility ball) per player

ORGANIZATION:

- Explain and demonstrate the following ball-handling skills; then have players get a volleyball and scatter in free space.

DESCRIPTION OF ACTIVITY:

1. Stand with feet shoulder-width apart and hold the ball with both hands. Pass the ball around your ankles and then spiral higher and higher around your body until it is overhead. Repeat, passing the ball in the opposite direction.
2. Hold the ball overhead in both hands. Bend from side-to-side and then from front-to-back. Roll the ball from hand-to-hand around your legs in a figure-eight.
3. Place the ball on the floor. Try to jump over the ball from side-to-side and then from front-to-back. Can you jump while holding the ball between your knees? your ankles? Try turning to left and right.
4. Can you V-sit while holding the ball between your knees or ankles? Try to turn in a circle while in this position. Show me how you can swing your legs overhead, hold them high, and drop the ball behind you.
   — From the sitting position, practice tossing and catching the ball from your forehead.
5. Find a partner, return one ball, and sit three meters (ten feet) apart. Show me how you can lightly pass the ball from your forehead back and forth to each other, 20 times, using both hands.
   — Make up another volleyball task with your partner.

GS–86 READY POSITION

FOCUS: Body and foot work

EQUIPMENT: Whistle

ORGANIZATION:

- Have players find a free space where they can all see you. Children stand in the ready position; the wide position of the feet gives stability; keeping the weight forward allows quick movement in any direction to get under the ball.

DESCRIPTION OF ACTIVITY:

1. *Technique:* Stand with your feet slightly wider than shoulder-width apart; step one foot slightly ahead of the other, bend your knees comfortably, and bring your weight forward onto the balls of your feet. Hold hands at chest level in a relaxed position with palms facing forward.
2. *Heads-Up Drill:* Stand in the ready position and watch me for directions. Whatever direction I point, shuffle step in that direction; to the left, to the right, forward, backwards! Continue for one minute. Whenever I blow the whistle, "pitter patter" (small quick steps) on the spot.
3. *Outlining the Court:* Find a partner. One partner, stand on the boundary of the court facing your partner, who stands inside the court, one meter (three feet) away; both in the ready position. Lead your partner CW around the boundary of the volleyball court. When you hear one whistle blast, "pitter patter." When you hear two whistles, find a new partner and shuffle CCW around the court.

GS-87 MEMORY DRILL CIRCUIT

FOCUS: Court awareness;
warm-up

EQUIPMENT:

Volleyball

net and poles (or long rope);

lively music (optional);
tape or record player

ORGANIZATION:
- Use the Memory Drill Circuit as a warm-up for your volleyball lessons. First review the ready position and the shuffle-step; then form groups of four to six players and have each group stand in single-file formation at one corner of the volleyball court. Use both sides of the court simultaneously.

DESCRIPTION OF ACTIVITY:
1. When the music starts, first player in each group, lead the other players through the following action:
   — Run forward to the net.
   — Block at the net by facing it and jumping straight up, arms extended high overhead with your thumbs touching.
   — Shuffle-step to the opposite corner while facing the net.
   — Block at the opposite corner.
   — Run backwards to the next corner.
   — Shuffle-step to the corner your group started at.
2. Leader, after the first time through, run to the end of your file so that the next player in line can lead the group through the circuit.
3. Continue until your group has gone through the Circuit five times.

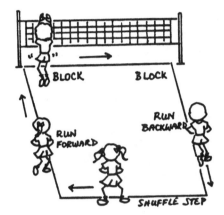

GS-88 THE OVERHEAD PASS (THE SET)

FOCUS: Volleying technique; hand-eye coordination

EQUIPMENT: One volleyball per player

ORGANIZATION:
- The overhead pass, also known as the "volley," the "set," or "face pass," is used to pass the ball among teammates during a game. To teach the set, have players get a volleyball and scatter.

DESCRIPTION OF ACTIVITY:
1. ***Body and Hand Position:*** Stand in the ready position. Spread fingers of both hands in a cupped position with thumbs and index fingers forming a triangle above your face. Look through the "little window" made by your hands. ***Movement:*** Stand directly under the ball as it comes toward you, with knees and elbows bent and hands in front of your face. Watch the ball constantly and distribute your weight evenly on both feet.
2. ***Making Contact:*** Contact the ball with the pads of your fingers and thumbs, relaxing your fingers so that you cushion the ball's impact with the cupped fingers, bent arms and legs. After contact, extend your arms and legs upward and flick your wrists out in the line of direction of the ball.
3. ***Practice:***
   — Put the ball on the floor. Spread your fingers in the cupped position, place them on the ball, and pick it up. Repeat several times, checking the hand position each time.
   — Bounce the ball, catch it, and check that your hands are cupped in the correct position. Repeat several times; then try to bounce the ball continuously.
   — Toss the ball into the air and catch it just in front of your forehead. Pause and check your hand positioning; then repeat the toss and catch several times. Gradually reduce the amount of time you pause while holding the ball so that you are continuously volleying the ball.

FOCUS: Volleying; body positioning; hand-eye coordination

EQUIPMENT: One volleyball per player; one beachball per group

ORGANIZATION:

- Players practice volleying skills individually, with a partner, and then within a group situation. To start, have each player get a volleyball and find a free space. Constantly remind players to volley and catch the ball while in the ready position.

DESCRIPTION OF ACTIVITY:

1. Toss the ball, set the ball once, and catch again.

   — Toss the ball, set twice, and catch again.

   — Can you set three times before catching the ball?

   — How many times can you do it in a row?

2. Toss the ball, set, let the ball bounce once, set again, and then catch it. Repeat this set-bounce, set-bounce pattern.

3. Toss the ball against the wall, let it bounce on the floor, and then set it back to the wall. Let the ball bounce and set again.

   — Do continuous wall sets to yourself, setting the ball at head level each time.

4. Find a partner, stand about three meters (ten feet) apart, and set the ball back and forth. At first, pause slightly after catching the ball; then gradually eliminate the pause so that you are continuously setting the ball to each other.

5. **Partner Setting Challenge:** Which pair can set the ball for the longest time? Count the number of sets aloud.

6. **Space Ball** (Form groups of six to eight players. Have each group stand in a circle, with players in ready position. Give a beachball to a player in each group.): On signal "Volley!" try to keep the ball in the air for as long as possible by volleying or setting the ball to each other. Keep alert! If the ball comes near you, move into the ready position and call "Mine!" Count the number of volleys out loud, continuing to call out the score until the ball hits the floor. Start counting from zero again if the ball does touch the floor or if the same player volleys the ball twice in a row.

VARIATIONS:

a. Have players play Space Ball while sitting or kneeling in a circle.
b. Have players number off around the circle. Players call out the number of the player to whom they intend to set the ball.
c. Play with a volleyball instead of a beachball.

GS-90 THE BUMP

FOCUS: Bumping (forearm passing) technique; hand-eye coordination

EQUIPMENT: One volleyball per player

ORGANIZATION:

- Players learn the forearm bumping technique, at first pantomiming the action, and then later using a volleyball. To start, have players each collect a volleyball, and then scatter around the play area. Ensure that players can see and hear your instructions.

DESCRIPTION OF ACTIVITY:

1. **Body and Arm Position:**
   - Place the ball on the floor beside you and show me your ready position. Good! Now place the knuckles of one hand into the palm of your other hand. Thumbs should be side by side with knuckles up, resting on top of your index fingers. Try to rotate your forearms forward so that your elbows almost touch.
   - Look at the flat surface formed by the fleshy insides of your forearms, that soft, round area just above your wrists and below your elbows. This is the place where you should contact the ball.
   - Find a partner and show each other your body, hand, and arm positions. Check each other for correct technique.

2. **Making Contact:**
   - Now pretend that a low ball is coming toward you. Move toward the ball, bending your knees to get under it. Watch the ball! Follow its flight and watch its contact.
   - Keep the arms together and extended, with the elbows straight. Drop the wrists to absorb the force of the ball on the inside of your forearms.
   - Now lift with your legs and follow through with your arms in the direction of the ball's flight. Keep the motion smooth and continuous.

3. **Practice:** Mime the action of bumping the ball, using the correct body, hand, and arm positions.

GS-91 FOREARM BUMPING TASKS

1. **Wave Drill Warm-Up:** Pretend to bump a ball that is coming from different directions. Start in the ready position. Move your body and arms in the direction I call. On signal "Bump Right!" pretend to bump a ball on your right. Continue for "Bump Left!" "Bump Forward!" and "Bump Backward!" Repeat in any order.

2. **Moving to the Ball:** Get a volleyball, scatter in free space, and do these Bumping tasks:
   - Toss the ball in the air and move into position under it with your arms in the bumping position. Let the ball contact your forearms, bounce off, and then bounce onto the floor.
   - Toss the ball again and try to bump the ball twice in a row before tossing it again.
   - Toss the ball into the air some distance away from you. How quickly can you move into position under it with your forearms in the bumping position?
   - Toss the ball overhead, let it bounce on the floor, bump it with your forearms, and then catch it again.
   - Bounce the ball on the floor, bump it overhead, let it bounce again, bump it again, and then catch the ball.
   - Continue this pattern: throw-bump-catch; throw-bump-bump-catch; throw-bump-bump-bump-catch.
   - Bump the ball overhead for as long as possible!

GS-92 PARTNER BUMPING TASKS

FOCUS: Bumping technique; hand-eye coordination; partnerwork and groupwork

EQUIPMENT: One volleyball per pair; one beachball per group

ORGANIZATION:

- Have players find a partner, get a volleyball to share, and scatter.

DESCRIPTION OF ACTIVITY:

1. Knee-sit about 3 meters (10 feet) away from each other and hold your arms in the bumping position. One partner, stand ready to bump the ball. Toss it to your partner so that he or she can bump it back to you. Remember to position yourself directly under the ball, watching it constantly. Contact the ball on the fleshy part of the forearms. Change roles after ten bumps.

2. Step back so that you are standing 4 meters to 5 meters (13 feet to 16 feet) apart. Toss the ball to your partner, who will bump it back to you. Catch the ball and toss it again. Repeat ten times; then change roles.

3. Toss the ball to one side of your partner so that he or she must quickly move into position under it in order to bump the ball back to you. Your partner then returns to his or her original spot. Change roles after five bumps; then toss the ball to your partner's other side.

4. Toss the ball to your partner, who will bump it to himself once, and then bump it back to you; then try to bump it back and forth as long as you can. Change roles after five tosses.

5. Toss the ball to your partner, who will bump it back to you. Bump the ball back to your partner. How many times can you bump it back and forth before the ball touches the floor?

6. *Space Ball:* Play game in groups of three to four, each group with a beachball. On signal "Bump!" try to keep the ball in the air for as long as possible by bumping the ball back and forth to each other. If the ball comes near you, move into ready position and call "Mine!" Count the number of bumps your group can make before the ball touches the ground. Which group will get the most?

   — Play the game again, allowing players to set or bump the ball to keep it in "orbit!"

GS-93 INTRODUCING COURT POSITIONS

FOCUS: Court positioning

EQUIPMENT: Volleyball net and poles;
one whistle;
one coin

ORGANIZATION:

- Form teams of six players and have each team take up the following court positions: Right Forward (RF), Right Back (RB), Center Back (CB), Left Back (LB), Left Forward (LF), and Center Forward (CF) as shown.

DESCRIPTION OF ACTIVITY:

1. When you hear the whistle, rotate CW from one position to the next until you are back in your starting positions. During volleyball games, you will rotate one court position CW each time your team wins the serve.

2. As you rotate from one position to the next, shuffle-step in the ready position while facing the net. Check the location of the players on either side, in front, and behind you; know where the boundary lines are in relation to your court position.

3. During volleyball games, cover the area around your court position. The other players will cover their areas also! Players at the back of the court, if the ball comes at or above your shoulder, let it go! It is on its way out-of-bounds!

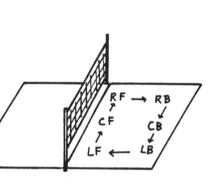

GS-94 NEWCOMB

FOCUS: Lead-up game; court positioning; teamwork

EQUIPMENT: See activity GS–93.

ORGANIZATION:

- Divide the class into teams of six to eight players. Each team positions itself on one side of the net, with players in their court positions. Adjust the height of the net to suit the players' ability. Toss a coin to determine which team starts with the ball.

DESCRIPTION OF ACTIVITY:

1. The team with the ball, start the game by throwing the ball over the net. Players on the receiving team, try to catch the ball before it touches the floor. After catching the ball on the fly, without moving from the spot, throw it back over the net.

2. The throwing team scores one point if an opposition player tries to catch the ball but drops it or the ball touches the floor.

3. The receiving team scores one point if the thrower throws the ball out-of-bounds or into the net, causing the ball to hit the floor on his or her side of the net. The boundary lines of the court are considered in-bounds.

4. Rotate one court position every three points. The game continues until one team has 15 points.

VARIATIONS:

a. Use a beanbag or deckring instead of a ball.
b. Cover the net with a sheet or parachute so that only the feet are showing.

GS-95 INTRODUCING THE UNDERHAND SERVE

FOCUS: Serving technique; hand-eye coordination

EQUIPMENT: One volleyball per player; volleyball net and poles; masking or floor tape

ORGANIZATION:

- Have players get a volleyball and experiment with different ways of striking it: with the heel of the open hand, a semiclosed hand, or a closed fist. Have them decide which hand position they prefer; then explain and demonstrate the underhand serve.

DESCRIPTION OF ACTIVITY:

1. *Stance:* Stand with feet shoulder-width apart facing the net. Step forward on the foot opposite your serving hand. Bend your knees slightly, and lean forward. Hold the ball at waist level in the palm and fingers of your nonserving hand.

2. *Movement:* Open your hand, straighten your serving arm, and swing it back and then forward to contact the ball. Shift your weight onto the front foot as your arm swings forward to hit the ball slightly below center with the heel of your serving hand, as the other hand drops away. Swing your serving hand up and forward to follow through. Step forward to complete the movement.

3. *Practice:*
   - Take the ball and find a free space at the wall. Serve the ball to the wall so that it hits above a line that is three meters (ten feet) from the floor. Gradually step farther away from the wall as you continue to serve the ball.
   - Find a partner, return one ball, and serve the ball so your partner can catch it. Coach each other in the correct serving technique.
   - Serve the ball over the net to your partner. Stand three meters (ten feet) away from the net; then gradually step back to increase the distance between you and your partner.

GS-96 SHOWER BALL

FOCUS: Underhand serve; lead-up game; visual tracking; catching

EQUIPMENT: See activity GS-95.

ORGANIZATION:

- Use floor tape to mark off half of each court as the serving area. Appoint two scorekeepers, who stand at opposite ends of the volleyball net; then form teams of six to twelve players and have them scatter on either side of the volleyball court. Distribute two or three volleyballs to each team.

DESCRIPTION OF ACTIVITY:

1. The object of the game is to serve the ball over the net so that it lands in the other team's court. Your team then scores one point. Each scorekeeper will keep track of one team's score.

2. You may serve the ball at any time, but only from the serving area at the back of the court.

3. Any player on the other team may try to catch your ball after it crosses the net. If a player catches your serve, your team does not score a point.

4. When the time limit is up, the game will stop and the scorekeepers will announce each team's total to determine who won the first round.

5. Who will volunteer to replace the scorekeepers so they can join the next game? Change ends, and let's play another round.

GS–97 BEACHBALL VOLLEYBALL

FOCUS: Lead-up game; teamwork; setting, serving and bumping skills; court awareness

EQUIPMENT: One beachball; volleyball net and poles

ORGANIZATION:

- Divide the class into teams of six to nine players and have each team position itself on one side of the net, with players in their court positions. Because a beachball is more difficult to serve than a volleyball, have players serve closer to the net, but still from the back right-hand court position. Emphasize that players should call "Mine!" if they intend to take the ball; play their court positions; keep alert and in the ready position.

DESCRIPTION OF ACTIVITY:

1. The player at the back right-hand side of the court serves first. One teammate may help you send the ball over the net after it has been served.

2. The ball is then in play. The ball may touch the net during play but not on a serve.

3. Each team is allowed no more than three tries to send the ball back over the net, but no player may hit the ball twice in a row. Play continues back and forth over the net until the ball hits the floor.

4. The serving team earns one point if the receiving team fails to return the ball over the net within three hits; the receiving team hits the out-of-bounds; or the ball hits the net during play and lands in the receiver's court. Only the serving team can score points.

5. The same server continues to serve as long as he or she scores points.

6. The receiving and serving teams change roles whenever the serving team fails to serve the ball over the net; the ball hits the net after it is served; or the ball is served out-of-bounds. The serving team rotates one position clockwise each time there is a new server.

VARIATIONS:

a. Players may hit the ball any number of times on their side before hitting it over the net.

b. Change server after he or she has served three consecutive points so that everyone will get more opportunity to serve.

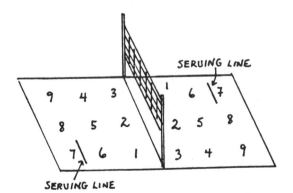

GS-98 DUAL CONTESTS

FOCUS: Leg, arm, and shoulder strength; balance

EQUIPMENT: One mat per pair

ORGANIZATION:

- Combative play should be introduced in the spirit of friendly competition. Encourage fair play and good sportsmanship at all times. Have players find a partner of equal size and ability.

DESCRIPTION OF ACTIVITY:

1. **Rooster Fighting:** Squat, facing your partner, and clasp your hands behind your knees. Now bump your partner with shoulders only, so that he or she releases the clasped hands. Repeat, holding your heels with your hands.

2. **Hoppo Bumpo:** Stand on your left leg and hold your right ankle with your left hand behind your back. Grasp your left arm behind your back with your right hand. Now try to gently bump your opponent off the mat so that he or she touches the floor with one or both feet. Reverse leg/hand positions and repeat. Challenge your partner to best two out of three tries.

3. **Team Hoppo Bumpo:** Have players hook four mats together to form one large mat area. Teams of four players challenge each other to see who is last still standing on the mats.

GS-99 REACTION CHALLENGES

FOCUS: Quick reactions; agility

EQUIPMENT: One flag per player; one folding mat per pair

ORGANIZATION:

- Have players find a partner of equal size and ability and find a free space.

DESCRIPTION OF ACTIVITY:

1. **Knee Boxing:** Stand facing your partner in a semicrouch position, holding your hands out in front. Try to touch your partner's knees while protecting your own with your hands and arms and quick, short steps. No body contact is allowed. Score one point for each successful tap on your partner's knee. Play to three points; then challenge someone else.

2. **Tiger Tails:** Get a flag and tuck it into the back of your waistband so that most of the flag shows. Try to grab your partner's flag while protecting your own. Repeat three times; then challenge a new partner.

VARIATIONS:

a. **Hand Boxing:** Have partners grasp right hands and Knee Box with the open free hand. They then repeat, grasping left hands.

b. **All-Fours Tiger Tails:** On all-fours on a folding mat, partners face each other head-to-head. Each partner has a flag tucked into the back of his or her waistband. Partners try to grab each other's flags while staying in the all-fours position throughout the activity.

GS-100 PLAY WRESTLING

FOCUS: Leg, arm, and shoulder strength

EQUIPMENT: One mat per pair; one sponge ball per pair

ORGANIZATION:

• Have players find a partner of equal size and stand together in free space.

DESCRIPTION OF ACTIVITY:

1. **Arm Wrestling:** Lie face down, head-to-head with your partner. Interlock your partner's right thumb and close your right hand around it. Pressing your right elbow to the mat, reach your left hand under your right elbow and join hands. Now force your partner's right hand to the mat. Change hands and repeat. Find a new partner and repeat.

2. **Leg Wrestling:** Facing opposite directions, sit side-by-side with hips touching. Lie back with your knees bent and lock your inside elbows; then raise your inside legs three times. On the third time, hook your partner's leg at the knee or ankle so that you pull your partner over. Repeat with the other leg; then challenge someone else.

3. **Back-to-Back Wrestling:** Sit with your backs touching and your legs spread. Interlock elbows with your partner; then try to force one of your partner's elbows to the mat. Challenge someone else and repeat.

4. **Shoulder Wrestle:** Get a mat and face your partner while kneeling on all-fours on the mat. Touch right shoulders and try to drive your partner off the mat. Repeat, pushing with left shoulders.

5. **Turn the Turtle:** Kneel on all-fours facing your partner. Try to turn your partner over onto his or her back. Change roles and repeat; then challenge another player and try again.

6. **Turn the Eagle:** One partner, lie face down on your mat with your arms and legs spread while your partner kneels alongside you. Challenge your partner to try to turn you over onto your back. Change roles and repeat; then challenge others!

7. **Ball Wrestle:** Collect a ball to share. Both partners, hold the ball firmly. On the signal "Wrestle!" try to wrestle the ball from each other.

GS–101 PARTNER TUGS

FOCUS: Arm, shoulder, and leg strength; partnerwork and groupwork

EQUIPMENT: One short rope per pair; one beanbag per pair

ORGANIZATION:

• Have players find a partner of equal size and stand facing each other on either side of a line or short rope.

DESCRIPTION OF ACTIVITY:

1. **One-Hand Tug:** Grip your partner's right wrist, turn sideways, and try to pull each other across the line. Best two out of three tries. Repeat using a left wrist-hold; then challenge a new partner and repeat.

2. **Two-Hand Tug:** Gripping the fingers of both hands, try to pull your partner across the line. Best two out of three tries. Challenge a new partner and repeat.

3. **Hopping Tug:** Hopping on only one foot and gripping right index fingers, try to pull each other across the line. Repeat with a left finger grip while hopping on the other foot.

4. **Rope Tug:** Together get a short rope and hold onto it with both hands. Now try to pull each other across the line; then hold the rope with first only your right hands and then only your left hands. Try pulling with your backs to each other and the rope between your legs.

5. **Floor Touch Pull:** Double the short rope and then double it again. Grasping the rope in your right hands, lean away from each other and try to be the first to touch your free hand to the floor. Repeat, holding the rope with left hands. Can you be the first to touch one hand and one knee to the floor?

VARIATION: In both the Rope Tug and Floor Touch Pull, have partners try to pick up a beanbag placed on the floor behind them.

GS–102 GROUP TUGS

ORGANIZATION:

• Have each player get a short rope and a beanbag and then form groups of three players and find a free space.

EQUIPMENT: One hoop per group; one beanbag; one short rope per player

DESCRIPTION OF ACTIVITY:

1. **Poison Hoops:** Place the hoop on the floor and stand around it holding hands. Try to force each other to step on the hoop or inside it. Who will be the last player to touch or step inside the hoop?

2. **Triangle Tug-o-War:** Tie three short ropes together with figure-eight knots, in which you knot right over left and then left over right. Space yourselves evenly around the rope, pulling it taut to form a triangle. Now place a beanbag one meter (three feet) behind you and try to grab your beanbag with your free hand while pulling on the rope to prevent the other players from reaching their beanbags.

3. **Tug-o-Peace:** Stand facing another team on the other side of a line. Join hands with the two players who are directly opposite you, using a finger or a wrist grip. The end players will have a free hand. On signal "Pull!" try to pull the other team over the line.

— **Team Tug-o-Peace:** Form teams of six to eight players and challenge each other.

GS–103 INTRODUCING BASKETBALL

FOCUS: Ball handling; manipulation; control

EQUIPMENT: One junior basketball per player

ORGANIZATION:

- Have players get a basketball and bounce the ball to a free space; then hold it in both hands.

DESCRIPTION OF ACTIVITY:

1. *Tape-the-Ball Drill:* Hold the ball in front of your chest with your elbows slightly bent. Can you tap the ball back and forth from hand to hand?
2. *Fingertip Drill:* Hold the ball overhead using only your fingertips. Pass the ball from the fingertips of one hand to those of the other hand. Try to pass the ball in time to the music. Can you pass the ball overhead without watching it?
3. *Circling:* Pass the ball from hand to hand and, at the same time, circle the ball around your waist. Now step one leg forward. How many times can you pass the ball around that leg before I say "Freeze"? Change legs and repeat.
4. *Figure-Eight Drill:* Stand with your feet wide apart and crouch slightly as you lean forward. Pass the ball under and around one leg and then under and around the other leg in a figure-eight. Try not to move your feet as you pass the ball. How many times can you make a figure-eight without looking at or dropping the ball?
5. *Butterfly Drill:* In the same position, hold the ball between your legs with one hand in front of your body and the other behind. Quickly change hands and grasp the ball again before it drops to the floor. Repeat as many times as you can.
6. *Roller Ball:* Can you roll the ball down your back, catch it behind you, and then bounce the ball through your legs so that you catch it in front?
7. *Floor Touch:* Stand, toss the ball in the air, and slap both hands on the floor before catching it again. What other stunts can you do while the ball is in the air? Try turning around.

GS–104 DRIBBLING

FOCUS: Technique; right and left dexterity; control

EQUIPMENT: Same as activity GS–103.

ORGANIZATION:

- Explain and demonstrate the dribbling technique; then have players get a basketball, scatter, and practice using either hand.

DESCRIPTION OF ACTIVITY:

1. *Technique:* Lean forward and bend your knees, keeping your weight evenly distributed on the balls of both feet. Push the ball toward the floor with the fingers and wrist of one hand, not **palms**. Do not slap the ball! Your wrist and fingers should be relaxed, with fingers spread, and your hand cupped. Push ball out in front of you. Ball should rise no higher than your hips. Dribble **heads up**—try not to watch the ball.
2. *Pocket Dribble (Protection Dribble):* Bend your knees and place opposite foot to dribbling hand forward. Keeping low and bending over the ball, dribble the ball in the triangular space "pocket" formed by your feet and body. The ball should bounce beside back leg. Keep your free arm up; protect the ball with your body and this free hand. The top of the ball should not rise higher than your knees. Practice. Switch hands and forward foot. Remember, heads up—do not watch the ball while you dribble!

GS–105 DRIBBLING TASKS

FOCUS: Control dribbling; right–left dexterity

EQUIPMENT: One junior basketball per player; music in 4/4 time; tape or record player

ORGANIZATION:

- Have players get a basketball, dribble it to a free space, and then practice each of the following dribbling tasks, using first one hand and then the other.

DESCRIPTION OF ACTIVITY:

1. *Low Dribble:* Place your left hand on your knee and bend both knees slightly. Dribble the ball rapidly with your right hand so that the ball stays below knee level. Now low-dribble with your left hand. Can you low-dribble with your eyes closed?

2. *Yo-Yo Dribble:* Stand with your feet apart and your knees slightly bent. Dribble the ball below knee level from one hand to the other in a V-pattern. Can you walk around the ball as you yo-yo dribble?

3. *One-Hand Yo-Yo Dribble:* Stand with your feet apart and your knees slightly bent. Dribble the ball below knee level in a V-pattern using only one hand. Change hands; then walk forward while yo-yo dribbling with only one hand.

4. *Combination Dribble:* Alternately low-dribble with one hand, yo-yo dribble with both hands, and yo-yo dribble with the other hand.

5. *More Dribbling Challenges:*
   - Stand and dribble the ball around your body without moving your feet.
   - Now travel around the ball while it bounces on the same spot.
   - Try to dribble the ball with one hand and touch the floor with the other. Now reverse dribbling and touching hands.

   - Can you bounce yourself up and down on both feet while dribbling the ball? Change hands and repeat; then yo-yo dribble while you are bouncing.
   - Hold one ankle. Dribble the ball on the spot with your free hand; then change hands and ankles and repeat.
   - Can you place one foot out in front and dribble around it? Now change dribbling hand and foot and repeat.

   - Standing with your legs wide apart, dribble in, out, and around your legs in a figure-eight pattern. Now dribble in the other direction.
   - Slap your heel with the free hand while dribbling the ball with the other hand. (Reverse hand roles and repeat.)

   - Show me how you can dribble the ball high and then gradually dribble lower and lower. Then dribble from low to high. Do the same with the other hand.
   - Stand while dribbling the ball; then kneel on one knee, kneel on both knees; sit, without stopping your dribble. Kneel, and then stand again, still dribbling the ball. Repeat dribbling with other hand.

   - Dribble the ball with your left hand; then, continuing to dribble, shake hands with as many players as you can. Greet each player by name and smile; for example "Hi, Jason!" or "Hi, Nikki!"
   - Who can dribble the ball and dance to the music?
   - Make up a dribbling stunt of your own!

GS–106 DRIBBLING ON THE RUN

FOCUS: Control dribbling; peripheral vision; offense and defense

EQUIPMENT: One junior basketball per player; four hoops per team; several cone markers; lively music (optional); tape or record player

ORGANIZATION:

• Have players get a basketball and dribble anywhere in the play area.

DESCRIPTION OF ACTIVITY:

1. *Jog and Dribble:* Dribble slowly around the play area, and then change to different speeds: quickly, normal speed, walk, run, on the spot. Change your dribbling hand often. Dribble high and slow; then dribble low and fast. Dribble at a medium height.

   — Repeat, using other locomotion movements: skipping, side-stepping, galloping, walking backwards, etc.

2. *Line Dribble:* Stand on any line on the floor. On signal "Dribble!" dribble your ball along the floor lines in any direction. When you come to a corner or where two lines cross, change hands and direction. If you meet another player, pass each other right shoulder to right shoulder and dribble with your left hands.

3. *Dribble-the-Hoops Relay* (Form teams of four to five players. Have each team stand in single-file formation behind a starting line. Place a row of four hoops in front of each team, and have the leader of each team get a basketball.): On the signal "Go!" leader, zig-zag dribble the ball in and out of each of the hoops, bounce the ball five times in the last hoop; then dribble directly back to your team to give the ball to the next player. Make sure you dribble with your outside hand as you pass each hoop. Continue until everyone has had two turns.

4. *Dribble Tag* (Have players find a partner, get a basketball, and run to a free space. The player holding the ball is on offense; the other is on defense.): On signal "Tag!" players on offense, try to dribble the ball so that the player on defense cannot touch the ball. Protect it by positioning yourself between the ball and your partner. You may dribble the ball with either hand but not both at the same time. Defensive player, stay close to your partner. Try to touch the ball with an upward flick of the hand without touching your partner. Stay low with your feet spread and hold one hand out in front and the other out to the side, ready to touch the ball. Change roles whenever the ball is touched, or when the dribbler dribbles with two hands. Remember to watch where you are going!

5. *Partner Knock-Away:* Play in a confined space. You must not go outside of this area. Dribble your ball while trying to knock away your partner's ball to score one point. Play to three points; then challenge another player. Remember, you are not allowed to dribble with two hands or hold the ball.

GS-107 SPEED DRIBBLING CHALLENGES

FOCUS: Control dribbling; speed

EQUIPMENT: Two junior basketballs per player; two cone markers per team; three hoops per team; one stopwatch; chalkboard and chalk or paper and pen

ORGANIZATION:

- Through relays and a challenging game, players learn to dribble the ball while moving quickly, yet in control.

DESCRIPTION OF ACTIVITY:

1. **Shuttle Dribble Relay** (Form teams of six and stand in shuttle formation, each file of three facing the other 15 meters [45 feet] away. The Leader has the ball to start.): On signal "Dribble!" each player in turn dribble the ball across to the opposite file and hand the ball to the first player there; then join the end of the file. Which team can make the most crossings in two minutes?

2. **Circle Dribble Relay** (Divide the class into two equal teams and have both teams number off consecutively. Teams then form one large circle, each team making up one half of the circle as shown. The leader of each team gets a basketball.): On signal "Go!" leaders, dribble the ball in a CCW direction around the outside of the circle, return to your starting position, and pass the ball to the second player on your team, who does the same. Continue until all players have had a turn.

3. **Speed Dribble Relay** (Form teams of four to five players and have each team stand in single-file formation at one end of the play area, facing a cone marker at the opposite end. Leaders of each team get a basketball.): On signal "Go!" leaders, dribble to the cone marker using your right hand, change

hands as you dribble around the cone, and continue to dribble back to the team using your left hand. Pass the ball to the next player and join the end of the file. Continue until each player has had four turns. Remember to dribble heads up!

— In 90 seconds, how many round trips can your team make by dribbling the ball to the turning cone and back? Which team will have the best record?

4. **Figure-Eight Scramble** (Divide the class into two equal teams and have teams stand side-by-side, facing each other on opposite sides of the play area as shown. Have teams number off; then set a hoop on the floor between the teams and place two basketballs in the hoop. Place a cone marker at each end between the two teams. Keep the score on the chalkboard for all to see.): Listen for your number. When it is called, run quickly toward the hoop, grab a basketball, and dribble it in a figure-eight pattern around the two cone markers. Return the ball to the hoop and run back to your starting position. Your team scores one point if you are the first to return to your starting position. Continue until everyone has had a turn.

5. **Hoop Dribble Game** (Form teams of three players. Have each team collect three hoops and three balls, lay the hoops on the floor in a file, about 5 meters [15 feet] apart, and place a ball in each hoop. Team members, stand in a file behind a starting line facing their hoops.): On signal "Go!" each player in turn run to the first hoop, pick up the ball, and dribble it to the second hoop. Put first ball in this hoop, grab the other ball in the hoop, and dribble to the third hoop. Put the second ball in the third hoop, grab the third ball, and dribble back to the first hoop, placing this ball in the first hoop. Then return to "give five" to the next player, who repeats the task. Game finishes when everyone has gone twice and team is sitting cross-legged in their file.

GS-108 BODYWORK/FOOTWORK FUNDAMENTALS

FOCUS: Basic body and footwork skills; terminology   **EQUIPMENT:** One junior basketball per player

ORGANIZATION:

- The ready position in basketball is introduced, followed by the fundamental body and footwork movements and a Signals game to reinforce these skills.

DESCRIPTION OF ACTIVITY:

1. **Triple-Threat Position** (The "ready position" in basketball.): With both feet planted, hold the ball close to your body at waist level, pull your elbows in, bend your knees, crouch and lean forward over the ball. Now you are ready to pass, shoot, or dribble.
2. **Cutting:** To change direction quickly, plant one foot firmly, bend your knees and lower your body, and then push off the planted foot to take a step in the new direction with your other foot.
3. **Jump Stop:** To do this two-foot stop, jump off either left or right foot so that you land with both feet together at the same time. Plant feet about shoulder-width apart, bending at the knees to absorb any forward movement and to keep balance. Keep head up and eyes forward. Your hands should be up in the ready position to receive the ball; otherwise, protect the ball in the triple threat position.
4. **Stride Stop:** Run in a slightly crouched position. Stop suddenly with one foot contacting the floor first; then land the other foot to ensure stopping and good balance. Feet should be spread about shoulder-width apart, knees bent. The first foot to touch the floor becomes the "pivot" foot and must remain in contact with the floor. Use this one-foot stop to receive a pass while running or to finish a dribble. Remember to keep head up, eyes forward, and hands in the ready position.
5. **Pivoting:** Do a Jump Stop. Pivot on the ball of one foot (for good body balance) while the other foot (stepping foot) moves in any direction by taking short steps to the right, to the left, forward, or back. Keep the pivot foot in contact with the floor; knees bent, body crouched low, and feet about shoulder-width apart. Keep head and eyes up and protect the ball with your body. Use this fundamental foot to protect the ball and for passing, faking, driving to the basket, and getting good rebounding position.
6. **Jumping:** Keep head and eyes on target. Bend your knees just before take-off; use your arms to swing forward and upward and extend your body upward. Jump off both feet. Land on the balls of your feet, bending knees to absorb the impact. Both feet should hit the floor at the same time.
   - Toss a ball overhead; jump straight up to catch the ball at the top of your jump; land in a Jump Stop, then crouch with the ball close to your body in the Triple-Threat position. Do this five times; then repeat using the Stride Stop.
7. **Footwork Signals:** On signal "Dribble!" dribble the ball in general space with good technique. On signal "Stop!" catch the ball and Jump Stop. On Signal "Triple Threat!" hold the ball in the Triple-Threat position. On signal "Right Pivot!" plant on the ball of your right foot and pivot around on the left foot. On signal "Jump!" toss ball upward, jump up, and catch it at the top of your jump before your feet touch the floor; land in Triple-Threat position.
   - Other signals: "Left Pivot!"; "Stride Stop!"; "Cutting!"

FOCUS: Chest passing technique;
catching; peripheral vision

EQUIPMENT: One junior basketball per player

ORGANIZATION:

- The Chest Pass is the most frequently used basketball pass and is mainly used to pass over short distances. The ready position or "Triple-Threat Position" is introduced in order to execute the pass. Have each player get a basketball, explain and demonstrate the technique, and then have players scatter to practice.

DESCRIPTION OF ACTIVITY:

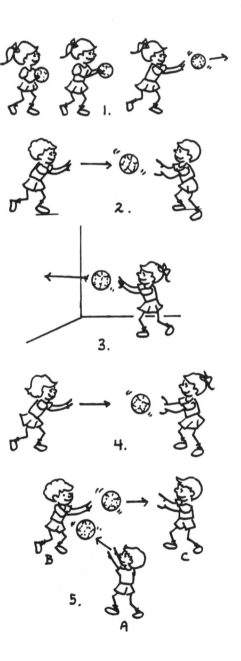

1. **Chest Passing:** Begin by holding ball close to chest, with elbows into the sides of your body. Stand with one foot slightly ahead of the other, knees bent, and body crouched low. This is called the "Triple-Threat Position" (to pass, shoot, or dribble). Hold ball with hands on the side of the ball, keeping your fingers relaxed and spread. Your thumbs should be pointing upward, in line behind the ball; the palms should not touch the ball. Step toward the target (for power) and thrust your arms forward. As you release the ball, snap your wrists; follow through with thumbs pointing to floor and fingers pointing to the target—the receiver's chest. Keep your head up, eyes on the target.

2. **Receiving:** Position feet about shoulder-width apart, knees bent, body crouched low (weight evenly distributed on both feet). Give a hand target for the passer. Step toward the ball in flight. Keep your eyes on the ball all the way into your hands. The "target hand" acts like a glove, while the other hand tucks the ball into the glove or blocking hand. Reach for the ball, bending your elbows upon contact. "Give" with your fingers, wrist, and arms to absorb the force. Keep balanced and ready for triple-threat position upon receiving the ball.

3. **Wall Practice:** Stand about three meters (ten feet) from a wall. Chest pass the ball to the wall and receive it with good technique, as it comes off the wall.

4. **Partner Chest Passing:** Stand facing a partner about three or four giant steps apart from each other. Practice chest passing and receiving with good technique.

5. **Split-Vision Challenge** (Form groups of three players: A, B, and C. Have each group collect two utility balls and stand side-by-side.): Player B, holding one ball, step forward three meters (ten feet) and turn to face the other two players. Players A and C, stand three meters (ten feet) apart, facing B. Player A, hold the second ball. Player B, signal "Pass!" and chest pass to C; at the same time, A pass to B. Continue with C chest passing back to B, while B passes back to A. Throw at the same time, calling out in unison "Pass," "Pass," . . . Throw slowly at first; then gradually increase speed.

GS-110 MORE PASSING SKILLS

FOCUS: Bounce passing; baseball passing techniques; receiving; partnerwork

EQUIPMENT: One junior basketball per player; one 30-centimeter (1-foot)-square wall target per pair; floor or wall tape

ORGANIZATION:

- Explain and demonstrate the techniques for Bounce Passing and later Baseball Passing. Have players practice these passes at a wall and with a partner. Then introduce bounce and chest passing combination tasks. Have players find a partner, get a ball to share, and stand about 3 meters (10 feet) apart.

DESCRIPTION OF ACTIVITY:

1. *Bounce Passing:* Hold ball in the triple-threat position as for the Chest Pass. Step toward your target and thrust your arms forward and down. Snap your wrists as you release the ball. The target area for the bounce pass is about waist level. Aim your ball to hit the floor two thirds of the distance toward receiver.

2. *Partner Bounce Passing:* Stand facing a partner about 4 meters (12 feet) away. Bounce pass back and forth to each other, sending and receiving the ball with good technique.
   — Now using one ball, one partner chest pass the ball while the other partner bounce passes it. Switch roles after 12 good passes.
   — Each partner bounce pass to the other partner at the same time.
   — One partner chest pass while the other partner bounce passes, at the same time.

3. *Target Practice:* Stand 3 meters (10 feet) from a wall target. How many times can you chest pass to the target in 30 tries?
   — Who can be the first to make 50 passes at the target? Sit down when finished.

4. *Wall Shuffle:* Stand about 1 meter (3 feet) from a wall at one end of the court. Side-step (shuffle) along the length of the wall as you Chest Pass the ball to the wall, rebounding as you go. Putting a little top-spin on the ball will make the ball rebound at the correct height. Send the ball slightly ahead to the wall to allow for your speed. Repeat using the Bounce Pass.

5. *Baseball Passing:* Stand with feet about shoulder-width apart, knees bent and body crouched low. Bring the ball back behind the ear with your best hand. The other hand is on the side of the ball for balance, with fingers spread. The pass is made like a baseball throw—a forward motion of the arm and wrist. During this motion, shift weight from the back foot to the front foot as you step forward toward the receiver. Snap wrist and release ball off the fingertips. The wrist follows straight through, creating a slight spin on the ball. Keep eyes focused on your target throughout the throw.
   — Practice at a wall, positioning about four giant steps away. Baseball pass and receive rebound with good technique.
   — Throw Baseball passes back and forth to a partner.

GS–111 PARTNER AND GROUP PASSING GAMES

FOCUS: Chest and bounce passing;
partnerwork and groupwork

EQUIPMENT: One junior basketball per pair;
one set of pinnies

ORGANIZATION:

• Passing skills and footwork fundamentals are reinforced through these drills and related games. The Lead pass is also introduced. To start, have players pair off and get one ball to share.

DESCRIPTION OF ACTIVITY:

1. **Shuffle and Pass** (Have partners stand facing each other 3 meters [10 feet] apart at one end of the basketball court.): Side-step (shuffle sideways) to the other end of the court, chest-passing the ball back and forth. When you reach the end, run back to the start, change sides, and repeat.

2. **Ten-Times-Three** (Form groups of three players. Have leaders collect a ball for their group; then have each group stand in a triangle formation, with players about 3 meters [10 feet] apart.): On signal "Pass!" player A, with the ball, chest-pass to B. B pass back to A. A pass to C, C pass back to A, and so on, until A handles the ball ten times. Change positions until each of the three players have had a turn in the middle. Repeat using the Bounce Pass.

3. **Circle Keep Away** (Form circles of seven to ten players. Have one or two players stand in the center of the circle.): Circle players, try to pass the ball across the circle without having the ball touched or intercepted. Do not pass to the player on your immediate left or right, or to the previous passer. Use Chest or Bounce Passes. Center player, if you touch the ball, change places with the circle player who passed the ball.

4. **Lead-Pass Drill** (A lead pass is a pass thrown just ahead of another player who is on the run. Have players pair off, get a ball to share, and stand in files on the endline of the play area, facing their partner about 3 meters [10 feet] apart.): Player with the ball, Chest-Pass the ball just ahead of your partner, who will run forward to catch it with a Jump Stop; then you run down the court ahead of your partner. Jump-Stop as you catch your partner's pass. Continue until you reach the opposite end of the court and return. At first move slowly to ensure good lead passes. Repeat using the Stride Stop.

5. **Three-Passes Game** (For each game, form two teams of six to eight players. One team wears pinnies. The game is started by a jump ball at the center.): The object of the game is for a team to complete three consecutive passes to three different players in order to score one point. When the ball touches the floor or is intercepted, the other team gets the ball. Pivoting is allowed, but dribbling or running with the ball is not. You may not hold the ball for more than three seconds.

6. **Four Corners** (Form groups of twelve players. Divide the twelve players into four smaller groups of three players: groups A, B, C, and D. Each smaller group stands in single-file formation in each corner of a 5-meter [16-foot] square, facing inward.): First player in groups A and B, get a ball. On signal "Pass!" Chest Pass the ball to the opposite corner, A to C, B to D; then run CCW to join the end of the next file. Continue. Repeat catching with the Jump Stop; the Stride Stop. Repeat using the Bounce Pass.

GS-112 INTRODUCING DEFENSE

FOCUS: Defensive stance and movement; man-to-man concept; partnerwork

EQUIPMENT: Cone markers

ORGANIZATION:

- Children are introduced to the individual defensive fundamentals of basketball. The basic defensive stance and movement of "man-to-man" defense is explained and demonstrated. These skills are then practiced and reinforced through several drills.

DESCRIPTION OF ACTIVITY:

1. *Basic Defensive Stance—The Boxer's Stance:*

   — Take a position between the offensive player and the basket.

   — Keep the weight evenly distributed on the balls of the feet; feet shoulder-width apart; one foot slightly ahead of the other.

   — Keep your seat low and your back straight.

   — Keep one hand up and the other hand down; palms up, fingers spread.

   — Keep your eyes on your opponent's waistband and hips (midriff). Watch everything else out of the corner of your eye.

   — Keep your feet moving all the time; body low, knees bent.

   — Never cross your feet or let feet come together. Use the side-step to move from side to side, and the shuffle step to go back and forward.

2. *Hands-Up Drill:* Find a spot alone in a free space, facing me in the Boxer's Stance, with both hands up. When I point and give a direction—forward, back, right side, left side—I want you to move in that direction. When I point to the floor, I want you to do the Stutter Step (run quickly on the spot).

3. *Slide Drill:* Form groups of four to ten players. Choose a leader for each group. In follow-the-leader style, side-step along any of the lines on the court. Don't cross your feet, and keep your seat low at all times.

READY POSITION

LEADER   3.

4.

4. *Corridor Dribble* (Use cones to mark off "corridors" or lengthwise sections of the play area from one endline to the opposite. Have players pair off and evenly distribute pairs to a corridor area.): One partner, be the defensive player; the other, the offensive player. Offensive player, shuffle down your corridor using "cutting" movements—not too quickly, but enough changes of direction to make your partner work hard on defense! Defensive player, keep good defensive position as you shuffle-step down the corridor, always keeping in front of your partner, watching his or her middle area. Switch roles once you reach the opposite end.

FOCUS: Lay-up and Set Shot techniques; hand- and footwork; listening

EQUIPMENT: One junior basketball per player

ORGANIZATION:

- A "Lay-Up Shot" is the basic basketball shot taken directly in front of or to either side of the basket. It is generally made after a player dribbles the ball to the basket or receives a pass near it. Players should learn to perform a lay-up with either hand. The "Set Shot" is the basic outside shot. Explain and demonstrate the right-hand lay-up and set shot; then have players get a ball and practice.

DESCRIPTION OF ACTIVITY:

1. _The Lay-Up Technique:_
— Begin by holding the ball in both hands, Triple-Threat position, feet parallel and shoulder-width apart. Step forward with the left foot and let the ball bounce once near this foot. Catch the ball in both hands off the dribble, step right foot, then left foot, keeping the ball to the right side of your body. Now push upward off your left foot, driving the right knee up to increase the height of your jump.
— For right-hand lay-up, when ball is picked up in two hands, the right hand is on top of the ball, the left hand on the side for support. Keep both hands on the ball until you reach the height of your jump, bringing the ball up to a shooting position. Now your right hand wrist should be cocked back to release the ball off your fingers. "Lay-up" the ball softly against the backboard, with the target being the top right corner of the rectangle on the backboard. Eyes stay on target, fingers follow through, and left hand comes off the ball but stays in the air to protect the shot.

2. _Lay-up Progressions:_
— Pantomime the footwork and arm action "bounce-2-3-up."
— Now stand about two giant steps from a wall. Check for good spacing. Practice pushing off with the left foot, driving the right knee upward, and laying-up the ball against the wall.
— Now stand in front of and to the right of the basket and about 1.5 meters (5 feet) away from it. Push upward on your left foot and carry the ball upward as high as possible with both hands. Lay the ball softly against the "target" on the backboard so that the ball falls softly into the basket. Remember to take off with your inside foot and shoot with your outside hand.
— "Walk-through" the "bounce-2-3-up!" pattern using your basketball. Practice several times.
— Now practice the whole sequence at a controlled speed. (Equally distribute players to a basket, depending upon the number of baskets available.)

3. _The One-Hand Set Shot:_
— Start in the triple-threat position. Square your body to the basket with knees bent and feet about shoulder-width apart. (Foot under the shooting hand is slightly forward.) Place your shooting hand under the ball, letting it balance on your fingerpads, not palms. Place your other hand on the side of the ball where it helps to balance and control the ball. Shooting arm should be at a right angle, with your elbow and arm in straight line with the basket, wrist cocked back. Push the ball up, not out, with your shooting hand, snapping your wrist forward, and releasing the supporting hand. Fingers follow through to the basketball ring (gives slight back-spin to the ball); eyes never leave target. As you bring ball up to shooting position, straighten your legs, rising onto toes.

4. _Set Shooting Progressions:_
— Pantomime action: thumbs make a "T"; palms face upward.
— Practice set shooting technique at a wall.
— Face a partner and practice set shot to each other.
— Position in semicircles around basketball key and practice set shooting. Start in close; then gradually get further away.

GS-114 LEAD-UP GAMES TO BASKETBALL

FOCUS: Basketball skills; positional play; offense; defense; teamwork

EQUIPMENT: One junior basketball; two sets of pinnies; two wastepaper bins; two mats

ORGANIZATION:

- For each game form two equal teams of about six to eight players, distribute the pinnies, and have teams scatter around the court. Each team selects a goalie to hold the garbage can in the goal area at the opposite end of the court or to stand on a mat placed at each end of the play area. Change goalies frequently throughout the game. Have each player select an opponent to guard whenever the other team has the ball. Emphasize that players guard this person and not clutter the ball!

DESCRIPTION OF ACTIVITY:

1. *Garbage Ball:*
   - The game starts with a jump-ball in the middle of the play area. The ball is tossed upward between two opposition players. These players jump for the ball, trying to tip it to a teammate. Each team must start in its own half.
   - The player with the ball is allowed only three dribbles and then must pass to a teammate or shoot at the garbage can.
   - To score a point, you must be in the other team's half of the court before taking a shot, and the ball must land in your goalie's can.
   - The goalie may move freely inside the goal area. All other players must remain outside the goal area.
   - After a goal is scored, the game is restarted by a jump-ball at the center.
   - The other team gets the ball whenever it is intercepted or goes out-of-bounds.

2. *Mat Ball:*
   - The game starts with a jump-ball at center between the smallest players on each team. All others must stand outside the jump-ball circle, two meters (six feet) away. The two players jumping for the ball try to tip it to a teammate.
   - The only way to move the ball is by passing. No dribbling is allowed.
   - The rule of three applies: You cannot hold the ball for more than three seconds; you must complete three passes in a row before attempting a goal; you may travel three steps in any direction with the ball.
   - To score a point, you must be in the other team's half of the court before taking a shot, and the goalie must catch the ball while standing on the mat.
   - Only the goalie is allowed on the mat or behind the endline.
   - After a goal is scored, the game is restarted by a jump-ball at the center.
   - The other team gets the ball if a player drops it, the ball is intercepted, or goes out-of-bounds.

VARIATION:

Have teams challenge each other, playing games for a fixed time to a certain number of points.

1.   2.

FOCUS: Basketball skills;
positional play;
offense; defense;
teamwork

EQUIPMENT: One junior basketball per game;
two hoops per game;
two bleach bottles (or cone markers) per game;
one set of pinnies per game;
two backboards per game

ORGANIZATION:

- Divide the play area to create several courts and thus have several games going on at the same time. Form teams of four to six players and distribute pinnies. Assign two teams to a court area. To make goals for Game 1, set a hoop in the middle of each end of the play area and place a bleach bottle inside each hoop. For Game 2, use regulation backboards or tape large sheets of chart paper to the wall at each end as goals.

DESCRIPTION OF ACTIVITY:

1. *Bleach Bottle Basketball:*
- The object of the game is to throw the ball so that it knocks over the bleach bottle in the opposition's hoop.
- The game begins with a jump-ball at center between the tallest players on each team, who try to tip it to a teammate.
- If you receive the ball, pass or dribble toward your goal at your opponent's end. You may not run with the ball ("travel"), and your team must complete three consecutive passes before shooting at the bleach bottle.
- Scatter around the play area and play one-on-one, so that you are guarding an opposing player. Try not to clutter the ball!
- Score one point for knocking over the bleach bottle. Play to ten points.
- After a point is scored, or whenever the ball goes out-of-bounds or is intercepted, the other team is given the ball outside the side line.

2. *Backboard Basketball:*
- Two opposing players, come to the center to "jump the ball." Try to tap the ball to a player on your team; then have the team move the ball toward your backboard (in the opposition's team half) by passing or dribbling.
- Once the ball is in your opponent's half of the court, you may attempt to score a point by throwing the ball at the backboard or target. However, your team must make three consecutive passes to three different players before taking a throw at the backboard.
- Score one point for each successful hit. After a score, the game is restarted once more with a center jump.
- If the ball goes out-of-bounds, it is awarded to the opposing team at that spot.
- If a player "travels" or "fouls" an opponent, the ball is taken out-of-bounds by the other team.
- The first team to make five points is the winner; then challenge another team.

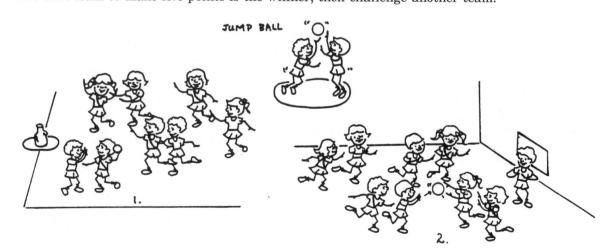

JUMP BALL "O"

1.

2.

GS-116 STICK EXPLORATION

FOCUS: Manipulation; familiarization; partnerwork

EQUIPMENT: One hockey stick per player

ORGANIZATION:

- Children explore using a hockey stick in a variety of movement tasks individually, and then with a partner. Have each player get a stick and take it to a home space. Check for good spacing. Discuss the importance of using the stick safely at all times.

DESCRIPTION OF ACTIVITY:

1. Put your stick on the floor in front of you. Show me how many different ways you can travel along your stick:
   —Hopping back and forth over the stick.
   —Jumping from side-to-side over the stick.
   —Stride-jumping over the stick, crossing your feet.
   —Walking on the stick like a "tightrope walker."
   —Zig-zag walking along the stick from one end to the other.
   —Leaping over the stick and landing on two feet; on one foot.
   —Building a bridge over the stick with one part on one side, and one body part on the other side.

2. **Balances:** Balance the stick on different parts of your body. Use the back of your hand, your palm, fingers, one finger, knee, and foot.

3. **Transfers:** Balance your stick on one body part. Now transfer it to another body part and still keep it upright. Can you toss the stick from hand to hand? What other transfers can you make?

4. **Stretches:** Invent ways of stretching, using your sticks. Copy each other's actions.

5. **Thread the Needle:** Hold your stick in both hands horizontally in front of you. Step one leg over the stick, and then the other. Step one leg back, and then the other, without breaking your hand-hold.

6. **Scottish Sticks:** On the floor, make a letter "X" with your sticks. Show me how you can move your feet in and out of the "X" without touching the sticks.

7. **Stick Tug-o-War:** Find a partner. Both grip one stick horizontally so that one hand is between your partner's hands. Try to pull your partner across a line between you.
   —Hold the stick vertically and have a tug-o-war.
   —Grip the stick with one hand and pull; grip with the other hand and pull.
   —Challenge another player to the above tugs.

8. **Stick Windmills:** Each partner hold one stick horizontally, with both hands wide apart. Lower shoulders on one side to turn outward as the stick turns under. While one end of the stick is lowered, the other is raised. Turn like a windmill.

9. **Jumps:** One partner, hold the stick at various heights. The other partner, try to jump over the stick.

10. **Limbo Sticks:** One partner, hold the stick at different heights while your partner tries to move under the stick, keeping belly-button upward. How low can you limbo?

FOCUS: Stick and puck manipulation; control; footwork

EQUIPMENT: One hockey stick per player; one plastic puck per player; one whistle; several cone markers; hoops; several chairs; one to two benches

ORGANIZATION:

• Review and demonstrate the grip, ready position, carrying the stick, and stick-handling technique. Allow players time to practice; then set up obstacles in the play area. To start, have players get a floor hockey stick and a puck before scattering around the play area.

DESCRIPTION OF ACTIVITY:

1. **Grip Technique:** Place one hand at the top of your stick and the other hand 15 centimeters to 20 centimeters (6 inches to 8 inches) below it. Now reverse hands and repeat. Which position feels the most comfortable to you?
2. **Ready Position:** Holding the stick with both hands, let the edge of the blade of the stick rest on the floor. Bend your knees slightly.
3. **Holding Stick on the Run:** Hold your stick in both hands with the blade as low to the floor as possible. Keep your knees bent and your back straight, and look up. Keep the stick below hip level; otherwise, you are "high-sticking," which is dangerous.
   — Practice holding the stick this way while running straight ahead; in a zig-zag; slowly; quickly with a sudden burst of speed. Keep your head up, watch where you are going, and run to empty spaces.
   — When I call "Change!" change direction every three steps, pushing off your back foot. When I call "Freeze!" stop immediately in the ready position.

4. **Carry the Puck:** Move the puck along the floor so that it always stays in contact with the blade, on one side only.
5. **Stick-Handling Technique:** Use this technique to control the puck when you change direction. Move the puck in front of you rather than to the side. Keep your head up and try to "feel" the puck on your stick by using short taps. Move forward quickly, pushing the puck from side-to-side in the middle of the blade.
6. **Practice:**
   — Carry the puck with your stick as you move around the play area. Change direction frequently, keeping the blade of your stick on the floor at all times.
   — Dribble your puck along the lines on the floor with good control.
   — Can you push the puck on your forehand going forward and pull the puck toward you with your backhand as you go backwards?
   — When the whistle blows once, stop in ready position. The puck should be touching the blade of your stick. When the whistle blows twice, continue dribbling the puck in general space.
7. **Obstacle Field** (Scatter several cones, chairs, benches, and hoops throughout the play area.): Carry or dribble the puck in and around the obstacles: around the benches or chairs; in and out of cone markers or hoops; along the lines; through the chair legs.
8. **Shuttle-Stick Relay** (Form teams of four to six players, each team in shuttle formation facing the other half about 10 meters [30 feet] apart. Each first player of one line has a puck.): First player in line, stick-handle the puck across to the first player of the opposite file, leave the puck for this player, who then repeats your action, and go to the end of the file. Continue until all players have had three turns.
9. **Zig-Zag Relay** (Form teams of four players and have each team stand in a single file behind a starting line facing a row of four cones spaced 2 meters [6 feet] apart.): On "Go!" signal, each player in turn stick-handle a puck through the cones, around the end cone, and directly back to the file to give the puck to the next player in line. Relay ends when everyone has had three turns.

GS–118 STICK-HANDLING GAMES

FOCUS: Stick-handling control;
defense; alertness

EQUIPMENT: One hockey stick per player;
one puck or ball for two thirds of the class;
floor tape;
chalkboard;
chalk;
brush;
whistle

ORGANIZATION:

- These action games reinforce the stick-handling skills and teach players the concept of playing defense.

DESCRIPTION OF ACTIVITY:

1. *Hockey Pirates* (Select one third of the class to be the Hockey Pirates, who each have a stick and stand in the center of the play area to start. Have the remaining two thirds of the class, the Free Players, each get a stick and ball and then scatter throughout the play area.): On the signal "Pirates are coming!" Hockey Pirates, try to stick-handle the puck or ball away from the Free Players. Free Player, as soon as you are without a puck or ball, you become a Pirate and must now try to get the puck away from any free player. Who will still have their puck or ball at the end of the game? Remember to keep your head up and sticks down as you move around! No body contact is allowed. Play fairly—you cannot step on the puck or pin it against a wall.

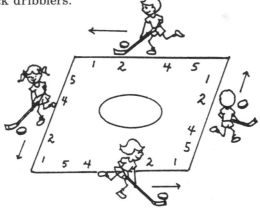

2. *Square-Box Hockey* (Form four teams with an even number of players on each team. Have each team stand on one side of a 10-meter [30-foot] square. Each team numbers off. Mark a 30-centimeter [1-foot] circle in the middle of the floor and place four pucks inside it. Record team scores on the chalkboard.): When a number is called, all players with that number, run to the middle, dribble a puck out of the circle, through the spot just vacated, CCW around the square, and back through your vacant spot to place the puck back in the circle. The first player back scores four points for the team; the second player scores three points; and so on. Which team will score the most points by the time all numbers have been called? Players on the square, cheer for your teammates but do not interfere with the puck dribblers.

VARIATION:

Hockey Team Pirates: Divide the class into two teams, identified by the color of stick each team player has. Players of one team each have a puck. Players of the other team try to "capture" as many pucks as they can before the whistle blows to signal stoppage of play. The number of captured pucks are counted and a score recorded. The two teams switch roles and the game continues.

FOCUS: Passing technique; receiving; control; partnerwork

EQUIPMENT: One floor hockey stick per player; one plastic puck per pair

ORGANIZATION:

- Have players find a partner. Each pair gets two floor hockey sticks and one puck and stands 3 meters (10 feet) apart.

DESCRIPTION OF ACTIVITY:

1. *Passing Technique:* Keep your stick blade upright and use a smooth, sweeping motion. Try not to raise the stick above your waist in the backswing or when swinging it forward. Pass slightly ahead of your receiver on his or her stick side. This is called a "lead pass." You will have to judge how fast the receiver is travelling so that you know where to place the puck.

2. *Receiving Technique:* Watch the puck. Tilt your stick blade over the puck to trap it. Cushion the pass by allowing your stick blade to "give" at the moment of impact.

3. *Practice:*

   — While standing still, pass the puck to your partner. Concentrate on passing the puck directly onto your partner's stick. Receiver, field the puck first, get it under control, and then pass it back to your partner. How quickly can you pass the puck back and forth and still pass it directly to your partner?

   — While standing still, pass the puck to your partner, who is on the move; your partner stops the puck and passes it back to you while you are on the move.

   — Can you and your partner both move while passing the puck back and forth?

4. *Passing Shuttle Relay* (Form equal teams of four to six players and have one half of each team stand in shuttle formation, facing the other half, 10 meters [30 feet] away. Mark a passing point for each half.): Each player, in turn, dribble the puck forward to this point; then pass it to the opposite file player, who fields the puck and repeats the action.

5. *Wall Passing:* Taking turns with your partner, hit a ball against a wall: one partner, hit the puck; the second partner, receive the rebound and hit the puck back again. Begin close to the wall; then gradually move farther away.

6. *Truck 'n Trailer Passing:* Stand behind your partner; the player in front with the puck is the Truck and the player behind is the Trailer. Truck, stick-handle the puck while your Trailer follows close behind. Truck, tap the puck backwards or "drop pass," the puck to your Trailer and continue to travel forward. Trailer, receive the puck, stick-handle it ahead, and then "drop pass" it back to the Truck. Continue in this way, always watching where you are going!

GS-120 SHOOTING SKILLS—THE WRIST SHOT

FOCUS: Shooting technique; forehand and backhand

EQUIPMENT: One floor hockey stick per player; one plastic puck per player; wall targets; floor targets; various obstacles, such as chairs, cones, hoops, and nets; floor and wall tape

1.

ORGANIZATION:

- Review the technique for executing a "Wrist Shot," then introduce "Forehand" and "Backhand" wrist shots. To practice shooting accuracy, tape several 1-meter (3-foot) wall targets, 15 centimeters (6 inches) from the floor. Tape a shooting line 3 meters (10 feet) from each wall target. Gradually increase shooting distance as player's ability improves. Have players get a floor hockey stick and a puck and stand facing a wall, about 4 meters (12 feet) away.

DESCRIPTION OF ACTIVITY:

1. **The Wrist Shot:** Shoot the puck at the wall. Recover the puck and repeat. Gradually move farther away from the wall and repeat. Explore keeping the stick along the floor and using your wrist to send the puck to the wall. This is called the Wrist Shot. Remember to:

   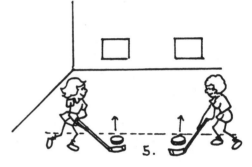

   5.

   — check the puck, and then concentrate on the target.

   — be sure that the blade and the puck are touching before shooting.

   — be careful not to raise the stick above the waist on the follow-through.

   — allow the lower hand to guide the stick down and "through" the puck. The hands are the same distance apart as they would be in the carrying position.

2. **Forehand Shooting:** Shoot the puck from the same side as your lower hand, with the nonhitting shoulder facing the wall. Slightly bend your elbows, snap your wrists, and push the stick through the puck. Point your stick at the target on the follow-through. Keep your eyes on the target!

3. **Backhand Shooting:** Turn so that your shooting shoulder faces the wall. Use your lower hand to pull the shot from the left side, and snap your wrist through.

4. **Individual Practice:** Take ten Forehand wrist shots at the wall; then take ten backhand wrist shots. Gradually increase shooting distance.

5. **Partner Target Practice:** Find a partner and take turns shooting at a wall target. Take ten Forehand wrist shots; then ten Backhand wrist shots. How many times can you hit the target in ten tries? (Use as a Performance Check and record results for each player.)

6. **Target Hockey** (For each game, mark out a middle line in a rectangular play area [10 meters by 10 meters or 30 feet by 30 feet]; then divide the class into teams of six to eight players. On each court have a team take up position on one side of the middle line. Equally space five cone markers on each endline of the play area and give each team an equal number of pucks.): On signal "Shoot!" each team try to shoot as many pucks into the opponent's half of the play area as possible. Try to hit the opponent's cone markers as well. You may not enter your opponent's half of the play area. On the signal "Stop!" each team count one point for each puck in your team's play area. Count two points each time a cone marker was hit. The team with the lowest score wins. Play fairly. (You may wish to keep score, or have a player who is unable to participate keep score.) Remember, sticks should not be raised above hip level and pucks should travel low to the floor.

GS–121 GOALTENDING

FOCUS: Shot blocking technique; visual tracking; partnerwork

EQUIPMENT: One floor hockey stick per player; one soft puck or ball per group; two cone markers per group

ORGANIZATION:

- Have players pair off and have each player get a stick, a puck, and two cone markers. Assign each pair to a wall area where they set up the cones as goals two meters (six feet) apart and one meter (three feet) from the wall.

DESCRIPTION OF ACTIVITY:

1. *Goalie Ready Position:*
   - Crouch slightly, holding the stick in front of your body with one hand. Use the other hand to catch or knock the puck away.
   - Place the stick squarely in front of the puck to stop it. Use your feet, legs, stick, and even your chest to stop the puck.
   - Clear the puck by hitting or kicking it to the side.
   - Watch the puck at all times!

2. *Practice:*
   - One partner be the goalie and stand between the cone markers, your goal. Be in the goalie ready position to block shots coming at you. The other partner, take wrist shots at the goal. Practice forehand and backhand wrist shots. Try short and long shots. Stick-handle toward your goal and pick the open spaces to shoot at, not the goalie! Remember to keep your stick blade lower than hip level and send the puck along the floor.
   - After ten shots, change roles.

GS–122 FACING OFF

FOCUS: Technique; alertness; visual tracking

EQUIPMENT: One floor hockey stick per player; one plastic puck per group

ORGANIZATION:

- Form groups of three players and have each player get a stick. Give each group one puck. Explain that the face-off is used to start a game or to restart it after a goal has been scored or a rule has been broken. Have one group demonstrate the face-off procedure.

DESCRIPTION OF ACTIVITY:

1. Two players, stand facing opposite sides about a stick-length apart. Place your stick blades on the floor so that they are almost touching; then slide them one blade length away from each other. Slide the lower hand down the stick shaft for more powerful control of the stick.
2. Third player, drop the puck between the two players. Each player, immediately try to gain control of the puck.
3. After every four puck drops, change roles until everyone has had a turn dropping the puck.

VARIATIONS:

a. Have the third player place the puck on the floor between the two players before the face-off and then simply say "Go!"

b. *Hickey-Hockey:* Place the puck on the floor. When the number is called, each player hits the floor on his or her side of the puck, and then the opponent's stick. Do this three times, calling "hickey-hockey 1!" the first time; "hickey-hockey 2!" the second time; and "hickey-hockey 3!" the third time the stick hits the floor. On the third hit, each player tries to get control of the puck.

GS-123 HOCKEY LEAD-UP GAMES _____

FOCUS: Lead-up games; stick skills;
     team play

EQUIPMENT: One floor hockey stick per player;
     one soft puck (or tennis ball) per game;
     one whistle per game;
     floor tape;
     cone markers

ORGANIZATION:
- The hockey stick skills learned are now reinforced through the following lead-up games.

DESCRIPTION OF ACTIVITY:

1. ***One-on-One Face-Off*** (Divide the class into two equal teams and have each team stand on opposite sides of the play area, about 10 meters [30 feet] apart and facing each other. Players on each team should space themselves at arm's length. Starting at opposite ends, have players number off. Mark a face-off circle, 60 centimeters [2 feet] in diameter, at the middle of the play area. To start the game, stand ready to drop the puck at the face-off circle.) When a number is called, the two opposing players with this number face off at the circle. The player who gains control of the puck, either dribble or pass it back to a teammate to earn a point for your team. The game continues until everyone has had a turn facing off; then add the scores to determine the winner.

VARIATIONS:

a. For a large class, have more than one game going on at the same time. Instead of dropping the puck for the face-off, have the puck placed on the floor between the two players, who must be outside the face-off circle. Blow the whistle for the face-off signal.

b. ***Side-Line Hockey:*** Play as for Face-Off game, but whoever gains control of the puck at the face-off tries to shoot it past the opposition's side-line players, who act as goalies.

c. ***Pair-Up Hockey:*** Call two or more numbers at a time, and add the rule that at least one pass must be made between the two players before attempting to score.

2. ***Mini-Hockey*** (The skills of stick-handling, shooting, checking, and goaltending are reinforced in a game-like situation of three-on-three. Have each player get a hockey stick to start; then form groups of six. Each group collects four cone markers and one puck or ball. Using floor tape or the existing floor lines, divide the play area into five mini-courts [for a class size of about 30]. Assign each group to a court and have them set up the goals at each end, using the cone markers. Each group of six plays a game of three-on-three in the assigned court. Observe the play closely, watching for dangerous swinging or raising of the sticks. Take immediate action!): In your group of six, make two teams of three players. One player of the threesome is the Goalie; the other two players try to score a goal. Change roles often or after every goal that is scored. Remember, there is no body contact! Don't bring your stick any higher than hip level or swing it dangerously. Always know where you are going and who is around you. On my whistle signal, immediately stop the play. Rotate to the next court and play a game of three-on-three with the new team!

VARIATION: Divide the play area into three or four courts and play four-on-four mini-hockey.

FOCUS: Hockey skills; team play; court awareness; fair play

EQUIPMENT: One floor hockey stick per player;
one plastic puck per game;
several bleach bottles (cone markers or bowling pins);
two sets of colored pinnies;
four hockey nets or eight cones;
one whistle

ORGANIZATION:

• These challenging lead-up games further reinforce hockey skills and team play.

DESCRIPTION OF ACTIVITY:

1. ***Bleach-Bottle Hockey*** (Divide the play area into smaller courts so that games of three-on-three can be played. For each game, have the two teams collect one floor hockey stick per player and three bleach bottles. One team will wear pinnies. Teams scatter on each half of the court area. Each team chooses its goalie; change goalies frequently throughout the play. For each game, set up the three bleach bottles, equally spaced apart, in the middle of each endline of the play area as goals. Only the goalie is allowed to guard the bleach bottles; the other two players are forwards. Each forward will guard an opposition forward.): Start the game with a face-off at the middle; then pass or dribble to shoot the puck to hit the bleach bottles. Score a goal every time a bleach bottle is hit.

2. ***Mad Ball Hockey*** (Position hockey nets in the middle of both ends and at each side of the play area. Divide the class into two equal teams and distribute one set of pinnies to each team. Assign each team one end net and one side net to defend. At the start of the game use two pucks; then as skill improves, add another and then another until four pucks are in use. Position each puck in the middle of the play area. Have two goalies for each team stand in front of the nets. All other players scatter.): To begin the game, four players, two from each team, stand on either side of the pucks ready to face-off. When the whistle blows, try to gain control of the puck and pass it to your teammates to try and score in either of the opposition's goals. Goalies, keep track of how many goals the other team has scored. After five minutes of play, the team with the fewest goals scored against it wins. Play a new five-minute game with new goalies.

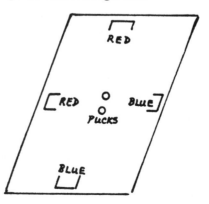

GS–125 FOUR-STATIONS HOCKEY

FOCUS: Stick-handling; accuracy shooting; passing; goaltending

EQUIPMENT: Four hockey nets;
seven deckrings;
six plastic bleach bottles;
eight bladeless hockey sticks;
six hockey sticks;
three folding mats;
three hockey pucks or balls;
floor tape or cone markers;
one whistle

ORGANIZATION:

• Partition the play area into four equal smaller areas and set up the suggested stations in each area. (If available, use benches turned over on their sides to mark off the four areas.) Then divide the class into four equal groups and assign each group to a station. Rotate groups every five to seven minutes on the whistle signal. Demonstrate the skill involved at each station. Emphasize safety at all times. At the finish, have each group put away the equipment.

DESCRIPTION OF ACTIVITY:

1. *Area 1, Ringette Hockey:* Play three-on-three or four-on-four hockey using a deckring, bladeless hockey sticks, and a net at opposite ends for each team.

2. *Area 2, Hockey Shoot* (Position two nets in one quarter of the play area so that they are well spaced apart. Mark a shooting line 5 meters [15 feet] away from one net and another shooting line 6 meters [20 feet] away from the other net.): Take turns trying to score a goal using the Wrist Shot.

3. *Area 3, Deckring Shot* (Set up two identical stations with three plastic bottles in a triangle formation about one giant step from a wall. Use floor tape or cones to mark off the shooting line four giant steps away.): Take turns using the bladeless stick to send the deckring toward the bottles. How many bottles can you knock over in three tries?

4. *Area 4, Goalie Challenge* (Position three folding mats, standing upright so they won't fall over, as goalie nets. Ensure that they are well spaced apart.): Each player, in turn, take five shots on goal to try and score. Goalie, how many saves can you make? Take turns goaltending and shooting.

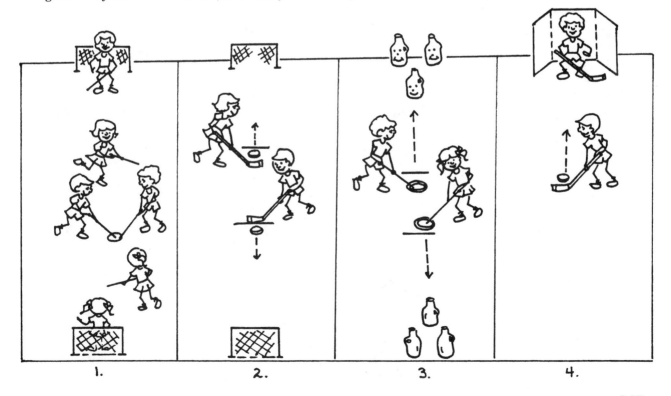

1.   2.   3.   4.

FOCUS: Throwing and catching; gripping the ball

EQUIPMENT: One softball per player; one softball glove per player

ORGANIZATION:

- Introduce and demonstrate the techniques for gripping the ball and using a glove to catch a ball. Review the overhand throwing technique. Allow players to practice at a wall. Have each player get a ball and stand about 4 meters (12 feet) from a wall. Check for good spacing.

DESCRIPTION OF ACTIVITY:

1. *Full-Hand Grip:* If you have smaller hands, use this grip. Space your thumb and fingers evenly around the ball and hold it with your finger pads, not in the palm of your hand. You should be able to see "daylight" between the ball and your hand.

2. *Two-Finger Grip:* Place your thumb on the underside of the ball and your index and middle fingers on top. Your third and fourth fingers support the ball along the side.

3. *Using a Glove:* Put the glove onto your nonthrowing hand. Put your fingers into the four glove fingers. Check that your fingers are not too deep in the glove: The back strap should come across your knuckles. The glove will protect your hand and increase the catching area.

4. *Practice Tasks:*
— "Snap" the ball into the pocket of your glove with short hard throws. Repeat several times.
— Toss the ball into the air and catch it in your glove. Repeat. How high can you toss the ball and still catch it?
— Underhand-throw the ball at a wall and catch the rebound with your glove.

5. *Overhand Throwing:*
— *Stance:* Stand with your nonthrowing shoulder to the wall and your feet comfortably apart. Hold the ball in the full-hand or two-finger grip.
— *Overhand Throwing Action:* Shift your weight to the rear foot. At the same time, swing your throwing hand up behind your shoulder so that the ball is just above your ear. As you step forward with your front foot, bring your throwing arm forward with your elbow leading. Snap your wrist forward and down as you release the ball and follow through in the direction of the wall. Keep your eyes on an imaginary target throughout the throw.

6. *Catching the Ball:* Stand with your feet comfortably apart and your knees slightly bent. Move in front of the oncoming ball, watch it, and catch with both hands. If the ball is low, catch with your fingers pointing down. If the ball is high, catch with your fingers up. Watch the ball enter your glove and trap it with your free hand, bending your elbows to soften the ball's impact.

7. *Practice Tasks:*
— Mime the throwing and catching actions several times; then, overhand-throw the ball at a wall at an imaginary target. Can you catch the ball before it hits the ground?
— How quickly can you make the catch, then throw the ball back to the wall? Try low throws; higher throws.
— Turn your back to the wall. Show me how quickly you can pivot to face the wall and still throw a ball at your target.

GS-127 FIELDING GROUNDERS

FOCUS: Ready position; throwing; visual tracking; fielding

EQUIPMENT: One small ball per player; one glove per player

ORGANIZATION:

- Review what it means to "field a ball" (to catch it, or stop it, to get control of the ball). Ask "what is a grounder?" (a ball that travels low along the ground). Guide players to discover what is the best "ready position" to field a grounder; then let them practice against a wall or with a partner. Vary the type of ball used: utility ball, sponge ball, whiffle ball, tennis ball, rubber ball. To begin, have players find a home space and face you. Check for good spacing.

DESCRIPTION OF ACTIVITY:

1. Let's pretend that an imaginary grounder is coming toward you. Show me your "ready position" to field the grounder:
   - position yourself so that you are directly in front of the oncoming ball and kneel on one knee
   - form a basket with your hand and glove, and hold it between your raised and lowered knee, just off the ground; little fingers touching and pointing down
   - keep your head up and eyes on the ball until you "feel" the ball in your glove
   - let the ball roll into your glove and trap it with the other hand
   - "give" with the force of the rolling ball

2. *Practice Tasks:*
   - Get a ball and stand about three giant steps from a wall. Overhand-throw your ball toward the wall so that it rebounds off the wall low, along the floor. Field the ball in the ready position as it comes toward you.
   - Find a partner. Practice fielding grounders with your partner. Start five giant steps away; then take another step back after you each field three grounders. At first throw slow grounders; then try to make the ball travel faster.

GS-128 FIELDING FLY BALLS

EQUIPMENT: See activity GS–127.

ORGANIZATION:

- Explain and demonstrate the Ready Position and catching technique; then allow players to practice fielding skills. Have each player get a ball and find a free space.

DESCRIPTION OF ACTIVITY:

1. *Catching a Fly Ball:*
   - To catch a fly or high ball, put your thumbs together and raise them to your chin.
   - Follow the path of the ball until it hits your glove; then "give" with your hands. Bend your knees slightly as you make the catch.

2. *Practice Tasks:*
   - Go to a wall. Underhand-throw the ball high on the wall. Field the rebound with your glove as it comes off the wall.
   - Find a partner, put one ball aside, and stand facing each other about five giant steps apart in a free space. Check for good spacing. Practice fielding a high ball. Use either underhand or overhand throws to send the ball high into the air.

3. *Fielding Triangle:* Form groups of three and stand in a triangle formation. First player, throw the ball along the ground toward the second player, who quickly fields the ball and throws a grounder to the third player. Move into the ball's path each time and strive to catch the ball with both hands. Repeat with high throws. Remember to watch the ball constantly until it falls into the glove; then trap with both hands! "Give" with your hands and arms to cushion the ball's force.

FOCUS: Fielding skills; groupwork

EQUIPMENT: One small ball per group;
one softball glove per player;
two bases per game;
cone markers

ORGANIZATION:

• The fielding games reinforce the fielding skills learned. Players do not have to use gloves, if unavailable.

DESCRIPTION OF ACTIVITY:

1. *Leader Ball* (Form groups of four to five players and have each group find a free area. Members stand arm's length apart in a line facing a leader with the ball who is 10 meters [30 feet] from the line of players. Increase the distance as ability improves.): Leader, throw a grounder to the first player in line, who will field the ball and throw it back to you. Continue to throw grounders to each player in turn. If a player misses the ball, everyone must do five jumping jacks while that player runs to retrieve the ball; then carry on. When the last player has fielded the ball, the player at the head of the line becomes the new leader and the former leader goes to the end of the line. The game continues until all players have been the leader. Repeat with Leader throwing a fly ball to each player, who fields the ball and throws back a grounder.

2. *Beat Ball* (For each game, mark off a large rectangular playing field about 20 meters by 10 meters [60 feet by 30 feet] in size. Then divide the class into two equal teams: the "Throwing Team" and the "Fielding Team." Place a home base or cone in the middle of one end of the play area, and a second base or cone in the middle of the playing area, about 10 meters [30 feet] from the home base. Have the Throwing team stand just outside one sideline, near the home base endline. The Fielding team scatter throughout the play area, except for one player, who is the Catcher and stands just behind home base.): Each Thrower, in turn, stand with one foot on home base and throw the ball into the field area as far as you can; then run to the second base and home before the Fielding team can retrieve the ball and throw it to the Catcher at home base. Thrower, if you beat the ball to home base, you score a run for your team. Fielder, if you catch an air ball, the Thrower is out. After each player of the Throwing team has had a turn to throw, the two teams then exchanges places. We will rotate the catcher after every three throws.

VARIATION:

Allow the Fielding Team to throw the ball at the Runner and put him or her out by hitting the Runner below the waist. The Fielder with the ball can only take three steps before making the throw.

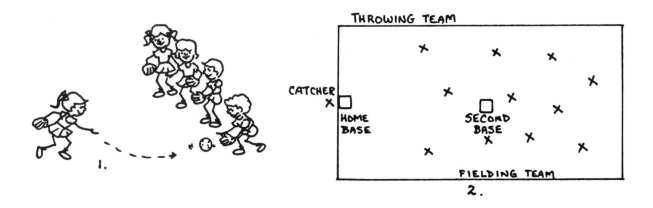

270 / *Game Skills*

GS-130 BASE RUNNING

FOCUS: Base-tagging technique;
infield awareness;
agility; teamwork

EQUIPMENT: Four bases or carpet squares or cone
markers per team;
one large utility ball;
chalkboard;
chalk;
brush

ORGANIZATION:

- Review the Infield Base positions and softball terms "Diamond," "Infield," and "Outfield." Also review the technique of "tagging up" or touching the inside of the base with one foot; then making a sharp turn to the next base. Players practice base tagging through team activities and a related game.

DESCRIPTION OF ACTIVITY:

1. ***Base-Running Warm-Up*** (Form teams of six players. Have the leader of each team collect four cones or carpet squares, which are positioned in a large diamond shape. All team members stand in a line behind leader at home base.): Start at home base and follow your leader to first, second, third bases and then back to home. (Repeat three times.) Practice "tagging up" or touching the inside of each base with one foot as you come to it; then making a sharp turn to the next base. What direction are you travelling in? (CCW)
   — What shape do the four bases make? (Diamond shape)
   — The area inside the four bases is the Infield; the area outside of the diamond is the Outfield.

2. ***Round-the-Bases Relay*** (Place one base in each corner of a 15-meter [50-foot] square; then place a cone in front of each base. Form four equal teams and have each team stand in single-file formation behind a cone inside the square.): On signal "Run!" each player, in turn, run CCW to touch all four bases with one foot, and then return to your team to tag the next runner. The first team to complete the relay and sit cross-legged wins.

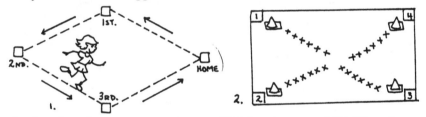

3. ***Manoc*** (Divide the class into two even teams: Kicking team and Fielding team. Have each team number off consecutively for kicking order. Have the Kicking team stand off to one side at a safe distance away; have the Fielding team scatter throughout the diamond area.)
   — First Kicker, place the ball on home base; then kick the ball forward into the field. Now run as quickly as you can around the bases until you reach home.
   — Meanwhile any fielding team player, retrieve the ball and quickly stand at that spot holding the ball up above your head. Fielders, this is your signal to quickly form a file behind the fielder with the ball and stand with your legs wide apart.
   — Kicker, if you can make it home before the Fielding team can roll the ball through the legs of each player in the file and the last fielder holds the ball up high, then you earn one point for your team; otherwise, the Fielding team earns a point. I will record the scores.
   — After everyone on the Kicking team has had a turn, the two teams exchange roles. Which team will earn the better score?

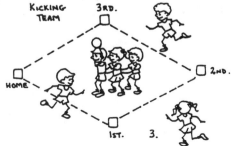

GS-131 UNDERHAND PITCHING AND BACK-CATCHING _____

FOCUS: Pitching technique; accuracy;
catching technique;
partnerwork and groupwork

EQUIPMENT: One small ball per player;
two bases per groups;
one softball glove per player;
catcher's mask and body protector;
wall tape

ORGANIZATION:

• Review and demonstrate the pitching technique; then have players practice pitching to targets taped to the wall 60 centimeters (2 feet) from the floor. Review the "Catcher" and "Pitcher" positions. Demonstrate how to wear a catcher's mask and body protector; then have players in pairs practice pitching and back-catching. To start, have players find a free space.

DESCRIPTION OF ACTIVITY:

1. **Pitching Action:** Let's mime the pitching action. Begin with your feet together, hold an imaginary ball in both hands, and face an imaginary target (batter).
   — Bend forward slightly at the waist. Now separate your hands, hold the ball between your fingers and your thumb, and swing your pitching arm back.
   — Keep your arm close to your body as it swings back; then swing the ball forward and, at the same time, step forward on the foot opposite your throwing arm. Watch your target as you deliver the ball.
2. **Pitching Practice:** Now pair up, get a ball each, and stand 5 meters (15 feet) from a wall target. Take turns pitching your ball to the target. Practice good technique. Partner, watch the pitcher and comment on his or her pitching action. How many times can you hit the target in ten tries? Now take a step back and pitch to your target again.
3. **Catcher Position:**
   — Position yourself just beyond the range of the swinging bat.
   — Squat with your feet shoulder-width apart and one foot ahead of the other.
   — Watch the ball and hold up your glove as the target for the pitcher.
4. **Pitcher Position:**
   — Stand about 6 meters (18 feet) away and face the catcher.
   — Aim the ball at the catcher's glove, which should be over the plate and between the batter's knee and shoulder.
5. **Pitching/Back-Catching Practice:** Partners, you will need a ball to share, a glove each, and a base. Place this base near a wall. Check for good spacing. One partner will be the catcher, who squats down just behind the base. The other partner will be the pitcher, who stands six giant steps away. Pitch the ball to your partner ten times, change roles, and repeat.
6. **Triangle Bases:** Form groups of three: catcher, pitcher, and first base player. Collect two bases: one for the catcher and one for first base. Form a triangle 5 meters (15 feet) away from each other.
   — Pitcher, pitch the ball to the catcher; catcher, throw the ball to first base; first base player, throw the ball back to pitcher. Repeat ten times; then rotate one position.

GS-132 LEAD-UP GAMES

FOCUS: Underhand pitching accuracy; fielding; base running; team play

EQUIPMENT: One small ball per player; one bleach bottle per player; four bowling pins; one base; sand; several benches

ORGANIZATION:

- The following games reinforce skills learned to this point: fielding, pitching, base running, infield positions.

DESCRIPTION OF ACTIVITY:

1. **Bleach Bottle Pitch** (Add 5 centimeters [2 inches] of sand to each bleach bottle for extra stability; then have each player get a ball and a bleach bottle. Form groups of three players and have each group arrange the bleach bottles on half of a bench. Ensure that the bleach bottles are well spaced along the benches. Two groups should be able to use the same bench. Players in each group take turns pitching at the three bleach bottles from a distance of 5 meters [15 feet].): One player pitches the ball; another player retrieves the ball; and the third player sets the bleach bottles in place again. Each player has three pitches to knock down all three bleach bottles. Rotate positions every three throws.

   — As the player's skill improves, increase the pitching distance.

VARIATIONS:

a. Give each player five pitches to knock over the three bleach bottles.

b. Challenge groups to knock down as many bottles as they can in two minutes by using the correct pitching technique.

c. Use bowling pins, tin cans, or wooden blocks instead of bleach bottles.

2. **Kick-Pin Softball** (Set up four bowling pins as first, second, third base and home, each 8 meters [25 feet] apart; then place the pitcher's base 5 meters [15 feet] from home plate. Form two equal teams: kickers and fielders. Number the players consecutively to establish kicking order and fielding positions. Kickers stand to one side, boy-girl, in single-file formation. Fielders stand in regular softball positions and the pitcher gets a ball and stands at the pitcher's base.): Pitcher, roll the ball to the first kicker, who kicks it and runs outside the bases to grab the home pin before the fielders can retrieve the ball and pass it to players at first, second, to third base, and then to home. Fielder, you must knock down the bowling pin at your base before throwing the ball to the next base. Score one run for each player who makes it home before all the pins are knocked down. Kicker, you are out when a fielder catches a fly ball, or all the pins are knocked over before you reach home. Change roles when everyone on the kicking team has had a turn. Which team will earn the better score?

FOCUS: Stance, grip, swing and hitting technique; groupwork

EQUIPMENT: One small ball per group; one home plate per group; one softball glove per player; one bat per player

ORGANIZATION:

• Review and demonstrate batting technique, and then allow players to practice in small groups.

DESCRIPTION OF ACTIVITY:

1. *Grip:* Hold the bat firmly, with your hands together near the "butt" of the bat, with your dominant hand on top of the other. Move your hands up the bat (called "choking up" on the bat) if more comfortable. Hold the bat off your shoulder with the trademark facing up. Do not cross your hands as you grip the bat!

2. *Stance:* Stand with your feet shoulder-width apart and your knees slightly bent. Turn your nondominant side toward the pitcher so that you face home plate. Point the bat over your rear shoulder, bend your elbows, and hold your hands out from your body. Practice a swing to see that the end of the bat reaches just past the far side of home plate. Step back if it reaches too far over the plate.

3. *Swing:* Focus your eyes on the ball. Swing your bat parallel to the ground. As the ball leaves the pitcher's hand, shift your weight to your back foot. Watch the ball and, as you swing the bat forward, step forward onto your front foot. Hit through the ball, continuing to swing the bat in a wide arc around your front shoulder. Your swing should be a smooth continuous motion.

4. *Batting Practice* (Form groups of four to five players: batter, catcher, pitcher, and one or two fielders. Number players consecutively to establish the order of rotation.): With batter standing at a base, pitcher throw one practice pitch, which the batter will not try to hit. Now throw five more pitches, which the batter will try to hit. Then rotate positions: batter to fielder, fielder to pitcher, pitcher to catcher, catcher to batter. Watch for and correct the following common batting faults:
   — stepping back while swinging the bat forward
   — chopping the bat down on the ball
   — swinging up and under the ball
   — not looking at the ball
   — pulling the elbows in to the sides
   — resting the bat on the shoulder
   — standing too far away from or too near home plate

5. *Bat Ball* (Form groups of five players: a batter, a catcher and three fielders. Each group gets a bat, softball, and home plate. The fielders stand in a semicircle about 10 meters [30 feet] from the batter. The catcher stands safely behind the batter.): Fielders, throw underhand pitches to the batter, who will try to hit grounders back to you. Each batter will try to hit at least five pitched balls. After the fifth pitch, you may stay at bat as long as you continue to hit grounders. Rotate one position CW when the batter is out, until all have had a turn at bat.

VARIATION: Batters are out after five pitches when they strike at the ball and miss; hit a fly ball over the fielder's heads; hit a foul ball that lands behind home plate.

GS-134 SOFTBALL STATIONS

FOCUS: Reinforcing basic softball skills; stationwork

EQUIPMENT: One small ball per pair; softball gloves (if possible); two bats per group; four bases per group; one batting tee per group; one whiffle ball per group

ORGANIZATION:

- Set up six to seven softball stations as illustrated; then form groups of four players. Assign each group to a station. Rotate groups to the next station every five to six minutes. Throughout the activity, observe players closely and correct poor skills where necessary.

DESCRIPTION OF ACTIVITY:

1. *Station 1—Baton Base Running:* Each player, in turn, run the bases in order to pass a baton to the next player. How many home runs will your team make before the signal to rotate is given?

2. *Station 2—Fielding Fly Balls:* One player throws fly balls to the other players, who call for the ball and try to catch it. Change throwers every five throws.

3. *Station 3—Pitching:* Working in pairs, one partner pitches while the other catches. Pitch the ball back and forth ten times; then change roles. Gradually increase the pitching distance until you are 6 meters (18 feet) apart.

4. *Station 4—Pepper Batting:* Fielders toss the ball to the batter, who hits grounders back. Change batter every five hits.

5. *Station 5—Fielding Grounders:* Pair off in your group and share a ball. Partners, stand facing each other about 5 meters to 8 meters (15 feet to 25 feet) apart. Throw grounders and fly balls to each other.

6. *Station 6—Mini T-Ball:* Play T-Ball in your area, changing positions after every three hits of the ball. Batter must run to a base and back to touch his or her T-ball plate to score a point. Each batter keeps track of his or her score.

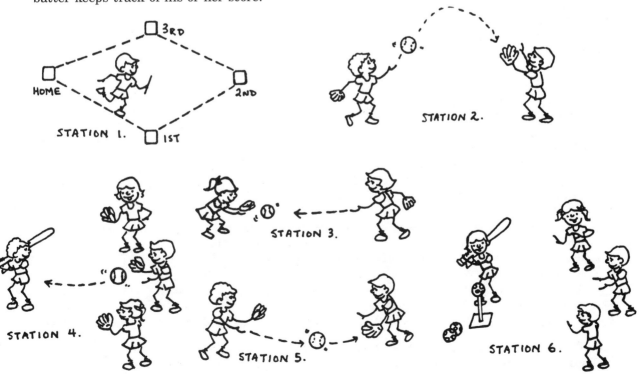

GS-135 LONG BASE

FOCUS: Lead-up game; batting; fielding; base running

EQUIPMENT: One bat;
two bases;
one small utility ball

ORGANIZATION:

- Set up home plate and another base 10 meters (30 feet) apart; then form two equal teams, batters and fielders. Number each team consecutively to establish batting order and fielding positions. Rotate fielding positions frequently.

DESCRIPTION OF ACTIVITY:

1. The pitcher pitches underhand to the batter, who tries to hit the ball and then runs to touch the "long base" and home again before a fielder retrieves the ball and throws it to hit the batter below the waist.
2. Batter, if you are tagged, you are out, but if you reach home without being tagged or hit, your team scores one run.
3. You may hit the ball in any direction and must run as soon as you hit it. If you miss the ball twice or hit a fly ball that is caught, you are out.
4. Change roles after all batters have had a turn at bat. After three innings, the team that scores the most runs wins the game.

VARIATIONS:

a. The teacher is the pitcher.
b. Allow each team to have three outs before fielding and batting teams change roles.
c. Allow the runner to stop at the base until the next batter hits the ball; then the first runner may return home. Establish running lanes for safety.
d. Play to five, seven, or nine innings.

GS-136 TEE-BALL PLAY

FOCUS: Stance; grip; swing; group play

EQUIPMENT: One plastic bat per group;
one base or carpet square per group;
one whiffle ball per group;
one batting-tee per group

ORGANIZATION:

- Batting skills are further developed through hitting the ball off a "batting-tee," which can be a purchased regulation batting-tee or a whiffle ball sitting on top of a cone marker. Demonstrate the positioning at the batting-tee plate; review the stance, grip, and swing. Form groups of four and have each member of the group number off 1, 2, 3, or 4. Each group then collects a bat, one ball, one base, and a batting-tee. Designate an area for each group to set up its batting-tee station. Check that groups are well spaced apart. Place the base or carpet square 4 meters (12 feet) to one side of the batting-tee.

DESCRIPTION OF ACTIVITY:

1. First player, you are the Batter; second player, the Catcher; and third and fourth players, Fielders.
2. Batter, do not crowd the plate or get too far away from it. Stand far enough behind the tee so that you can step forward into the swing. Hit the ball in front of you. Don't throw your bat after you hit the ball! Drop it. Keep your eyes on the ball!
3. Batter, when you hit the ball off the batting-tee, run to the base and back to score one run. If it is safe, go again to score another run! Meanwhile, Fielder, retrieve the hit ball and either touch the Batter or home plate. Each Batter, keep track of the number of runs you make in three hits.
4. After the Batter has made three hits, everyone rotate one position: Batter to fourth player's position; fourth player to third player's position; third player to Catcher; and second player to the Batter's position.

GS–137 ENDLINE KICKBALL

FOCUS: Lead-up game; fielding positions; kicking, throwing and catching

EQUIPMENT: Four bases; four cones; one small utility ball; floor tape

ORGANIZATION:

- Endline Kickball is a modified softball game that can be played indoors or outdoors. Divide the class into two equal teams: a kicking team and a batting team. Have each team stand in single-file formation, alternating boys and girls, and number off consecutively to establish the order in which they will kick the ball. Before beginning the game, mark a Kicking line and an Endline as illustrated, and an "X" where players will stand to kick the ball.

DESCRIPTION OF ACTIVITY:

1. Pitcher, roll the ball toward the first kicker, who may kick the ball past the Kicking line anywhere in the play area. Kicker, run quickly to the Endline without being hit below the waist by the ball. Try to get back to the Kicking line, if you can, to score one run.
2. Fielders, retrieve the ball and, without taking any steps, throw the ball at the runner to hit him or her below the waist before he or she can reach the safety of the Endline. A hit runner is out. A caught fly ball does not put the runner out. If indoors, play the ball off the wall.
3. Fielders, you cannot run with the ball, but you may pass it to a teammate to throw, or throw at the runner yourself from that point.
4. Runners, you may stay over the Endline as long as no more than two runners are there at any time. When a third runner arrives, the first runner must try to run back to the Kicking line. You could all try to run back if you dare!
5. Teams exchange roles after all members of the team have kicked the ball. After even innings, the team with the best score wins.

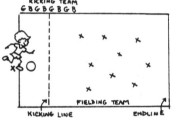

GS–138 KICKBALL

ORGANIZATION:

EQUIPMENT: Four bases; cones; kickball

- Divide the class into two equal teams: the kicking team and the fielding team. Number the players for fielding and kicking order; then teach the fielding positions and location on the field: 1—catcher; 2—pitcher; 3—first base; 4—second base; 5—third base; 6—short stop; 7, 8, and 9—fielders. Have players rotate one field position after every three kickers; for example, 2 rotates to catcher position; 3 to pitcher; 1 to fielder; and so on.

DESCRIPTION OF ACTIVITY:

1. To start the game, pitcher roll the ball toward the first player on the kicking team. The first kicker, standing in front of home base, kick the ball between first and third base; then run to first base.
2. The runner is out if a fielder catches a fly ball. Other runners on base cannot advance to the next base if a ball is thrown to the base before the runner reaches it; the runner is hit below the waist with the ball.
3. While on base, runners are not allowed to lead-off a base or steal a base while the pitcher is holding the ball.
4. The kicking team scores one run for each player who reaches home plate. Both teams change roles after each member of the kicking team has had a turn.

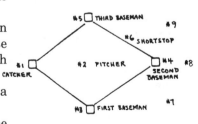

VARIATION: If playing indoors, use a partially deflated soccer ball and draw a line high on the wall behind second base. A ball kicked above this line is a home-run for the kicker.

GS-139 FREEZE SOFTBALL

FOCUS: Lead-up game; batting; fielding; base running

EQUIPMENT: One small ball; one softball glove per fielder; one bat; four bases

ORGANIZATION:

- Set up the bases as for softball. For each game divide the class into two equal teams of six to eight players: batting team and fielding team. Have the fielders position themselves around the bases and in the field area. The pitcher is a member of the batter's team.

DESCRIPTION OF ACTIVITY:

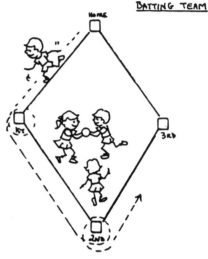

1. Pitcher, pitch to your batter. Batter, hit the ball into the field; then run to first base, circling around it completely without touching it, and continue to the next base and so on. Change the pitcher for every new batter, so that everyone gets to bat and pitch.
2. Fielder, field the ball, and then move quickly around so that every fielder touches the ball. The fielder who is last to catch the ball shouts "Freeze!" This is the signal for the base runner to immediately stop and stay in that position, even if caught between bases.
3. After the next batter hits the ball, the frozen base runner (or runners) continue to circle around each base until reaching home plate and score one run, but must stop again on the signal "Freeze!"
4. After everyone on the batting team has had a turn at bat, the fielding team will bat. There are no outs—everyone wins!

GS-140 SCOREBALL

EQUIPMENT: One small ball; one bat; four bases

ORGANIZATION:

- Form two equal teams of eight to ten players. Number the players consecutively to establish batting and fielding positions. Have the batting team stand off to one side, at a safe distance away. Follow regular softball rules; however, score points for each base players reach: first base—1 point; second base—2 points; third base—3 points; and home plate—4 points.
- Explain that a ball landing in the infield between and including the first and third base lines is called a "fair ball"; a ball landing outside this area is a "foul ball," and the batter gets another hit.

DESCRIPTION OF ACTIVITY:

1. I will be the Pitcher for both teams. Batter, you have three tries, or "strikes," to hit the ball into fair territory between first and third baselines. Then run the bases in order. Score points for each base you reach safely. Batting team, shout out your score as a team each time your runner scores a point.
2. Fielders, try to put out the Batter by tagging the Batter with the ball before he or she reaches a base. The Batter is also out if he or she hits a fly ball that is caught by a fielder.
3. After everyone on the batting team has had a turn, then the two teams change roles.

VARIATIONS:

a. Have batting and fielding team change roles after every four outs.
b. Allow players to pitch with a new pitcher for every three batters.

GS-141 INTRODUCTION TO FRISBEE™ THROWING

FOCUS: Throwing and catching technique

EQUIPMENT: One Frisbee™ per pair; one hoop per pair

ORGANIZATION:

- Explain and demonstrate Frisbee™ throwing and catching techniques. Have players find a partner and practice together. Encourage them to throw and catch with either hand.

DESCRIPTION OF ACTIVITY:

1. *Grip:* Place thumb on top of Frisbee™ and index finger along rim. Other fingers are under Frisbee™ and grip is relaxed, as if you were going to use the Frisbee™ to fan yourself.

2. *Backhand Throw:* Stand sideways to partner and step toward partner on the closer leg. Reach across your body in a full back swing, draw the Frisbee™ forward across your body again, snap wrist, and release. Try to keep Frisbee™ flat as you release it. Let your hand follow through in the line of direction.

3. *Underhand Throw:* Face partner and hold Frisbee™ close to the side of your body. Step forward with leg opposite to throwing arm. At the same time, bring Frisbee™ forward, snap wrist, and release, trying to keep Frisbee™ flat as you release it.

4. *High Catch:* Watch Frisbee™ as it leaves thrower's hand. If Frisbee™ is coming toward you at a height above the waist, catch it with both hands, pointing thumbs down and fingers up. Reach for the Frisbee™ and close thumbs and fingers over it.

5. *Low Catch:* If Frisbee™ is coming toward you at a height below the waist, point thumbs up and fingers down. Watch Frisbee™, reach for it, and close hands over it.

6. *Catching Challenge:* How many throws and catches in a row can you make as a pair? Start over if you drop the Frisbee™.

7. *Underhand Throw:* Face your partner and hold Frisbee™ close to one side of your body. Step forward with the leg opposite your throwing arm. At the same time, bring the Frisbee™ forward, snap your wrist, and release. Keep the Frisbee™ flat as you release it.

8. *Hoop Target Throw:* One partner, get a hoop and hold it vertically at waist level about 3 meters (10 feet) from a wall. Other partner, collect a Frisbee™ and pace out five giant steps away from your partner. How many times can you throw the Frisbee™ through the hoop? Take turns and try throws with either hand. Repeat, holding the hoop at different levels.

9. *Distance Throw:* When outdoors, select a distant point, such as a tree at the end of the schoolyard. Challenge players: "How many throws will it take you to hit the tree?"

VARIATION:

Finger Catch: Explore catching the Frisbee™ on the pointer finger.

FOCUS: Foot-eye coordination; dribbling technique; control

EQUIPMENT: One soccer ball per player; several cone markers

ORGANIZATION:

- Foot-dribbling is a series of short kicks or taps along the ground, usually alternating the feet to contact the ball. This allows the dribbler to maintain possession of the ball. Scatter several cone markers throughout the play area; then have players get a ball and dribble it to a free space.

DESCRIPTION OF ACTIVITY:

1. *Dribbling Technique:* Use the inside of the foot, not the toe, and keep the ball close in order to maintain better control. Short kicks or taps should be used so that you can "feel" the ball at all times without actually looking at it.

2. *Practice:* Dribble the ball around the play area without touching a cone, another ball, or another player. Try not to break your running stride as you move in a straight line.
   — Use only the inside of either foot.
   — Use only the outside of either foot.
   — Use the inside and outside of either foot.
   — Dribble the ball slowly; dribble quickly.
   — Dribble the ball in different patterns: zig-zag, circular, rectangular.
   — On signal "Change!" exchange your soccer ball with another player and continue to dribble in and out of the cones.

3. *Bubbles:* Dribble your ball ("bubble") around the play area. Do not let your bubble touch another bubble or cone; otherwise, your bubble will "burst" and you must do ten jumping jacks before rejoining the game.

4. *Pirates:* Every third player, return your soccer ball. You are the Pirates. Go to the middle of the play area and on signal "Ahoy Mateys!" try to steal the balls from the dribblers. A player without a ball becomes a new Pirate.

5. *Poison Trees:* All girls stand still in a home space holding your ball in both hands. You are the "Trees." Boys, dribble through the forest without touching the trees or any other boys. Dribbler, if your ball touches a Tree, then you become a Tree; Tree you become a Dribbler.
   — Play the game again except that if a Dribbler's ball touches a Tree, then that Dribbler becomes a Tree (or a point is awarded to the Tree team).

6. *Shuttle Dribble Relay* (Form teams of five or six players and have them stand in shuttle formation, one half facing the other about 15 meters [50 feet] away, standing in single-file formation.): First player, dribble the ball to the opposite line, pass the ball to the next player, and go to the end of the line. How many crossings can your team make in two minutes?

GS-143 TRAPPING THE BALL _____

FOCUS: Foot-eye coordination; ball control; terminology   **EQUIPMENT:** One soccer ball per player

ORGANIZATION:
- At first have the players explore different ways to "trap" a ball. Have them throw the balls at different heights at a wall and then try to trap the ball. After some experimentation, present the following techniques and have players practice them.

DESCRIPTION OF ACTIVITY:

1. **Sole of Foot:** Keep your heel close to the ground and raise your toe. Crouch slightly with body relaxed. Trap and then quickly prepare to pass.

2. **Inside of Foot:** Lean slightly toward the oncoming ball. Bend your knee to form a wedge with the ground and draw your foot back as it contacts the ball.

3. **Trap with Shins:** Use this trap when you have plenty of time. Face the oncoming ball, and bend both knees toward the ground forming a wedge between shins and ground.

4. **Inside of Leg:** Use this trap to control a low bouncing ball or low pass. Keep the trapping foot close to the ground; then turn toward the oncoming ball, crouch slightly with a bent knee, and wedge the ball between your lower leg and ground.

5. **Chest:** Use this trap to control a high pass. Arch your back to contact the ball. Let your body sink down and backward so that the ball will drop slowly to the ground. Girls, you may cross your arms for protection, but your arms cannot be used to play the ball.

6. **Stomach:** At contact, lean forward and draw in your abdominal muscles to cause the ball to drop forward.

7. **Top of Foot:** Use this trap to control a dropping ball. Raise your foot and stop the ball in the wedge made by your instep. At contact, draw your foot downward.

8. Practice trapping a low ball:
   - Dribble the ball around the play area, avoiding other dribblers. On signal "Trap!" use the sole-of-the-foot trap to stop the ball. Continue using a different trap each time.
   - Kick your ball along the floor into an open space, run after it, get in front, and trap the ball with the sole of your foot. Bring the ball under control before you kick it again. Do this again, trapping with the sole of the other foot. Repeat using the Inside-of-the-Foot Trap.
   - Now stand about two meters (six feet) from the wall. At first, kick the ball gently to the wall and trap the rebound with sole of your foot; inside of your foot; outside of your foot; your shins. Do each trap five times.

9. Practice trapping a high ball:
   - Stand about three meters (ten feet) from the wall. Toss the ball up the wall and trap the rebound after the first bounce with the inside of your leg; your shins; your chest; your stomach. Repeat each trap five times.
   - With a partner, take turns throwing the ball to your partner's chest, stomach, and thighs. Trap the ball, control it, and kick it back to your partner. After five throws, change roles.

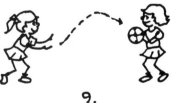

FOCUS: Kicking techniques; footwork; partnerwork   **EQUIPMENT:** One soccer ball per player

ORGANIZATION:

• The "Instep Kick" is the most powerful kick in soccer and, along with the Toe Kick, is used for distance kicking. The "Inside-of-the-Foot Kick" is generally used for passing but may also be used to score goals. Demonstrate these kicking techniques; then allow players to practice in pairs.

DESCRIPTION OF ACTIVITY:

1. *Inside-of-the-Foot Kick:* Place your nonkicking foot beside the ball; then draw your kicking foot back, turning the toe outward. The inside of your foot is now at right angles to the ball's line of flight and the sole is parallel to the ground. Contact the ball with the inside of your foot and follow through in the direction of the kick, straightening the knee.

2. *Practice:* Find a partner and stand 5 meters (15 feet) apart. Kick a ball back and forth to each other, using the inside-of-the-foot kick. Receiving partner, trap the ball with the inside-of-the-foot trap. Can you kick-pass the ball so that your partner does not have to move? Remember to trap the ball before you kick it. Now try to kick the ball with the inside of the other foot and trap the ball with the inside of this foot. Who can kick the ball with one foot and trap with the other?

   — Moving in general space, kick-pass the ball to each other. Remember to get the ball under control before you pass the ball back.

3. *Center-Kick Game:* Form groups of three players and collect two soccer balls. First and second players, each with a ball, stand facing about 10 meters (30 feet) apart; the third player, stand in the middle. First player, kick to the middle player, who will trap the ball and return it to you; then second player, kick to the middle player. Change places every ten kicks that the center player is able to return. Try to use either foot to kick the ball. Use the sole-of-the-foot trap.

4. *Instep Kick:* Approach the ball from an angle, two or three steps behind the ball. Place your nonkicking foot beside the ball about 15 centimeters (6 inches) away from it. Swing your kicking foot from the hip, back and then forward. Point the toe down and heel up, keeping your ankle rigid. Contact the ball with the lower part of the shoelaces underneath the ball, snapping the lower leg forward at the knee. Follow through in the direction of the kick and straighten the knee. Hold your arms out to the side for balance.

   — Show me how you can kick the ball with the toes of your foot. This is called the "Toe Kick."
   — Face a wall about 6 meters (20 feet) away. Practice the Instep Kick by kicking the ball to the wall and trapping the rebound. Practice Toe Kicks as well. After every ten kicks, move another giant step away from the wall until you are 10 meters (30 feet) or ten giant steps from the wall.
   — Face a partner about 10 meters (30 feet) away. Practice these kicks using your favorite foot; then your other. Can you kick the ball directly to your partner? Use different traps to bring the ball under control.

5. *Target Kicking* (Use hockey nets, low wall targets, cones, plastic bleach bottles, boxes on their sides and open at one end, and chairs as targets. Have players pair off and assign them to a starting target. They then practice, in turn, the basic kicks above. After a few minutes, have partners exchange targets.)

TOE KICK

GS-145 TARGET KICKING CHALLENGES

FOCUS: Accuracy kicking; trapping; cooperation

EQUIPMENT: One soccer-type ball per pair;
two cones per pair;
one hoop per group;
one wall target per pair

ORGANIZATION:

- Have players pair off. Each pair collects a ball and two cones and then finds a free space. Check for good spacing.

DESCRIPTION OF ACTIVITY:

1. *Goal-Kicking:* Place the cones one giant step apart on the floor; then pace three giant steps away from the cones.
   — Try to kick the ball between the two cones to your partner.
   — Explore using the different kicks you have learned.
   — Explore placing the cones closer together, or stepping further away from them.
2. *One-on-One:* Now place the two cones about two giant steps apart for the goal (near a wall, if possible). One partner be the kicker; the other partner, the goalie. Kicker, take five kicks to try to score a goal; then change roles. Goalie, try to trap the ball with your legs or feet.
3. *Hoop Kick* (Form groups of three. Players in each group collect one ball and a hoop; then find a free space. Check for good spacing.): Player A, stand in the middle holding the hoop vertically on the floor and out to one side. Player B, try to toe-kick the ball through the hoop. Player C, trap the ball; then take a turn at toe-kicking the ball through the hoop. Start close enough so that your kicks go through the hoop. Gradually move further away. Change the hoop holder after every five kicks. Continue until everyone has had a turn at holding the hoop. Repeat using Instep Kicks and the Inside-of-the-Foot Kicks. Kick with either foot.
4. *Kicking a Moving Ball* (Mark off several 1-meter [3-foot] square targets on the walls, 30 centimeters [1 foot] above the ground; also mark off a line 4 meters [12 feet] from the target. Have players find a partner, get a ball each, and stand about 6 meters [20 feet] from the wall targets.): In turn, dribble your ball to the line; then kick it at the target using the instep kick. Watch the ball as your foot contacts it; then field the ball and take nine more kicks. Repeat ten Instep Kicks with the other foot; then repeat using Inside-of-the-Foot Kicks.
5. *Passing Shuttle* (Form teams of six players. Divide each team in half and have each half stand facing the other 10 meters [30 feet] apart. Set up two cones, 2 meters [6 feet] apart and between the two groups.): The first player, dribble the ball forward; then kick it between the cones to the second player and run to the end of the opposite file. Second player, repeat the pattern, and so on.
   — Which team can be the first to complete 30 kick-passes through the cones?
6. *Performance Checking:* Have one partner make ten Inside-of-the-Foot Kicks at a low wall target or hockey net, while the other partner keeps track of the number of kicks that hit the target. Teacher records the scores; then the partners switch roles. Repeat for the Toe Kick and Instep Kick.

2.

3.

4.

5.

FOCUS: Dribbling; kicking; trapping; cooperation; fair play

EQUIPMENT: One soccer-type ball per pair; two cone markers, hockey nets, or plastic bleach bottles per pair; six to eight bowling pins

ORGANIZATION:

• Dribbling, kicking, passing, and trapping skills are reinforced through game play in small groups.

DESCRIPTION OF ACTIVITY:

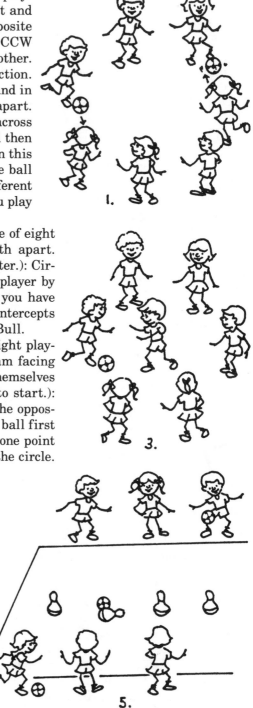

1. **Chase Ball** (Have players form circles of six to eight players, with players spacing themselves arm's length apart and facing inward. For each circle, give a ball to any two opposite players.): On the signal "Chase!" kick-pass the ball in a CCW direction to the next player to make one ball chase the other. Play the game again, but send the balls in a CW direction.

2. **Keep It In** (Form groups of six to eight players, who stand in a circle formation. Ensure that groups are well spaced apart. Have a leader from each group get a ball.): Kick the ball across the circle to another player, who traps the ball first and then kicks it across the circle to a different player. Continue in this way, trying to keep the ball in the circle. Each time the ball comes to you, try to trap it, and then kick it, in a different way, using the traps and kicks you have learned. Can you play this game while moving CW slowly around the circle?

3. **Bull in the Ring** (For each game, form one large circle of eight to ten players, with players spaced about arm's length apart. Choose one player to be the Bull, who stands in the center.): Circle players, try to keep the ball away from the center player by passing it from one player to another using the kicks you have learned. If the ball goes outside the circle, or the Bull intercepts the ball, then the player responsible becomes the new Bull.

4. **Circle Soccer** (Divide the class into teams of six to eight players. Have two teams form a large circle, with each team facing the other across the circle. Players should space themselves about arm's length apart. One team is given the ball to start.): On signal "Kick!" kick the ball, trying to send it past the opposing players, below the knees. Opposing players, trap the ball first to get control; then kick. No hands may be used. Score one point each time the ball is kicked past the opponent's side of the circle. Play to five points; then challenge another team.

5. **Pin-Ball Soccer** (Each game requires two teams of six players. Have the players of each team stand side-by-side facing the other team players on lines that are about 10 meters [30 feet] apart. To start the game, place a row of bowling pins across the middle of the play area between the teams and distribute three soccer balls to each team.): Each player, kick a ball from behind the line trying to knock down the pins. Before kicking, trap the ball to control it. Keep the kicks at ground level. The team knocking down more pins is the winner. When all the pins are knocked down, reset them and start again. You may pass the ball to a teammate who is in a better position for a kick at the pins.

GS-147 TACKLING

FOCUS: Defense; footwork; control   **EQUIPMENT:** One soccer ball per player

ORGANIZATION:
- Players explore different ways of taking the ball off an opponent or "tackling," through partner, small group, and large group play. Have players pair up, one partner get a ball, and together find a free space. Check for good spacing.

DESCRIPTION OF ACTIVITY:

1. You have explored different ways of dribbling, trapping, and kicking the ball. Now let's explore different ways of taking the ball off another player. This is called Tackling. One partner start with the ball. Dribble toward your partner. Partner without the ball, keep your eyes on the ball as you move toward it. Using only your feet, try to get control of the ball. Dribbler, how can you dodge and fake with the ball so that the tackler cannot get control of the ball?

2. **Keep Away** (Form groups of three; one player with the ball.): Two players try to keep the ball away from the third player, who is IT. If the third player does get the ball, then that player who was tackled becomes IT.

3. **Bull in the Square** (Form groups of five players and have each group get a ball. Four players stand at the corners of a 5-meter [15-foot] square. The fifth player, the Bull, stands in the middle.): Corner players, kick-pass the ball among yourselves while the Bull tries to intercept it. Use both the inside and outside of your feet to trap the ball. Bring it under control before kicking again. If the ball is kicked out of the square or is intercepted by the Bull, the player responsible becomes the new Bull. The old Bull runs to retrieve the ball and then kicks it from the vacated corner.

4. **Pirates** (Choose four or five players to be "pirates," who do not have a ball. Everyone else dribbles a ball to a free space.): On signal "Pirates are coming!" pirates try to tackle the ball away from dribblers.

GS-148 GOALKEEPING

FOCUS: Technique; kicking accuracy   **EQUIPMENT:** One large utility ball per pair; two cone markers per pair

ORGANIZATION:
- Have players pair off. Each pair collects a ball and two cones. Explain and demonstrate the stance and technique of stopping a ground ball and a chest-high shot at goal.

DESCRIPTION OF ACTIVITY:
1. **Technique:** Stand with feet shoulder-width apart and lean forward slightly with your weight on the balls of your feet. Raise your hands in front of your body at chest level, ready to stop the oncoming ball. Keep yourself between the goal and the ball. Watch the play and move out from the goal to stop the ball.

2. **Practice:** Place your cones near a wall and space them 2 meters (6 feet) apart. This is your goal. One partner is the goalie; the other is the kicker and stands 6 meters (20 feet) in front of the goal. Change roles after every five kicks.
   - Goalie, when stopping a ground ball, kneel on one knee, positioning yourself directly in front of the ball. "Give" with the hands as the ball contacts your fingers. When stopping a ball at chest height, move quickly into the path of the ball. As contact is made, pull the ball toward your chest. Smother the ball with your chest to secure the ball.

3. **Two-on-Two Soccer:** Each pair, set up your own goal, 15 meters (16 yards) away from the other pair's goal. On each team, one partner plays the goalie; the other is a forward. Change roles often. Play to five points; then challenge another pair.

GS-149 PUNT KICKING _____

FOCUS: Technique; distance kicking

EQUIPMENT: One soccer ball per player; one beanbag per player

ORGANIZATION:

- The punt kick used by the goalie can be made from the stationary position or on the run. Explain and demonstrate the punt kick, allowing players to practice outdoors if possible. Get a ball and find a free space, facing me.

DESCRIPTION OF ACTIVITY:

1. **Keep the Ball Up (Warm-Up):** Toss the ball in the air and let it bounce. Can you keep the ball bouncing without touching it with your arms or hands? Use your feet, lower legs, knees, and thighs.

2. **Punt Kick Technique:**

   — Hold the ball with both hands at waist level in front of your body and directly over your kicking leg.

   — Take three steps forward, starting with your non-kicking foot.

   — Look at the ball. Lean over it as you guide it down over your kicking foot.

   — Swing your kicking foot forward and contact the middle of the ball with your instep (shoelaces).

   — It should feel as though you are kicking "through the ball," with your foot pointing toward the target. Finish by rising on the toes of your nonkicking foot.

3. **Punting Practice:** Find a partner, get a ball each, and stand facing each other about 10 meters (30 feet) apart. Punt the ball back and forth to your partner. Observe each other's technique and coach each other.

4. **Partner Punting and Receiving Game:** Each pair collect two beanbags of different colors. Punt the ball to your partner, who will try to catch it and punt it back to you. If you are both successful at punting and catching, each take a step backwards and repeat. How far back can you go and still punt and catch the ball? Use a beanbag to mark the spot for your next kick.

5. **Kick and Mark:** One partner is the Kicker; the other, the Fielder. Kicker, punt each of the two soccer balls in turn, while the Fielder places a beanbag where your farthest punt lands, and then fields the ball for you. Take six punts; then change roles, marking the farthest punt this time with the other beanbag. Repeat. Can you punt the ball farther than you did the first time?

VARIATIONS:

a. Have players use their nondominant foot to punt.

b. Have players punt while on the run.

GS–150 FORCING BACK

FOCUS: Lead-up game; punt kicking; receiving; fair play

EQUIPMENT: One soccer ball;
soccer field (or open area);
cone markers;
one coin

ORGANIZATION:

- For each game, form two teams of six to eight players and have each team scatter on opposite sides of a large play area divided in half by a middle line. Use cones to mark out the play area (end goal-lines and middle line). Toss a coin to see which team will be the first to punt the ball.

DESCRIPTION OF ACTIVITY:

1. Try to punt the ball across the other team's goal-line to score a point. The first team to get three points wins the game.

2. To start, the team with the ball may choose any player to punt the ball. The first kick is taken at a point 18 meters (20 yards) back from the middle line. The player who fields the ball must also take the kick; however, after the receiver has made three kicks, give the ball to another teammate to kick until everyone has had a turn.

3. Players on the other team, you must kick the ball back from the spot where the ball was first touched. If the ball is caught, the receiving player may advance five paces to take the kick. If the ball is caught by a receiver in the endzone, no point is awarded to the punting team.

GS–151 ONE-ON-ONE SOCCER

FOCUS: Lead-up game; tackling; goalkeeping; kicking

EQUIPMENT: One soccer ball;
four cone markers

ORGANIZATION:

- Use cones to mark out two parallel lines that are 10 meters (30 feet) apart. Then for each game form teams of six to eight players and have each team stand facing the other on one line. Have each team number off from 1 to 8; then place a ball in the middle of the play area, between the two lines. To begin the game, call a number. Vary the order in which numbers are called and ensure that all players' numbers are called during the game.

DESCRIPTION OF ACTIVITY:

1. When your number is called, run forward, get control of the ball, and try to kick the ball through the opposition side-line players to score a point.

2. If the side-line player does trap the ball, then a point is awarded to his or her team.

VARIATIONS:

a. Call two numbers and play Two-on-Two.

b. If the ball goes out-of-bounds, the ball is out of play and another number is called.

GS–152 TWO-ON-TWO MINI-SOCCER

FOCUS: Lead-up game; offense and defense

EQUIPMENT: One soccer-type ball per game; two cone markers per team

ORGANIZATION:

- Through a soccer game-like situation, players reinforce kicking, trapping, tackling, and goalkeeping skills and learn offensive and defensive play and team play. Divide a large play area into four smaller areas. Form two teams of four players and have each team occupy half of their area. Each team collects two cones as the goals and sets them about two meters (six feet) apart at each end of the play area. In each team of two, one partner is the Goalie; the other partner, the Dribbler.

DESCRIPTION OF ACTIVITY:

1. Start the game with a kick-off at center: Place the ball in the middle between the two opposing players. Tap each other's leg, then the ground three times, and then try to get control of the ball. Then try to score a goal by kicking the ball between the opposition's cones.
2. After each goal, have a kick-off at center. Goalie and Dribbler change roles. Only Goalies may punt kick, but they are not allowed to score goals.
3. The other team is awarded a free kick after rough play, or when an opposition player touches the ball with the hands.

VARIATIONS:

a. *Three-on-Three Mini-Soccer:* Form teams of three with one goalie and two dribblers. Change goalies often.

b. Play Kickball. (Refer to activity GS–138.)

GS–153 FOUR-A-SIDE SOCCER

ORGANIZATION:

- Use a 12-meter by 20-meter (13-yard by 22-yard) play area and place two cones 3 meters (10 feet) apart in the middle of each endline as goals. Form two teams of four players and have each team occupy half of the play area. Toss a coin to see who kicks off first.

EQUIPMENT: One soccer ball per game; four cone markers per game; one set of pinnies per game; one coin

DESCRIPTION OF ACTIVITY:

1. Start the game with a kick-off at center; then try to score a goal by kicking the ball between the opposition's cones. The other team, try to intercept the ball and score. After a goal, the opposite team kicks off from the center.

2. The kick-off must be kicked to a teammate first; from then on, the ball may be kicked by any player.

3. The other team is awarded a free kick after rough play, or when an opposition player touches the ball with the hands.

4. The opposition team throws the ball back into the play area if it goes out over the sidelines or endlines. To throw the ball in, a player must hold the ball overhead in both hands and have both feet in contact with the ground throughout the throw.

GS-154 KICKING STATIONS

FOCUS: Foot-eye coordination; ball control; stationwork

EQUIPMENT: Soccer-type balls;
cone markers;
plastic bleach bottles;
wall targets;
hockey nets;
large cardboard boxes

ORGANIZATION:

- Through participating in the following stations, players further reinforce their soccer skills learned as well as interacting with each other. Set up six to eight stations around the perimeter of the play area. Number each station in CW order, and tape a sign to indicate the activity. Divide the class into groups of three or four players and assign each group to a starting station. After four or five minutes, use a stopping signal; then have groups rotate CW to the next station. Circulate around to the stations, observing children's performance and providing help as needed.

DESCRIPTION OF ACTIVITY:

1. **Dribble Maze:** Dribble your ball in and out of the cones. Try not to let the ball touch a cone!

2. **Soccer Hockey:** Take turns kicking the ball into the net, using the different kicks you have learned. Increase your kicking distance to give you more challenge.

3. **Bleach Bottle Kick:** You may stand the bleach bottles any way you like; then try to kick the bleach bottles over. For example, stand the bottles in a triangle; make a pyramid; place them in a line; etc. Use either foot.

4. **Soccer Juggle:** Explore different ways of bouncing the ball off your knees; off your feet. How many times in a row can you keep the ball in the air using your knees or feet?

5. **Punt Kick:** Punt kick the ball to a partner. Use either foot. Increase the punting distance.

6. **Wall Target Kick:** Kick the ball into low wall target and trap it as the ball comes off the wall. Use either foot to kick and trap.

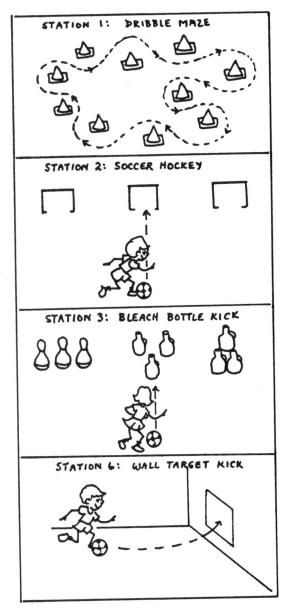

GS-155 THE READY POSITION

FOCUS: Stance; bodywork; footwork

EQUIPMENT: Several cone markers

ORGANIZATION:

• Review the ready position, which players will use in all paddle and racquet sports. To begin, have players find a free space. Check for good spacing.

DESCRIPTION OF ACTIVITY:

1. ***Ready Position:*** Plant your feet shoulder-width apart, bend the knees; keep your head up and weight evenly distributed on both feet.
2. ***Practice:***
   — Run anywhere in the play area. On the signal "Ready!" stop and face me in the ready position. On signal "Go!" continue running.
   — (Use cones to mark two lines 10 meters [30 feet] apart.) Side-step back and forth between the two lines. On the signal "Ready!" stop in the ready position. On the signal "Go!" continue side-stepping.
3. ***Hands-Up Drill:*** Find a spot alone and face me. Raise hands in front at shoulder level, bend knees, and watch me. When I point in a direction, I want you to side-step in the ready position in that direction: forward, backwards, to the side, to the other side. Do not cross your feet. On the signal "Ready!" stop in the ready position. On the signal "Go!" side-step in the direction I point. Remember, do not cross your feet.
4. ***Shadow Game:*** Find a partner. One partner is the leader; the other is the follower. As the leader moves around the play area in the ready position, follower move in the same way, trying to stay only one step away. Change roles on the signal "Change!" and continue.

GS-156 SERVING THE BALL

FOCUS: Technique; cooperation; right–left dexterity

EQUIPMENT: One small utility ball per pair

ORGANIZATION:

• Have players find a partner. Each pair gets a ball and stands side-by-side in the Ready Position, facing a wall. Explain the term "serve."

DESCRIPTION OF ACTIVITY:

1. ***Bounce Serve:*** Step forward with the foot opposite your serving hand. Allow the ball to bounce once; then swing your arm forward to strike the ball against the wall with the open palm of the hand. Take turns with your partner. Repeat with the other hand.
2. ***Drop Serve:*** Hold the ball at chest level in your nondominant hand. Drop the ball in front of your body and, as it drops, use an underhand swing to strike the ball before it hits the floor, with the palm of your hand. Take turns hitting the ball.
3. ***Serving Practice:***
   — Take turns using the bounce serve to serve the ball to the wall. One partner serves the ball; the other catches it and serves it again.
   — Drop-serve the ball to the wall. As the ball bounces off the wall, let it bounce once before your partner serves it back. Take turns serving until someone misses; then start again. Try serving with your nondominant hand as well.
   — Stand facing your partner across a line. One partner, drop-serve the ball; other partner, allow it to bounce once before you catch it, and then serve it back to your partner. Repeat using the bounce serve.

GS-157 HAND PADDLE PLAY

FOCUS: Hand-eye coordination; footwork; dexterity; visual tracking

EQUIPMENT: One 15-centimeter (6-inch) utility ball per player; one wall target per pair; floor tape

ORGANIZATION:

- Players explore striking the ball with an open hand. Have each player get a ball and stand facing a wall, about 3 meters (10 feet) away.

DESCRIPTION OF ACTIVITY:

1. Let the ball bounce once; then hit it against the wall. Hit the ball high against the wall; medium height; low. Catch the ball in two hands each time. Change hands and repeat.
   — Can you hit the ball to the wall, let it bounce once off the wall, and then hit it back to the wall? How many times can you do this without missing?

2. Try to hit the ball with your right hand, then with your left, then the right, etc. Can you keep this going without stopping? Start close to the wall; then move further away from the wall. Always be in control!

3. *Handball Target* (Tape targets on the wall so that two can share a target.): Try to hit the target with your right hand five times; then left hand five times. Bounce the ball first; then strike it.

4. *Circle Pass* (Form groups of six to eight players. Each group gets a ball, forms a circle, and stands in the ready position.): Use the bounce serve to send the ball across the circle to another player.
   — Challenge other groups to be the first to serve and catch the ball 30 times.

5. *Two Square* (Use floor tape or paint to mark out as many 1-meter by 2-meter [4-foot by 8-foot] courts and a center line as needed. Have players pair off. Each pair gets a ball; players then stand facing each other in one side of the two-square court.): One partner, start the game by bounce-serving the ball: drop the ball and hit it on the first bounce with your open hand into the other player's square. Continue hitting back and forth until one player misses. Play to five points. Then challenge another player.
   — *Rules:* On the line is in; ball must clear the center line and bounce in the other player's side; either hand or both hands may be used; ball must be hit after the first bounce.
   — Remember to be in Ready Position and keep your head up. Try to use either hand to hit the ball. Referee yourselves and keep your own score. Play fairly.

6. *Four Square* (Use masking tape to mark out as many 2.5-meter [8-foot]-square courts as you have groups of four players. Divide the court into four smaller squares and name each square A, B, C, and D. Form groups of four players; then have each player stand in the ready position in one of the squares of the court.): Player in Square A, bounce-serve the ball with one or two open hands to a player in any of the other three squares. Whoever receives the ball, allow it to bounce; then hit it with one or two open hands to a player in any other square. You may go out of your square to hit the ball. The game continues with players hitting the ball after one bounce, from square to square, until one player fails to return the ball or a point is scored. The receiver scores a point whenever the previous player's ball hits a line or goes out-of-bounds; the previous player strikes the ball down (the ball must be arched); the previous player hits the ball with a fist. The server scores a point whenever the receiver misses the ball or the receiver holds the ball.
   — The game is restarted after a point is scored by a bounce serve from the player in Square B, then Square C, Square D, and then by Square A again. The first player to earn five points wins the game.

FOCUS: Handshake grip; visual tracking; footwork; cooperation

EQUIPMENT: One paddle per player; one large balloon ball per group

ORGANIZATION:

- Review and demonstrate the handshake grip; then allow players to practice the grip while in the ready position. To reinforce grip, use a large balloon that players can easily strike with the paddle. Have each player get a paddle and stand facing you in a free space.

DESCRIPTION OF ACTIVITY:

1. **Handshake Grip:**

   — Hold the paddle out from your body, waist high, so that the head is vertical to the ground and the handle is pointing to your belly button.

   — Grip the paddle handle as if you were shaking hands with it; thumb and forefinger form a V-shape along the top of the handle and point to the edge of the paddle head.

   — Spread your fingers so that they are comfortable.

   — Hold the throat of the paddle with the other hand.

2. **Practice:** Hold your paddle in the handshake grip in the ready position at all times as you side-step around the play area. When I call the name of an object, such as the door, chalkboard, bench, that wall, stop quickly in the ready position and face the object. Do not cross your feet as you side-step. Do not hold the paddle with a "frying pan grip" (horizontal to the ground)!

3. **Circle Bat** (Form circles of six to eight players. Each group gets a large balloon ball and all players stand in the ready position, holding the paddle in the handshake grip.): Using the bounce serve, bat the ball to any player across the circle. Players, allow the ball to bounce once before you hit it back across the circle. Challenge other groups to be the first to hit the ball 30 times.

4. **Pivoting Technique:**

   — Stand in the ready position. Without moving your left foot, step forward with your right foot; then step backwards and to the side with your right foot and return to the ready position.

   — Stand in the ready position. Without moving your right foot, step forward, back and to the side with your left foot. Return to the ready position.

   — Run in free space. On the signal "Pivot!" stop and pivot around in a circle on one foot until you face me.

5. **Mirror Game:** Find a partner and face each other in the ready position, about two meters (six feet) apart. One partner, side-step around the play area in any direction, pivoting often, using either foot. Other partner, copy the moves while staying in front of your partner. Change roles and repeat.

GS-159 BALLOON, BEACHBALL, AND BEANBAG PADDLE PLAY

FOCUS: Hand-eye coordination; visual tracking; right–left dexterity

EQUIPMENT: One paddle per player; one balloon per player; one beachball per pair; one beanbag per player

ORGANIZATION:

- Children explore using the paddle to strike different-sized objects beginning with balloons and beachballs, and then beanbags. To begin, have each player get a paddle, blow up a balloon, and find a free space. Check for good spacing.

DESCRIPTION OF ACTIVITY:

1. Show me how you can bat the balloon with your paddle. Don't let your balloon touch the floor! Switch hands and repeat.
2. Find a partner and try to bat the balloon back and forth to each other with your paddles. Hold the paddle in your favorite hand; then in your other hand.
3. *Circle Balloon Bat:* Form groups of five or six players, who stand in a circle, spaced arm's length apart. How many times can your group bat the balloon before it touches the floor? Call "Mine!" if you are going to bat the balloon.
4. Find a partner and collect a beachball to share. Use your paddles to roll the beachball to each other. Use either hand. Now take turns bouncing the beachball with your paddle. Use either hand. Can you bounce your beachball to your partner to hit back to you?
5. *Paddle Weave Relay* (Form teams of four; each team stand in a line facing a row of four cone markers or chairs. The Leader has a beachball and paddle to start.): On signal "Weave!" each player, in turn, use your paddle to roll the beachball in and out of the cones, around the last cone, and straight back to the line; then give the paddle and ball to the next player, who does the same. The relay ends when everyone has gone twice and is sitting cross-legged. Which team will be first?
6. *Beanbag Paddle Play:* Now collect a beanbag and take it to a free space. Try the following tasks:
   — Walk with your Beanie on the paddle. Try to run; skip; gallop; side-step. Look for open spaces!
   — With your Beanie on the paddle, try to sit down; then stand up again without dropping the beanbag. Can you stand still and move the paddle all around your body; from hand to hand; high to low?
   — Place your beanbag on the paddle. Can you toss Beanie up off your paddle and catch it in your free hand? Can you catch Beanie between the paddle and your free hand? Switch hands and try this.
   — Who can toss the Beanie up with your free hand and catch it on the paddle? Can you toss it higher and still catch it? Can you use your other hand and still do this?
      —Show me how you can toss Beanie up off your paddle and catch it on your paddle. How many times can you toss and catch in this way without dropping the beanbag? Can you toss and catch the beanbag using your other hand?
      —Now try to toss Beanie up off your paddle as you hold it palm up (Forehand Position) and catch it on your paddle as you hold it palm down (Backhand Position). What other trick can you do using the paddle and your Beanie?
      —Find a partner. Stand facing each other about one giant step apart. Place Beanie on your paddle. Can you toss Beanie back and forth and catch it with the paddle and hand? Can you catch it on the paddle only? Remember to watch the beanbag!

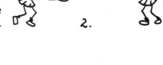

GS-160 PADDLE TASKS

FOCUS: Striking and bouncing; visual tracking

EQUIPMENT: One paddle per player; one whiffle ball, racquetball, or tennis ball per player; several benches

ORGANIZATION:

- Review the Ready Position, Handshake Grip, the Bounce Serve, and Drop Serve (activities GS–155, GS–156, and GS–158). Have players get a paddle and a ball and move to a free space. Players crouch in the Ready Position, holding the paddle in the handshake grip, and practice the following tasks.

DESCRIPTION OF ACTIVITY:

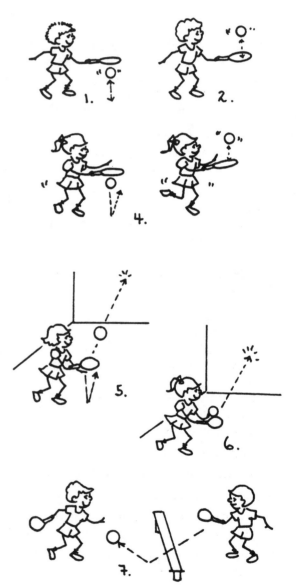

1. Bounce the ball to the floor. Start low to the floor; then gradually bounce the ball higher and higher. Keep the ball under control at all times.

2. Now place the ball on your paddle. Try to bounce the ball about 30 centimeters (12 inches) in the air each time.

3. Alternately bounce the ball against the floor and then off your paddle into the air. How long can you alternate bounces without stopping?

4. Walk around the play area while:

   — bouncing the ball on the floor with your paddle

   — bouncing the ball off your paddle into the air

   — alternately bouncing the ball on the floor and into the air

5. Find a free space about four big steps from a wall. Bounce the ball once, and then hit it against the wall. As the ball comes off the wall, let it bounce, and then hit it again. How many times in a row can you keep the bounce-hit pattern going?

6. *Serve and Catch:* Stand about 2 meters (6 feet) from a wall. Using a Bounce Serve, drop the ball and serve it to the wall at about waist level. Catch the ball with your free hand after each serve. When you can do this five times without a miss, take one step back and repeat.

   — After five times without a miss, step back again and repeat.

   — How many times can you serve and catch the ball in two minutes?

   — Repeat all of the above using the Drop Serve.

7. *Partner Serve:* Find a partner. Stand facing each other about 4 meters (13 feet) apart on either side of a balance bench. Serve the ball to your partner using the Bounce Serve; then hit the ball back and forth over the bench as if it were a net. Allow the ball to bounce only once before hitting it back. How many times can you hit the ball back and forth without a miss?

   — Repeat, using only the Drop Serve.

GS-161 FOREHAND AND BACKHAND STROKES _____

FOCUS: Stroke technique; footwork;
visual tracking; partnerwork

EQUIPMENT: One paddle per player;
one whiffle ball, racquetball, or
tennis ball per player;
several benches;
wall targets

ORGANIZATION:

- Introduce and demonstrate the forehand and backhand strokes, one at a time. Constantly remind players to use the Handshake Grip. Check for "frying pan" grip and correct. Emphasize that players return to the Ready Position after making each stroke, and keep their eyes on the ball. To start, have players find a partner, get a paddle each and a ball to share, and then stand facing each other without the ball, about 4 meters (12 feet) apart.

DESCRIPTION OF ACTIVITY:

1. *Forehand Stroke:* Hold the paddle in the handshake grip with a firm wrist. Turn the shoulder of the nonhitting arm toward your partner. Place the foot opposite your hitting hand in front and the other foot behind. Now holding the paddle vertically, pull it back and then swing it forward toward an imaginary ball and follow through. Keep your head down throughout the hit.

2. *Backhand Stroke:* Hold the paddle in the handshake grip and turn the shoulder of your hitting arm toward your partner. Step forward on the foot that is on the same side as your hitting arm and hold your paddle vertically. Practice pulling your arm across your body and then following through toward your partner.

3. *Stroking the Ball:* Stand sideways to the wall with your nonhitting shoulder closer to the wall. Bounce the ball with your nonhitting hand; then hit it with the forehand stroke to the wall. Catch the ball on the rebound and repeat. After ten Forehand strokes, repeat using Backhand strokes.

4. *Target Stroking* (Tape as many 1-meter [3-foot]-square targets to the wall as needed; targets should be 1 meter [3 feet] from the floor. Review the Forehand and Backhand techniques; then have players find a partner, get one paddle and one ball per pair, and stand behind a line 3 meters [10 feet] from a target.):

   — *Forehand Stroking:* First player, stand sideways to the wall, bounce the ball with one hand, and use a Forehand stroke to hit the target. Repeat until you have had ten tries. Your partner, your "coach," will watch you and count the number of times you hit the target. Your coach may help you by giving hints on technique: Watch the ball at all times; use the Handshake Grip; return to the Ready Position after each stroke; catch the ball on the rebound; let the ball bounce once, and then make the stroke; follow through after each stroke; stand behind the 3-meter (10-foot) line when making a stroke. Change roles and repeat.

   — Both players, have ten more tries each; then report your best score to me.

   — *Backhand Stroking:* Repeat the procedure using the Backhand stroke.

5. *Partner Practice:* One partner, get a ball and stand opposite your partner about 5 meters (15 feet) apart. Toss the ball so that it bounces in front of your partner's paddle side. Your partner makes a forehand stroke and hits it back to you. Repeat five times, catching the ball each time.

   — Toss the ball to your partner's other side, so that your partner can make a backhand stroke on that side. Repeat five times.

   — Change roles after ten hits.

   — Alternating turns, hit the ball to the wall. Decide which stroke you will use—forehand or backhand. How many hits in a row can you and your partner make?

   — Hit the ball across a bench while practicing the strokes.

FOCUS: Lead-up games; forehand and
backhand stroking;
partnerwork and groupwork

EQUIPMENT: One paddle per player;
eight cone markers;
one whiffle ball or tennis ball per player;
low net (or several benches);
wall and floor tape

ORGANIZATION:

• The following games further reinforce the paddle striking skills.

DESCRIPTION OF ACTIVITY:

1. **Clean Out** (Divide the play area into three equal zones: two end zones and a net zone. Then form two
equal teams of five or six players. Have each player get a paddle and a ball and take up position in
teams in opposite end zones.): On signal "Play!" hit the ball from your end zone, across the net zone,
and into the other team's end zone. Try to hit as many balls into the other team's end zone as you can,
using forehand and backhand strokes. A ball in the net zone must stay there and may not be served
again. On signal "Freeze!" stop and count the number of balls in your end zone. The team with the
fewest balls in their end wins the game. To restart the game, everyone retrieve a ball and start again.

VARIATION:

Set up a low net or benches across the net zone and play the game as above.

2. **Partner Wall Ball** (Tape lines on the walls
about one meter [three feet] above the floor;
then tape other lines on the floor in front of the
wall lines and about three meters [10 feet] from
the wall. Have each player find a partner, collect a paddle and one ball, and then go to a wall
line.): First player, serve the ball so that it hits
the wall above the line. Partner, hit the ball on
the first bounce or play it as it comes off the
wall. Each time your partner does not return
the ball, score one point and serve again. Play to
ten points. Challenge a new partner.

3.

3. **Group Wall Ball:** Form groups of three or four players. Each group, stand in single-file formation
behind the floor line and face the wall line. First player, bounce the ball and serve it to the wall
above the line; then quickly step aside so that the second player can hit the ball after it bounces
once. Third player do the same, and continue. Join the end of the file after you play your shot. Count
the number of times your team hits the wall above the line in one minute.

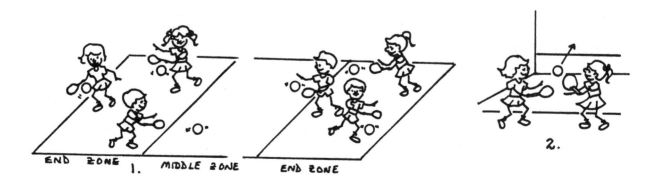

END ZONE   1.   MIDDLE ZONE   END ZONE   2.

GS-163 FLOOR PING-PONG

FOCUS: Lead-up game;
hand and paddle stroking;
partnerwork

EQUIPMENT: One tennis ball or whiffle ball per game;
one paddle per player;
floor tape

ORGANIZATION:

- Play Floor Ping-Pong according to the basic rules of ping-pong. Tape as many 3-meter by 1.5-meter (10-foot by 5-foot) courts as you will need for pairs; then have players find a partner and get a ball to share.

DESCRIPTION OF ACTIVITY:

1. Begin the game with a bounce serve from your right-hand court. Hit the ball with the open hand over the center line (the net) and into your opponent's right-hand court. Either hand may be used to hit the ball.

2. Your opponent may then return the ball so that it lands anywhere in your court.

3. Continue to play according to the basic rules of ping-pong:

   — Each player serves for five points and then the serve changes after each five points.

   — The ball must be hit with the open hand, and not held.

   — A player may go anywhere to return a ball.

   — The ball must arch before landing: It cannot be struck downward.

   — Play to 11, 15, or 21 points.

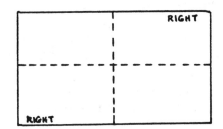

4. Lose a point if:

   — The ball hits a line or goes out-of-bounds.

   — The ball is hit with a closed fist.

   — A player fails to return a ball.

VARIATIONS:

a. Play with paddles and whiffle or tennis balls.

b. Play doubles. Either player may hit the ball.

c. Arrange a tournament.

FOCUS: Accuracy in rolling, underhand
and overhand throwing,
and kicking; visual tracking;
cooperation

EQUIPMENT: Five wooden or plastic bowling pins;
three 15-centimeter (6-inch) utility balls;
three 20-centimeter (8-inch) utility balls;
several benches;
three beanbags;
six cone markers;
one tennis ball and can per player;
three small garbage containers;
three lightweight mats;
three batting tees and whiffle balls;
floor and wall tape

ORGANIZATION:

- This Station activity reinforces all the balls skills learned to this point, including rolling, accuracy underhand and overhand throwing, fielding, kicking, and striking. (See activity GS–154 for organization of these stations.) If possible, set up two identical activities at each station to increase the participation level! Add Station ideas of your own! Stations 5 and 6 are ideally suited for field play.

DESCRIPTION OF ACTIVITY:

Station 1, Five-Pin Bowling (Near a wall, set up five bowling pins in a pyramid formation and mark off a rolling line 5 meters [15 feet] away from the head pin. Place two benches on edge to act as the "sides of the bowling alley."): Each player, in turn, bowls three balls at the pins, trying to knock over as many as possible. Other players field the ball, clear pins away, and then reset them.

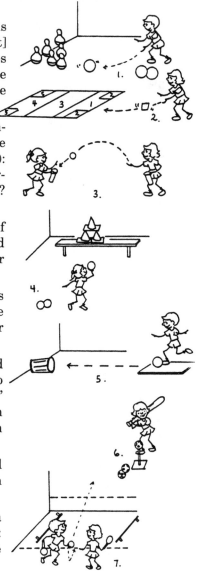

Station 2, Beanbag Shuffleboard (Use floor tape to mark out a simple grid on the play area floor or use chalk on a tarmac. Number the grid as shown. Also mark out a tossing line 3 meter [10 feet] away.): Each player, in turn, toss three beanbags using the one-handed underhand throw toward the shuffleboard. How many points will you score? On your next try, toss with your weaker hand.

Station 3, Tennis Ball and Can Trick: Explore different ways of tossing a tennis ball and catching it in the tennis can. Pair up and toss one tennis ball to each other, catching it in the can. What other trick can the two of you invent?

Station 4, Three for One (Balance one cone marker on top of two others on a bench. Use floor tape to mark out a throwing line.): Each player, take one overhand throw to try to knock all the cones off the bench. Use your favorite hand to throw; then on your second try, use your other hand!

Station 5, Three-Hole Golf Kicking (Set up three golf holes around the perimeter of the play area. Place a garbage container on its side to act as the "hole." Use a light mat as the "tee-off" place. Space the "hole" and "tee-off" about 10 meters [30 feet] away from each other.): Each player, count the number of kicks you will make to sink the ball in each hole. Try to equal or better your score for each hole.

Station 6, Batter's Box (Set up three batting tees well spaced apart.): Each player, hit three balls off the batting tee. How far can you hit? Try to equal or better the distance hit each time.

Station 7, Paddle Ball (Use wall tape to indicate a hitting line and a serving line. Place a bench on its side on each side of the court area.): Partners, hit the ball above the wall line and serve from behind the serving line as you play a game to five points.

GS-165 TRAINING RUNS

FOCUS: Running technique

EQUIPMENT: Track, open area, or gymnasium

ORGANIZATION:

- Explain and demonstrate good running technique. Encourage runners to concentrate on good running form rather than speed: Run on the balls of the feet; drive with the arms; run with the body leaning forward; run with the head up and still. Have players run side by side in groups of four or five. As soon as one group reaches the halfway point of the play area, the next group may start.

DESCRIPTION OF ACTIVITY:

1. *Technique:* Run in an upright position, looking directly ahead of the finish line. Bend your elbows at right angles and brush your hips with your hands as you drive them forward. Place the thumb of each hand on your forefinger and relax your hands. Use a high lift of the thighs and pump your arms while running. Run with a forward lean on the balls of your feet and use a stamping motion.
2. *Sewing Machine:* Run lightly on the spot on the balls of your feet. Start slowly, gradually increasing speed and using the correct running technique; then gradually decrease your speed. Repeat several times.
3. *High Knee Lift:* Start by running on the spot, lifting your knees high with each step. Hold your hands out in front at waist level and try to hit the palms with your knees on each step. Move forward, stepping on the balls of your feet and lifting with knees. Keep your head up and look straight ahead.

GS-166 STRIDING

FOCUS: Accelerating while running

EQUIPMENT: Track, open area, or gymnasium; several cone markers

ORGANIZATION:

- Explain and demonstrate the Striding technique; then have players practice. Have players stand side-by-side along a starting line in groups of four or five, on a 100-meter (300-foot) track or in a gym. As soon as one group reaches the halfway point, the next group may start, and so on. Remind runners to run on the balls of the feet, lifting the knees high; breathe naturally as they run; drive forward with their arms; run with the body leaning forward; and run with the head up and still.

DESCRIPTION OF ACTIVITY:

1. *Striding Technique:* From a standing start, slowly run forward with an exaggerated stride and arm action. Kick your feet out in front as you run, reach forward with your foot, and snap your foot down on the track. Gradually increase the pace of the halfway mark; then gradually slow down until you reach the finish. Stride back to the starting line and repeat.
2. *Jogging and Striding:* Start with an easy jog; then stride. Alternate jogging and striding to the finish line; then stride back to the starting line at a strong pace, pumping your arms and increasing your pace to full speed at the starting line.
3. *Run Through:* Start by running on the spot; then move forward, gradually gaining speed. At the halfway mark, you should be running at close to top speed. Gradually slow down until you are running on the spot again at the finish line. Slowly stride back to the starting line down the side of the track. Repeat four times.

GS–167 THE STANDING START

FOCUS: Starting position; running form   **EQUIPMENT:** One baton per group (optional)

ORGANIZATION:

- Explain and demonstrate the starting position and have runners experiment to see which foot they would rather have in front.

DESCRIPTION OF ACTIVITY:

1. *Upright or Standing Start:* Place the toe of your leading foot just behind the starting line. Place your other foot a comfortable distance behind. Lean forward slightly. Push off quickly with your back foot and bring it forward to take the first step. At the same time, throw your opposite arm forward. Take small quick steps at first as you move forward, pumping with the arms.
2. *Practice:* Try the standing start with your right foot forward; then experiment with your left foot forward. Take off from each position, run for a short distance, and then jog back. Which feels better?
3. *Shuttle Relay* (Form teams of six to eight runners and have them stand in shuttle formation; each half about 20 meters [60 feet] apart.): The first runner in each group, get into the standing start position. On signal "Go!" first runner, run to touch the second runner; second runner, run to touch the third; and so on. After each run, join the end of the line. Continue until you are in your original position.
   — *Baton Relay:* Repeat Shuttle Relay with runners exchanging a baton.

GS–168 SPRINTING

FOCUS: Accelerated start   **EQUIPMENT:** Track, open area, or gymnasium; two hoops per group; one beanbag per group

ORGANIZATION:

- Form groups of three or four runners and have groups line up behind the starting line.

DESCRIPTION OF ACTIVITY:

1. *Sprint Technique:* First group, run on the spot, slowly at first; then gradually increase speed as you run down the track, keeping upright and lifting your knees high. Get to top speed at about the 30-meter (100-foot) mark; then gradually slow down. Jog together back to the starting line. Repeat.
2. *Quick Off the Mark:* Take a standing start position. On signal "Go!" explode into your run and sprint to the 30-meter mark. Pretend to run through a tape at top speed with your head up and your knees high. Jog back to the starting line. Repeat.
3. *Beanbag Race* (Each group collects two hoops and a beanbag and stands about 18 meters [60 feet] apart.): Stand in single-file formation behind the first hoop with the beanbag inside the hoop. On signal "Go!" first runner, pick up the beanbag, sprint to the second hoop, place the beanbag in the hoop, sprint back to tag the second runner, and join the end of the line. Second runner, sprint to the second hoop, pick up the beanbag, and return it to the first hoop. Continue until all players have had two turns.
4. *Overtaking:* Find a partner and stand behind the starting line. One runner, run behind your partner, speed up to sprint past your partner; then your partner sprints past you.

GS-169 SPRINT START—FINISH _____

FOCUS: Start and finish technique

EQUIPMENT: Finish-line tape (wool yarn)

ORGANIZATION:
- Explain and demonstrate the Crouch Start and Finish techniques. Explain the three starting commands: "On your mark!" "Get set!" "Go!" Have players practice on their own and in pairs.

DESCRIPTION OF ACTIVITY:

1. **The Crouch Start:**
   - **Position:** Place the toe of your front foot about 20 to 30 centimeters (5 to 12 inches) behind the starting line and the knee of the rear foot beside the front foot.

   ON YOUR MARK

   - **"On Your Mark!":** Place the thumb and forefinger of each hand behind and parallel to the starting line, shoulder-width apart. Your remaining fingers form a high arch so that your shoulders are as high as possible. Straighten your arms and fix eyes on a spot 1 meter (3 feet) ahead.

   GET SET

   - **"Get Set!":** On the word "Set!" take and hold a deep breath. Raise your hips so that they are slightly higher than your shoulders. Shift your weight forward onto your hands and extend your rear leg. Your front knee should form a right angle. Continue to look at a spot 1 meter (3 feet) ahead.
   - **"Go!":** On "Go!" or the clap of my hands, push off with your back leg. Quickly swing your leading leg through and take a short stamping step as you lean forward. At the same time, vigorously throw your leading arm (same side as your leading leg) forward. Rise gradually as you pump your arms and run forward, taking quick steps.

   GO!

   3.

2. **Individual Practice:** Find a spot and practice the sprint start on your own. Say to yourself "On your mark!" "Get set!" "Go!" Run about 20 meters (60 feet) three or four times.
3. **Finish Technique:** Run "through" the finish line as if you had another 20 meters (60 feet) to run; then gradually slow down. Do not lunge at the tape.
4. **Sprint Challenge** (Set up a finish-line tape 30 meters [100 feet] from the starting line.): Race a partner to the finish line; then jog back to the start. Change partners and repeat.

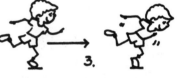

4.   FINISH

GS-170 WIND SPRINTS _____

FOCUS: Sprinting; jogging; endurance

EQUIPMENT: Six cone markers; finish-line tape (or wool yarn)

ORGANIZATION:
- Review sprint start and finish techniques and sprinting form; then have runners find a partner and line up in pairs behind the starting line. Runners run together, alternating sprinting and jogging down the track. Place cone markers about 30 meters (100 feet) apart and have each runner hold the finish line for the next pair. Remind runners to run on the balls of their feet and to lift knees high when sprinting. Have them pump vigorously with the arms to gain maximum speed quickly.

DESCRIPTION OF ACTIVITY:
1. When your pair is called to the starting line, get into the sprint start position.
2. On the signals "On your mark!" "Get set!" "Go!" sprint at top speed to the first marker; then gradually slow to a jogging pace until you reach the second marker. Accelerate to top speed again. When you reach the third marker, slow to a jog for another 30 meters (60 feet). Finally, sprint at top speed to run through the finish line.

VARIATION: Move the markers to increase the sprinting distance and decrease the jogging zone.

FOCUS: Standing and crouch starts; sprinting; baton changing

EQUIPMENT: One baton per team; watch

ORGANIZATION:

- Review the Standing Start and the Sprint Start; then explain and demonstrate the shuttle method of exchanging batons. Form teams of four to six runners and have one player on each team get a baton. Allow players to practice with their team.

DESCRIPTION OF ACTIVITY:

1. ***Baton-Changing Shuttle Relay, Standing Start:*** Half of each team stand in a file facing the other half behind a line about 30 meters (100 feet) away. First runner, hold the bottom of the baton in your right hand. On the signal "Go!" run to the other file and pass the baton to the receiver's right hand with a downward motion. Receiver, stand behind the line with your right palm open and facing upward. Watch the baton as it approaches. Make the exchange, passing each other right shoulder to right shoulder and staying behind the starting line. If the baton is dropped, you must stop to pick it up and then continue.
   — Which team can finish first after every runner has had a turn?

2. ***Sprint Start Relay:*** Repeat the Shuttle Relay using the sprint start. When it is your turn to run, go down on the mark, get set, and go when the incoming runner touches you on the right shoulder.

3. ***Twenty Crossings:*** Repeat the Shuttle Relays until the teams complete 20 laps. Waiting teammates, count the number of crossings run.

4. ***Circular Relay*** (Explain and demonstrate the left-to-right baton-changing technique; then form teams of four runners; number the runners 1, 2, 3, and 4, and have them stand one behind the other about 16 meters [50 feet] apart. The first runner on each team gets a baton. At first, have runners practice with their team at a slow pace to learn the baton-exchange technique.) Here is the "Left-to-Right Baton Exchange Technique":

   — First runner, hold the bottom of the baton in your left hand, run, and pass it into the right hand of the runner ahead with an upward motion.
   — Continue to the other three runners, passing with the left hand and receiving in the right.
   — Receiver, while facing the front, reach back with the fingers and thumb of the right hand facing down, and start to run when the incoming runner is about 4 meters (13 feet) away. Shift the baton to your left hand as you run.
   — Exchange the baton while both runners are near top speed with both arms fully extended.

VARIATIONS:

a. Time the runners; then have teams try to improve their times.

b. Increase the distance run.

c. Repeat the relays so that each runner runs three, five, or seven times. This is a form of interval running and conditioning.

d. ***Walking Practice:*** To learn the technique, first have the four runners space themselves one behind the other as above but only about 8 meters (25 feet) apart. Have them walk to pass the baton to each other, concentrating on correct technique, and then take turns being the first runner.

GS-172 STANDING LONG JUMP

FOCUS: Technique; jumping using the arms

EQUIPMENT: One small mat per player; one piece of chalk per player; one short rope (optional); two cone markers (optional); long-jump pit with take-off boards

ORGANIZATION:

• Use the guided discovery method to teach the standing long jump. Ask the following questions.

DESCRIPTION OF ACTIVITY:

1. *Exploration Questions:* Stand at your mat.
   — Can you jump a long way if you stand up straight to start? ("No!")
   — Tell me what your legs should do to get ready to jump across your mat. ("They should bend at the knees!")
   — What other part of your body could help you jump? ("The arms!")
   — What must your arms do to help you jump forward? ("They must swing back and then forward!")
   — How would you start if you wanted to jump a long way from the standing position? ("Start with the knees bent and arms back; then swing arms forward to jump!")
   — Good! Now let's all find a line and practice the standing long jump across the mat.
2. *Upward Spring Practice:* Stand with your feet behind a line, shoulder-width apart. As you squat, swing your arms forward and back. On the third swing, spring upward and outward as high as you can. Repeat ten times.
3. *Standing Long Jump Practice:* Repeat the squat and arm swings again, but on the third swing overbalance forward to leap as far forward as possible. Swing your arms forward and upward vigorously and push with your legs to help you leap. While in mid-air, bend your knees; then land with arms forward. Try nine more long jumps.

VARIATIONS:

a. Give each player a piece of chalk. Have them practice upward springs beside a wall. On the first spring, they reach up to mark the wall at the height of their jump. On their next jumps, they try to beat that mark.
b. Practice at a long-jump pit.

GS-173 RUNNING LONG JUMP

ORGANIZATION:

• Have Jumpers gather around the long-jump pit. Explain and demonstrate technique; then have them form groups of four to six jumpers. Set up other track and field practice stations to increase participation. Have each group in turn come to the long jump pit. Other groups practice previously taught skills. Rotate stations every five minutes.

DESCRIPTION OF ACTIVITY:

1. *Technique:*
   — *Approach:* Start from the same spot each time with both feet together. Increase your speed to reach the take-off board at top speed.
   — *Take-off:* Hit the board with the same take-off foot each time. Spring off that foot, rolling from your heel, to the ball of your foot, to your toe. Prepare for the take-off by "gathering" with your arms (throwing them upward vigorously with a circular motion.) At the same time, bring your rear leg up and forward, and look up.
   — *Flight:* Try to gain as much height as you can. "Hang" in mid-air with your arms up and back, leading with your belly button. Look up.
   — *Landing:* Reach forward with your legs, arms, and trunk. As your heels hit the sand, quickly fling both arms back to force your whole body forward.
2. *Jump and Measure:* Find a partner and get a measuring tape. Take turns practicing long jumps and measuring the distance jumped. Can you beat your best jump? Encourage jumpers to gain as much speed and height as they can. *Speed + Height = Distance.*

GS-174 TAKE-OFF, FLIGHT, AND LANDING

FOCUS: Running long jump

EQUIPMENT: Long-jump pits with take-off boards;
several long ropes;
several measuring tapes;
several hoops (optional)

ORGANIZATION:

• Explain and demonstrate the long-jump stages: the approach, take-off, flight, landing; then allow jumpers to practice.

DESCRIPTION OF ACTIVITY:

1. *Take-Off Foot Practice:* Stand with your feet together. Break into a slow run; then hit the take-off board with your left foot and land on both feet. Repeat, jumping from the right foot. Which foot would you rather jump from? Use it as your take-off foot each time.

2. *Flight:* Run toward the pit; then as you take off, try to gain as much height as possible as you leave the board. Jump from the same take-off foot each time.

3. *Height and Distance:* Sprint down the track toward the pit. Try for height and distance. Try to jump over a rope held lightly across the pit. Can you jump over it if we raise it higher? Take turns holding the rope.

4. *Jump the Creek* (Set two long ropes on the ground about 1 meter [3 feet] apart at one end and widening to about 2.5 meters [8 feet] at the other end.): Run to the creek, take off on one foot, and land on both feet. Decide which part of the creek you wish to jump. Use your arms to increase the height as you jump.

VARIATIONS:

a. *Stepping Stones:* Widen the creek and use hoops in the middle as stepping stones to reach the other side.

b. *Jump the Creek Standing:* To practice the standing long jump, reduce the width of the creek. Jumpers line up along the creek and jump off both feet and land on both feet.

GS-175 INTRODUCING HIGH JUMPING

FOCUS: Scissors technique; straddle technique

EQUIPMENT: Two or more sets of high-jump standards; two or more plastic or metal training bars; foam landing pits (or freshly dug sand pits)

ORGANIZATION:

- Most high jump styles today require a foam landing pit; however, the scissors style can be taught using only a sand pit. Explain the scissors technique and have players practice; then form groups of four or five players. Have them gather near a high-jump pit.

DESCRIPTION OF ACTIVITY:

1. **Scissors Technique:** Approach the bar at about a 30-degree angle. If you take off with your left foot, approach the bar from the right. Move to the opposite side for a right-foot take-off. Choose whichever side you prefer. Take five to ten springing steps as you approach. Take off at about arm's length from the bar. Kick high the leg nearest the bar and swing your arms up as if you are about to sit on the bar, lifting your rear leg over the bar in a scissors movement. Straighten your legs as you go over the bar to complete the scissors action. Land on your leading foot, followed by your take-off leg.

2. **Practice:** Stand three to five steps away from the bar on the side you prefer. With the bar set at waist level, run and jump using the scissors style. If you knock the bar, replace it, and continue. As you improve, raise the bar.

3. **Scissors Relay** (At least two jumping pits are required. Each group stands in single-file formation at a pit.): On signal "Go!" first player in line, run in and jump the bar using scissors style, run back to the line, touch next player, and go to end of line. Continue until all jumpers have had a turn. Replace the bar if you knock it down and continue. The first team to finish wins.

4. **Straddle-Style High Jump** (The straddle-style is also called the "Belly Roll." When a foam landing pit is available, the straddle and the flop styles are preferred high-jumping methods. Explain the four stages of the straddle-style; then, to allow for maximum participation, allow at the most only five or six jumpers at each set of standards during practice. Rotate groups to other events while waiting.):

   - **Approach:** Run toward the bar from the left side at about a 30- to 45-degree angle. Take five to seven steps as you approach, running high on the balls of your feet until the next to last step. As the right foot rocks from heel to toe, lower yourself for the "gather" (circle the arms upward), plant your left foot (take-off foot), and bend at the knees. The last three steps are longer and quicker as you prepare to "gather."

   - **Take-Off:** Swing your right leg up and begin to turn your tummy toward the bar. Swing both arms up in front of the bar, leading with the left arm.

   - **Clearance:** At the top of your jump, look down at the bar and roll over onto your tummy to "lie along the bar." Your right leg is the first to go over the bar. Lift your left leg high and out of the way.

   - **Landing:** Land on your right leg or on your right side and back.

GS-176 FLOP-STYLE LEAD-UPS

FOCUS: Flop-style technique

EQUIPMENT: Two or more sets of high-jump standards and crossbars;

foam landing pits;

three or four folding mats

ORGANIZATION:

- To introduce jumpers to the feeling of arching backwards when jumping, have them practice the flop-style without high-jump standards or bar. Jumpers take turns practicing the technique.

DESCRIPTION OF ACTIVITY:

1. ***Standing Flop:*** Stand at the edge of a foam landing pit with your back to the pit. Throw your arms up and back, spring off both legs, and throw yourself backward. Arch your back as you fall backwards and land on your upper back. Roll off the pit and repeat, taking turns.

2. ***Running Flop:*** Stand facing the pit. Take only three to five steps as you run to the pit in a slightly curved path. Throw your arms up and back and spring off both feet to gain as much height as you can. Land on the pit on your upper back and shoulders, with both legs and feet dangling overhead. Roll off the pit and repeat. Ensure that landing pits are in position before jumpers jump.

GS-177 FLOP-STYLE HIGH JUMPING

EQUIPMENT: Foam landing pits of standard size;

crossbars;

folding mats

ORGANIZATION:

Safety: Because the jumper lands on the back and shoulders, the flop-style high jump should only be allowed if foam landing pits of standard size and quality are used. Place the pit directly below the crossbar with the front edge in line with the jump standards. Place folding mats on the sides and behind the foam pit as well. Explain and demonstrate the technique; then practice.

DESCRIPTION OF ACTIVITY:

1. ***Approach:*** Place the bar at about waist level. Approach the bar from the same side as you would for the scissors-style high jump. If you are using a left-foot take-off, approach the bar from the right. For a right-foot take-off, approach from the left. Take three to five steps as you run to the bar at a 30- to 45-degree angle and with a slightly curved path so that you rotate naturally during your jump.

2. ***Take-Off:*** The take-off is similar to the basketball lay-up. Swing the inside knee up high as you swing your arms upward. Rotate your body so that your back is to the bar; arch your back as you rise over the bar; raise your hips and flick your legs up and over the bar as you fall toward the landing pit.

3. ***Landing:*** Look toward the bar as you land on your upper back and shoulders. Roll backwards off the landing pit.

4. ***Practice:*** Stand facing a low bar at a distance of one meter (three feet). Take one step, plant your foot, and rotate to clear the bar. Land on your upper back, flipping your feet out of the way to prevent knocking the bar. After several successful tries, raise the bar another two or three centimeters (one inch).

5. ***More Practice:*** Try the flop after a three- to five-step running approach to the bar. Raise the bar again after several successful jumps.

   — Gradually lengthen the run-in to seven to nine steps and have jumpers approach in a full semicircle. Remember to jump over the "middle" part of the bar.

Special Games

Special Games activities develop leadership, cooperation, self-esteem, creativity, and a sense of fair play. The emphasis throughout these activities is on fun and teamwork, not winning or losing.

The 47 Special Games in Section 7 are organized into Relays, Low-Organized Games, and Play Day Activities. They include:

RELAYS

SG–1 Touch and Go Relay
SG–2 Roly-Poly Beanbag Relay
SG–3 Animal Walk Relay
SG–4 Zig-zag Relays
SG–5 Around-the-World Relays
SG–6 Beachball Shuttle
SG–7 Fortune Hunt Relay
SG–8 Rescue Relay
SG–9 Chain Relay
SG–10 Two-Legged Relay
SG–11 Chariot Relay
SG–12 Spoke Relay
SG–13 Hoop Line Relay
SG–14 Obstacle Relay
SG–15 Snowshoe Race
SG–16 Three-Stunt Relays
SG–17 Jump-and-Crawl Relay

LOW-ORGANIZED GAMES

SG–18 Pip, Squeak, and Wilber
SG–19 Spud
SG–20 Worm Grab
SG–21 Mother Carey's Chickens
SG–22 Everyone for Yourself
SG–23 Line Dodgeball

LOW-ORGANIZED GAMES
(*Continued*)

SG–24 Team Dodgeball
SG–25 Cross-Over Dodgeball
SG–26 British Bulldog
SG–27 Chinese Wall
SG–28 Star Wars
SG–29 Battlestar Galactica
SG–30 Spaceships
SG–31 King's Court
SG–32 Touchdown
SG–33 Lost Treasure
SG–34 Base-Ket-Ball
SG–35 Rocketball
SG–36 Jump the Shot

PLAY DAY ACTIVITIES

SG–37 Introducing Play Days
SG–38 Play Day Stations 1, 2, 3, and 4
SG–39 Play Day Stations 5, 6, 7, and 8
SG–40 Play Day Stations 9, 10, 11, and 12
SG–41 Play Day Stations 13, 14, 15, and 16

PLAY DAY ACTIVITIES
(Continued)

SG-1 TOUCH AND GO RELAY _____

FOCUS: Speed running; agility

EQUIPMENT: Four cone markers

ORGANIZATION:

- Use four cones to mark the starting line and turning line, 10 meters (30 feet) apart. Form teams of four to five players and have each team stand 2 meters (6 feet) apart in single-file formation behind their starting line. If there is an unequal number of players in the files, have a member of that file go twice. Emphasize that players wait for their turn *behind* the starting line, not crossing it until they receive the hand touch. Encourage team members to cheer for each other.

DESCRIPTION OF ACTIVITY:

1. On signal "Go!" each player of each team run, in turn, to the turning line, touch it with the palms of both hands, return to the right side of your file, touching the left hand ("Give Five") of the next player, and then go to the end of the file.
2. The first team to complete the relay and sit cross-legged in their file is the winner.

VARIATIONS:

a. Have players touch the turning line with other body parts: right hand and left knee; nose; two elbows; seat.

b. Instead of running, have participants perform other locomotor movements: hopping, slide-stepping, skipping, walking backwards.

c. Repeat the relay in pairs.

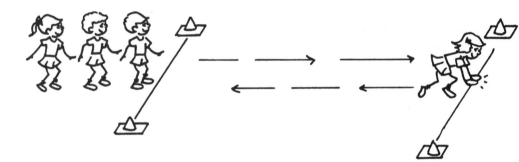

SG-2 ROLY-POLY BEANBAG RELAY _____

FOCUS: Coordination; cooperation

EQUIPMENT: One beanbag (or deckring) per team; two cone markers

ORGANIZATION:

- Form teams of five or six players. Have each team long-sit in single-file formation, with each player equally spaced one meter (three feet) apart. The first player has a beanbag (or deckring) gripped between his or her feet. Ensure that teams are well spaced.

DESCRIPTION OF ACTIVITY:

1. On the signal "Go!" the first player, keeping the beanbag between your feet, roll backwards and pass it over your head to the next player behind you. The second player grip the beanbag between your feet, roll onto your back, and pass it over your head to the next player behind you.
2. Continue passing the beanbag in this way down the line to the last player, who grips it between his or her feet and then hops to the front of the line, where he or she sits down and starts the beanbag passing down the line again. All the other players in the line, move back to allow space at the front for the last player to sit down.
3. The first team to complete the relay and long-sit in starting position is the winner.

SG–3 ANIMAL WALK RELAY

FOCUS: Agility; arm-shoulder strength; fair play

EQUIPMENT: Four cone markers

ORGANIZATION:

- Use cones to mark out a starting line and turning line that are 10 meters (30 feet) apart. Form teams of four to five players, who stand in single-file formation just behind the starting line; each team about 2 meters (6 feet) from the other. Adjust the "walking distance" according to the ability level of the players. If there are unequal teams, a player may have to go twice. In performing the "Wicket Walk," have players bend slightly at the knees to avoid any stress to the lower back.

DESCRIPTION OF ACTIVITY:

1. Each player, in turn, perform an "Animal Walk" to the turning line and back to your file in this way:

    — First Player: ***Lame Dog Walk*** on hands and feet, with your trunk facing downward and one foot in the air;

    — Second Player: ***Spider Walk*** on hands and feet, with your trunk facing upward and head leading;

    — Third Player: ***Wicket Walk*** by bending forward and grasping legs just above ankles and stepping forward without releasing your grip;

    — Fourth Player: ***Alligator Walk*** by using only your lower arms to move forward and dragging your feet;

    — Fifth Player: ***Bear Walk*** by moving forward with your right hand and foot, and then your left side.

2. The first team to complete the relay and sit cross-legged is the winner.

VARIATIONS:

a. *Animal Walk Shuttle:* Arrange teams in shuttle formation and perform relay as above.

b. Include other "walks" such as:

    —***Chicken Walk:*** In squatting position, place your elbows between your legs and grasp ankles on the outside.

    —Refer to activity FA–12 in Section 2 and the activities in Section 3 for more examples.

SG–4 ZIG-ZAG RELAYS

FOCUS: Agility; equipment manipulation

EQUIPMENT: Four to five cone markers per team; one playground ball per team; one hoop and one rope per team; one ball and one scooter per team; lively music (optional); tape or record player

ORGANIZATION:

- Arrange each team of four to five players in single-file formation behind a starting line and facing a row of four or five cone markers, spaced about three meters (ten feet) apart. Have the first player of each team hold a playground ball. If there is an unequal number of players in the teams, have a player go twice for his or her team. Emphasize that players wait behind the starting line until they receive the ball.

DESCRIPTION OF ACTIVITY:

1. On the signal "Zig-Zag!" the first player of each team, bounce a ball in and out of the cone markers, around the end cone, and directly back to your file. Hand the ball to the second player, who repeats the zig-zag course, bouncing the ball.
2. Continue until every player has had a turn. The first team to complete the course and sit cross-legged in their file is the winner.

VARIATIONS:

a. **Soccer Zig-zag Relay:** Have players, in turn, dribble a ball using only their feet in and out of the cones.
b. **Skipping Zig-zag Relay:** Have players, in turn, jump rope in and out of the cones.
c. **Hoop Zig-zag Relay:** Have players, in turn, roll a hoop in and out of three cones.
d. **Scooter Zig-zag Relay:** Have players take turns pushing each other on a scooter in and out of the cones.

SG–5 AROUND-THE-WORLD RELAYS

FOCUS: Speed running; fair play

EQUIPMENT: Deckrings, beachballs, or playground balls (optional)

ORGANIZATION:

- Form teams of five or six players. Have teams make one big circle, with each team being one-quarter of the circle and all circle players facing outward, spaced arm's length apart. Each team numbers off its members: 1, 2, 3, . . . , 5 or 6.

DESCRIPTION OF ACTIVITY:

1. On the signal "Go!" the first players, run CCW around the outside of the circle to your starting position and tag the second players, who repeat the circle run. Continue until everyone on your team has had a turn.
2. The first team to complete the activity and sit cross-legged in their quarter of the circle is the winner.

VARIATIONS:

a. Have players run CW around the circle.
b. Repeat relay using manipulative equipment such as deckrings, beachballs, or playground balls that must be handed off from one player to the next.
c. **Circle Bounce Relay:** Have players, in turn, bounce a large playground ball around the circle.
d. For a smaller class, form a large circle with one team occupying each half of the circle. Number each team off and perform the relay as above.

SG-6 BEACHBALL SHUTTLE

FOCUS: Speed running; shuttle formation

EQUIPMENT: Four cone markers;
one beachball per team;
lively music (optional);
tape or record player

ORGANIZATION:

- Use cones to mark out two lines that are 20 meters (60 feet) apart. Form equal teams of four to six players. To arrange teams in "Shuttle Formation," have half the players standing facing the other half behind each of the lines. Have the first player of each team get a beachball.

DESCRIPTION OF ACTIVITY:

1. On signal "Go!" the first player, run with the beachball toward the other half of your team. Hand the ball to the second player, then go to the end of that file. The second player, carry the beachball across to the opposite file and hand it to the third player; then go to the end of that file.

2. The relay continues until everyone has had a turn and all players are in their starting positions, sitting cross-legged.

VARIATIONS:

a. Use a variety of locomotor movements: skipping, slide-stepping, hopping, walking backwards.
b. Have players carry other objects (beanbag, deckring, baton, football, medicine ball) to the opposite player.
c. Challenge teams to see which team can make the most number of crossings in two minutes.

SG-7 FORTUNE HUNT RELAY

FOCUS: Cooperation; running

EQUIPMENT: Two hoops per team;
several beanbags, deckrings, and short ropes;
lively music;
tape or record player

ORGANIZATION:

- Form teams of four or five players and have each team stand in single-file formation at one end of the play area. Set a hoop in front of each team and another 10 meters (30 feet) away. Then have leaders of each team place at least as many different objects as there are team members in the far hoops.

DESCRIPTION OF ACTIVITY:

1. On signal "Fortune Hunt!" all players on each team, join hands, and run to your far hoop. Try to move together safely and quickly.

2. When you reach the far hoop, the leader, pick up one object. Your team then runs back to the first hoop and the leader places the object inside it.

3. Each team, then run back to your far hoop to pick up another object. Continue the relay until your far hoop is empty and the first hoop is full. Change leaders each time an object is placed in the first hoop, so that everyone has a turn at being a leader.

4. The first team to complete the relay and sit cross-legged behind the first hoop is the winner.

SG-8 RESCUE RELAY

FOCUS: Running; teamwork; fair play

EQUIPMENT: Two cone markers per team; lively music (optional); tape or record player

ORGANIZATION:

- Use cones to mark a starting and turning line, 10 meters (30 feet) apart. Form teams of four or five players in each team. Arrange teams in single-file formation behind the starting line and spaced about 2 meters (6 feet) from each other. The Leader of each team stands on the turning line, facing his or her team. Remind players to keep the hand-hold throughout the rescue. Emphasize that players wait for their turn *behind* the starting line until they are "rescued." If there is an unequal number of players in a team, have one player go twice.

DESCRIPTION OF ACTIVITY:

1. On the signal "Go!" the Leader, run to the first player of your team, grasp him or her by the wrist, and both run back to the leader's turning line.

2. While the Leader remains at this line, the rescued player run back and get another player.

3. Continue the relay in this way until all the players are rescued. The first team to complete the task and sit cross-legged wins the relay.

VARIATION: Vary the way the players are rescued, such as: linking elbows; holding both hands while slide-stepping; hopping together on one foot each; dragging by the ankles the player to be rescued, across the floor; pushing the rescued player on a scooter.

SG-9 CHAIN RELAY

FOCUS: Running; teamwork; fair play

EQUIPMENT: Cone markers

ORGANIZATION:

- Use cones to mark each team's starting line and turning line, 10 meters (30 feet) apart. Form teams of four or five players and have each team stand in single-file formation behind their starting line.

DESCRIPTION OF ACTIVITY:

1. On signal "Go!" first player, run forward, around the far cone marker, and back to the cone marker at the starting line. Grip the wrist or hand of the second player on your team and run around the far cone marker together.

2. Upon returning to your team, grip the third player's hand. All three players, run around the far cone marker together.

3. Continue until your entire team is running as a chain. The first team to complete the activity and sit cross-legged in your file is the winner.

VARIATION:

Zig-Zag Chain Relay: Place a row of cone markers in front of each team, spacing the cones 1 meter (3 feet) apart. Have players run a zig-zag course through the cone markers.

SG–10 TWO-LEGGED RELAY

FOCUS: Cooperation

EQUIPMENT: Two cone markers per team;
lively music;
tape or record player

ORGANIZATION:

- Use cones to mark a starting line and turning point, 10 meters (30 feet) apart. Form teams of six to eight players. Players pair up with a teammate of equal size; partners stand side-by-side, and pairs stand in a single-file formation behind the starting line. Adjust the hopping distance according to the ability level of the class.

DESCRIPTION OF ACTIVITY:

1. On signal "Go!" first pair, hold each other around the waist, raise your inside legs, and hop together toward the cone marker. Change sides there and hop back to your team.

2. The second pair will repeat your action as soon as you cross the starting line. Sit cross-legged at the end of the file.

3. The first team to finish with all players sitting cross-legged in file formation wins the relay.

VARIATION:

Three-Legged Relay: Form teams of six or nine players and have three players at a time hold each other around the waist, raise their right legs, and repeat the relay together.

SG–11 CHARIOT RELAY

FOCUS: Cooperation

EQUIPMENT: Cone markers

ORGANIZATION:

- Use cones to mark a starting line and turning post, 10 meters (30 feet) apart; then form teams of six to nine players. Each team forms several chariots of three players: two players form the chariot by standing side-by-side and joining inside hands; the third player is the driver and stands behind them, holding the players' outside hands. Each team should have at least two chariots. Emphasize that players hold each other's hands tightly. Remind chariots of the traffic pattern: Go around the marker from the right side (counterclockwise) and return to cross the finish line on the right side.

DESCRIPTION OF ACTIVITY:

1. On signal "Go!" first chariot, run forward, around the marker, and back across the starting line. The second chariot may then go.

2. Continue the race until each chariot has made three round trips and each player of the group of three has been a driver. The first team to finish wins.

VARIATION:

Zig-Zag Chariot Relay: Set up a zig-zag course of cone markers or chairs so the chariots must maneuver in and out.

SG-12 SPOKE RELAY _____

FOCUS: Cooperation; agility

EQUIPMENT: Lively music (optional); tape or record player

ORGANIZATION:

- Form teams of six to eight players. Each team forms a circle and players lie face down with their heads toward the middle of the circle and their legs spread apart. Have players join hands to form the hub of the wheel; their bodies are the spokes. Players on each team then number off.

DESCRIPTION OF ACTIVITY:

1. On signal "Spokes!" first player, stand up and carefully run CW over the other players' legs until you reach your spot. Lie down there. As soon as you are lying down again, the second player will quickly stand up and repeat your action.

2. Continue in this way until each teammate has repeated the relay twice. The first team to sit in a circle with legs outstretched wins the game.

SG-13 HOOP LINE RELAY _____

FOCUS: Cooperation; coordination

EQUIPMENT: One hoop per team

ORGANIZATION:

- Form equal teams of five or six players and have each team stand in single-file formation holding hands with the players on either side of them. The leader of each team gets a hoop and hangs it over his or her free arm.

DESCRIPTION OF ACTIVITY:

1. Leader, put your head into the hoop and step through it; then the next player will do the same. Pass the hoop down the line in this way so that everyone on your team steps through the hoop.

2. You may use your hands to steady the hoop as you step through it as long as you do not let go of the next player's hand.

3. When the last player passes through the hoop, that player takes it to the front of the line and repeats the action until the team is standing in the starting positions. The first team to finish in starting order wins the relay.

VARIATIONS:

a. **Circle Hoop Relay:** Have all players join hands to form a circle. Players step through the hoop as it passes around the circle.

b. **Circle Hoop Race:** Have two teams form one half of a large circle, with players facing inward and joining hands. The leader of each team starts the hoop moving in a CW direction around the circle as described above. The object of the race is to try to catch the other hoop.

SG-14 OBSTACLE RELAY

FOCUS: Agility; speed running

EQUIPMENT: Two chairs, one bench, and one table or box horse per team;
hurdles or high jump standards and poles;
three hoops per team;
two cone markers;
lively music;
tape or record player

ORGANIZATION:

- Arrange each team of four or five players in single-file formation behind a starting line. Each team collects several obstacles (two chairs, one bench, one table or box horse, three hoops and two hurdles) and arranges them in a row in front of their file, spacing them about three meters (ten feet) apart.

DESCRIPTION OF ACTIVITY:

1. Each player, in turn, go through the obstacle course and back around your team to your starting position. Return to tag the next player in line. The first team to complete the course and sit cross-legged in their file is the winner.

2. *Suggestions for the Obstacle Course:* Go over one chair; under the second chair; hop along the bench from one end to the other; over the first hurdle; under the second hurdle; climb up and over the table or box horse; and in and out of three hoops.

VARIATIONS:

a. *Doubles Obstacle Course:* Have players pair off in their teams and go through the obstacle course twice, holding hands with their partner.

b. Have class design their own obstacle course using the equipment above.

SG-15 SNOWSHOE RACE

FOCUS: Agility; coordination; fair play

EQUIPMENT: Twelve beanbags per team;
four benches

ORGANIZATION:

- Place benches parallel to each other and about three meters (ten feet) apart; then form three equal teams of six to eight players. Have each player get two beanbags and hold one beanbag in each hand. The beanbags are the player's "snowshoes." Each team then stands in single-file formation behind a line that is three meters (ten feet) from the first bench.

DESCRIPTION OF ACTIVITY:

1. On signal "Snowshoe!" the first player, put a beanbag under each foot and snowshoe toward the first bench. When you reach it, pick up your beanbags, jump over the bench, and put your snowshoes under your feet again.

2. Continue to the next bench and repeat the action. As soon as you reach the second bench, the next player in your team may go. When you reach the last bench, run around the outside of the benches and back to your team. Jog in place until it is your turn again.

3. When all players on your team have completed the course twice, jump up together and yell "Shazam!" Who will be the first team to finish?

SG-16 THREE-STUNT RELAYS

FOCUS: Agility; strength; coordination

EQUIPMENT: Eight cone markers;
one basketball per team;
one hoop per team;
one jump rope per team;
one bench per team

ORGANIZATION:

- Form teams of four or five players and have each team stand in single-file formation behind a starting line. Mark three lines in front of and parallel to the starting line, all spaced three meters (ten feet) apart.

DESCRIPTION OF ACTIVITY:

1. On signal "Go!" each player, in turn, run forward and perform a different stunt at each of the three lines; then return to your team and tag the next runner. Continue until all players have performed the stunts. The first team to complete the relay and sit cross-legged in single-file formation at the starting line is the winner.
2. Suggestions for stunts:
   — Jump and do two heel clicks at the first line.
   — Lie down and jump up four times at the second line.
   — Place one hand on floor and pivot around it twice at third line.

VARIATIONS:

a. *Equipment Stunt Relay:* For each team, place a jump rope on the first line; a hoop with a basketball inside, on the second line; and a bench on the third line. Each player, in turn, runs to the first line and jumps the rope 30 times; dribbles the basketball twice around the hoop in each direction at the second line; and vault-jumps over the bench five times at the third line.

b. *Partner Stunt Relay:* Partner Wheelbarrow to the first line; Partner Two-Leg Hop to second line; Partner Rope-Jump to third line.

SG-17 JUMP-AND-CRAWL RELAY

FOCUS: Agility; coordination

EQUIPMENT: Cone markers

ORGANIZATION:

- Mark a starting line with cones and form teams of four to six players. Each team stands in single-file formation behind the starting line with each player standing one meter (three feet) apart.

DESCRIPTION OF ACTIVITY:

1. On signal "Go!" the end player of each team, jump over the back of the player in front of you, crawl through the legs of the next player, and then jump over the back of the next player in front of that player. Continue in this way until you reach the front of the file.
2. When you reach the front, yell "SHAZAM!" which is the signal to the last player that it is his or her turn.
3. Waiting players, help the moving player reach the start of the file quickly by either crouching on all-fours or standing with your legs wide apart, alternating these two positions in the file. Continue until each player has had two turns.

SG-18 PIP, SQUEAK, AND WILBER

FOCUS: Agility; teamwork; fair play

EQUIPMENT: One hoop;
several large playground balls

ORGANIZATION:

- Arrange players in groups of three, evenly spaced around a large circle. Ensure that groups are well balanced. In each group, players sit cross-legged, side-by-side, facing the center of the circle. The player on the right of each group is called "Pip"; the middle player, "Squeak"; and the player on the left, "Wilber." Place several balls (one fewer balls than the number of groups) inside a hoop placed in the center of the circle.

DESCRIPTION OF ACTIVITY:

1. Listen carefully. I will call out one of the three names; for example, "Wilber!" All the Wilbers, run CCW around the outside of the circle, go underneath the arch formed by the other two members of your groups, and into the center. Grab a ball and dribble it to your group.

2. Now Wilbers, return your balls to the hoop and everyone listen for the next name I will call. Remember to place, not toss, the balls back into the hoop each time.

3. Groups, keep track of the balls you get. Which group will collect the most?

VARIATION: Use other objects to be picked up from the center such as: beanbags, deckrings, small balls, knotted short ropes.

SG-19 SPUD

FOCUS: Alertness; throwing accuracy; catching; fair play

EQUIPMENT: One Nerf™ ball

ORGANIZATION:

- Have players stand in a circle formation, spaced arm's length apart and facing inward; then number off around the circle. Select one player to get a ball and stand in the center of the circle.

DESCRIPTION OF ACTIVITY:

1. Circle players, start jogging CCW around the circle. Center player, toss the ball overhead and call a number. Circle players, quickly move as far away from the center player as possible.

2. The player whose number is called, catch the ball on one or no bounces and yell "Iceberg!" All players must then stop immediately and hold their positions.

3. Now player with the ball, throw it so that the ball hits a "frozen" player below the waist. If you miss, you get one "spud" and must toss the ball overhead again, calling a new number. If you hit a player, that player gets one "spud" and becomes the new center player.

4. When you have collected three spuds, you must come to me to perform a task before you can rejoin the game.

VARIATION: If playing the game in a gym, have players stay on or inside the basketball boundary lines.

SG-20 WORM GRAB

FOCUS: Alertness; agility; fair play

EQUIPMENT: One short rope per player;
one hoop per game

ORGANIZATION:

- For each game, form two equal teams and arrange the teams in two lines about 6 meters (20 feet) apart, standing and facing each other. For a larger class, set up two games and conduct them simultaneously. Give each team a bird's name; for example, "Robins" and "Blue Jays." Have the players in each team number off: 1, 2, 3, etc. Use a 1-meter (3-foot) circle, or hoop, in the middle between the two lines. Place a rope in the circle. Discuss the meaning of "fair play" and why players must be behind the line when the numbers are called.

DESCRIPTION OF ACTIVITY:

1. When I call out a number, such as "3!", the two players with that number, run to the circle and try to grab the worm (rope) first and return with it to your starting line.

2. Then I will add another rope to the circle and call another number.

3. When all players have had a turn (or several turns), each team will count the worms it has collected and we will see which team has more.

SG-21 MOTHER CAREY'S CHICKENS

FOCUS: Throwing accuracy; running and dodging

EQUIPMENT: One set of banners;
three sponge balls

ORGANIZATION:

- Choose three players to be the "Foxes." Each Fox gets one ball and goes to the middle of the play area. Form teams of four players and have each team stand in single-file formation with players holding at the waist of the player in front of them. The first player of each team is called "Mother Carey"; the other players are her "Chicks."

DESCRIPTION OF ACTIVITY:

1. On signal "Go!" Foxes, throw your ball trying to hit the Chicks below the waist. Mother Carey, protect your brood of chicks by swinging them away from the ball or using your hands to block it.

2. Any Chick who lets go of the brood or who is hit by the ball becomes that Fox's helper and must wear a banner. The helper's job is to retrieve the ball after each throw and pass it back to the Fox.

3. Foxes, as soon as you have a helper, you must throw the ball from where you caught it.

4. Play continues until all Chicks are hit and only the Mother Carey's are free.

VARIATION: Foxes must hit only the end Chick of the brood.

SG–22 EVERYONE FOR YOURSELF

FOCUS: Throwing; running and dodging; alertness

EQUIPMENT: Two or three Nerf™ balls; several cone markers; three to four benches

ORGANIZATION:

- Use cones to mark off a large rectangular play area. Players scatter throughout this area. To begin the game, toss two balls into the play area.

DESCRIPTION OF ACTIVITY:

1. Any player may try to grab a tossed ball.

2. The player with the ball has three seconds and may take three steps in any direction before throwing the ball at another player. The ball must hit below the waist.

3. If you are hit, you must sit on a bench until the player who hit you is also hit; then you may re-join the game. Remember who hit you and watch the play closely so you can get back into the game.

4. A loose ball may be picked up by any player.

VARIATIONS:

a. After six players are sitting on the benches, allow them all to return to the game.
b. Toss three Nerf™ balls into the play area and watch the activity level increase!
c. Establish the rule that a player with the ball may take only one "pivot step" in any direction.

SG–23 LINE DODGEBALL

FOCUS: Throwing accuracy; catching; dodging; fair play

EQUIPMENT: One Nerf™ ball per group; four cone markers per group; one long rope per group

ORGANIZATION:

- Divide the class into groups of seven to eight players. For each group assign an area and use cones to mark out two parallel lines that are 6 meters (20 feet) apart. Use rope to mark out a circle 1.2 meters (4 feet) in diameter and midway between the two lines. Have one player stand in the circle; half of the remaining players stand just behind one line, facing the other half who stand just behind the opposite line. Give one ball to a line player to start the game. Remind line players that they must stay *behind* the line when throwing the ball. Encourage players to take turns throwing the ball.

DESCRIPTION OF ACTIVITY:

1. Line players, take turns trying to hit the middle player below the waist.

2. Center player, try to dodge the ball but never be caught with both feet out of the circle at any time. If you are hit, change places with the ball-thrower. Continue the game in this way.

VARIATIONS:

a. Use two balls instead of one and extend the distance between the two parallel lines up to 10 meters (30 feet).

b. Have circle player keep both feet in the circle at all times.

SG-24 TEAM DODGEBALL

FOCUS: Throwing accuracy; dodging; fair play

EQUIPMENT: Two Nerf™ balls per circle; several cone markers or one 10-meter (30-foot)-long rope

ORGANIZATION:

- Mark out a large 6-meter (20-foot) diameter circle using cone markers or a long rope. Form two equal teams and have the players of one team stand inside the circle, and the players of the other team space themselves arm's length apart just outside the circle markers. Give two circle players a ball each to start the game.

DESCRIPTION OF ACTIVITY:

1. On the signal "Go!" players with the ball, throw it at the players inside the circle and try to hit them below the waist.
2. Circle players, you may enter the circle to retrieve a loose ball, but must throw it to another circle player before it can be put into play again.
3. Circle team, score one point for every player you hit below the waist. Remember that the ball must be thrown from *behind* the circle markers; otherwise, a point will not be awarded for hitting a player below the waist. Take turns throwing the ball.
4. After three minutes, circle players and inside players change places, and play another three-minute game. The team with the best score at the end of the game wins.

VARIATIONS:

a. For a large class, divide the class into four teams and have two games occurring at the same time.
b. **Squat Dodgeball:** Have a hit player squat inside and near the circle perimeter and stay in this position until the game ends. Circle players try to get all the inside players squatting in two minutes. At the end of two minutes, the squatters are counted and the circle team's score recorded; then the circle and inside players change places and play another two-minute game.

SG-25 CROSS-OVER DODGEBALL

FOCUS: Throwing accuracy; dodging; fair play

EQUIPMENT: Two sponge balls per team; several cone markers

ORGANIZATION:

- In this game, no one loses. The cross-over structure, together with the extra balls, small teams, and the moderately sized play area, ensure that all players are continuously involved. Form teams of five or six players. Have each team get two balls and stand on either side of the play area, marked out with cone markers.

DESCRIPTION OF ACTIVITY:

1. The object of the game is to avoid being hit by the ball.
2. Each team will throw its two balls at the players on the other team, trying to hit them below the waist.
3. If you are hit, you must run to the opposite side and join the other team. The game continues until all players are on the same side.

SG–26 BRITISH BULLDOG

FOCUS: Running and dodging

EQUIPMENT: Several cone markers;
one flag per player;
one set of banners

ORGANIZATION:

- Have players tuck a flag into the back of their waistband and stand side-by-side at one end of the play area; then choose one player to be IT, who wears a banner. That player runs to the middle of the play area and starts the game.

DESCRIPTION OF ACTIVITY:

1. IT, shout "British Bulldog!" On this signal, all players, try to run to the opposite end without getting your flag pulled.

2. A player with a pulled flag must bring it to me and exchange it for a banner. Now you join the IT team and help to catch other free players.

3. Players, you may only run when the signal "British Bulldog!" is given.

4. The game continues until only one player is left. That player becomes the new IT in the next game.

SG–27 CHINESE WALL

FOCUS: Running and dodging; alertness

EQUIPMENT: Eight cone markers

ORGANIZATION:

- Using the cones, mark out two parallel endlines that are 20 meters (60 feet) apart. Then mark out two parallel lines, 3 meters (10 feet) apart, across the center of the play area to represent the wall. Select three players to stand on the wall to defend it, and have the remaining players start on one of the endlines.

DESCRIPTION OF ACTIVITY:

1. On the signal from the wall defenders, "Scale the wall!" players run and try to cross the wall to the opposite endline without being tagged with a one-hand touch by the defenders.

2. Remember to watch where you are going at all times. Do not attempt to cross the wall to the other endline until defenders give the signal.

3. Defenders, you may not leave the wall, but may travel anywhere along it.

4. Players, if you are tagged by a defender, you must remain on the wall and help to defend it on the next crossing.

VARIATIONS:

a. Have players wear flags (tucked into the back of their waistbands) that the defenders try to pull out as players run across to the opposite endline.

b. Connect folding mats across the middle of the play area that stretch from one sideline to the other. This becomes the "wall."

SG-28 STAR WARS

FOCUS: Running and dodging

EQUIPMENT: Four cone markers; three beanbags

ORGANIZATION:

- Mark out a large rectangular area with the cones. Select one player to be Darth Vader, who is IT, along with two helpers, who are called Stormtroopers. Have these players each hold a beanbag and stand across the middle of the play area, facing one end line. Divide the rest of the class into three or four groups (depending upon the size of the class) and call the groups: R2D2s, Chewbaccas, C3POs, and Luke Skywalkers. Have groups stand side-by-side on the endline facing the IT group. Designate an area just outside of the play areas as the Trash Compactor. (This area is controlled by the Teacher and perhaps a student who is unable to actively participate.) Remind Darth Vader and the Stormtroopers that they start in the middle of the play area each time, before calling another group. Emphasize that players must run inside the boundaries of the play area; otherwise, they are automatically caught.

DESCRIPTION OF ACTIVITY:

1. Darth Vader, call one group at a time to run across the play area to the safety of the opposite endline. As they move across, you and your two helpers, the Stormtroopers, try to tag these players by touching them with your beanbags.

2. Those players tagged must go to the "trash compactor," miss one turn, and perform a task such as jumping jacks, push-ups, sit-ups, etc.

3. Darth Vader, after each group has been called to cross the play area, then call each group, in turn, to cross the play area again.

4. Then I will choose a new Darth Vader and two Stormtroopers, and we will play the game again.

VARIATIONS:

a. Use other names for the groups such as Hans Solos, Princess Leias, Wickets.

b. Have players wear flags, tucked into the waistbands at the back of their shorts or sweat pants, which are pulled by Darth Vader and the Stormtroopers to make a capture.

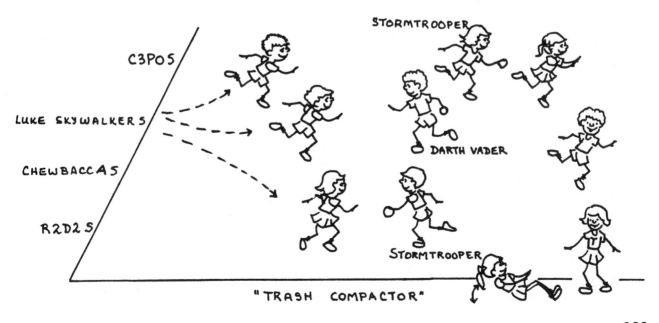

SG–29 BATTLESTAR GALACTICA

FOCUS: Throwing accuracy;
running and dodging

EQUIPMENT: 16 to 30 beanbags or fleece balls;
four cone markers

ORGANIZATION:

- Use cones to mark out a rectangular area with 20-meter (60-foot) sidelines and 6-meter (30-foot) end-lines. Form two equal teams. The players on the first team are Cylons, who each get a laser (beanbag), and evenly space themselves along the sidelines of the play area. The players on the second team are Viper Spacecraft, who stand side-by-side at one end of the play area. You are the Commander of the Galactica Spaceship and control the launching of Viper Spacecraft with the signal "All Vipers, go!"

DESCRIPTION OF ACTIVITY:

1. The object of the game is for the Cylons to hit the Viper Spacecraft below the waist, as they run from one end of the play area to the other.

2. Hit Vipers, you must freeze on the spot. I will count how many Viper Spacecraft are hit and then thaw them out so that they can continue to the opposite endline.

3. Cylons, you may run to pick up the lasers only after all Viper Spacecraft have reached the other end. Viper Spacecraft, you cannot be launched again until the play area is clear and I give the signal.

4. After three runs, Viper Spacecraft and Cylons change roles and the game continues. The team that scores more points wins the game.

VARIATION: Have each Viper who hits a Cylon exchange roles with that Cylon.

SG–30 SPACESHIPS

FOCUS: Throwing accuracy; running and dodging; fair play

EQUIPMENT: Three hoops;
three small utility balls

ORGANIZATION:

- Equally space three hoops lengthwise through the middle of the play area (galaxy). Choose three players to be the aliens. They each get a ball (meteorite) and stand with both feet inside the hoop (space station). The other players are the spaceships and stand in a line formation at one end of the play area.

DESCRIPTION OF ACTIVITY:

1. As Commander of the universe, I will call the spaceships to fly from one end of the galaxy to the other. Spaceships, as you travel through space, watch out for aliens who will try to zap you with their meteorites. If a meteorite hits you below the waist, you are stranded in space and must sink to your knees.

2. Aliens, you must have both feet inside your space station when throwing a meteorite. Quickly retrieve a thrown meteorite and return to the space station before throwing it again.

3. Any spaceships who run out-of-bounds or fly outside the galaxy will become stranded there. Stranded spaceships, try to touch a flying spaceship to change roles with that player. Remember, you can only move your upper body; your lower body is frozen to the spot! Continue until all spaceships are stranded in space.

VARIATION: Use different signals to call the spaceships across the galaxy: all girl spaceships; all boy spaceships; all spaceships wearing green; all spaceships wearing sweatpants or shorts.

SG-31 KING'S COURT

FOCUS: Throwing and catching; dodging; fair play

EQUIPMENT: Three sponge balls; several cone markers

ORGANIZATION:

- Use cones to mark out a large rectangular play area and center line. Form two equal teams and assign each team to one half of the play area. To begin the game, have players stand on the endline of their court. Place balls equally spaced apart on the center line.

DESCRIPTION OF ACTIVITY:

1. On the signal "Go!" players, run to the center to grab the balls and, staying in your court, throw the balls at your opponents. The object of the game is to be the first team to hit all the opposition players.
2. Players hit below the waist, go to the opposition's end. There you may field any ball that comes into the end zone and throw it back to your court players.
3. Court players, you are not allowed to step outside your court to retrieve a ball; end players, you are not allowed to step inside the court.
4. If you catch a ball while it is travelling through the air, you may bring one of your end players back to your court. However, if you drop an air ball, you are considered hit.

SG-32 TOUCHDOWN

FOCUS: Running and dodging; alertness

EQUIPMENT: One set of banners; several cone markers; small object such as a marble, piece of chalk, button, or ping-pong ball

ORGANIZATION:

- Use cones to mark a play area with a center line that suits the players' level of running ability. Form two equal teams and have one team wear the banners. Each team stands side-by-side in its half at the center line facing the other team. Flip a coin or choose a number to decide which team receives a small object (the Football) at the start of the game.

DESCRIPTION OF ACTIVITY:

1. The offensive team, with the Football, has ten seconds to meet in a circular huddle to decide on the team's game plan: Who will carry the object in his or her hands? How can you fake it to look like everyone in your team is carrying it?
2. On the signal "Go!" offensive team players, run toward the opposite end of the play area. Meanwhile, defensive team players, try to tag the opposition with a one-hand touch.
3. Offensive players, if you are tagged, open your hands and show what you are carrying. If your hands are empty, freeze on the spot. If you have the object, the teams change roles and the other team gets the Football.
4. Offensive player, if you are carrying the Football and reach the end of the play area without being tagged, shout "Touchdown!" Your team then earns one point. The other team gets the football and the game continues.

FOCUS: Running and dodging; fair play

EQUIPMENT: 40 beanbags;
several cone markers;
one set of banners;
two to four hoops;
two baskets or boxes

ORGANIZATION:

- Divide a large rectangular play area in half using cone markers, and mark a line across each end and at center. Evenly distribute 20 beanbags (the Treasures) behind each line. Place a hoop on two diagonal corners of the playing area. These are the Prisons. Place a basket on the other two diagonal corners. These are the Treasure Boxes. Then form two equal teams and have one team wear banners. To start, the players on each team stand side-by-side in their half at center, facing the opposition.

DESCRIPTION OF ACTIVITY:

1. On the signal "Go!" both teams, attempt to run to the other end of the play area and cross your opponent's goal line without being tagged. If you succeed, you may pick up one of the opponent's treasures and carry it on your head back to your half. No one can tag you as you walk back. Place your treasure in the Treasure Box.

2. If you are tagged in the opponent's half of the play area, you become a prisoner. Go to the opponent's Prison and remain there until a teammate frees you with a hand-touch. When freed, both you and the player who freed you may then return safely to your half by walking on the outside of the playing area.

3. A player can only free one prisoner at a time. Only one beanbag at a time can be taken from the opposition's line. The prison can be guarded by only one player at a time.

4. As soon as one team has collected all the treasures, or after a certain time, the game ends. The team with more beanbags wins.

VARIATIONS:

a. Place a hoop in the middle of each half. The hoop is a "safe" place for opponents.

b. Establish the rule that as long as a team has members in Prison, no treasures can be taken.

c. For outdoors, scatter obstacles (mats, cone markers, cardboard boxes, etc.) throughout the play area so that players can dodge around, over, under, or through them.

SG–34 BASE-KET-BALL

FOCUS: Retrieving and passing; shooting; running

EQUIPMENT: One mini-basketball; chalkboard and chalk; several cone markers

ORGANIZATION:

- Form two equal teams of "Batters" and "Fielders." One fielder, the "Shooter," stands at the foul-line of each basketball key. The other fielders, the "Retrievers," scatter throughout the play area. One Batter gets a basketball and stands at home plate, which is in the middle of one side of the play area. The other batters stand in batting order just outside the sideline and wait their turn to bat. Mark a throwing line parallel to and three meters (ten feet) from the batter's sideline. Place cones at each corner of the play area. Adjust the shooting distance to the ability level of the class. After every four throws, change the Shooters, so that everyone in the fielding team gets a chance at this position.

DESCRIPTION OF ACTIVITY:

1. Batter at home plate, throw the ball over the "throw-line," and then run CCW around the cones. Try to reach home before a retriever can catch the ball and throw it to the nearest Shooter, who will try to make a basket.

2. If the Shooter shoots the ball into the basket before you reach home plate, you are out. If the Shooter misses, the ball is passed to another Shooter, who will try again. Fielders, continue retrieving and shooting the ball until the Batter reaches home.

3. You score one point for your team if you reach home plate before the other team can make a basket.

4. After all Batters have had a turn, change roles. The team with the better score wins.

VARIATION:

Have Batting and Fielding teams change roles after every three outs.

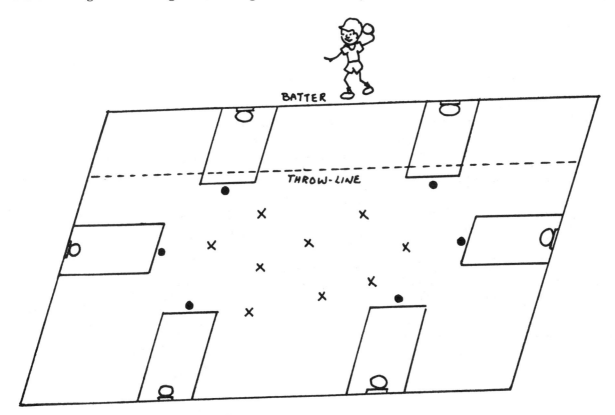

SG-35 ROCKETBALL

FOCUS: Throwing and catching; alertness

EQUIPMENT: Six cone markers; tube socks tennis balls;

ORGANIZATION:

- This game is best played outdoors. Make up six Rocketballs by knotting tennis balls in the toes of tube socks. Demonstrate how to throw a rocketball by circling it twice around in a CW direction, and then tossing it up and outward with an underhand motion. Allow time for players to practice this throwing action. Use cones to mark out a large rectangular area, 20 meters by 10 meters (60 feet by 30 feet), with a center line. Form two equal teams, and have each team scatter on one half of the play area. Give each team three Rocketballs.

DESCRIPTION OF ACTIVITY:

1. The object of the game is to catch the Rocketballs before they hit the floor or ground in your half of the play area. When I signal "Go!" throw the Rocketballs into open spaces in the other team's half.
2. Call "Mine!" when you intend to catch a Rocketball. It must then be thrown from the spot where it was caught.
3. The other team scores a point whenever:
   — a Rocketball touches the floor in your half or the ceiling;
   — your team throws a Rocketball out-of-bounds; or
   — your Rocketball does not make it into the other team's half.

SG-36 JUMP THE SHOT

FOCUS: Leg strength; alertness

EQUIPMENT: One long rope per team; one slightly deflated tether ball or deckring per team

ORGANIZATION:

- To make a Jump-the-Shot rope, attach a tether ball to a rope that is about 5 meters (15 feet) long. If you do not have an old tether ball, any soft object such as a deckring or beanbag will do. Form equal teams of six to eight players. Each team stands in a circle, with players spaced at arm's length. One player on each team gets a Jump-the-Shot rope and stands in the center of the circle.

DESCRIPTION OF ACTIVITY:

1. Middle player, swing the rope CW slowly at first, so that the circle players know how far away from it they should stand to be able to jump over it. The rope should just pass under their legs. As you swing the rope, keep it low to the ground so that it is easy to jump.
2. Circle players, jump the rope each time it swings past you. If the rope hits your leg or you miss a jump, leave the circle and jog once around the play area; then rejoin the game. Change rope turners every five turns.

VARIATIONS:

a. Have rope turners swing the rope counterclockwise.
b. Vary the speed of the rope according to the ability level of the jumpers.
c. Have circle players join hands with a partner.

SG–37 INTRODUCING PLAY DAYS

FOCUS: Teaching guidelines; organization

EQUIPMENT: Equipment list for each station; description of each event; posterboard and marking pens; stopwatch or digital watch; whistle; litter cans; list of senior groups, leaders and teams; participation certificates or ribbons; treats (optional); music (optional)

ORGANIZATION:

- The purpose of a primary Play Day is to provide an opportunity for everyone to participate and enjoy various fun-filled, low-skilled, and fitness-oriented activities. The emphasis is on cooperation, sportsmanship, and team spirit, rather than on winning and individual performance. Therefore, the stations could be scored but the results not recorded. At the closing, a participation certificate or ribbon could be given to every child to acknowledge their efforts.

- The number and types of stations will depend upon the overall objective or theme of the Play Day; the number of children and staff involved; the facilities available (indoor or outdoor); availability of equipment; and the availability of a senior class as officials to run the Play Day. A notice concerning the date, time, and location of the Play Day; appropriate dress for the event (T-shirts, shorts, running shoes, sun-hat, sunscreen, and insect repellent); and invitations for parents to watch could be sent home a week in advance.

ORGANIZING PLAY DAYS Grades 1, 2, and 3 should be combined to participate in the Play Day and placed on teams of eight to ten players. The number of stations required for the Play Day is one half of the number of teams. The senior class is divided into four groups of leaders: Team Leaders, Station Leaders, Rest Station Leaders, and Clean-Up Gang. Their duties are as follows:

—*A Team Leader* is assigned to each team and is responsible for choosing a team name; making name tags for the team players and team name; and looking after the team and getting the players from one station to the next.

—*Station Leaders* are responsible for setting up the equipment needed for each station; making the appropriate sign; explaining how the activity is performed; and effectively and safely running the station. The rules for each station should be simple and easily scored.

—*Rest Station Leaders* are responsible for the Rest or Break Station where treats, such as frozen fruit bits or nutritious drinks, are given to the children.

—*Clean-Up Gang* is responsible for setting up litter cans as needed; picking up any litter on the playground; and putting away the equipment at the completion of the Play Day.

SETTING UP A PLAY DAY

—The senior class groups should be briefed of their duties. A list of events including rules, procedures, and a diagram should be prepared and distributed to all Station and Team Leaders and Teachers. A list of equipment should be prepared and checked at least three days in advance. The diagram should show the placement of the events and the rotation order. Have the Station group organize each station about two hours beforehand.

—Prior to the start of the Play Day, have all teams assemble to meet their Team Leaders and be taken to their starting stations. The activities at each station should be duplicated, if possible, as two teams will be participating at the same time at each station: teams 1 and 2 will start at Station 1; teams 3 and 4 at Station 2; teams 5 and 6 at Station 3; and so on. Have the station activity last for about five minutes. Use a whistle signal or music signal to indicate when teams rotate to the next station.

CLOSING

—At the closing of the Play Day have teams again assemble at the starting area. During this time, Leaders give participation certificates or ribbons to each of their team members, and then dismiss their team. Now the Clean-Up Gang goes quickly into action under your supervision.

—Following the Play Day, meet with the Senior Class and teachers involved to discuss and evaluate the overall event, the planning and organization, the station activities, and children's reactions. Hopefully suggestions will be made for implementing an even better Play Day the next time!

FOCUS: Equipment manipulation

EQUIPMENT: Cone markers;
two tablespoons;
one small potato;
two paddles;
one ping-pong ball;
two potato sacks;
two laundry baskets;
eight hoops or deckrings;
eight beanbags

DESCRIPTION OF ACTIVITY:

Station 1, Potato Spoon Relay (Have team stand in single-file formation behind a starting line, facing a turning cone 6 meters [20 feet] away. The first two players of each team hold a spoon with a potato in the spoon.): Each player, in turn, carry the potato on a spoon while travelling to the turning cone, around it, and back to your team to hand the potato to the next player in line. If you drop the potato, pick it up and keep going!

Station 2, Paddle Ball Race (Use the same formation as above, but have the first player hold a paddle and a ping-pong ball and the second player hold a paddle.): Each player, in turn, balance a ping-pong ball on your paddle as you travel to the cone marker and back to hand the ball to the next player in line. If the ball slides off, pick it up, put it on your paddle, and continue running.

Station 3, Potato Sack Relay (Have each team in shuttle formation with each half facing the other half, 10 meters [30 feet] away. The first player stands inside a potato sack holding the sides.): The first player, hop across to the opposite line, quickly step out of the sack to let the second player step inside, and then join the file. The second player hop in the same way across to the opposite file to give the sack to the third player. Continue in this way.

Station 4, Junk Relay (Have each team stand in single-file formation behind a starting line, facing a row of four hoops [or deckrings] spaced 1 meter [3 feet] apart and 2 meters [6 feet] from the line. In each hoop place a beanbag, and on the starting line place a laundry basket.): The first player, run to the first hoop, pick up the beanbag, carry it back to your team and drop it in the basket, and then run to the second hoop, pick up the beanbag, and return to drop it in the basket. Continue to the third and fourth hoop to do the same. The second player, grab one beanbag out of the basket, and place it in a hoop. Return to the basket to grab a second beanbag and place it in another hoop. Repeat in this way until all the beanbags have been returned to the hoops. The third player then collect all the beanbags, one at a time. The fourth player, return the beanbags, one at a time, to the hoops, and so on.

VARIATION:

Garbage Relay (Have each team stand in single-file formation behind a starting line, facing a pile of "garbage" [two beanbags, two skipping ropes, two sponge balls, two scoops, two banners, two batons, etc.] 6 meters [20 feet] away.): First player runs to the "garbage pile," picks it all up, and carries it back to the starting line to dump it there. The second player picks it all up and carries it back to its original place, and then runs quickly back to tag the next player, who runs and repeats the first player's actions. If a player drops an object, it must be picked up before continuing.

SG–39 PLAY DAY STATIONS 5, 6, 7, AND 8

FOCUS: Equipment manipulation; accuracy throwing and rolling

EQUIPMENT: Two large beachballs;
one two-meter (six-foot) cageball or innertube;
several cone markers;
six ice cream pails;
eighteen clothespins;
nine small utility balls;
nine bowling pins or bleach bottles;
nine beanbags

DESCRIPTION OF ACTIVITY:

Station 5, Keep-It-Up (Have players of each team form a circle. One player gets the beachball.): The object of the activity is to keep the beachball in the air. Don't let it touch the ground! How many times in a row can your team hit the ball upward before it touches the ground?

Station 6, Weave and Roll (Place a line of five cones about two meters [six feet] apart from a starting line. Have players pair off in each team and stand in single-file formation behind the starting line, facing the cones. The first pair gets the cageball.): Each pair, in turn, roll the ball in and out of the cones, around the end cone, and directly back to pass the ball to the next pair, who does the same.

Station 7, Clothespin Toss (Have players stand behind a throwing line and face an ice cream pail placed three meters [ten feet] away. Give each of the first players three clothespins. For each team, set up three duplicate activities to provide more participation.): Each player, in turn, take three tries to toss the clothespins in the ice cream pail. Can you get all three in the pail? Keep track of how many good tosses you make in all.

Station 8, Three-Pin Bowling (Place three bowling pins in a triangular formation about 6 meters [20 feet] from a rolling line. Place three small utility balls near the rolling line. For more participation, set up as many of these three-pin bowling activities as you have equipment available.): Each player, in turn, bowl three balls at the pins trying to knock them all down. How many pins will you knock down altogether?

VARIATIONS:

a. ***Shuttle Roll:*** Arrange each team in pairs in a shuttle formation and have each pair roll an innertube across to the opposite pair, who does the same.

b. ***Three for a Quarter:*** Have two team players hold a bucket and stand in a spot about 10 meters (30 feet) from a throwing line. The other players stand in a file just behind the throwing line. Have each player, in turn, toss three beanbags toward the bucket-holder, who tries to catch the beanbags in the bucket. After every two players have thrown, change the bucket-holder.

FOCUS: Accuracy throwing and kicking; agility running; teamwork

EQUIPMENT: Several cone markers; six plastic rings or small hoops; two to four benches; eight safety mats; 20 beanbags; 20 deckrings; 22 batons; eight bases; four nets; eight soccer balls; eight tennis balls; eight hockey sticks

DESCRIPTION OF ACTIVITY:

Station 9, Hoop-La (Place three large cone markers in a triangle formation, equally spaced one meter [three feet] from each other, and three meters [ten feet] from a throwing line. Set up a duplicate activity if equipment is available.): Each player, in turn, toss three plastic rings toward the cone markers. How many cones will you ring?

Station 10, Long Play (Place two benches butted against each other and two long folding mats on either side of the benches.): Each team, arrange yourself on the bench in any order. Can you, without stepping off the bench, reverse your positions so that the last player now becomes the first player?

Station 11, Base Run (Set up the bases in a diamond pattern. Have each team start at home plate, standing in a file in the infield. The first player holds a baton.): Each player, in turn, hold the baton and run as fast as you can around the bases, tagging each cone in order with your foot as you go past. When you reach home plate, hand the baton to the next player, who repeats the activity.

Station 12, Soccer Kick (Place four nets near a wall spaced two meters [six feet] apart. Mark out a kicking line using cones. Place two soccer balls on the kicking line for each net. Designate each team to kick into any two of the four nets.): Have players stand in a file at the kicking line, facing either of the two nets. Each player, in turn, kick a soccer ball into the net, and then retrieve your ball before the next player goes. How many goals will you score?

VARIATIONS:

a. *Ring Toss:* Have players in pairs. Each partner holds a baton in one hand and a deckring in his or her throwing hand. Partners face each other about 3 meters (10 feet) away to start. Each partner, in turn, tosses his or her deckring toward the other partner's stick. The receiving partner tries to catch the deckring on his or her stick.

b. *Horseshoes:* Partners face a deckring that is 5 meters (15 feet) away from them. Each partner, in turn, tosses a beanbag toward the deckring. Which partner will come closer to the ring?

c. *Hockey Shoot:* Set up the same equipment as for "Soccer Kick," except use tennis balls instead of soccer balls, and give each team hockey sticks. Each player, in turn, shoots the ball at the net.

SG-41 PLAY DAY STATIONS 13, 14, 15, AND 16

FOCUS: Agility; strength; teamwork

EQUIPMENT: Chairs;
tables;
ropes;
hoops;
benches;
cones;
box horse;
mats;
crash pad;
high jump standards and poles;
various balls;
two sets of old clothes;
10 meters (30 feet) of thin rope;
several clothespins;
two laundry baskets;
one parachute;
one tug-o-war rope;
three flags;
two long ropes

DESCRIPTION OF ACTIVITY:

Station 13, Obstacle Course Relay (Have two identical courses set up. Refer to activity FA–30 in Section 2 for suggestions. Set up obstacles that players must move under, over, around, through, across, in and out, on and off or use equipment that they must manipulate.): Each player, in turn, move through the obstacle course as safely and quickly as you can, and then join the end of your file. As soon as the player in front of you has reached the halfway point, you may go.

Station 14, Obstacle Clothes Relay (Collect two sets of old clothes such as a hat, a pair of boots, baggy overalls, and coat. Place these on a starting line and have each team stand in a file behind the line. Use a rope to mark a turning line 20 meters [60 feet] away.): Each player, in turn, quickly put on the old clothes, run to the turning line where you just as quickly remove the clothes, and then carry them back to hand to the next player in your file, who does the same.

Station 15, Parachute Play (Refer to "Parachute Play" in Section 6. Choose one of the many activities using a parachute. Spread the parachute flat along the ground. Have players spread themselves evenly around the parachute and grab onto the edge with an Overhand Grip.)

Station 16, Team Tug-O-War (Extend the tug-o-war rope flat along the ground. Use flags knotted around the rope to mark the center and a point 60 centimeters [two feet] on either side of the center marker. Draw a line directly under the center marker. Have each team stand alongside one half of the rope with players evenly spaced apart. The first player of each team is at his or her marker.): Each team, grip the rope on your side of center. On the signal "Tug!" try to pull the other team's marker over center to win. All players, stay on your feet throughout the pull. Which team will do better out of three Tug-O-Wars?

VARIATIONS:

a. ***Clothesline Relay*** (Erect a clothesline at a height above the ground that all players can reach. Place four different clothes on it with clothespins and place a laundry basket on the starting line. Have each team stand in single-file formation behind the starting line and face the clothesline 10 meters [30 feet] away.): The first player runs to the clothesline, quickly removes the clothes, runs back to the starting line and puts them in the basket; then tags the second player, who takes the clothes out of the basket, runs to the clothesline, and hangs them back up; then runs back to tag the third player, who repeats the first player's actions. The relay continues in this way.

b. ***Long Rope Play:*** Each team gets one long rope. Players should take turns being jumpers and rope turners. Challenge the team to see how many players can jump at the same time in the middle of the rope! (Refer to "Rope Play" in Section 6 for activities using a long rope.)

SG–42 INTRODUCING TABLOID SPORTS

FOCUS: Teaching guidelines; class organization

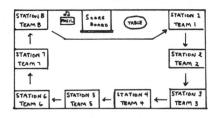

EQUIPMENT: Station equipment;
stopwatch and calculator;
posterboard and marking pens;
chalkboard and chalk;
floor or masking tape;
selection of lively music;
tape or record player

ORGANIZATION:

• Tabloids are circuits of high-interest, low-skill, mass-participation activities that are challenging and fun! Choose eight activities from the following for each Tabloid and add ideas of your own. Set up equipment in stations around the play area, posting a sign at each station that can be easily read from a distance. Set up the scoreboard, mark starting lines with floor or masking tape, and select the music to be played. To begin, form as many teams of five to eight players as you have stations. Choose a leader for each team, and assign each team a number from one to eight. Explain the rules. Demonstrate the task to be performed at each station, or have each team demonstrate the task at its starting station. Allow each team to decide how it will organize itself at each station.

VARIATIONS:

a. Choose sports or seasonal themes such as the Olympic Games, a Circus or Carnival, Christmas, Easter, or Halloween.

b. Practice game skills in tabloid format. Set up a Volleyball Tabloid; a Basketball Tabloid; a Soccer Tabloid; a Hockey Tabloid; a Track and Field Tabloid.

c. Adapt the tabloid activities so that they can be used outdoors as in a Winter Carnival or Beach Carnival Tabloid.

d. *Integration:* Combine several Grade 5 classes and run a Tabloid. As an Art project, have the children draw and paint pictures, depicting the theme of the tabloid and the station ideas.

SG–43 SETTING UP A TABLOID

ORGANIZATION:

• The objective is for each team to score as many points as possible within a time limit of two minutes or more at each station. When the music starts, players take turns at their activity. The leaders keep score for their team. When the music stops, everyone quickly sits cross-legged at their station in single-file formation, behind their leader and facing the scoreboard. The first team to do this earns three bonus points; the second team earns two points; and the third team earns one point. These points are added to the team score.

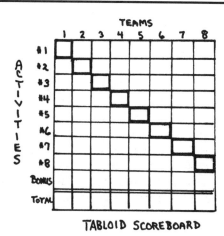

TABLOID SCOREBOARD

DESCRIPTION OF ACTIVITY:

1. Each team in turn, call out your score when I call your team number. The team who yells the loudest and clearest score gets three bonus points!

2. After the scores are recorded on the scoreboard, rotate CW to the next station. Your team has 20 seconds to get organized before the music starts again.

3. When the music begins, try to score as many points as possible within the time limit at your new station. Be honest in keeping score!

4. After you have completed all eight activities, assemble near the scoreboard. Points will be tabulated and scores announced. Everyone, cheer for every team!

(The following activities give eight Station Ideas for a "general" Tabloid, followed by eight Station Ideas for a Carnival or Circus theme.)

SG–44 TABLOID SPORTS STATIONS 1, 2, 3, AND 4

FOCUS: Volleying; agility; passing; rolling

EQUIPMENT: One beachball;
eight to ten hoops;
one medicine ball;
one cageball;
five cone markers;
masking or floor tape

DESCRIPTION OF ACTIVITY:

Station 1, Keep-It-Up (Have players form a circle. One player holds a beachball.): The object of this activity is to keep the beachball in the air. Don't let it touch the floor! You cannot hit the ball twice in a row. Score one point every time the ball is hit five times in a row.

Station 2, Stepping Stones (Place pairs of hoops in a row, with rows about 1.6 meters [5 feet] apart as shown. Tape each hoop to the floor. The team stands in single-file formation just behind a starting line.): The object of this activity is for each player to walk through the hoops on both hands and feet. Hands walk through the hoops on one side and feet walk through the hoops on the other side. When you reach the last hoop, stand up, run to your team to tag the next player, and then go to the end of the file. Score one point for each player who finishes the task.

Station 3, Hot Potato (Mark a 3-meter [10-foot] circle with tape or ropes. Have players equally space themselves around the circle with the leader holding a medicine ball.): Pass the ball with control in a CW direction around the circle. Score one point each time the ball passes the leader.

Station 4, Cageball Weave (Place a line of five cones about 2 meters [6 feet] apart and in front of a starting line. Place the cageball behind the starting line. The team is in pairs in file formation behind the line.): Each pair, in turn, roll the ball in and out of the cones, around the end cone, and back again the same way. Pass the ball to the next pair, who repeats the rolling pattern. Score one point for each round trip with the ball.

FOCUS: Throwing accuracy;
arm and leg strength

EQUIPMENT: One hoop or tire;
three sponge footballs or deckrings;
three junior basketballs or volleyballs;
basketball hoop and backboard;
two short ropes;   horizontal ladder;
four large cone markers;   several mats;
three plastic rings;   landing pit;
climbing frame;   floor or masking tape

DESCRIPTION OF ACTIVITY:

Station 5, Hoop-a-Basket (Tape a throwing line about 3 meters [10 feet] from a basketball hoop or use the foul-line of the basketball key. Players stand in single-file formation behind the throwing line with the first three players holding the balls.): Each player, in turn, try to shoot the ball through the basketball hoop. Score one point for each basket.

Station 6, Flying Ace (Use a short rope to suspend a hoop from a basketball backboard and tie a second rope to the bottom of the hoop. Secure that rope to the floor with tape so that the hoop will not sway. Tape a throwing line 3 meters to 4 meters [10 feet to 12 feet] away from the hoop.): Each player, in turn, try to throw a football through the hoop. Score one point for each successful throw.

Station 7, Rickshaw Ride (Place a cone marker 10 meters [30 feet] away from a starting line. All players are just behind and facing the starting line. Three players stand side by side and a fourth stands in front of the team): Middle player, put your arms around the neck and shoulders of the other two players, who will join their outside hands beneath you. Fourth player, stand in front, lift the legs of the middle player, and hold the player's ankles at waist level. Move as a team in this way toward the cone marker, around it, and back to the starting line to score one point. Take turns in each of the four positions.

Station 8, Cross-the-River (Secure a ladder to the climbing frame in a horizontal position and at a height that is above the players' heads; then place mats directly below the ladder. Have each team stand in single-file formation beside the ladder.): Each teammate, in turn, swing from hand-to-hand beneath the ladder. If you must drop, continue crossing the ladder from that point. When you reach the end of the ladder, land softly on the mat, bending your knees; then the next player may go. Score one point for each crossing.

VARIATIONS:

a. In *Flying Ace,* have a player spin the hoop to increase the challenge level.

b. *Hoop-La:* Place three large cone markers in a triangle formation, equally spaced 1 meter (3 feet) from each other and 3 meters (10 feet) from a throwing line. Each player, in turn, tosses three plastic rings toward the cone markers. Score one point for each ring that encircles a cone.

c. *Cat Walk:* Each player, in turn, climbs up the frame to the horizontal ladder, walks across it using his or her hands and feet on the other end of the frame, and jumps into the landing pit; then the next player goes. Score one point for each crossing.

SG-46 CARNIVAL TABLOID STATIONS 1, 2, 3, AND 4 _____

FOCUS: Running, arm and
leg strength;
teamwork

EQUIPMENT: One broomstick;
five cone markers;
four scooters;
two short ropes;
two folding mats;

one long jump rope;
one beachball (optional);
one plastic spider (optional);
floor or masking tape

DESCRIPTION OF ACTIVITY:

Station 1, Wild Bronco Ride (Place four
cones in a row, each 3 meters [10 feet] apart
and 3 meters [10 feet] from a starting line.
Have players in pairs, standing in single-file
formation just behind the starting line. The
first pair gets a broomstick.): Each pair, in
turn, straddle the broomstick and ride it like
a horse, weaving in and out of the cone markers, around the end cone, and directly back
to the starting line. Score one point for each
round trip.

Station 2, Dog Sled Race (Have a rider lie on his or her
front on two scooters [joined together by a rope], and hold
onto a looped rope which is pulled by one or two team players.
Place a cone as a turning point about 10 meters [30 feet] in
front of the starting line.): Pull each Dog Sled around the end
cone and directly back to the starting line so that the next
sled can go. If the cone marker is knocked over, it must be set
upright before continuing. Take turns at being pulled and being the puller. Score one point for each Dog Sled that completes the course.

Station 3, Clown Carry (Place two folded mats about 4 meters [12 feet] apart. Tape a direction arrow between the
mats.): One player, lie down on your back on the first mat.
Any number of players may hold onto the lying player's arms
and ankles, safely carry that player to the other mat, and
gently place the player on the mat; then run back to the first
mat to pick up the next Clown. Everyone on your team should
have a turn at being carried and being a carrier. Score one
point for each Clown carried from mat to mat.

Station 4, Jack-Be-Nimble (Place a long
rope on the floor. Two players stand at either end of the rope and start turning it.
The other players stand in single-file formation nearby.): Each player, in turn, perform five jumps in the middle to score one
point for your team, while all other players
sing: "Jack be nimble, Jack be quick, Jack
jump over the candlestick!" You may jump
in "front door" or start in the middle. Everyone on your team should take turns at
being the jumper and the rope turner.

FOCUS: Agility; shooting and throwing accuracy; hanging and swinging

EQUIPMENT: Two parachutes;
three deckrings;
five bleach bottles;
one broom handle or bladeless hockey stick;
floor or masking tape;
two box horses;
one or two climbing ropes;
crash pad or landing pit;
one nonskid mat;
four large mats;
two small utility balls;
two large plastic garbage pails;
three softballs;
two plastic laundry baskets

DESCRIPTION OF ACTIVITY:

Station 5, Haunted Maze (Stand several mats upright in a zig-zag position to create the sides of the tunnel and a maze effect; then cover the tunnel with one or two parachutes.): Score one point each time you travel from one end of the tunnel to the other end. Be careful not to touch any of the sides!

Station 6, Deckring Shot (Place five bleach bottles on crosses that you have taped in a pyramid pattern about 4 meters [12 feet] from a shooting line. Place a broom handle and three deckrings near the shooting line.): Each player, in turn, take three tries to knock over the bottles by shooting at them with the deckrings and broom stick. Other players, keep setting up the bottles as they are knocked over. Score one point for each bleach bottle knocked over.

Station 7, Cannon-Ball Drop (Place a box horse about 2 meters [6 feet] from the climbing rope; then lengthwise position a crash pad on a nonskid mat under the rope. Check that the climbing rope is short enough to swing clear of the box horse. Place a laundry basket, with two utility balls in it, in the middle of the crash pad and under the rope. Lay a folded mat on either side of the crash pad. Players stand in single-file formation behind the box horse.): Each player, in turn, hold a utility ball between your ankles while standing on the box horse; then swing forward, dropping the ball into the laundry basket and landing safely on the crash pad. Score one point for each ball that lands in the basket.

Station 8, Softball Toss (Place two plastic garbage pails side-by-side, about 1 meter [3 feet] from a wall as shown. Tape a throwing line 3 meters [10 feet] from the wall, and place a laundry basket containing the three softballs, on one side of the line. Have players stand in single-file formation behind the throwing line.): Each player in turn, take three tries to throw a softball at the wall so that it rebounds off the wall into either garbage pail. Score one point for each ball that lands in the pail.

VARIATIONS:

a. ***Bottle Bowling:*** Set up the bleach bottles as for Deckring Shot. Tape a rolling line 10 meters (30 feet) from the front bottle. Have each player, in turn, bowl one ball toward the bottles. Count one point for every bottle knocked down.

b. ***Flying Trapeze:*** Lengthwise position a crash pad on a nonskid mat between two short box horses. The climbing rope should hang in the middle between the two boxes. Place folding mats on either side of the crash pad and behind each box horse. Have each player, in turn, stand on the box horse, grab the rope, and swing forward; land safely on top of the other box horse. Swing back to land on the first box. Score one point for each round trip.

Closing Activities

After a vigorous physical workout, the Closing Activity serves as a quiet, cool-down activity and leaves children ready to continue with classroom work. The 43 Closing Activities in Section 8 include:

CA–1 FRIENDSHIP BUILDERS

FOCUS: Self-worth; positive feelings

EQUIPMENT: Quiet background music; tape or record player

ORGANIZATION:

- These promoters of self-esteem show the children that you really do care for them as persons. Used often, they will help to promote a warm and friendly atmosphere in your lessons. Choose one or two of these Friendship Builders to use at the beginning, during, or at the end of the lesson. To teach, have children stand and face you. For homework, have the children teach the Friendship Builders to at least one other person. Have partners design a "friendship greeting" of their own and teach it to other partners.

DESCRIPTION OF ACTIVITY:

1. *Hug Yourself:* Wrap your arms around yourself and say "I love me!"
2. *Hugging Huddle:* Put your arms around the shoulders of the players on either side of you and chant a favorite cheer, such as "Awesome!"
3. *I Love You:* Say "I love you!" in sign language. With thumb and fingers extended, close your third and fourth fingers to your palm.
4. *I Really Love You:* Say "I really love you!" in sign language. With thumb and fingers extended, close your third finger to your palm and cross your first and second fingers.
5. *Respectful Greeting:* Stand tall facing the person or persons to be honored. On the signal "1, 2, 3!" form a fist, slap it into the palm of your other hand, and bow graciously from the waist. (Use to greet your class each morning and during the day.)
6. *High Five's:* Greet a partner by together jumping upward and slapping each other's hand. Now find another partner and give each other Low Five's. How would you give each other Medium Five's?

CA–2 PLAYER OF THE DAY

FOCUS: Class recognition; self-esteem

EQUIPMENT: None

ORGANIZATION:

- Use this self-esteem activity at the end of every physical education lesson. Have class gather in a listening circle. Recognize a child (children) in your class as the "player of the day" and have this person stand facing the class. Tell the class why you think this player of the day is so special: perhaps for cooperating with others; playing fairly; sharing equipment; being cheerful; helping others; helping you; or trying hard to improve at a skill. When you have finished telling them, have the class give the player of the day a big "round of applause" by clapping their hands while moving CW or CCW in a large circle. Ensure that each player in the class is given recognition at some time during the school year. You may wish to give a "Player of the Day" certificate to the boy or girl you have recognized.

CA-3 HEALTHY HABITS

FOCUS: Health concepts; listening skills; fair play

EQUIPMENT: Four cone markers

ORGANIZATION:

- Mark two endlines about 6 meters (20 feet) apart. Have the players stand side-by-side in a line, at one end of the play area, facing you. Explain that the object of the game is for each player to reach the other end of the play area and, to help them do so, you will ask them various questions.

DESCRIPTION OF ACTIVITY: If you can honestly answer "Yes" to any of the questions that I am going to ask about a healthy lifestyle, you may take one step forward. If you answer "No," stay where you are:

— Did you brush your teeth before coming to school?
— Did you floss your teeth last night before going to bed?
— Do you wash your hands before you eat?
— Do you drink at least a glass of milk a day?
— Did you exercise yesterday?
— Did you eat fruit (vegetables) yesterday?
— Did you make your own bed this morning?
— Did you hug your mom or dad today?
— Did you eat no junk food yesterday?
— Did you get at least eight hours' sleep last night?
— Have you done someone a good deed today?
— Have you combed your hair today?
— Did you eat a healthy breakfast this morning?
— Did you walk or bike to school this morning?

FLOSS YOUR TEETH?

VARIATION: Ask children several True and False questions about a specific health topic such as Smoking, Heart and Circulatory System, or Nutrition. For every correct answer, one step forward may be taken.

CA-4 "OLE MOTHER O'LEARY"

FOCUS: Cool-down; singing; miming

EQUIPMENT: Song titled "Hot Time in the Old Town Tonight"; tape or record player

ORGANIZATION:

- This favorite action song is about how Mrs. O'Leary's cow kicked the lantern over in the barn and burned down much of Chicago in 1871. Have the children sit cross-legged inside a circle reasonably close to each other, facing you. Go over the song and the actions two or three times. Have them join in and sing along with you until learned.

DESCRIPTION OF ACTIVITY:

Follow me as I sing and do the actions of the song "Ole Mother O'Leary":

— "Oh! Oh!, one fine night, when we were all in bed!
(*lean head on hands and pretend to go to sleep*)
— Ole Mother O'Leary left the lantern in the shed!
(*hang out a lantern*)
— The cow kicked it over and winked her eye and said!
(*lean back, kick one leg, and wink*)
— There'll be a hot time in the Old Town Tonight!
(*rub both hands together*)
— Fire! Fire! Fire!"
(*stand quickly, raise one fist in the air as you yell "Fire!" "Fire!" "Fire!" and then quickly sit down*)

FIRE! FIRE! FIRE!

CA-5 TAP HEADS

FOCUS: Cool-down; relaxation

EQUIPMENT: None

ORGANIZATION:

- For this Cool-Down activity, lead the line, weaving in and out in a snake-like formation among the lying children. When the last child has been tapped, lead the line through the door into the change-room. Stress that there must be no talking while the line moves among the children. Have the children lie on the floor in the front-lying position, well spaced apart from each other.

DESCRIPTION OF ACTIVITY:

1. Stretch your arms forward and your legs back to make yourself as long as you can. Hold the stretch until I count to ten. Relax.

2. Now, rest your head on your hands and close your eyes. Without talking, relax and breathe in through the nose and out through the mouth. Think of lying on a lovely beach in the warm sun. You are getting drowsy!

3. I am going to walk around, and when I tap you on the head, get up, join the line, and quietly follow me. Remember, do not get up until I tap you on the head.

VARIATION:

Have the team leaders tap the heads of members of their own teams and lead them to the door.

CA-6 PINK PANTHER

FOCUS: Concentration; self-control

EQUIPMENT: Music: "Pink Panther Theme" by Henry Mancini; record or tape player

ORGANIZATION:

- Choose one player to be the "Pink Panther." All other players scatter in well-spaced positions around the play area, lie on their backs with legs straight and hands folded across their chests, and pretend to be asleep.

DESCRIPTION OF ACTIVITY:

1. When the music starts, Pink Panther, prowl around the play area, trying to wake the other players. You may speak to them to try to wake them, but you may not touch them! Hold your hands behind your back and lean over as you speak to them.

2. Sleeping players, if you move in any way, such as opening your eyes, changing your expression, smiling, or giggling, you must stand up, join the Pink Panther, and try to wake the other players.

3. The challenge is to stay asleep without being awakened by the Pink Panthers, until the music ends. Remember, there is absolutely no talking during Pink Panther.

VARIATION: Have more than one Pink Panther at the start of the game.

CA-7 RAINBOW GAME

FOCUS: Listening skills; cooperation

EQUIPMENT: None

ORGANIZATION:
- Form six equal teams and give each team a color of the Rainbow: Red, Orange, Yellow, Green, Blue, Indigo, or Violet.

DESCRIPTION OF ACTIVITY:

1. On signal "Rainbow!" everyone begin to walk around the play area so that all the colors are mixed up.

2. On signal "Freeze!" stop immediately, close your eyes, and hold your arms out in front. Without opening your eyes, slowly walk around the play area, trying to find the other players in your group. Call out your color so that other players can find you.

3. When you find another player who has your color, link elbows. Together, continue calling your color until all the players who have your color are linked.

4. When everyone is together, sit cross-legged and open your eyes. Have you found everyone in your group?

VARIATION:

Silent Numbers: Instead of colors, give each team a number, 1 through 6. Then have players, still keeping their eyes closed, use "sign language" to find players with the same number.

CA-8 BARNYARD MADNESS

FOCUS: Cooperation; listening; fair play

EQUIPMENT: None

ORGANIZATION:
- Form five or six equal groups. Name each group after farm animals, such as pigs, cows, ducks, sheep, and chickens. Then choose a leader for each group.

DESCRIPTION OF ACTIVITY:

1. On signal "Barnyard Madness!" everyone scatter, close your eyes, and carefully walk around the play area reaching out with your hands to guide you. Try to find the other members of your group by making your animal noise: chickens "cluck"; cows "moo"; ducks "quack"; sheep "baa"; and pigs "oink."

2. When you find someone who sounds like you do, hold hands and move together looking for other members of your group.

3. Which group can collect its members together and sit cross-legged in a circle the quickest? Remember, no peeking! Play fair!

CA-9 COOPERATION GAMES

FOCUS: Cooperation; alertness

EQUIPMENT: Cone markers; one large mat per group

DESCRIPTION OF ACTIVITY:

1. **Big Foot** (Form equal groups of six to eight players; then use the cone markers to indicate a start and finish line, spaced 10 meters [30 feet] apart.): On the signal "Go!" first player, stand with one heel on the starting line and place your other foot ahead of it so that you are standing heel to toe. The next player in your group, place one heel at the toes of your front foot and then stand heel to toe. Other players repeat, until the whole group is standing heel to toe in a long line. Which team can go the farthest? That is, which team has the biggest feet?

2. **Tall to Small** (Form groups of six to eight players and have each group scatter in a limited area, and stand still.): Close your eyes and keep them closed throughout the game. Now, while keeping your eyes closed and by feeling only, arrange yourselves in order of height, from tallest to smallest in a straight line, without talking to each other. When you have all found each other and linked elbows, open your eyes and see if you are lined up correctly. If you are, stay linked and walk to the exit door.

3. **The Big Turtle** (Form groups of six to eight players. Have each group kneel on all-fours and place a large mat over their backs. The mat is the Turtle's shell.): Show me how your group can move together in the same direction. Move as slowly as a Turtle would move. Can your Turtle move in different directions without stopping? Move to the right; move to the left. Move backwards. Move in a circle. Move diagonally. Show me how your Turtle can dance to the music. Try not to lose your shell!

4. **Zig, Zag, Zoop** (Have players sit cross-legged around a circle. Explain the signals; then call them quickly throughout the game.): Listen for the following signals and respond as I suggest:
   — If I point to you and say "Zig!" quickly name the player on your right.
   — If I point to you and say "Zag!" quickly name the player on your left.
   — If I point to you and say "Zoop!" name yourself!
   If I call your name and you cannot tell me another player's name before I count to three, then run once around the circle before rejoining the game.

VARIATIONS:

a. **Big Foot Race:** Have players stand in single-file formation as for Big Foot. On the signal "Go!" groups race to reach the finish line as follows: The player at the end of each group runs forward and stands heel to toe at the front of the file; the new last player repeats, and so on until the whole group reaches and crosses the finish line.

b. For **Tall to Small,** have boys form one group, the girls another; have the whole class arrange themselves from Tall to Small.

c. For **Big Turtle,** challenge each group to climb over a mountain (a balance bench) or move through an obstacle course without losing its shell. Hold Turtle races over a short distance.

CA-10 LION HUNT

FOCUS: Singing game; concentration

EQUIPMENT: None

ORGANIZATION:
- Have the players sit cross-legged in a listening circle, facing you. Chant the following story while players repeat each line and imitate your actions.

DESCRIPTION OF ACTIVITY:
1. Repeat after me as I chant and do the actions:
   — "Going on a lion hunt"
   Players repeat.
   — "Come on . . . here we go!"
   Alternate knee slaps, as if walking.
   — "I wonder where the lions are."
   Continue the walking knee-slaps.
   — "Going through the tall grass . . . Swish, Swish!"
   Brush hands together, gradually lifting your hands higher and brushing them together more slowly.
   — "The grass is getting taller"
   Brush your hands faster as if you are running.
   — "Wading through the water"
   Clap your hands quickly.
   — "Creeping into a dark cave"
   Slap your knees slowly and quietly.
   — "Brrr!—it's cold in here!"
   Shiver and shake all over.
   — "Do you see any lions?"
   Hold a hand above your eyes, look right and left.
   — "Oh, oh, . . . there's a lion"
   Point in any direction.
   — "Let's get out of here!"
   Slap your knees as fast as you can.
2. Reverse all the motions until you are back at the beginning.

CA-11 THE A-B-C-D-E-F-G SONG

FOCUS: Singing; friendly competition

EQUIPMENT: None

ORGANIZATION:
- Split the class into two even teams: team A and team B; sitting about two meters (six feet) apart, facing each other. Have each team choose a leader to lead the singing for his or her team. Have the leader face the team. You will need to conduct the overall singing. Sing the Chorus to the tune of "Here We Go Gathering Nuts in May."

DESCRIPTION OF ACTIVITY:
1. Everyone start by singing the chorus:
   "A-B-C-D-E-F-G, H-I-J-K-L-M-N, O-P-Q-R-S-T-U, V-W-X-Y-Z."
2. As soon as the whole class stops singing the Chorus, team A, you have to be ready to sing the first verse of a Nursery Rhyme. When team A is finished, the whole class, sing the Chorus again. Then it is team B's turn to sing a Nursery Rhyme.
3. Continue, with the whole class singing the Chorus; then each team takes turns to sing a Nursery Rhyme, until one team cannot think of a new one or they sing a Rhyme that has been sung before.

CA–12 HANDS-ON SONG

FOCUS: Coordination; alertness　　　　**EQUIPMENT:** None

ORGANIZATION:

- This action song can be used as a closing activity or as a break after a long period of inactive class-work. Have the children scatter around the play area or stand in an aisle or open space, facing the front. Then have the children respond as you read the words aloud. Repeat the song several times, increasing the speed each time.

DESCRIPTION OF ACTIVITY:

1. As I read the words, do the actions:
   - Hand on your hips, hands on your knees,
   - Put them behind you, if you please.
   - Touch your shoulders, touch your nose,
   - Touch your ears, touch your toes.
   - Raise your hands high in the air,
   - At your sides, on your hair.
   - Raise your hands as before,
   - As you clap 1, 2, 3, 4.
   - My hands upon my head I place,
   - On my shoulders, on my face;
   - Then I raise them to the sky
   - To make my fingers quickly fly;
   - Then I put them in front of me,
   - And gently clap them 1, 2, 3!

   Repeat the reading as quickly as it seems the children are able to respond with the correct actions.
2. Give yourselves "a Round of Applause" by clapping your hands while moving around in a large circle.

CA–13 I SPIED

FOCUS: Creative thinking; dramatization　　　　**EQUIPMENT:** None

ORGANIZATION:

- Have the players sit cross-legged in a circle facing the center. Choose one player to be the "Storyteller," who stands at the edge of the circle.

DESCRIPTION OF ACTIVITY:

1. Storyteller, start your story by saying, "While I was walking down the street, I spied with my little eye a. . . . " Instead of telling what you saw, go to the center of the circle and mime it out by using gestures. You must not make any noises.

2. *Suggestions:* a speeding car; a running dog; a fire engine; an airplane; a parent pushing a baby carriage; a mail carrier delivering mail; etc.

3. Circle players, try to guess what the Storyteller saw. Raise your hand if you have an answer. If you guess correctly, then you become a new Storyteller and the game starts again.

VARIATION: Have the Storyteller tell the story in whatever way he or she chooses, such as: "As I was walking . . . through the park; . . . along the beach; . . . through the zoo; . . . through the store."

CA-14 HEAD BALL

FOCUS: Cooperation

EQUIPMENT: One large utility ball (or beachball) per group

ORGANIZATION:

- Form groups of three players and have each group get a utility ball.

DESCRIPTION OF ACTIVITY:

1. Place the ball on the floor in the middle of your group and lie face down with your heads toward it.

2. Press your heads against the ball and rise to all-fours. If the ball drops to the floor, lie face down again and start over.

3. Can you return the ball to the floor using your heads only? Remember, three heads are better than one!

VARIATIONS:

a. Challenge players to stand up while pressing their heads against the ball.

b. Increase the size of the group.

CA-15 CHUCKLE BELLY

FOCUS: Togetherness

EQUIPMENT: None

ORGANIZATION:

- This activity gets the whole class "splitting their sides" with laughter. Arrange the players, one at a time, in the lying position, with each player's head resting on someone's belly.

DESCRIPTION OF ACTIVITY:

1. On the signal "Go," keep your eyes open and see if you can go 30 seconds without giggling, smiling, or laughing. Meanwhile, I am coming around to try to make you giggle by making faces, making weird sounds, telling funny jokes, and making funny actions. (It is almost impossible for the class to go for 30 seconds without giggling. As soon as one starts, they all start.)

2. **"Laugh and Pass It On"** (Have players get into back-lying position in a straight line in groups of six or eight. Check for good spacing. While players are in the "Chuckle Belly" position, have everyone keep a serious face to start.): First players start laughing, then pass it on to the second, who passes it on to the third, and so on, until all are roaring with laughter. Then have the first player quit and go to the exit, then the second, the third, and so on, until they are all lined up.

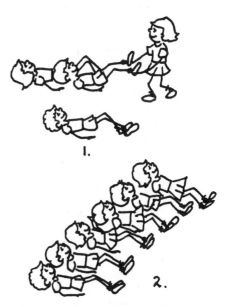

CA-16 MUSICAL MATS

FOCUS: Cooperation; alertness

EQUIPMENT: One mat per player; popular music with a strong beat; tape or record player

ORGANIZATION:

• Have each player get a mat and then stand on it anywhere in the play area.

DESCRIPTION OF ACTIVITY:

1. When the music starts, walk around the mats in time to the music. Do not step on a mat or touch any of the other players as you move. Meanwhile, three or four mats will be removed.

2. When the music stops, quickly but safely land on the mat nearest you. When you hear the music again, continue to walk around the mats. Meanwhile, three more mats will be removed. When the music stops again, stand on a mat. You may have to share your mat with another player.

3. Continue until only three or four mats are left. Can you cooperate with each other so that several players are able to squeeze together on one mat?

CA-17 NUMBERS CHANGE

FOCUS: Alertness; listening

EQUIPMENT: None

ORGANIZATION:

• Choose one player to be IT. All other players form a single circle, facing inward, with IT standing in the center. Give each player a different number, from 1 to ?, including IT. Have the players count off around the circle.

DESCRIPTION OF ACTIVITY:

1. When I call out two numbers, the players whose numbers are called must attempt to change places, but IT, you may also try to get into one of the open places in the circle.

2. IT, you must remain in the center until both numbers are called.

3. The player who is left out is the new IT when the game continues.

VARIATIONS:

a. Have the circle players sit.

b. Call three numbers instead of two.

CA-18 FOUR CORNERS

FOCUS: Alertness; honesty

EQUIPMENT: None

ORGANIZATION:

- Have players sit cross-legged in a circle and explain that each corner of the play area has a number from 1 to 4. To check that players know how corners are numbered, call each corner and have them point to it. One player, who will be IT, sits in the middle of the circle.

DESCRIPTION OF ACTIVITY:

1. IT, cover your eyes and count aloud to ten. While IT counts aloud, circle players, quickly scatter to any of the four corners. You must be in a corner before IT counts to ten.

2. At the number ten, IT, shout "Freeze!" and call the number of any corner. All players in that corner are caught, must join you in the circle, and help you count to ten again; however, you are the only player who may call the number of a corner and give the signal "Freeze!"

3. When there are only four or less players left in the game, each player must go to a different corner. Continue until only one player is left to run to a corner. That player is IT during the next game.

VARIATIONS:

a. Have IT count backwards from ten.

b. Have IT count in French or some other language.

CA-19 ELECTRIC SHOCK

FOCUS: Concentration

EQUIPMENT: None

ORGANIZATION:

- Form a circle with players sitting cross-legged and holding hands. Choose one player to be the "Inspector," who sits in the center of the circle.

DESCRIPTION OF ACTIVITY:

1. Inspector, close your eyes while I select a player to begin passing the Electric Shock around the circle. The shock is passed by squeezing the hand of the player on the right or left.

2. Inspector, try to guess where the Electric Shock is, but remember that the Shock can be reversed at any time. If you guess where the Shock is, that player becomes the new Inspector.

3. Circle players, keep a straight face and try not to let the Inspector know where the Shock is.

VARIATION: Have the players sit in the circle with feet wide apart and touching, and leaning back on the hands. Have them pass the Shock by tapping their neighbor's foot.

CA-20 SPORTS MIMING

FOCUS: Leadership; pantomiming

EQUIPMENT: None

ORGANIZATION:

- Discuss the meaning of the term "pantomiming." Have a player demonstrate how to pantomime an action such as "skating." Have players scatter around the play area; then start the game going and let the players take over the miming action.

DESCRIPTION OF ACTIVITY:

1. Can you think of a sports activity or exercise that you can mime? Keep your sport in mind throughout the game because each player, in turn, is going to lead the class in miming the actions of a sport.

2. When I call your name, mime the actions of the sport you have chosen; the other players, copy the actions.

3. If another player mimes the actions of the sport or exercise you planned to do, mime another. If you cannot think of a sport to mime, a friend or I will try to suggest one. The game continues until everyone has had a turn.

VARIATION: Do all the actions in slow motion.

CA-21 TOUCH AND NAME

FOCUS: Memory; concentration

EQUIPMENT: Various objects such as balls, benches, hoops, ropes, beanbags, deckrings, and mats

ORGANIZATION:

- Have players sit cross-legged anywhere in the play area. Scatter several objects around them.

DESCRIPTION OF ACTIVITY:

1. We are going to play a memory game in which you must remember every object that has been touched. I will begin the game by touching an object, naming it, and then tagging a player.

2. The tagged player must get up, touch and name the first object, and then touch and name a second object. Before sitting down, this player then tags another player, who must touch and name the two previous objects, touch and name a third object, and then tag another player.

3. The game continues in this way until the last player touches and names every object that has been touched and named. If you cannot name the objects touched, you may ask a player who has not had a turn to help you.

VARIATION: Play the game in groups of ten to twelve players. Gradually increase the size of the group until the whole class is involved.

CA-22 ANGELS IN THE SNOW

FOCUS: Relaxation; rhythm breathing

EQUIPMENT: Quiet background music; tape or record player

ORGANIZATION:

- Have children begin in back-lying position, with feet together, arms at sides, and eyes closed. Count the breathing pattern aloud: As children's arms and legs open, have them inhale four counts; as their arms and legs close, have them exhale four counts.

DESCRIPTION OF ACTIVITY:

1. Relax as you listen to the music. Your body should feel very loose.
2. We are going to make "Angels in the Snow." Slowly move your arms along the floor to shoulder level. Hold them there; then, just as slowly, return them to your sides.
3. Repeat the arm movement, but this time breathe in for four counts as you move your arms away from your sides. Breathe out for four counts as you pull your arms in toward your sides.
4. Now add your legs to the movement. Move your legs apart and together, breathing in and out as before.

VARIATIONS:

a. Have players lie face down to repeat the activity.
b. Have players move the arm and leg on the same side of their bodies each time; move opposite arms and legs while continuing the breathing pattern.

CA-23 PUPPETS ON A STRING

FOCUS: Relaxation; body control; listening

EQUIPMENT: None

ORGANIZATION:

- Have the "Puppets" (players) lie on their backs in their homes, with legs extended, feet together, and arms at their sides. Encourage puppets to be relaxed, floppy, and limp and to move only when the string is pulled. Have them move with slow, jerky movements.

DESCRIPTION OF ACTIVITY: I am the "Puppeteer" and you are all my "Puppets-on-a-String" as you lie still on the floor. I control the strings of each puppet. When I pull the strings and call out an action, show me how you will move (in four counts):

—I am pulling up your right knee; lowering it. Now I'm raising your left.
—I am slowly lifting your head forward off the floor; gently lowering.
—I am raising your shoulders off the floor (balance on your lower back and seat).
—I am lifting you slowly to the sitting position; your legs bend at the same time; now gently curl down to a long position on the floor.
—I am raising (lowering) your left arm, now your right.
—I am pulling you to the kneeling position (without using the arms).
—I am now springing you to the standing position; flop your head to one side and stand still.
—Now I am making you dance. While you are dancing, I am lining you all up. Now I am dancing you all to the exit door.

VARIATION: Use stretching movements from "Angles in the Snow" and Section 2.

CA-24 PIRATE'S TREASURE

FOCUS: Agility; fair play

EQUIPMENT: One beanbag;
four cone markers

ORGANIZATION:

- Mark out the play area with traffic cones. Have the "Sailors" (players) stand in the safe zone at one end of the play area. Choose one player to be the "Pirate," who sits at the other end of the play area with his or her back to the Sailors, both hands covering the eyes, and the "Treasure" (beanbag) placed about two meters (six feet) behind him or her.

DESCRIPTION OF ACTIVITY:

1. When I say "Treasure Hunt," Sailors, creep toward the Pirate and try to steal the Treasure. Pirate, quietly count to yourself: "One Treasure, Two Treasures, Three Treasures, . . ." If you think that the Sailors are close by, take your hands off your eyes and quickly turn around.

2. Sailors, carefully watch for the Pirate to turn around. When you see the Pirate turn, immediately "freeze" on the spot. Pirate, if you see anyone moving, point to him or her: That person is "grounded" and must return to the starting line.

3. Sailors, you may make a break for the Treasure at any time, but if the Pirate sees you moving, you can be sent back to the starting line.

4. Sailor, if you capture the Treasure, you must get it back to the safe zone before the Pirate can catch you. If you are successful, you become the Pirate for the next game.

CA-25 BLINDMAN'S BLUFF

FOCUS: Cool-down game; challenge

EQUIPMENT: One blindfold per circle;
quiet background music;
tape or record player

ORGANIZATION:

- Form circles of eight to twelve players; circle players space about arm's length apart, facing inward. Choose one player to be IT, who is blindfolded and taken to the center of the circle.

DESCRIPTION OF ACTIVITY:

1. IT, while you count to ten, the circle players move CW in time with the music. When you call "Freeze," they will immediately stop. Then ask them to move three steps in any direction and stand still.

2. IT, walk carefully among the players until you touch one. If you can guess who it is, you swap places with that player. If you are unsuccessful, you can have two more guesses. After this I will pick another player to be IT and continue the game.

CA-26 FALLING WAND

FOCUS: Listening; reaction

EQUIPMENT: One wand per group

ORGANIZATION:

- Form circles of six to eight players. All players number off, stand facing the middle of the circle, and step forward on one foot, ready to move when called. Choose one player to be IT. That player stands in the middle of the circle and places one finger on top of an upright wand to steady it as it rests on the floor. Increase or decrease the size of the circle to match the players' ability.

DESCRIPTION OF ACTIVITY:

1. IT, start the game by calling the number of any player in the circle; then release the wand. The player whose number was called must try to catch the wand before it hits the floor.

2. If successful, that player becomes the new IT, goes to the middle of the circle, and calls another number. The first IT joins the circle and the game continues.

VARIATION:

Spin the Platter: Spin a deckring, a plastic plate, or a Frisbee™ and play the game as above.

CA-27 THE LAUGHTER GAME

FOCUS: Leadership

EQUIPMENT: One nylon scarf

ORGANIZATION:

- Have the players sit cross-legged, close together in a circle; then choose a good-natured player to lead the game. That player gets a nylon scarf and stands in the middle of the circle.

DESCRIPTION OF ACTIVITY:

1. Leader, toss the scarf into the air and immediately break into a fit of laughter. Try to make everyone else laugh, too. Continue laughing as long as the scarf floats in the air.

2. As soon as it touches the floor, everyone must immediately stop laughing and put on a sad face. Anyone who shows even the slightest hint of a smile after the scarf touches the floor is "out."

3. Out players must now lie down with chin on hands; they join in the laughter and try to make other players laugh. Remember, no touching!

4. I will change the middle player after every three throws. Who will last the longest without laughing?

VARIATION: Use a balloon instead of a scarf.

CA-28 THREAD THE NEEDLE

FOCUS: Cooperation

EQUIPMENT: None

ORGANIZATION:

- Have the players form lines of about eight players, holding hands. The first player in the line is the "Needle."

DESCRIPTION OF ACTIVITY:

1. Needle, begin by leading the "thread" (line of players) under the raised arms of the last two players, who turn in to face each other. This is called a "stitch."

2. Needle, continue down the line, going under the arms of each of the thread players to form more stitches. When you get to the end, turn under your own arm, and now the whole line has been stitched.

3. Everyone raise your arms, and we will "Rip the Stitches." Continue to hold hands and turn back to your original positions. Be careful not to pull the line too fast and break the thread.

4. Continue until everyone has had a turn as Needle.

VARIATIONS:

a. Form larger groups and "thread the needle."

b. Have the whole class "thread the needle."

CA-29 SUBMARINE

FOCUS: Cooperation; trust

EQUIPMENT: None

ORGANIZATION:

- Form groups of six to eight players and have each group stand in single-file formation. Players place their hands on the shoulders of the player in front of them. The file is a "Submarine," and the last player in the line is the "Captain."

DESCRIPTION OF ACTIVITY:

1. Everyone, except the Captain, close your eyes. Captain, steer your Submarine around the play area without making a sound!

2. If you want the Submarine to turn right, gently press the right shoulder of the player in front of you. If you want the Submarine to turn left, gently press that player's left shoulder. Each player in turn will gently press the shoulder of the player in front of them until the first player gets the signal; then the line moves slowly and carefully together in that direction.

3. Continue moving around the play area in response to your Captain's signals. The challenge is to avoid hitting another Submarine!

4. On signal "Regroup!" Captain, go to the front of the line; end player, you are the new Captain.

CAPTAIN

CA-30 TWEETIE

FOCUS: Listening skills; alertness; fair play   **EQUIPMENT:** None

ORGANIZATION:

- One player is secretly chosen as the "Tweetie." The other players scatter around the play area and stand with their eyes closed. If the tempo of the game is slowing, have the Tweetie give out a high-pitched chirp now and then. Emphasize that the players be honest—no peeking!

DESCRIPTION OF ACTIVITY:

1. On signal "Move!" everyone walk slowly around the play area with your eyes closed.
2. Find someone's hand, shake it, and ask "Tweetie"? Other players will answer you with "Tweetie"? but the Tweetie will remain silent throughout the game.
3. If both you and the player you shake hands with speak, asking "Tweetie"?, drop hands and find someone else to ask "Tweetie"? Obviously you have not found the Tweetie yet!
4. If you find a player who does not answer, you have found the Tweetie. Join hands and remain silent for the rest of the game. Continue until everyone is holding hands with the Tweetie.

VARIATION: To play a short game of Tweetie, reduce the size of the play area.

CA-31 THE MAD DOCTOR

FOCUS: Alertness; fair play   **EQUIPMENT:** None

ORGANIZATION:

- Secretly choose one player to be the "Mad Doctor." All other players walk around the play area, shaking hands with every player they meet.

DESCRIPTION OF ACTIVITY:

1. When shaking hands with the other players, be careful of the Mad Doctor. The Mad Doctor will press your wrist with a thumb as if injecting you with deadly poison!
2. If you are poisoned, take several steps and "collapse dead" on the floor. Now you must lie quietly for the rest of the game.
3. If you think you know who is acting as the Mad Doctor, raise your hand. After I point to you, say "The Mad Doctor is _____." If your guess is correct, the game is over. If your guess is incorrect, fall to the floor dead and remain silent for the rest of the game.
4. Continue until the Mad Doctor is discovered or only one player remains alive.

CA-32 COOPERATIVE ROPE PLAY

FOCUS: Cooperation

EQUIPMENT: One short rope per player

ORGANIZATION:

- Form groups of six to eight players and have each player get a rope. Groups knot their ropes together with square knots, in which right is folded over left and left over right. Suggest different shapes, letters, and numbers into which players can then pull their knotted ropes. Remind players that this activity is not a tug-o-war. Players should *pull with* rather than *against* each other.

DESCRIPTION OF ACTIVITY:

1. To make a square with your knotted ropes, four players space yourselves evenly around it and, holding onto the rope, pull to make four corners. Try not to pull too hard! Extra players can join any one of the four corner players.

2. How would you make a triangle? Show me a rectangle. Can you make an X? Make an N.

3. Untie one knot and reknot it with another group's rope. Together try to make an 8. Join yet another group and reknot your rope with that group's rope. Now together, try to make a 6.

4. Continue until the whole class is making shapes with one continuously knotted rope.

VARIATION: Have groups sit and then pull the rope into different shapes as they rise and stand.

CA-33 TANGLES

FOCUS: Cooperation

EQUIPMENT: None

ORGANIZATION:

- Form groups of ten players and have each group stand in a circle.

DESCRIPTION OF ACTIVITY:

1. *Human Knot:* Reach across the circle and join hands with any two players except those who are standing on either side of you. Now work together to untangle your hands so that everyone is standing around the circle again holding hands. While you are untangling yourselves, remember not to let go of each other's hands.

2. *Human Pretzel:* Everyone but two players join hands around the circle. Twist yourselves over, under, and through each other without letting go of each other's hands; meanwhile, the two outside players will turn their backs so they cannot see how you have tangled yourselves together. Then the outside players turn around and try to untangle the group.

3. *Triangle Tangle:* Break into groups of three players. Each group, tangle yourself together by holding hands under your arms, over your shoulders, and between your legs. Once you are tangled, try to move together. Continue to hold hands while moving around the play area.

VARIATION:

Triangle Tangle: Repeat in groups of four or five players, or have the whole class tangle together.

CA-34 ROCK, PAPER, SCISSORS

FOCUS: Concentration

EQUIPMENT: None

ORGANIZATION:

- In this game, "Paper covers rock," "Rock covers scissors," and "Scissors cut paper." Everyone must choose to be either "Rock," "Paper," or "Scissors." Have players find a partner and sit facing each other. This game can be played in pairs or in teams.

DESCRIPTION OF ACTIVITY:

1. *Pairs:* Find a partner and a free space. On the signal "1, 2, 3, Show!" show either a Rock, by placing one fist on top of the other; Paper, by spreading one hand flat; or Scissors, by extending two fingers forward. Decide who wins and award one point. Play the game for the best out of three tries; then challenge another player.

2. *Teams* (Form equal teams and appoint a Leader for each team. Players on each team stand side-by-side in a line, with the two teams facing each other.): Leader, hold a huddle with your team and decide whether your team will be Rock, Paper, or Scissors; then line up again facing the other team. On the signal "1, 2, 3, Show," check to see which team earns one point. The game continues until each player has had a turn at being Leader.

CA-35 SLAP, CLAP, SNAP

FOCUS: Concentration

EQUIPMENT: None

ORGANIZATION:

- Form groups of eight players and have them sit cross-legged around circle. Each group numbers off; the player with the number one is the Leader. Practice the "Slap, Clap, Snap" hand rhythm: players slap knees twice, clap hands twice, and then snap fingers twice. Continue to practice until players have got the rhythm: "Slap-slap, clap-clap, snap-snap."

DESCRIPTION OF ACTIVITY:

1. Leaders of each group, start the rhythm. When you hear "Snap-snap," call your number and number of another player in your group.

2. The player whose number is called, wait until you hear "Snap-snap"; then call your number and the number of another player. You may call the number of the player who just called your number.

3. Keep the rhythm going. If I repeat the hand signals quicker, can you still do the hand actions and call the other players' numbers? Let's give it a try!

CA-36 LIMB STRETCHES

FOCUS: Flexibility; cross-lateral mobility

EQUIPMENT: One mat per player; quiet background music; tape or record player

ORGANIZATION:

• In this cool-down activity, children slowly raise and lower limbs in different combinations. Emphasize that players should hold each stretch without bouncing, and move arms and legs smoothly, taking the full four counts. To begin, players get a mat, find a free space, and lie on their backs on the mat with legs together and arms at sides.

DESCRIPTION OF ACTIVITY:

1. Take four slow counts to raise your right leg (1-2-3-4). Then gently hold your right ankle with your right hand for another four counts. Now lower your leg to the mat for the final four counts. (Repeat with left leg and left hand.)

2. Take four slow counts to raise your right leg; hold your right ankle with your left hand for four counts; and then lower your leg to the mat for four counts. (Repeat with left leg and right hand.)

3. Continue this four-count movement while raising both legs; hold your ankles with both hands; and then lower them to the mat.

4. Raise and lower your right leg and right arm at the same time. (Repeat with the left limbs.)

5. Raise and lower your right leg and left arm. Raise and lower your left leg and right arm.

6. Relax in back-lying position on your mat. Make yourself as long as you can and hold the stretch for eight counts. Roll over onto your front and stretch again for another eight counts. Totally relax. Now slowly take eight counts to stand up. Bring your heavy head to a high level, last!

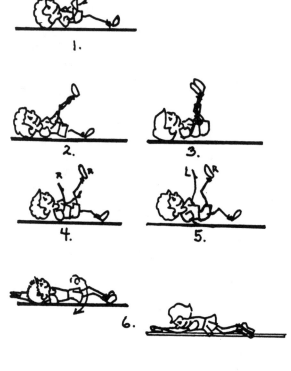

CA-37 A TO Z

FOCUS: Body control; cooperation

EQUIPMENT: None

ORGANIZATION:

• Have the players lie on the floor.

DESCRIPTION OF ACTIVITY:

1. Can you make the letter "O" with your body?

2. Well done! Now, show me how you can make these letters:
   A-X-S-C-F-J-U-V-K-Z.

3. Find a partner. Can the two of you make a two-letter word? Suggestions: ON, TO, OF, IT, NO, OH, SO, HI, IF, DO.

4. Choose up teams of three players. While lying on the floor, in three letters, use your bodies to spell the name of an animal; a girl's name; a boy's name; the name of a tree; the numbers 369, 172, 504.

CA-38 ORBIT BALL

FOCUS: Cooperation; visual tracking; hand, foot, eye coordination

EQUIPMENT: One oversized beachball or cageball per group

ORGANIZATION:

- Form two groups of ten to twelve players and have groups form a double circle; one circle inside the other. Players in the outer circle stand with arms ready to tap the beachball. Players in the inner circle lie on their backs, heads pointing to the middle of the circle and legs raised overhead, ready to tap the beachball with their feet. Emphasize control of the ball. It should be tapped gently rather than kicked or punched.

DESCRIPTION OF ACTIVITY:

1. Circle players, work together as you pass the beachball around the circle to put it into "orbit."

2. Try to keep the ball between the inside players, who tap it with their feet, and the outside players, who push it back with their hands. Do not allow the ball to touch the ground. Call "Mine!" when you want to hit the ball.

3. Can you count the number of times the ball orbits the circle? Count out loud each time.

4. Inner and outer circles, change places. Put the ball into orbit again. Can you beat your previous score?

VARIATIONS:

a. For a large class, set up two games.

b. Time the ball's orbit rather than counting the number of taps.

CA-39 WALL SIT

FOCUS: Cooperation; leg strength

EQUIPMENT: Wall (or fence)

ORGANIZATION:

- Form groups of five to seven players and have each group stand close together in single-file formation near a wall. The last player in each line leans back against the wall. All players hold onto the waist of the player in front of them.

DESCRIPTION OF ACTIVITY:

1. On signal "1, 2, 3, Sit!" sit in the lap of the player behind you so that everyone is comfortably seated. Do not lean back as you sit down. Now stand up.

2. Try the Wall Sit again, but this time, hold your hands above your head instead of around another player's waist.

3. Regroup and repeat the challenge.

WALL SIT!

"WALKING CHAIR"

VARIATION:

Walking Chair: After giving the signal "1, 2, 3, Sit!" give the signal "Left, Right, Left, Right!" upon which the group slowly walks forward, beginning with the left foot. Challenge groups to try to walk the farthest without breaking their hold of another player's waist.

CA-40 BALANCE FEATHERS _____

FOCUS: Coordination and balance

EQUIPMENT: One balancing feather per person; relaxing background music

ORGANIZATION:

- A "balance feather" is a peacock feather that can be purchased from Physical Education equipment suppliers. Have each player get a balance feather and take it to a free space. Emphasize the importance of handling the feathers with gentleness, as they are quite fragile. Ensure that players are well spaced to avoid any interference with other players. Emphasize that players need to concentrate on the feather, never letting their eyes leave it!

DESCRIPTION OF ACTIVITY:

1. Balance your feather in the palm of your right hand; in the palm of your left hand. Now balance it on the back of each hand in turn. Balance your feather on your index finger of your right hand; your left hand. Try balancing it on each of the other fingers.

2. Balance your feather on other body parts: elbow; shoulder; wrist; knee; forehead; nose; foot. On how many different body parts can you balance your feather?

3. Try to balance your feather while slowly moving; while bending and straightening your knees; while moving around in a circle; while touching the floor or wall or some other object.

4. Now try to transfer your feather from one body part to another without having the feather touch the floor. For example, can you transfer your feather from an elbow to the back of your hand?

5. Invent other balancing challenges. We will all try to perform your challenge.

VARIATIONS:

a. *Feather Challenge:* Set up a contest to see who can balance their feather the longest. Time the event, and provide opportunity for the record to be broken.

b. Wands (which are one meter [three feet] in length and six millimeter [¼ inch] dowelling) can be substituted for balance feathers.

CA-41 BEACHBALL BALANCE _____

FOCUS: Cooperation; partnerwork

EQUIPMENT: Two beachballs per pair

ORGANIZATION:

- Have players find a partner of equal size and get a beachball to share in a free space.

DESCRIPTION OF ACTIVITY:

1. Which pair can balance the beachball between your bodies without using your hands? between your heads? between your hips? between another body part of your choice? move around play area balancing the beachball with different body parts?

2. Join another pair. Can your group of four players balance one beachball together? balance two beachballs? balance two beachballs between any two players without using hands? add another beachball and balance the three beachballs together?

3. *Beachball Chain* (Form groups of four or five players and have members of each group stand in single-file formation, holding a beachball between each player.): Can your chain move around the play area without dropping the beachballs?

CA-42 THE SPONGE

FOCUS: Progressive relaxation

EQUIPMENT: One mat per player;
quiet relaxing music;
tape or record player

ORGANIZATION:

- In this cool-down activity, players tense different muscle groups for ten seconds and then relax. Have each player get a mat and scatter around the play area. Players start by lying on their backs with legs slightly apart and arms at sides.

DESCRIPTION OF ACTIVITY:

1. Lie quietly on your mat and listen to the music. Try to relax every part of your body. Think of something pleasant.

2. Press your head against the mat; then relax. Now, frown and move only your scalp upward. Yawn very slowly; then relax.

3. Squeeze your shoulder blades together; then relax. Make fists with your hands and squeeze them tightly as you would a sponge; then relax.

4. Tighten your tummy muscles. Can you feel them tighten? Now relax. Squeeze your buttocks together; relax. Press your legs to the floor; relax. Point your toes away from you; then relax. Pull your toes toward you. Now completely relax again.

5. Close your eyes. Breathe in deeply; then slowly breathe out. Without making a sound, open your eyes, stand up slowly, and stretch tall.

CA-43 YOGA TIME

FOCUS: Relaxation; rhythmic breathing

EQUIPMENT: See activity CA-42.

ORGANIZATION:

- The following basic yoga routine includes a quick, gentle warm-up followed by balance, fitness, and breathing exercises. Have players get a mat and take it to a free space.

DESCRIPTION OF ACTIVITY:

1. *Warm-up:* Rub your body all over to increase its circulation; then, standing with knees slightly bent, bend at the waist and let yourself hang loose for ten seconds. Now lie on your mat in the back-lying position, hug your knees, and gently rock back and forth on your back four times.

2. *Sun Greeting:* Standing tall, with palms of hands gently pressed together at your chest, slowly breathe in as you raise your arms overhead; then slowly breathe out, bringing your arms forward and down and bending slightly at the knees. Repeat three times.

3. *Cat Stretch:* Begin on all-fours. Breathing in, rock backwards slightly and lower your chest to the floor. Breathing out, round your shoulders like a frightened cat. Now breathe in again, bringing your right knee toward your head. Breathe out as you bring your right leg backwards and upward. Finally, breathe in as you return your leg to its starting position. Repeat with the left leg.

4. *Rhythmic Breather:* In kneeling-sit position, straighten your back and slowly breathe in through your nose. Breathe in for about ten seconds, hold your breath for five seconds, and then slowly breathe out. Repeat three times.